Director's Handbook

A Field Guide to 101 Situations Commonly Encountered in the Boardroom

Praise for *Director's Handbook* . . .

"The need for boards of directors to shape the future of our corporations is greater today than ever. The *Director's Handbook* is an informative tool for directors to better understand their roles and responsibilities. The handbook offers insightful questions directors should be asking themselves on topics they commonly encounter in an effort to create effective corporate governance frameworks within corporations."
—Ira M. Millstein, senior partner at Weil, Gotshal & Manges LLP; author, *The Activist Director: Lessons from the Boardroom and the Future of the Corporation*

"The *Director's Handbook* provides insightful, prescient, and pragmatic assistance to directors in a straightforward and clear approach, which will aid directors in fulfilling their fiduciary duties . . . a must-read for directors of public, closely held, and nonprofit companies."
—Myron T. Steele, former chief justice, Delaware Supreme Court; partner, Potter, Anderson & Coroon, LLP

"With its cleverly selected and wide-ranging topics of focus, the *Director's Handbook* will be a valuable tool for directors and their counsel. There are offerings for almost every board situation imaginable, and with well-chosen authors for the subjects presented, it promises to occupy a prominent place on many bookshelves including mine."
—Charles M. Elson, Edgar S. Woolard Jr. Chair in Corporate Governance and director of the John L. Weinberg Center for Corporate Governance, University of Delaware

"The *Director's Handbook*, with its broad sweep and user-friendly format, promises to be a valuable addition to the resources available to educate directors and prepare them for the increasingly challenging but vital role they play."
—Martin Lipton, founding partner, Wachtell, Lipton, Rosen & Katz

"This handbook is an excellent tool to help guide directors through not only the challenges in exercising their fiduciary duties, but also in understanding the meaning of good corporate governance process. The *Director's Handbook* addresses most of the situations faced by boards and provides a litany of questions to assist in identifying and addressing the many challenges they may face."
—Larry W. Sonsini, founding partner, Wilson, Sonsini, Goodrich & Rosati

"Businesses are operating in a world defined by uncertainty, resulting in a rapidly widening scope of boardroom responsibilities. For directors who are feeling overwhelmed, the *Director's Handbook* makes the 21st-century director's multifaceted duty of oversight far more approachable. Editor and contributor Frank Placenti has assembled insights from legal and governance experts who provide the reader with the resources directors need to capably handle the most common and complicated governance issues."
—Peter R. Gleason, CEO, National Association of Corporate Directors

Corporate Governance Committee
ABA Business Law Section

Director's Handbook

A Field Guide to 101 Situations Commonly Encountered in the Boardroom

FRANK M. PLACENTI
EDITOR

Cover design by Cathy Zaccarine/ABA Design

Printed in the United States of America.

21 20 19 18 17   5 4 3 2 1

Library of Congress Cataloging-in-Publication Data

Names: Placenti, Frank M., editor. | American Bar Association. Section of Business Law. Corporate Governance Committee, sponsoring body.

Title: Director's handbook: a field guide to 101 situations commonly encountered in the boardroom / edited by Frank M. Placenti.

Description: First edition. | Chicago : American Bar Association, 2017. | Includes bibliographical references and index.

Identifiers: LCCN 2017003388 | ISBN 9781634258111 (print : alk. paper)

Subjects: LCSH: Corporate governance—Law and legislation—United States. | Directors of corporations—United States—Handbooks, manuals, etc.

Classification: LCC KF1422 .D57 2017 | DDC 346.73/06642—dc23

LC record available at https://lccn.loc.gov/2017003388

Discounts are available for books ordered in bulk. Special consideration is given to state bars, CLE programs, and other bar-related organizations. Inquire at Book Publishing, ABA Publishing, American Bar Association, 321 N. Clark Street, Chicago, Illinois 60654-7598.

www.ShopABA.org

CONTENTS

INTRODUCTION

The original *Boy Scout Handbook*, authored by Adam Baden Powell in 1910, offered confident guidance concerning the intricacies of knives, arrows, knots, woodcraft, plant identification, hygiene, citizenry, and navigation of trails by moonlight. A modern version of that handbook is still published and in use today.

Those who find themselves in a public company boardroom might welcome a similar ready reference, given a legal and business environment in which straying from the trail entails consequences far greater than a nasty case of poison oak.

There have been thousands of articles, hundreds of court cases, and dozens of treatises dealing with board responsibilities. Many have been written from a theoretical or legal perspective, while others suggest best practices.

This Handbook takes a different approach.

While bashing corporate directors and officers as irresponsible has become increasingly fashionable in both the media and governmental circles, my experience in boardrooms over the last three decades has convinced me that nearly all public company directors are honorable people trying to do the right thing by their shareholders, customers, and employees. Unfortunately, the "right thing" is not always clear, and discerning it requires identifying underlying issues that are, themselves, sometimes less than obvious.

Based upon that experience, the twin premises of this Handbook are that

- among the most powerful tools available to any director is the ability to ask the targeted questions; and
- when a group of intelligent, well-meaning people is presented with the relevant facts, it will generally come to a proper answer.

With those premises in mind, this Handbook identifies 101 topics commonly encountered by public company directors and devotes a brief chapter to each of those topics. The first portion of each chapter sets forth a general discussion intended to provide basic context. The second section of each chapter suggests a list of questions or issues that a director might consider in connection with the topic at hand, including information to be sought from the company's management or advisors to inform the board's deliberations.

The final portion of each chapter identifies additional resources to which the director might turn for a more in-depth analysis of the particular topic. Employing this format, this Handbook is intended as a ready-reference or field guide, rather than a definitive or exhaustive exposition on any particular topic.

The collective effort of the authors to arm directors with the right questions reflects a view that, while there is rarely a one-size-fits-all answer to the issues encountered by directors, in most cases there is a sound set of questions that will help lead an individual company to *its* right answer.

Frank M. Placenti
Editor
February 2017

FOREWORD

The legal description of director duties has not changed significantly for many years: Directors must act in good faith; in a manner reasonably believed to be in the best interests of the corporation (duty of loyalty); and with such care, including reasonable inquiry, skill, and diligence, as a person of ordinary prudence would use under similar circumstances (duty of care). However, for much of the past two decades, boards of directors of public, private, and nonprofit corporations organized in the United States have been subject to increasing scrutiny and expectations regarding how they govern and whether they do so effectively. Boards govern in a challenging environment of rapid technological and geopolitical change, business disruption, and economic and political uncertainty. The increased regulation of public companies in the aftermath of corporate scandals and the global financial crisis, the birth of the influential and concentrated proxy advisory industry, the growing influence of shareholders, and the enhanced power of shareholder activists adds to the complexity that boards face in their task of governing. Much has been written about the structures and practices that boards and their committees should consider to support effective governance, with a focus on issues such as board composition, leadership structure, committee structure, board and committee processes for agenda-setting and information flow, management relations, and board culture. Far less has been written about how individual directors can enhance their contributions to board effectiveness.

Yet, any serious effort to improve board effectiveness must focus not only on the board but also on the contributions and behaviors of individual directors. While the authority to govern lies with the board as a collective, it is through the application of informed judgment by individual board members that the board forms consensus and takes action. This is underscored by the fact that fiduciary obligations of care and loyalty are owed to the corporation by each individual director, and the related legal reality that liability for breach of fiduciary obligations is personal to the director.

Fundamentally, board effectiveness begins with informed judgment by individual directors, which requires that directors assess the quality and relevance of the information they receive, ask probing questions on the range of matters that come before the board, and seek from management and experts additional information when needed. And the range of matters that directors must attend to is broad: Directors must be prepared to come to informed judgments in a range of contexts on a wide range of topics, including corporate strategy and finance; management performance; risk management; cybersecurity; management development and compensation; financial reporting and related controls; legal and regulatory compliance; corporate ethics and related controls; corporate social responsibility and sustainability; relations with investors, including shareholder activists and institutional investors and other key stakeholders; CEO succession; and on and on.

This Director's Handbook has been written for the individual director who seeks to improve his or her own effectiveness with respect to an expansive set of 101 specific topics that boards most often face. The intent is to provide practical guidance for directors in preparing for meetings and participating in board decision making. Each of the concise 101 chapters provides a high-level overview of a topic and includes a set of suggested questions directors can ask of themselves and management to provide a useful starting point for discussion. Website links to relevant resources are also provided at the end of each chapter.

The Handbook is the brainchild of Frank M. Placenti, who came up with the overall concept and outline of topics and proposed that it become a project of the ABA Business Law Section's Corporate Governance Committee. In addition to its novel scope and approach, the Handbook is notable for the innovative "crowdsourcing" method by which it was created. Members of the Corporate Governance Committee were invited to draft one or more chapters and to invite colleagues from their firms to contribute. Members of the American College of Governance Counsel were also invited to participate. Among his many roles in shepherding his idea to fruition, Frank was our Tom Sawyer—convincing us how much fun it would be to help "paint the fence." He also nagged us, gathered and reviewed author contributions, and served as editor. My sincere thanks to Frank for his wonderful idea and masterful job in implementing it in record time. And special thanks to all the authors who contributed.

To say that boards and directors operate in a challenging environment understates the complexity and pressures of board service—and it is a service in the nature of public service, due to its importance to our economy, the commitment required, and the risks of liability that arguably outpace the rewards. As directors continue to grapple with ever-expanding agendas and complex issues in the boardroom, this Director's Handbook provides a valuable practical resource.

Holly J. Gregory
Chair, ABA Business Law Section Corporate Governance Committee
November 2016

ABOUT THE EDITOR

Frank M. Placenti chairs the U.S. Corporate Governance Practice at Squire Patton Boggs (US) LLP, where he practices from the firm's Phoenix, Arizona office.

Frank is no stranger to the boardroom and has more than 30 years' experience advising boards and management teams with respect to mergers and acquisitions, corporate governance, securities law, anti-takeover, and shareholder relations issues.

Frank has assisted public companies, broker/dealers, and private equity firms and their portfolio companies with mergers and acquisitions, capital formation, securities and corporate law, regulatory compliance, anti-takeover matters, and shareholder engagement and activism. He has represented clients, special committees, and audit committees in managing internal investigations, as well as with U.S. Securities and Exchange Commission and stock exchange investigatory matters.

Frank serves as the founding President and Trustee of the American College of Governance Counsel and as a Vice Chair of the Corporate Governance Committee of the American Bar Association. The 2013 International Global Law Experts Awards recognized him as the Corporate Governance Lawyer of the Year in Arizona.

Frank has been listed in Best Lawyers in America since 2006, Chambers USA since 2003, and is a multi-year member of the Lawdragon 500, an acknowledgment given to the top 500 lawyers in America. He has been recommended for corporate matters and mergers and acquisitions by the PLC *Which Lawyer Yearbook* since 2009 and is listed in the PLC *Cross-Border Mergers and Acquisitions Handbook*. Each year since 2007, Frank has been selected by his peers to appear in Southwest Super Lawyers, a distinction awarded to the top 5 percent of lawyers in the region.

Frank is a frequent speaker on governance and M&A topics at regional, national, and international conferences and has published extensively on those topics.

Frank's boardroom experience includes service as the lead director for a NASDAQ-listed healthcare company and as lead director for a private company based in Charlotte, North Carolina that serves the restaurant and hospitality industries. He currently serves as

ACKNOWLEDGEMENTS

This Handbook has been "crowdsourced," with the various chapters prepared by individual contributors, many of whom are members of the American Bar Association Corporate Governance Committee. The collective effort of this group of highly-skilled and knowledgeable boardroom counselors is consistent with the long tradition of service of ABA members to clients and the profession.

The contributing authors are identified in the individual chapters.

The editor extends his thanks to all of those who contributed to this Handbook and also wishes to acknowledge the support of Holly J. Gregory, chair of the ABA's Corporate Governance Committee. Recognition is also due to Bruce Dravis and Jayne Juvan, co-chairs of that Committee's Publications Subcommittee, as well as the dedicated staff of the ABA who assisted in the preparation and publication of this Handbook.

Special thanks to Pamela Wedemeyer of the Squire Patton Boggs (US) LLP research staff for her efforts to assist in locating supporting articles for many of the chapters.

Finally, a hearty and heartfelt thanks to my assistant, Jean Reynolds, without whose tireless support and organizational skills this volume would not have been completed within this decade, if at all.

Frank M. Placenti
Editor

SECTION ONE

BOARD DUTIES, ROLES, AND STRUCTURE

1.1 THE LEGAL DUTIES OF CORPORATE BOARD MEMBERS

CONTRIBUTED BY
Frank M. Placenti
Squire Patton Boggs (US) LLP[1]

The corporate laws of most states provide that a company's board of directors is responsible for the management of the company's business and affairs. Despite the use of the term "management," boards act in a supervisory or oversight role, while delegating day-to-day management to the officers of the corporation. This structure is intended to provide a balance between the managers of a company, who direct and control the corporation's daily activities, and the directors, who have the duty and power to supervise, oversee, retain, and replace the managers.

In their oversight role, directors are obligated to evaluate and select senior management, approve major expenditures, acquire and dispose of significant assets or businesses, issue securities, or change the company's fundamental direction. Through their supervisory powers, boards also frequently require managers to obtain board approval for events that, although are not fundamental to the business, are nevertheless sensitive or material, such as major acquisitions, licensing, joint venture, or other arrangements.

1. Frank M. Placenti is a partner in the corporate practice of Squire Patton Boggs (US) LLP, where he leads the firm's U.S. corporate governance practice.

Members of the board do not have the authority to act individually on behalf of the corporation, unless there has been a specific board resolution to grant such power. Instead, the board functions as a group, deliberating and acting collectively.

The law of every state requires business corporations to maintain a board of directors and imposes specific duties, typically referred to as "fiduciary duties," either by statute or court decision. Fiduciary duties are generally described as

- *Duty of Care*. This duty generally requires the director pay attention, ask questions, and act diligently in order to become and remain fully informed and to bring relevant information to the attention of other directors.
- *Duty of Loyalty*. This duty generally requires the director make decisions based upon the company's best interest, and not on any personal interest.

In determining whether directors have satisfied their fiduciary duties, courts will most often apply what is referred to as the "Business Judgment Rule." Under the Business Judgment Rule, the board's decision is protected unless it is proven the directors breached either their duty of care or their duty of loyalty.

In certain circumstances, the Business Judgment Rule gives way to more detailed scrutiny of the board's decisions, such as where one or more directors have an interest in the transaction, or where the company is being sold in a change of control transaction. These situations are dealt with elsewhere in this Handbook, including in the chapters comprising Section 6, Management and Oversight of Transactions.

In addition to these general fiduciary duties, boards of U.S. public companies have broad statutory duties under a variety of federal and state laws. Many of these duties have arisen pursuant to legislation passed since the collapse of Enron in 2001. The focus on corporate governance during what is often called the "post-Enron era," has brought with it an increasing set of new laws, as well as Securities and Exchange Commission and stock exchange mandates that have codified what previously had been thought of as best practices.

Key Questions

When considering the nature and exercise of a director's duties, key questions that a board member might ask include the following:

- ❑ Do I have enough information to make an informed decision? If not, what additional information do I need?
- ❑ How reliable are the sources of that information? Do any of the individuals providing it (e.g., management) have a personal interest that I should be aware of?
- ❑ Do the managers of my company have significant (or any) experience with the matters under consideration? Is it reasonable to rely on their recommendations?
- ❑ Would it be advisable to seek additional input from independent third parties or experts?
- ❑ With respect to any third party or expert who has provided information, what are their qualifications? What is their relationship to management, and how independent are they? Is their compensation structured to create any bias that I should consider?

- ❑ Are there any time constraints that would prevent the board from obtaining further information before making a decision?
- ❑ What alternatives have management considered? Has the case for those alternatives been fully explored?
- ❑ Do I or any of my fellow board members have (or appear to have) a personal interest in the transaction? Should that director participate in our deliberations? Abstain from voting?
- ❑ If so, does the full board understand the contours of that personal interest, has it been disclosed, and has it been recorded in the minutes of our deliberations?
- ❑ Have we received appropriate legal advice concerning any of these apparent conflicts of interest?
- ❑ Are there any legal or regulatory issues to be considered? Have we received proper advice?
- ❑ What are the accounting considerations or impacts of our discussion?

Additional Reading

1. ABA Business Law Section, Committee on Corporate Laws. *Corporate Director's Guidebook*. 5th ed. (See Section 3.).

2. Forrester, Christopher M., and Celeste S. Ferber. "Fiduciary Duties and Other Responsibilities of Corporate Directors and Officers." RR Donnelly Global Capital Markets, 2008.

   http://www.mainstreetforumnc.org/wp-content/uploads/2012/07/Fiduciary_Duties_and_Other_Responsibilities_of_Corporate_Directors_and_Offiers.pdf

3. What Does a Corporate Board of Directors Do?

   http://biztaxlaw.about.com/od/startingacorporation/a/boardduties.htm

Notes

1.2 DECIDING WHETHER TO SERVE ON A BOARD

CONTRIBUTED BY
Frank M. Placenti
Squire Patton Boggs (US) LLP[1]

Serving on a corporate board can be challenging, interesting, and satisfying. Starting in the 1980s, there has been an increasing emphasis on the role of boards of directors, and the standards for their performance have risen continuously. This increased pressure now means that board service generally requires significant personal time and attention. In addition, the specter of individual liability and reputational risk if things go wrong means that anyone considering board service should make the decision thoughtfully, after considering the nature of the company, its business, the composition of its board, the reputation and competency of its senior management, the reasons that the candidate is being considered for the board, and any particular role or function that is being requested.

Some steps a candidate might consider before joining a board include the following:

- ❑ Meeting with the senior management of the company, particularly the CEO and CFO, to determine whether they would welcome proactive and independent board judgment and activity.

1. Frank M. Placenti is a partner in the corporate practice of Squire Patton Boggs (US) LLP, where he leads the firm's U.S. corporate governance practice.

- ❑ Meetings with selected members of the board of directors, including corporate governance committee members to understand the principle issues facing the corporation, board practices, organization and procedures, and any contemplated committee memberships or other special functions.
- ❑ Determining whether there are any company-specific factors that are relevant, including financial distress, upcoming transactions, and other events that may require greater than usual time commitment.
- ❑ Getting a feel for the "tone at the top" of the company and the corporate culture.
- ❑ An evaluation of the company's protective mechanisms, including indemnification and exculpation arrangements and directors' and officers' liability insurance (see Section 3).
- ❑ The company's past litigation history, including any shareholder litigation.
- ❑ Reviewing examples of the "board book" provided to directors in advance of recent meetings to determine whether the board is receiving sufficient information or, alternatively, is being subjected to "information overload."

Key Questions

The American Bar Association "Corporate Director's Guidebook" suggests the following questions when an individual is considering joining a public company board:

- ❑ Whether the opportunity to serve on the board is sufficiently compelling to engage serious interests and attention.
- ❑ Whether the individual has sufficient time and flexibility to perform diligently the required duties, especially if a corporate crisis or major transaction arises.
- ❑ Whether the individual has any scheduling conflicts that would unduly interfere with a board's normal meeting schedule.
- ❑ Whether the individual has skills and experience to participate meaningfully as a director of the company.
- ❑ Whether there are any foreseeable or perceived conflicts of interest with the corporation or its business or senior management (e.g., material relationships with competitors, acquisition targets, or potential acquirers).
- ❑ Whether the individual has or can develop a sufficient depth of understanding of the corporation's business and business model in order to function effectively.
- ❑ Whether the individual believes that the senior management of the board has integrity and conducts itself in an honest and ethical manner.

Some additional questions could include the following:

- ❑ Why would I want to serve on this board? Why does the company want me? What can I contribute? Do I have the time available to make a worthwhile contribution?
- ❑ Am I comfortable with the people, and particularly the CEO and the other directors?

- ❑ How do the members of the board interact with each other, and with management?
- ❑ Is the location of most board meetings compatible with my personal and travel schedule? Will I be able to attend 75 percent or more of all board and committee meetings?
- ❑ Is there adequate exculpation, indemnification, and directors' and officers' insurance provisions in place to protect directors? (See Section 3.)
- ❑ Are the remuneration arrangements satisfactory? Are they generally aligned with shareholder interests?

Additional Reading

1. *The Boardroom Guide for New Directors* (publication of the National Association of Corporate Directors)
   http://www.directorship.com
2. *What to Ask and Know Before Becoming a Director*
   http://diversitymbamagazine.com/?s=what+to+ask+and+know+before+becoming+a+director&x=0&y=0
3. *Board of Directors*
   http://www.smallbusinessnotes.com/operating/leadership/board.html
4. *Qualifications to Serve on a Board of Directors*
   http://www.ehow.com/list_6569366_qualifications-serve-board-directors.html
5. *Board of Directors Corporate Governance Guidelines*
   https://www.ncr.com/sites/default/files/Corporate-Governance-Guidelines-2016.pdf

Notes

____

____

____

____

____

1.3 BOARD COMPOSITION AND RECRUITING

CONTRIBUTED BY
Frank M. Placenti
Squire Patton Boggs (US) LLP[1]

Boards function best when they deliberate openly, collaboratively, and collegially. Collegiality does not mean, however, that board discussions should become an exercise in "group think." Board members need to trust each other enough to constructively disagree, while trying to reach a decision that is in the best interest of the corporation and its shareholders.

For a board to function in this fashion, while addressing the panoply of complex issues facing modern business, board composition becomes a critical exercise. Although there was a time when corporate CEOs selected board members almost exclusively from their own social or business network, today's best boards are carefully assembled with the board's responsibilities and corporation's specific needs in mind.

Most well-managed boards of directors maintain nominating committees chaired by an independent director (i.e., not the CEO) charged with the responsibility to evaluate the performance of existing board members and recruit new ones.

1. Frank M. Placenti is a partner in the corporate practice of Squire Patton Boggs (US) LLP, where he leads the firm's U.S. corporate governance practice.

Recent changes to the Securities and Exchange Commission regulations mandate that the board's process for selecting and evaluating directors' qualifications be discussed publicly in the company's annual proxy statement, accompanied by disclosures as to which skills and attributes each director brings to the table.

Significant changes in the business of a company can also suggest the need to consider changes in the boardroom. When a company exits a business, goes into a new line of business, expands internationally, or undertakes other significant corporate activity, it may find that the existing board may no longer be composed of the right individuals going forward.

Shareholder activities, discussed elsewhere in this Handbook, can also play a role in shaping the constitution of a board.

Key Questions

When thinking about board composition, some important questions include the following:

- ❑ How large should the board of the company be in order to discharge its duties?
- ❑ What specific skills or attributes are necessary to serve on this board, including those needed to fill specific roles such as audit committee chair, audit committee member, compensation committee roles, etc.?
- ❑ What role should diversity play in the board's composition? How should we define diversity?
- ❑ What particular business backgrounds might be helpful in terms of understanding the company's operations or planning its future course of action?
- ❑ Would it be helpful to have one or more directors with key contacts that can assist in expanding the company's business?
- ❑ Should we consider having a written job description with respect to any board vacancies that we wish to fill at the present time?
- ❑ Do we have sufficient contacts in the boardroom to generate a list of suitable candidates, or should a search firm be retained?
- ❑ What process will be used to evaluate potential candidates?
- ❑ What process will be used to evaluate the current composition and performance of the board?
- ❑ How will we promote the retirement of board members at the appropriate time? Are term limits appropriate? What about a mandatory retirement age? Under what circumstances should we be willing to waive those limitations?
- ❑ Does our proxy disclosure accurately and transparently reflect our nomination process?
- ❑ Have any of our shareholders expressed a view about the composition of our board? Have they submitted nominees?
- ❑ Does our board need to be "refreshed"? Do we have any long serving board members who are no longer sufficiently contributing? What is the best way to effect any desirable change?

Additional Reading

1. Building the "Right" Board
   https://www.nacdonline.org/Magazine/Article.cfm?ItemNumber=36561
2. Strength in Diversity: The Changing Boardroom
   http://www.committee100.org/media/media_eng/JohnChiang_030210.pdf
3. Olson, John E., and Michel T. Adams. "Composing a Balanced and Effective Board to Meet New Governance Strategies." *The Business Lawyer* 59 (February 2001).
4. Board Composition and Director Criteria
   http://www.angelblog.net/Board_Composition.html

Notes

1.4 DIFFERENTIATING BOARD AND MANAGEMENT ROLES

CONTRIBUTED BY
Frank M. Placenti
Squire Patton Boggs (US) LLP[1]

While the corporate statutes of most states provide that the boards of directors are responsible for the "management" of the affairs of their companies, most well-functioning boards do not attempt to actively manage the business, but instead oversee the officers who do so. While it is appropriate for board members to collect enough information to perform their oversight function, board members must be careful not to involve themselves in the day-to-day operation of the business for a variety of practical as well as legal reasons. One formulation of this admonition that clients have found helpful over the years is that boards should follow the "NIFO Rule" (Noses In, Fingers Out).

Stating the need for this balance is easier than actually striking it. The board should give continuous consideration to its agenda and processes to ensure that it is sufficiently informed, thoroughly engaged, thinking seriously, and providing meaningful input, without becoming so involved in *minutia* that board meetings become an exercise in "Monday morning quarterbacking."

1. Frank M. Placenti is a partner in the corporate practice of Squire Patton Boggs (US) LLP, where he leads the firm's U.S. corporate governance practice.

Similarly, although directors are recruited for their background and experience, board meetings should not represent an opportunity for individual board members to share war stories of how "we do it at our company," to the annoyance and frustration of all present, including management. Even in board committees where the focus is, by design, on items of a more granular nature, board members should remember that their role is to oversee the management of the company, not run it.

A board can generally be comfortable that it is striking the balance correctly when it is focusing on selecting and mentoring key members of the management, providing guidance, responding to management's request for input, and exercising its prerogative to replace an underperforming management team, while refraining from functions that would customarily associate with the day-to-day management of the business.

Key Questions

In considering the board's role and differentiating it from that of management, some questions to consider include the following:

- ❑ Is our board receiving sufficient information in order to exercise its oversight function?
- ❑ Do our board books provide us with the information we need to know in the format we need to know it?
- ❑ Are we being deluged with too much information?
- ❑ Do our board meetings strike the right balance between management presentations and an opportunity for board deliberation and input? Are we suffering from "death by PowerPoint"?
- ❑ Are any individual board members "too deep in the weeds" during board discussions? What can be done to remedy that situation?
- ❑ Are we focused on the right things during our board meetings?
- ❑ Have we appropriately focused on strategy, the future, and long-term value creation?
- ❑ Do we have sufficient confidence in our management team to feel as if we can separate ourselves from day-to-day management decisions?
- ❑ Are our agendas organized to promote focus on the right topics?

Additional Reading

1. *Creating Value from the Owner-Board-Management Relationship*
   http://iveybusinessjournal.com/publication/creating-value-from-the-owner-board-management-relationship/
2. "Beyond 'Independent' Directors: A Functional Approach to Board Independence," 119 *Harvard Law Review* 1553–75 (March 2006).

Notes

15 THE BOARD'S ROLE IN STRATEGY DEVELOPMENT

CONTRIBUTED BY
Frank M. Placenti
Squire Patton Boggs (US) LLP[1]

A leading Midwestern insurance company promotes its products by reminding customers that "Life Comes at You Fast." That is certainly true in business where yesterday's Kindle™ can quickly be eclipsed by today's iPad™. Shifts in strategic direction, which formerly took place once in a decade can now be experienced every few months, particularly in technology businesses.

Recognizing that strategy is a huge determinate of long-term success or failure, boards are increasingly becoming involved in formulating corporate strategy, rather than simply ratifying strategies presented by management.

According to the National Association of Corporate Directors, strategy development entails "establishing overall destination, and making provisions for frequent mid-course correction. It involves perpetual redefinition that will—internally for strengths and weaknesses, and externally for opportunities and threats—focusing intently on competition."[2]

1. Frank M. Placenti is a partner in the corporate practice of Squire Patton Boggs (US) LLP, where he leads the firm's U.S. corporate governance practice.
2. National Association of Corporate Directors, *Report of the NACD Blue Ribbon Commission on the Role of the Board in Corporate Strategy* (Washington, D.C.: National Association of Corporate Directors, 2006), 6.

Stating the need for greater board involvement in strategy development does not necessarily guarantee successful participation. A 2007 article in *Strategy and Leadership* summarized the problem:

> Strategy work is an iterative process, not a big bang event. Yet, often we (boards) treat it as though it were a one-time even by scheduling the board's strategy meeting or making strategy the key agenda item at an annual board retreat. Absent rich context [however] directors are hard pressed to contribute effectively.[3]

Key Questions

For a board to play a meaningful role in strategy development, here are some items to be considered:

- ❑ What major strategic challenges are facing the company in the near term, mid-term, and long term? Has the board identified or even discussed them?
- ❑ What is the best model for the board's involvement in strategy for this corporation? Should management be developing strategic alternatives for consideration by the board? Should it be more collaborative?
- ❑ How frequently should the board be discussing strategy? Every board meeting? Is a board retreat helpful?
- ❑ Should the board establish a standing strategic planning committee, or is this better retained as a function of your full board?
- ❑ What information can be provided to the board on a regular basis (periodicals, industry materials, etc.) that can give the board the "rich context" in which to deliberate about strategic matters?
- ❑ What is the role of a lead director or outside chairman in developing the board's strategic role?
- ❑ Am I comfortable that the company has a good grip on strategic issues? Do I have confidence in management's ability to navigate a thoughtful strategic course?
- ❑ Should we have a Plan B in any area of our business?
- ❑ How much risk is appropriate for our company with respect to any new or untested strategic initiatives?
- ❑ How much capital can we afford to commit?
- ❑ What and when should we communicate to the market about our new strategic initiatives in order to create shareholder values?
- ❑ With respect to any new strategic initiatives, do we have the right senior management? The right board?
- ❑ Should we implement our new strategy organically, or would an acquisition make more sense?
- ❑ Do we need external advice with respect to any particular new strategy?

3. Donnelly Townsend, "Engaging the Board of Directors on Strategy." *Strategy and Leadership* 35, no. 5 (2007).

Additional Reading

1. *The Board's Role in Corporate Strategy*
   http://www.kslaw.com/Library/publication/12-08%20HLSCorporate GovernenceBlog%20Stein,%20Baxley.pdf
2. The Board and Strategic Change: A Learning Organization, *International Review of Business Research Papers* 3, no. 1 (March 2007): 125–46.
   http://www.bizresearchpapers.com/Paper%2010.pdf
3. Neil L. Drobney, "Strategy as a Governance Issue." *NACD Directors Monthly* (February 2004).
4. Robert R. Hallaghan, "The Board's Role in Strategy: Research and Action Points." *NACD Directors Monthly* (January 2009).
5. *Your Board's Generative Work*
   http://www.crenyc.org/_blog/News_and_Views/post/Your_Board%E2%80%99s_Generative_Work/
6. The Big-Picture Board: Creating a Culture for Generative Thinking
   http://www.nais.org/Magazines-Newsletters/ISMagazine/Pages/The-Big-Picture-Board.aspx

Notes

16 BOARD COMMUNICATION—BALANCING COLLEGIALITY AND CANDOR

CONTRIBUTED BY
Frank M. Placenti
Squire Patton Boggs (US) LLP[1]

There is an old story that, during the 1940s and 50s, board meetings often took place in private clubs. After dinner, board members would look under their plates to find one or more crisp one hundred dollar bills, which was the remuneration for their board service.

Those clubby days are gone forever. While corporate board service is not yet a full-time job, it is serious work done by serious people in an environment of enhanced scrutiny.

Now that board members are no longer drawn from a small pool of personal friends of the CEO, members may come into the boardroom knowing very little about each other. They generally spend little, if any, time together outside the formal board process. Moreover, as the board's work has become increasingly time consuming and granular, much of the work of the board occurs in separate committees.

All of these factors conspire to make it more difficult for board members to function as a high-powered, yet collegial team.

Much has been written in recent years concerning the dangers (on the one hand) and the virtues (on the other) of a "collegial" environment in the board. While most believe

1. Frank M. Placenti is a partner in the corporate practice of Squire Patton Boggs (US) LLP, where he leads the firm's U.S. corporate governance practice.

that collegiality is a necessary ingredient to a high-functioning board, others celebrate the role of constructive conflict in the boardroom. Striking the appropriate balance may ultimately provide the right answer for most corporations.

Key Questions

In thinking about your board's interpersonal relations, some issues to be considered include the following:

- ❑ Do we have trust in our boardroom?
- ❑ Are board members comfortable speaking their minds without fear of retaliation or being "cut from the herd"?
- ❑ What should we do to foster free and candid exchange of ideas?
- ❑ Do we have any individual board members whose conduct is impeding that goal?
- ❑ Does our CEO conduct himself/herself in a manner that fosters candid board discussion?
- ❑ Do our board members receive sufficient information to permit them to constructively challenge management recommendations and proposals?
- ❑ Do board members spend sufficient time with each other socially to build team spirit and camaraderie?
- ❑ Do our board members have shared values about the way in which board members should communicate and conduct themselves?
- ❑ Do we have appropriate diversity in our boardroom in all key dimensions (age, gender, cultural background, geography, industry experience, etc.)?
- ❑ Once decisions are made, do we "close ranks" behind a decision, or are grudges or factions maintained?
- ❑ Do we need any type of outside counseling with respect to the functioning of our board?
- ❑ Would outside board leadership (by a nonexecutive chair or lead director if not already present) foster better board dynamics?
- ❑ Would a board self-evaluation improve our functioning? (See Chapter 2.5 of this Handbook.)

Additional Reading

1. *The ABCs of Board Room Dynamics—Attitude, Behavior, Candor*
   https://www2.deloitte.com/content/dam/Deloitte/in/Documents/risk/Board%20of%20Directors/in-gc-the-abcs-of-boardroom-dynamics-noexp.pdf
2. *On Speaking Terms: Boardroom Communication*
   http://www.kaye.com/fambz/boardroom.pdf

Notes

17 DEALING WITH ACTIVISM IN THE BOARDROOM

CONTRIBUTED BY
Frank M. Placenti
Squire Patton Boggs (US) LLP[1]

Not all board members are recruited by the incumbent board. Shareholder activists of various types, and with varying agendas, have come to recognize that board representation can be one of the most effective ways in which to influence corporate activity. Hedge funds and other investors hoping to catalyze change either conduct or threaten to conduct proxy efforts as a vehicle for seating corporate directors. While proxy contests are successfully waged from time to time, more often, companies seek to avoid the expense and disruption of a proxy contest by negotiating with shareholder activists to seat one or more directors.

In 2010, the Securities and Exchange Commission adopted new "proxy access" rules that would have made it easier for significant investors of a corporation to gain board representation by nominating directors for election and presenting those candidates on the company's own proxy materials. These rules were struck down following judicial challenge and have not been readopted. However, as of this writing, over 100 major U.S.

1. Frank M. Placenti is a partner in the corporate practice of Squire Patton Boggs (US) LLP, where he leads the firm's U.S. corporate governance practice.

public companies have enacted some form of proxy access procedure, either voluntary or under pressure from investors, and that trend continues.

All of these factors combine to suggest that many boards will find themselves dealing with one or more board members who have been seated without the full-throated support of the company's management and incumbent board.

Whether to treat these new directors as "gate crashers" to be tolerated, or to instead welcome them as potentially valuable team members, will depend upon facts of the particular circumstance, the demeanor and agenda of those seated, their qualifications and ability to contribute to the board, and a variety of other factors. That said, the fact that a board member may have gained his or her seat at the table in a nontraditional manner does not change the fact that all board members share a fiduciary duty to the corporation and its shareholders and have certain rights that underpin their ability to disengage those duties. When one or more directors have their own agenda, however, it can complicate discussions and lead to both practical and legal problems.

Please see Chapter 5.6 of this Handbook for a further discussion of shareholder activism.

Key Questions

When a board includes one or more activists seated through negotiation or proxy election, some issues to consider are as follows:

- ❑ What are the agenda and goals of the new director(s)?
- ❑ Do they have a specific transaction or series of transactions they are sponsoring?
- ❑ Does the new director(s) have an allegiance to any particular shareholder that must be understood? Are they being separately compensated by a third party? What are the details of those arrangements and how do they influence that director's views?
- ❑ How independent is/are the new director(s) from the activists who sponsored them?
- ❑ What is the best method in which to orient the new director(s)?
- ❑ Does the new director(s) have positions or programs that are meritorious and should be considered? How can we create a constructive dynamic?
- ❑ What if the new director(s) refuses to follow pre-established board policies?
- ❑ Does the new director(s) have conflicts of interests or other legal impediments to their service?
- ❑ What should be done if a new director is disruptive? Breaches a confidentiality obligation?
- ❑ What advice of counsel may be necessary or appropriate in that regard?
- ❑ What committee assignments are appropriate for the new director(s)?
- ❑ Is the new director(s) focused upon transactional issues (such as acquisitions, dispositions, etc.) or more on social or labor relations issues?
- ❑ What are the implications of those orientations?

Additional Reading

1. Activist in the Boardroom: How Advocacy Groups Seek to Shape Corporate Behavior
   http://thepriceswrite.com/Activists%20in%20Boardroom.pdf
2. Directorial Activism in the Face of Alleged or Actual Officer Misbehavior
   https://www.complianceweek.com/blogs/harvey-l-pitt/directorial-activism-in-the-face-of-alleged-or-actual-officer-misbehavior#.WE9FYCMrJYI

Notes

1.8 MANAGING THE BOARD'S AGENDA AND CALENDAR

CONTRIBUTED BY
Frank M. Placenti
Squire Patton Boggs (US) LLP[1]

It is imperative that the board takes control of its own calendar and agenda. All too often, however, the board's agenda and annual calendar is a historical relic of past practice, as to which very little fresh or innovative thought has been given. Similarly, board meetings are too often dominated by a parade of management presentations on a variety of routine issues, leaving little time for the board to function creatively or effectively.

It is desirable that the board periodically step back and redesign its agenda and calendar. Thought should be given to the board's standing committees and their charter. Delegation of routine tasks to board committees is an effective way in which to ensure that the board itself creates the time and opportunity for meaningful discussion at the full board level. Similarly, matters can be dealt with in written reports provided to the board in advance of the meeting, with an opportunity to ask questions, but with no need to rehash material that the board has already read.

The chairman or lead director should meet with the CEO and/or corporate secretary to map out an annual meeting calendar, with a goal of spreading mandatory functions

1. Frank M. Placenti is a partner in the corporate practice of Squire Patton Boggs (US) LLP, where he leads the firm's U.S. corporate governance practice.

among various board meetings, so that no meeting is entirely dominated by mandatory or routine items.

Key Questions

To manage a board's program of work, some questions might include the following:

- ❑ Do we have the right board committees?
- ❑ Should any be sunset or should any new ones be created?
- ❑ Are our committee charters clear and correct? When were they last reviewed and updated?
- ❑ Do each of the committees know what they are expected to do? Are they doing it?
- ❑ What is the most effective way for board committees to communicate their output to the full board to avoid a complete rehashing of the committee process at the full board meeting?
- ❑ Is the composition of our board books optimal? Is there too much information? Too little?
- ❑ Is the information presented in an accessible manner?
- ❑ How could reports be reformatted to make them more meaningful?
- ❑ What key indicators could be employed to facilitate reporting?
- ❑ Where is "exception reporting" more appropriately used than full recitations on any given subject?
- ❑ What is the appropriate length for our board meetings?
- ❑ Should committee meetings be held the day before?
- ❑ Should we have an annual board retreat?
- ❑ If so, what topics should be covered?
- ❑ What is the appropriate balance at the retreat between social and business activity?
- ❑ Should the CEO produce a monthly (or periodic) written report to the board between board meetings?
- ❑ Would a monthly call with the CEO provide better context and input opportunities than a written board report?
- ❑ Is there an appropriate role for an executive committee with delegated authority to handle routine matters (transaction approvals, loan approvals, etc.) between full board meetings?

Additional Reading

1. Don't Bore the Board of Directors
   http://web.mit.edu/e-club/hadzima/pdf/dont-bore-the-board-of-directors.pdf

2. Time Management: Managing by Calendar
   http://bonnernetwork.pbworks.com/f/BonCurManagebyCalendar.pdf

Notes

1.9 COMMON STANDING BOARD COMMITTEES

CONTRIBUTED BY
Frank M. Placenti
Squire Patton Boggs (US) LLP[1]

The breadth and complexity of issues facing a modern board of directors is too great to permit all of the work of the board to be done as a committee as a whole. Virtually all major corporations employ a series of standing committees. In some cases, these committees have delegated authority to perform a particular board function, while in other cases they are expected to develop recommendations for action by the full board of directors. Certain committees and their composition are mandated by stock exchange listing rules.

Some common standing board committees and their functions include the following:

- *Nominating and Corporate Governance*. Sometimes a single committee, and sometimes two separate committees, the functions performed by the directors assigned to the nominating and corporate governance effort include recruiting, selecting, and nominating new directors; board self-assessment and performance; oversight of the public disclosure concerning board functions in the company's written proxy materials; and development, approval, and oversight of the corporate governance policies and procedures utilized by the company.

1. Frank M. Placenti is a partner in the corporate practice of Squire Patton Boggs (US) LLP, where he leads the firm's U.S. corporate governance practice.

Typically, this committee is comprised of all nonemployee (independent) directors and should not include the CEO.

- *Executive Committee.* Most often used for companies with large or geographically dispersed boards of directors, an executive committee receives delegated authority to perform routine functions, or to act on behalf of the entire board in emergency situations between board meetings. The company's CEO almost always serves on an executive committee, along with a small number of independent board members. Given modern communication and the prevalence of telephone meetings, fewer companies employ executive committees than in the past.
- *Audit Committee.* U.S. public corporations maintain audit committees by mandate. Rules and regulations governing audit committees are complex. Audit committees are comprised of all nonemployee (independent) directors, with strict independence tests mandated by Securities and Exchange Commission Rules. The audit committee provides oversight for the company's audit and financial reporting functions, and often performs the role of reviewing and approving related party or other conflict of interest transactions. Most U.S. public corporations have chosen to have their audit committees chaired by an individual who meets the Securities and Exchange Commission standard as a financial expert in order to avoid disclosing that they do not have such an expert available on the committee. Securities and Exchange Commission Rules contain detailed provisions on the qualifications and background necessary to be considered a financial expert for audit committee service.
- *Compensation Committee.* The compensation committee is usually comprised of independent directors to oversee the compensation programs for the company's chief executive officer and senior management. This includes oversight of the company's salary, incentive bonus, and long-term incentive compensation plans. The committee will also generally review and approve the company's public disclosure statement concerning its compensation programs. Compensation committees increasingly employ outside consultants to assist them in benchmarking and other functions necessary in order to have a well-thought-out and justifiable compensation program.
- *Strategic Planning Committee.* Some boards elect to appoint a strategic planning committee with particular responsibility for working with the company's management to develop strategy. The merits of delegating this strategic planning role to a subset of the board has been vigorously debated in academic and other literature.
- *Finance or Investment Committee.* When a company regularly engages in financing, hedging, investment, or acquisition activity, it may find that delegating decisions to a finance or investment committee can be appropriate.

Key Questions

Some important questions to ask regarding standing committees include the following:

- ❑ Besides legally mandated committees, what committees should we maintain?
- ❑ Should we have a separate executive committee?
- ❑ If so, what are the parameters of its authority?
- ❑ Are our committee charters accurate? When were they last reviewed?
- ❑ Do they "over promise" (i.e., are they so aspirational in their content as to set standards the committee will not meet)?
- ❑ Do we have the right members on each of our committees?
- ❑ Do they meet statutory and regulatory mandates?
- ❑ Are they appropriately independent of management?
- ❑ Do any of our committees need separate legal counsel or other independent advisors?
- ❑ Do the individuals on our audit committee understand our company's principal accounting policies and risks?
- ❑ Do our committee members spend an appropriate amount of time performing their functions?
- ❑ What is the appropriate remuneration for participation on each of our committees?
- ❑ Should committee chairs receive higher remuneration for service on any of our individual committees, particularly the audit and compensation committees?
- ❑ When should our committees meet?
- ❑ Should they be expected to meet in person or by telephone periodically, other than contiguously with board meetings?
- ❑ Do we have the right chairman in place for each of our committees?
- ❑ Should we have a policy of permitting/encouraging board members who are not serving on a particular committee to attend (or participate) in those committee meetings as an ex officio member?
- ❑ Who should formulate the slate of committee assignments for board consideration? The CEO? Lead director? Nominating and corporate governance committee?
- ❑ Do any of our board members serve on the compensation committee of companies where our compensation committee members are employed?
- ❑ Does our CEO serve on any board where any of our compensation committee members are employed?
- ❑ Do our committee members meet all legal and regulatory qualifications for independence and expertise?

Additional Reading

1. Principles of Corporate Governance, Business Roundtable, May 2002.
2. *Corporate Governance in the Board, What Works Best*, PricewaterhouseCoopers and the Institute of Internal Auditors Research Foundation, 2002.
3. All Big Four accounting firms routinely publish current materials regarding best audit committee practices, which should and can be requested from the companies' auditors.
4. *Typical Types of Board Committees*
   http://managementhelp.org/boards/brdcmtte.htm

Notes

1.10 SPECIAL BOARD COMMITTEES

CONTRIBUTED BY
Gregory V. Varallo
Richards, Layton & Finger, P.A.[1]

The work of most public company boards is largely accomplished through a number of committees of the board. From time to time, however, a situation arises that calls for the appointment of a "special" committee. Typically, a special committee is formed when some type of conflict transaction presents itself: a proposal from a controlling stockholder, for example, or the sale of the company to a management-led group where the CEO has a seat on the board.

Outside of the transactional context, special committees are sometimes formed to conduct investigations in circumstances where one or more members of the board might potentially be involved in the conduct being investigated, or in response to a shareholder demand that the board investigate and take action with respect to a particular topic. In addition, special committees are sometimes formed in the context of dealing with derivative litigation where nonconflicted directors are empowered to investigate the allegations

1. Gregory V. Varallo is a director and president of Richards, Layton & Finger, P.A., where he practices in the areas of complex business litigation, ADR, and corporate governance. The author wishes to acknowledge the assistance of his colleague John R. Fitzgerald in the preparation of this chapter.

of the pending action and to take action regarding whether the suit should continue, be dismissed, or be settled (in all events subject to court oversight).

The receipt of a shareholder demand to investigate triggers certain obligations on the board to do just that, lest the company be held to have surrendered the legal presumption of independence of a majority of the board, which arises, at least under Delaware law, by virtue of the shareholder having made the demand.

While special committees can be formed for vastly different purposes, they share several common denominators. First, the membership of a special committee needs to be entirely independent—indeed beyond reproach. Second, the special committee needs to not only be independent on paper, but also to act in a manner that simulates arm's-length bargaining or vigorous investigation. In short, the special committee has to act in a manner that bespeaks independence. Finally, the special committee must have a governing charter that is properly tailored to the circumstances.

The failure of the special committee to pay careful attention to the contextually specific independence of all of its members, to act independently, or to have an appropriate delegation of power from the full board could be fatal to the work of the committee. In any of these cases, the poorly formed, authorized, or functioning committee may wind up creating more trouble for the company in later litigation than it was created to solve. Put simply, it is almost always the case that a poorly conceived or executed committee is worse than no committee at all. We deal with each hallmark of the successful committee in the following sections.

Independence Beyond Reproach

The single most important common denominator in all special committee work is to populate the committee with truly independent directors. For this purpose, "independence" is not measured solely by the standards set out by the various exchanges, but instead is a context-specific inquiry. What ties does each member of the committee have with the person or circumstance that gives rise to the formation of the committee? If a controlling stockholder is involved, are there any longstanding social ties that may interfere with a finding of "independence"? While "mere friendship" is not enough to disqualify a special committee member, a particularly deep social relationship might. Does the director being examined vacation with the controlling stockholder? Do they have other business interests together? Are there other ties of a more subtle social nature that would suggest a lack of true independence? In all events, counsel chosen by the special committee will almost invariably begin by helping the committee ensure that all of its members are rigorously independent. Indeed, if that does not happen, the committee may wish to reconsider its choice of counsel.

What happens if the board (or the committee) concludes that there are no truly independent directors, or instead only one? The most straightforward answer is that the board should either consider expanding the board to add directors who are truly independent in the specific context presented, or instead consider proceeding without a committee. To be clear, at least in the view of the author, proceeding with a committee that lacks real independence is almost invariably a mistake.

Likewise, the law tends to disfavor single-person committees. While one-person committees are not prohibited, the law requires that the independence of a single-member committee be "beyond reproach." A director asked to be a sole-member committee is well advised to ask the board to consider either adding a second member or appointing a new member of the board to participate in the committee.

Independence in Fact

Special committees are called upon, in both the transactional and investigatory context, to attempt to simulate arm's-length bargaining or to approach an investigation at arm's length, typically because a conflict exists that would otherwise disqualify the full board from acting. Thus, committee members are charged with setting aside friendships or social ties and proceeding in the best interests of the company and all its constituencies, and not in the best interests of the conflicted party. Trying to find a solution that is "fair to everyone" is not the idea, and is likely to lead to criticism or liability of the committee members. The task is not to be "fair" but to negotiate or investigate vigorously and at arm's length. Directors who are not up to this challenge should decline to serve on the committee at the outset.

Charter

In reviewing the work of special committees, courts have often focused on the power given to the committee in the resolution establishing it, in other words, its charter. As a general matter, the committee's charter should empower the committee to investigate or negotiate and to say "no" if it determines that to be appropriate. Of course, all committees should be given both the power and the funding to hire counsel and such other experts as they deem appropriate in their discretion.

Circumstances may arise where it would be appropriate and desirable to delegate to the committee the entire power of the board to make a decision with respect to a matter. For example, the so-called special litigation committee chartered to take over conduct of a pending derivative suit, in order to be effective, must first have the full and complete delegation of the power of the board to take whatever action it deems appropriate after its investigation. On the other hand, a committee formed to investigate a shareholder demand (prelitigation) should almost always have the power to investigate and report back to the full board a recommendation, rather than the power to take final action. Likewise a committee formed to negotiate a merger often may not be given full power to approve the transaction, as the statutory corporate law in many jurisdictions, including Delaware, prohibits the delegation of power to a committee to take final board action with respect to a merger. In all circumstances, committee counsel typically will begin its representation of the committee with a careful review of the committee's charter and make changes as appropriate.

Importance of Advisors

While the retention of independent advisors is dealt with separately in this H
worth noting that special committee practice has emerged as a highly deve
As with any specialized area of the law, directors are well advised to re
with, and rely on the advice of credentialed advisors who are themse
independence by the committee and are in all events expert in specia

Key Questions

Members of a special committee should ask each other and counsel the following questions in organizing and carrying out their work:

- ❑ Am I likely to be found completely independent of the person on the other side of the transaction that I am being asked to work on, or free to investigate the subject or targets of the investigation I have been called to address, without concern about bias or lack of independence?
- ❑ Is each of the other members of the committee likewise independent in the context of the committee's work?
- ❑ What advisors are best suited to this work? Am I convinced that they are independent themselves and capable of guiding the committee through its work?
- ❑ What does the resolution appointing the special committee say about its authority? Has counsel carefully vetted that resolution to ensure that the committee has the proper charter, including the power to hire counsel and experts and the power to say "no"?
- ❑ As the work of the transactional committee goes forward, does the transaction that I am working on continue to make sense from the perspective of the company? Would I do this transaction if it were solely for my own account? If my retirement depended on it?
- ❑ As the work of the investigatory committee goes forward, am I convinced that the hard questions have been asked and that no punches have been pulled? Is the investigation being done in an appropriately thorough manner?
- ❑ In considering the correct path to take as a committee formed to investigate a shareholder demand, would I be proud of the decision I am making if it were exposed to public scrutiny on the front page of *The New York Times*? If not, shouldn't I carefully reconsider what the committee is doing and why?

Additional Reading

1. Varallo, Gregory V., Srinivas M. Raja, and Michael D. Allen. *Special Committees: Law and Practice* 2nd ed., LexisNexis, 2014.
2. Varallo, Gregory V., Daniel Dreisbach, and Blake Rohrbacher. *Fundamentals of Corporate Governance: A Guide for Directors and Corporate Counsel* 2nd ed. ABA, 2009. (Note: especially chapter 5 on managing derivative litigation.)
3. William T. Allen, "Independent Directors in MBO Transactions: Are They Fact or Fantasy?" *The Business Lawyer* 45, no. 4 (August 1990).
4. John M. Zeberkiewicz, "Revisiting the Special Committee Process: 'In re Southern Peru Copper Corporation,'" 26 *Corporate Counsel Weekly* 368 (2011), available at http://www.rlf.com/files/112011SouthernPeru.pdf.

Notes

1.11 DIRECTOR RESIGNATION ISSUES

CONTRIBUTED BY
Ning Chiu
Davis Polk & Wardwell LLP[1]

The recruitment, election, and onboarding of directors that mark the beginning of a director's term are carefully and thoughtfully managed, but sometimes the end of a director's tenure is less well-orchestrated if a director decides to leave the board unexpectedly. Directors should be aware of the circumstances that may lead to either voluntary or forced resignations, and the resulting impact to their companies of how those situations are handled.

Changes in Director's Circumstances

A director should be sensitive to any change in his or her individual circumstances that could lead to resignation from a board. A new business relationship may cause an independent director to no longer be viewed as independent, create a conflict of interest, or even result in an actual competitive issue with the company. The company must at least be informed of the change so that it can undertake the necessary analysis to ensure that it would be appropriate for the director to continue serving. For that reason, many companies' governance guidelines require that directors who change their employment inform the board and offer to resign.

1. Ning Chiu is counsel at Davis Polk & Wardwell where she practices in the corporate governance and securities regulation areas.

There may also be instances where director resignation is viewed to be appropriate if a director becomes too busy managing his or her own affairs to fully devote time and attention to the board, such as when a director's own company is engaged in significant business dealings or faced with major regulatory investigations. A director may also choose to resign when he or she becomes embroiled in a public scandal, or is accused of significant misbehavior or criminal activity, and wants to avoid entangling the board with these matters.

Company Events That May Lead to Resignations

Directors may decide to resign if they ultimately disagree with the other board members or management with regard to fundamental issues that affect their service. The board may be divided over the strategic direction of the company, and may split as to whether to pursue significant business decisions. Directors may disagree as to the right succession plans for management. In addition, directors who do not believe that they are receiving sufficient information to make good decisions may eventually resign out of concern that they cannot fulfill their fiduciary responsibilities.

Directors may also decide to resign if shareholder votes for their election are lower than they would like, and believe that their election is not widely supported by investors. In addition, sometimes a company may have changed over time and a certain director's skill set may no longer be as pertinent to the needs of the company. These types of issues may surface from director evaluations.

Majority Voting for Director Elections and Resignation Policies

In recent years many companies have adopted majority voting for the election of directors, which require incumbent directors to receive more votes cast in favor of their election than against their service. Due to the holdover statute of many state corporate laws that allows directors to remain on their boards until the earlier of resignation, retirement, removal, or a successor is appointed, majority voting for director elections is usually coupled with a director resignation policy. The policy requires that directors who received more "against" votes than "for" votes offer to resign. Usually the board's governance committee is charged with reviewing the circumstances leading to the resignation and makes a recommendation to the board as to whether or not to accept that resignation within a certain period, and that board decision is publicly announced. While boards may be criticized for not accepting such a resignation, it does occur, particularly when the reason for a failed election is viewed as a one-time event that a director can amend.

Public Disclosure of a Director's Resignation (Noisy vs. Quiet Resignations)

Directors should be well aware of the required public disclosure surrounding resignations. Public companies must file a Form 8-K within four business days after a director's resignation. Given that a director's decision to resign may be the subject of discussion over some length of time before the director actually resigns, or the director may decide not to resign, the SEC has acknowledged in its interpretations of the rules that a discussion about the possibility of a director's resignation does not trigger disclosure. Directors should be judicious, then, to start with a conversation about the prospect of resigning first, which could then allow a company ample time to prepare for public disclosure, rather than submitting an official resignation immediately that could cause a scramble to make disclosure prematurely. These discussions should also happen with the same person, either the chair of the board or the head of the governance committee, who are well-versed in the rules.

SEC rules require that if a director's resignation is due to a disagreement with the company that is known to management regarding the company's operations, practices, or policy, then that disagreement must be publicly disclosed along with any correspondence from the director surrounding the circumstances of his or her resignation. Directors should be mindful of the nature of their written resignations that may appear to suggest that such a disagreement exists, lest it require public disclosure.

Delaware courts have held that, in certain narrow circumstances, where a resignation would leave the company in the hands of persons who would inflict harm on the company's shareholders, a director's resignation could constitute a breach of fiduciary duty.

In other less-severe circumstances, a director may still want to consider whether a resignation from a financially distressed company is advisable in order to avoid being a director at the time the company actually files for bankruptcy. In some cases of distress, however, directors determine that it is best to continue service in order to have an opportunity to positively affect the fortunes of the distressed company and thereby mitigate the risk of exposure to liability even following resignation. Thus, whether to resign from a distressed company is often a complex decision requiring consideration of competing factors.

Other Impact on the Board from a Director's Resignation

A director's resignation could have far-reaching effects on board succession planning, especially if the director provided a crucial expertise for the board or served a key function. The director should provide the board with as much notice as possible so that it can begin discussing recruiting new directors. The company also needs to prepare its public relations and external communications teams.

Key Questions

When considering resignation from a board, key questions that a board member might ask include the following:

- ❑ Do I understand the board policies that may require me to offer to resign, including changes in employment and under an applicable majority voting director election standard?
- ❑ If my personal circumstances or responsibilities change, should I be considering whether continued board service remains appropriate?
- ❑ Should I discuss the possibility of a resignation with the board far in advance so that the board may appropriately tailor its board succession plans?
- ❑ Do I know who the point person on the board is to discuss the possibility of a resignation?
- ❑ Do I understand the SEC and stock exchange rules surrounding public disclosure of director resignations?
- ❑ Do I need personal legal advice with respect to the resignation (or the matter underlying the reason for the resignation) or do I feel comfortable relying on company counsel?

- ❑ If I am resigning due to a disagreement with respect to the company's management or policies, should I engage in a noisy resignation? What are the ramifications of that for the company? For me? For my ability to receive future board positions?
- ❑ In a distressed company environment, what are the factors that militate for and against resignation? Do I need personal legal counsel to advise me with respect to the decision?

Additional Reading

1. TheCorporateCounsel.net's *Director Resignation and Retirement Handbook* (subscription required)

   http://www.thecorporatecounsel.net/GreatGovernance/member/Handbook/DirectorResignations.pdf

Notes

____

____

____

____

____

1.12 BUSINESS SUSTAINABILITY

CONTRIBUTED BY
John H. Stout and Deborah Walker Kool
Fredrikson & Byron, P.A.[1]

Business sustainability is a relative newcomer to boardrooms, with its longer-term focus offering a counterbalance to a focus on quarterly and annual results. While the general subject of "sustainability" embraces many topics that will not be germane to directors' oversight of their companies, "business sustainability" refers to business models, strategies, and operations that balance long-term enterprise adaptability and viability with short-term performance objectives. This balance requires that a board and management take into account (i) risks and opportunities that could challenge a company's current business model, and (ii) economic, governance, ethical, environmental, energy, and social practices that are relevant to longer-term enterprise value creation.

Increasingly, the current impact of business strategies and activities are evaluated by various stakeholders against a global concern for meeting our current society's interests and needs without compromising the interests and needs of future generations.

1. John H. Stout is a shareholder at Fredrikson & Byron, P.A. in Minneapolis. He co-chairs the firm's Corporate Governance group with Melodie Rose and chairs its Business Sustainability and Social Responsibility group. Deborah Walker Kool is an associate at Fredrikson & Byron, P.A. She practices with its Mergers & Acquisitions, Corporate Governance, Business Sustainability and Social Responsibility, and Start-up and Rapid Growth Enterprises groups.

Reinforcing stakeholder interest in sustainable business strategies and practices is the increasing demand for business reporting, which includes financial and nonfinancial results and impacts.

Directors who are not familiar with the growing domestic and international interest in business sustainability, should consider the following:

- The Concept Release from the Securities and Exchange Commission (SEC) regarding Business and Financial Disclosure Required by Regulation S-K, which asks eight questions respecting possible sustainability disclosure subjects (Section F, pages 204–15). (See Additional Reading at the end of this chapter.)
- The increasing credibility of the Sustainability Accounting Standards Board (SASB) (http://www.sasb.org/) which to date has analyzed business sustainability subjects grouped into five categories (environment, social capital, human capital, business and model innovation, and leadership governance) for 79 industries (with more to come) in ten economic sectors (consumption, financials, healthcare, infrastructure, nonrenewable resources, renewable resources and alternative energy, resource transformation, services, technology and communications, and transportation). (See Additional Reading at the end of this chapter.)
- The work of the United Nations Sustainable Stock Exchange Initiative (23 stock exchanges around the world, including NYSE and Nasdaq) (http://www.sseinitiative.org/) and the Sustainability Working Group of the World Federation of Exchanges (WFE) (https://www.world-exchanges.org/home/index.php/news/world-exchange-news/wfe-launches-sustainability-working-group) (almost identical membership with SSEI).
- Sustainability commentaries on the websites of various investors and pension funds, including Vanguard (http://www.vanguardworld.us/photo_video_us/company/sustainability/), Blackrock (http://www.vanguardworld.us/photo_video_us/company/sustainability/), CalPERS (https://www.calpers.ca.gov/page/investments/governance/sustainable-investing), CalSTRS (http://www.calstrs.com/sustainability), New York City Comptroller (http://comptroller.nyc.gov/reports/shareowner-initiatives/), TIAA-CREF (https://www.tiaa.org/public/why-tiaa/how-we-invest/responsible-investment), AFL-CIO (http://www.aflcio.org/Learn-About-Unions/Global-Labor-Movement/Responsibility-Outsourced-Report), reflecting the interest of important long-term investors in the business sustainability awareness and practices of current and prospective investments.
- The International Global Governance Principles of the International Corporate Governance Network (ICGN) (https://www.icgn.org/policy), an investor-led organization committed to promoting "effective corporate governance to advance efficient markets and economics world-wide."
- The publications of the Conference Board's Center for Sustainability (https://www.conference-board.org/sustainability/).
- Materials produced by the National Association of Corporate Directors (NACD) reflecting the increasing needs of corporate directors for information that will educate them regarding the importance of sustainability considerations in assessing companies' strategic plans, business risks and opportunities, investor

interests in sustainability practices and reports, balancing long- and short-term enterprise value creation, oversight of companies' sustainability awareness and practices, and investor engagement on sustainability matters. (See Additional Reading at the end of this chapter.) (https://www.nacdonline.org/).

- The reporting platforms of the Global Reporting Initiative (https://www.globalreporting.org/information/sustainability-reporting/Pages/default.aspx) and the International Integrated Reporting Council (http://integratedreporting.org/).
- The growing number of laws and regulations, domestic and international, addressing corrupt practices, supply chain responsibility, contracting practices, and financial matters, for example, the U.S. Foreign Corrupt Practices Act (https://www.law.cornell.edu/uscode/text/15/78dd-1), the California Transparency in Supply Chains Act (http://www.state.gov/documents/organization/164934.pdf), the U.K. Modern Slavery Act (http://www.legislation.gov.uk/ukpga/2015/30/contents/enacted), the financing requirements of the World Bank (http://siteresources.worldbank.org/INTLAWJUSTICE/Resources/IBRD_GC_English_12.pdf), the procurement regulations of the U.S. Department of Defense and General Services Administration (http://www.gsa.gov/portal/category/21879), and the procurement regulations of numerous U.S. states and cities.
- The emergence of Environmental, Social and Governance (ESG) research, analysis, and ratings by organizations such as MSCI ESG Research (https://www.msci.com/esg-indexes), which rate companies on ESG and other sustainability factors independently and within defined industry groups. There is evidence that these ratings are being taken into consideration by shareholders and other stakeholders in their assessments of rated companies. ESG ratings are likely to gain rather than lose traction in this regard. (See Additional Reading at the end of this chapter.)
- The Model Business and Supplier Policies on Labor Trafficking and Child Labor (http://www.americanbar.org/groups/business_law/initiatives_awards/child_labor.html) adopted by the American Bar Association in 2015, which resulted from an ABA task force formed in 2013 under the leadership of E. Christopher Johnson. These principles address corporate responsibility for eliminating human trafficking, worker health and safety issues, and child labor from corporate supply chains. The implementation of the principles is the responsibility of the Principles Implementation Committee of the ABA Business Law Section's Corporate Social Responsibility Committee. (See Additional Reading at the end of this chapter.)
- The work, programs, and publications of the ABA Business Law Section's Corporate Governance and Federal Regulation of Securities Committee's Joint Committee of Governance and Sustainability.
- The work and annual reports of the United Nations Global Compact to which a member of national and multinational corporations are signatories (https://www.unglobalcompact.org/).

As is demonstrated by the breadth and nature of the listed resources, "business sustainability" can be viewed through the lens of a variety of interest groups, many of which are corporate stakeholders. These include long-term investors, organizations that represent the interests of investors, board-centric organizations, company-centric organizations, governance-centric organizations and advisors, accounting, law and consulting firms and organizations, environmental and social activists, legislatures, regulators, government contracting agencies, and international political and social bodies.

Clearly, directors need to be well-informed about the subject of sustainability as it impacts the business of their respective companies. Directors need a degree of sustainability literacy, and boards need one or more members who are quite knowledgeable about this rapidly developing subject. Boards and management need to agree on (i) a definition of "sustainability" as it applies to their companies, and their companies' strategies, practices, operations, compensation plans, and incentives; and (ii) executive responsibility for enterprise-wide compliance, goals, objectives, auditing, reporting, and engagement, internally and externally, on these matters. As with so many subjects that impact corporate activity, materiality is a critical determination for boards and management assessing those aspects of sustainability that deserve their companies' time and resources. As SASB uses the SEC definition of materiality in its work, the industry information on SASB's website will help boards understand the application of various sustainability considerations to their companies. NACD publications regarding the director's role as to sustainability will be immediately helpful to directors seeking to appropriately provide insight, oversight, and engagement with management and stakeholders on this critically important topic.

Key Questions

When considering sustainability matters, some questions for the board include the following:

- ❑ Are there one or more directors on the board reasonably well versed in the subject of business sustainability and its applicability to business plans and practices?
- ❑ What is the level of sustainability awareness of the board and management as it relates to the company?
- ❑ Have the board and management agreed on a definition of (or framework to understand) sustainability for assessing its impact on company plans and operations? Is the agreed-on definition of sustainability being utilized by management in company planning and operations?
- ❑ Has the board incorporated sustainability considerations in its review and approval of the company's strategic and operating plans?
- ❑ Has the board incorporated sustainability considerations in its oversight of the company's operations and practices, including its responsibility for ensuring an ethical and legally compliant culture, its oversight of enterprise business and reputational risk, and its review of financial and nonfinancial reports to regulators, shareholders, other stakeholders, and the public?

- ❑ Has management focused the responsibility for sustainability awareness and implementation on one or more individuals with executive authority in its senior leadership team?
- ❑ Does the company have key sustainability goals and metrics, and are these incorporated into management evaluations, compensation, and incentives?
- ❑ Are relevant sustainability goals incorporated into the company's values and compliance program, and are they a key component of the company's training programs?
- ❑ What are the company's most significant sustainability risks? For example, supply chain issues as to key suppliers, supplies, and logistics; liability and reputation for human rights misconduct; liability and reputation for the ESG consequences of its business activities; etc.
- ❑ What are the company's most significant sustainability opportunities? For example, cost savings, revenue generation, employee recruitment and retention, reputation with customers, suppliers, regulators, and the public.
- ❑ Do the board and management have a shareholder/stakeholder engagement program that thoughtfully engages the company's shareholders and other interested stakeholders on sustainability matters?

Additional Reading

1. SEC Concept Release regarding Business and Financial Disclosure Required by Regulation S-K (April, 2016)
   https://www.sec.gov/rules/concept/2016/33-10064.pdf
2. Sustainability Accounting Standards Board
   http://www.sasb.org/
3. SASB response to SEC Concept Release regarding Sustainability Disclosure
   http://www.sasb.org/wp-content/uploads/2016/09/Reg-SK-Comment-Bulletin-0913161.pdf
4. United Nations Sustainability Stock Exchange Initiative (SSEI)
   http://www.sseinitiative.org/
5. SSEI Model Guidance on Reporting ESG Information to Investors (November 2015)
   http://www.sseinitiative.org/wp-content/uploads/2015/09/SSE-Model-Guidance-on-Reporting-ESG.pdf
6. World Federation of Exchanges (WFE)
   http://www.world-exchanges.org/home/
7. WFE Sustainability Working Group Exchange Guidance and Recommendation—October, 2015
   https://www.ceres.org/files/wfe-guidance-recommendations-for-sustainability-disclosures/

8. ICGN Global Governance Principles, 4th ed., with particular reference to the Preamble and Article 7.5 of the Principles
   https://www.icgn.org/policy
9. "Sustainability Matters," a publication of the Conference Board
   https://www.conference-board.org/retrievefile.cfm?filename=TCB_R-1481-11-RR1.pdf&type=subsite
10. NACD Director's Handbook *Oversight of Corporate Sustainability Activities*, a publication of NACD's Director Handbook Series in collaboration with Ernst & Young's Center for Board Matters.
11. The UN Global Compact
    https://www.unglobalcompact.org/
12. The 2016 Annual Report of the UN Global Compact
    https://www.unglobalcompact.org/library/1171
13. Directors will find additional resources respecting ESG analysis and ratings by searching the Internet for "ESG ratings" and "ESG analysis."
14. Information pertaining to the Dow Jones Sustainability Indices available at http://www.djindexes.com/sustainability/.

Notes

SECTION TWO

SELECTED GOVERNANCE POLICY MATTERS

21 CORPORATE GOVERNANCE POLICIES AND CHARTERS

CONTRIBUTED BY
Bruce Dravis
Downey Brand LLP[1]

Audit Committee Policies and Charters

The audit committee has broad authority and broad responsibility. Its activities are subject to more specific regulatory requirements than the activities of any other board committee.

The audit committee must oversee the process by which the company's financial statements are prepared, audited, and communicated to investors. The committee's job is to ensure that the process is conducted without susceptibility to challenge, and that the financial statements that are the end product of that process are accurate and reflect fairly the financial position and financial results of the corporation. Both NYSE and NASDAQ require the audit committee to have a written charter.

1. Bruce Dravis acts of counsel to Downey Brand LLP, specializing in securities, corporate governance, and corporate finance matters.

Many audit committees have additional responsibilities. Some serve as the board's risk management committee. Often, audit committees are called upon to review related party transactions. The audit committee is also the committee most often called upon to manage internal, governmental, or regulatory investigations.

Key Questions

To ensure that the committee charter is appropriate and up-to-date, some questions to ask might be the following:

- ❑ Has the committee calendared an annual review of the charter? Has the review been conducted in each year and have all needed changes been adopted?
- ❑ Is the committee charter clear and does it meet the exchange and regulatory requirements?
- ❑ Does each member of the committee meet the requirements for committee membership? Has the committee designated at least one "financial expert" in accordance with exchange and regulatory requirements?
- ❑ Has the committee adopted required policies, such as policies on receipt of whistleblower communications? When was each policy last reviewed? Are there developments in the law that should be reflected in any policy?
- ❑ Has the committee operated in accordance with its charter and related policies?
- ❑ Has the committee had all necessary information before it at the times that it has acted?
- ❑ Has the committee experienced any recurring gaps in information, or delays in obtaining information, that the committee should address?
- ❑ Are committee actions, and materials presented to the committee, appropriately recorded in the committee's records (neither too much nor too little information)?
- ❑ Has the committee considered off-balance sheet arrangements that have or are reasonably likely to have a material current or future effect on the company's financial condition, results of operations, liquidity, capital expenditures, or capital resources, and that should be addressed in the company's MD&A disclosures?
- ❑ Are committee actions communicated to the full board effectively to avoid a complete rehashing of the committee process at the board meeting?
- ❑ In communicating to the board, does the committee present information in an accessible manner? Should reports to the board be reformatted to make them more meaningful?
- ❑ Has the committee conducted any self-assessments required by its exchange, its charter, or policies that it has adopted? If the self-assessment resulted in a recommendation to take any specific actions, has the committee taken them?
- ❑ Is the committee appropriately staffed to deal with all of its various functions?
- ❑ Should the committee have independent legal counsel to deal with any of those functions?
- ❑ Is the committee's compensation adequate given the scope of its activities and the associated time commitment?

Additional Reading

1. National Association of Corporate Directors Blue Ribbon Commission on Audit Committees
   https://www.nacdonline.org/Store/ProductDetail.cfm?ItemNumber=2877
2. *Possible Revisions to Audit Committee Disclosures* [SEC Release No. 33-9862 (July 1, 2015)]
   http://www.sec.gov/rules/concept/2015/33-9862.pdf
3. Audit Committee Dialogue [Public Company Accounting Oversight Board (May 2015)]
   https://pcaobus.org/sites/digitalpublications/audit-committee-dialogue

Notes

Nominating Committee Policies and Charter

The nominating committee evaluates potential director candidates, a list that typically should include incumbents, but in any year can also involve finding new or replacement directors, or evaluating nominations made by shareholders. Assembling an effective board requires not only an assessment of the skills and knowledge individual members can bring to the company, but also assessing the ability of the members to work well together.

The nominating committee may also be tasked with establishing internal governance processes, such as policies on tenure or on division of the role of CEO and board chair.

The efforts of the nominating committee to establish a board with a particular blend of skills, knowledge, and working relations may be affected—or disrupted—by the operation of mandatory proxy access (where companies have adopted it) or by activist investors putting forth nominees who join the board as a settlement to avoid a proxy contest. The nominating committee charter and policies adopted by the committee should include provisions flexible enough to accommodate director nominations arising from any source.

In recent years, nominating committees have come under increasing pressure to "refresh" boards by replacing long-serving directors or those of advanced age. In addition, nominating committees face demands to increase the diversity of those serving on their boards.

Key Questions

To ensure that the committee charter is appropriate and up to date, some questions to ask might be the following:

- ❑ Has the committee calendared an annual review of the charter? Has the review been conducted in each year and have all needed changes been adopted?
- ❑ Is the committee charter clear and does it meet any exchange and regulatory requirements?
- ❑ Does each member of the committee meet the requirements for committee membership?
- ❑ In conducting its work, is the committee subject to requirements beyond its charter, such as bylaw provisions on proxy access, or previously adopted policies on matters such as review of director nominations proposed by shareholders? When was each policy last reviewed? Are there developments in the law that should be reflected in any policy?
- ❑ Has the committee operated in accordance with its charter and related policies?
- ❑ Has the committee had all necessary information before it at the times that it has acted?
- ❑ Has the committee experienced any recurring gaps in information, or delays in obtaining information, that the committee should address?
- ❑ Are committee actions, and materials presented to the committee, appropriately recorded in the committee's records (neither too much nor too little information)?
- ❑ Are committee actions communicated to the full board effectively to avoid a complete rehashing of the committee process at the board meeting?
- ❑ In communicating to the board, does the committee present information in an accessible manner? Should reports to the board be reformatted to make them more meaningful?
- ❑ Has the committee conducted any self-assessments required by its exchange, its charter, or policies that it has adopted? If the self-assessment resulted in a recommendation to take any specific actions, has the committee taken them?
- ❑ Has the committee considered the need to replace long-serving board members who may no longer be serving with the required level of energy, commitment, or independence?
- ❑ What should be the diversity policy or goals of the board?

Additional Reading

1. The Nominating Process and Corporate Governance Committees: Principles and Commentary (Business Roundtable)
   http://businessroundtable.org/sites/default/files/Business%20Roundtable%20Nominating%20Committee%20Principles.pdf
2. Governance Committee: Driving Board Performance (NACD)
   https://www.nacdonline.org/Store/ProductDetail.cfm?ItemNumber=639

Notes

____

____

____

____

____

Compensation Committee Policies and Charter

Executive compensation decisions are unique to every company. Compensation choices can be affected by such factors as the company's size, profitability, industry, business prospects, personnel, and stage of business development, as well as on the individual attributes of the executives.

Executive compensation is initially a matter between the company and the executive, but it is also reviewed by an audience of shareholders, potential shareholders, securities analysts, and proxy advisors, each of which forms its own judgment as to the performance of the CEO and the equitability of his pay. These additional players also form judgments on the performance of the compensation committee and the board in assessing the CEO's performance and in setting pay. Executive compensation may be a topic on which key shareholders engage directly with the company or the committee, or on which they express themselves through a "say-on-pay" vote.

Compensation committees also deal with various detailed tax, securities, and exchange rules that are more appropriately handled at the committee level than by the entire board.

Compensation committees have come under fire in the last decade when executive compensation is not viewed as sufficiently linked to corporate performance.

In public companies, the compensation committee is responsible for a compensation report to be included in the company's proxy statement that should explain the company's compensation philosophy and how its various plans are consistent with corporate policy and goals.

Shareholder activists increasingly seek direct engagement with compensation committee directors when dissatisfied with executive compensation. Committee members must decide when and how to engage with shareholders and whether they are equipped and prepared to do so.

Public company compensation committees using compensation consultants should retain their own consultants who operate independently from management and must make disclosure to that effect in the company's proxy statement.

Key Questions

To ensure that the committee charter is appropriate and up to date, some questions to ask might be the following:

- ❑ Has the committee calendared an annual review of the charter? Has the review been conducted in each year and have all needed changes been adopted?
- ❑ Is the committee charter clear and does it meet the exchange and regulatory requirements?
- ❑ Does each member of the committee meet the requirements for committee membership? Has the independence of the committee members been determined by the board in accordance with exchange and regulatory requirements?
- ❑ Has the committee adopted required policies, such as clawback policies or hedging policies? When was each policy last reviewed? Are there developments in the law that should be reflected in any policy?
- ❑ Has the committee operated in accordance with its charter and related policies?
- ❑ At the time the committee acts on any matter, are there any necessary SEC disclosures required on a Form 8-K?
- ❑ If the committee engages a compensation advisor, are there procedures in place to render a determination on the independence of that advisor from management? If the committee engages an advisor that is not independent, has it documented the basis of its decision?
- ❑ Has the committee had all necessary information before it at the times that it has acted?
- ❑ Has the committee experienced any recurring gaps in information, or delays in obtaining information, that the committee should address?
- ❑ Are committee actions, and materials presented to the committee, appropriately recorded in the committee's records (neither too much nor too little information)?
- ❑ If the committee waives any condition to payment of compensation, or amends any terms in a compensatory arrangement or plan, is the committee dealing with a unique circumstance, or is it setting a precedent it may be obligated to follow in the future?

- ❑ Are committee actions communicated to the full board effectively to avoid a complete rehashing of the committee process at the board meeting?
- ❑ In communicating to the board, does the committee present information in an accessible manner? Should reports to the board be reformatted to make them more meaningful?
- ❑ What is our policy regarding direct engagement with shareholders?
- ❑ Are committee members sufficiently equipped and knowledgeable to successfully engage with shareholders? If not, what training or resources do they need?
- ❑ Should we use a compensation consultant?
- ❑ Does the consultant used by the committee qualify as "independent" under applicable rules? Do we need legal advice with respect to that issue?
- ❑ Has the board begun to consider the pay equity ratio requirements that the company will be required to disclose in future proxy statements and does the ratio suggest any changes that need to be made to the company's compensation policies for the upcoming fiscal year?

Additional Reading

1. NACD Blue Ribbon Commission Report on the Compensation Committee https://www.nacdonline.org/Store/ProductDetail.cfm?ItemNumber=15035
2. Mark A. Borges, *Executive Compensation Disclosure Rules*. ABA Publishing, http://shop.americanbar.org/eBus/Store/ProductDetails.aspx?productId=214003ct=20f03d35196aa1af1d1a95de21610c07722c9a9b0a3f4c14063bcefbdf164ab5010aef745f663cada1239fd1b7f628fa658536a7f3b6331e1872e556b3885b82&term=executive%20compensation

Notes

____

____

____

____

____

2.2 INDEPENDENT CHAIRS AND LEAD DIRECTORS

CONTRIBUTED BY
Avrohom J. Kess and Yafit Cohn
Simpson Thacher & Bartlett LLP[1]

Good corporate governance requires an attentive board of directors comprised primarily of independent directors who work constructively with, and provide oversight of, management. It also requires an empowered CEO with the authority to act decisively without undue board interference. There is no single board leadership structure that has been demonstrated to be superior in achieving the appropriate balance between the board and CEO functions and providing the oversight that leads to corporate success. Instead, each company must tailor its leadership structure to its particular facts and circumstances at any given point in time.

The Commission on Public Trust and Private Enterprise, convened in 2002 "to address the causes of declining public and investor trust in companies, their leaders and America's capital markets," concluded that there are three principal approaches that public companies can take to provide the appropriate balance between the powers of the CEO and those of the independent directors:

1. When this chapter was authored, Avrohom J. Kess was a partner at Simpson Thacher & Bartlett LLP, where he headed the Public Company Advisory Practice; he is currently Vice Chairman and Chief Legal Officer of The Travelers Companies, Inc. Yafit Cohn is counsel at Simpson Thacher & Bartlett LLP, where she practices in the Public Company Advisory Practice. The authors would like to thank Ari Pruzansky of NYU Law School for his valuable assistance in preparing this chapter.

1. Combine the CEO and chairman roles and establish a lead director position.
2. Separate the CEO and chairman roles, with the chairman being an independent director under stock exchange listing standards.
3. Separate the CEO and chairman roles and, where the chairman is not an independent director (often the former CEO), establish a lead director position to be occupied by an independent director.

Where the chairman is not independent, the lead director serves the critical role of ensuring there is sufficient independent oversight of management. Generally speaking, the lead director helps to coordinate the efforts of the independent and nonmanagement directors in the interest of ensuring that objective judgment is applied to sensitive issues involving the company's management and, in particular, the performance of senior management. The duties of the lead director should be clearly defined. The primary responsibilities of the lead director are generally to

- work closely with the CEO (and executive chairman, if the roles are separated) in framing issues for board consideration, setting the board agenda, determining the information to be provided to the board for board meetings, and ensuring that there is sufficient time for discussion of all agenda items;
- convene, set the agendas for, and chair the regular executive sessions of the independent and nonmanagement directors and provide any input to the CEO (and executive chairman, if the roles are separated) as may be appropriate, resulting from those sessions;
- serve as the principal liaison between the CEO (and/or a separate executive chairman) and the independent directors;
- depending on the facts and circumstances, assume a leadership role in times of crisis;
- preside at all meetings of the board at which the executive chairman is not present;
- communicate to the CEO (sometimes in conjunction with the executive chairman, if the roles are separated) the results of the board's evaluation of the CEO's performance (and, if the company has a separate executive chairman, communicate to the executive chairman the results of the board's evaluation of the executive chairman's performance); and
- when appropriate, take the lead role in the company's shareholder engagement efforts.

Like the duties of the lead director, those of the executive chairman should be clearly delineated. While the precise role of the executive chairman will depend on the specific facts and circumstances of the company, the executive chairman generally has the responsibility to

- preside over meetings of the board;
- promote effective relationships among directors;
- work closely with the lead director (and the CEO, if separate from the executive chairman) to establish the agendas and scheduling for board meetings and finalize information flow to the board;

- if the roles of CEO and executive chairman are separated, assist the board in evaluating the performance of the CEO and, in some cases, meet with the CEO together with the lead director to discuss the evaluation; and
- preside over the annual shareholders meeting.

Not every board leadership structure is equal in the eyes of the proxy advisory firms. Glass Lewis takes the position that having an independent chairman is a better governance structure than combining the CEO and chairman positions. Accordingly, Glass Lewis will typically support shareholder proposals that seek to separate the roles of CEO and chairman. Glass Lewis does not believe that the presence of an independent lead director provides "as robust protection for shareholders" as an independent chairman. Nonetheless, Glass Lewis does not recommend that shareholders vote against a CEO who chairs the board. Glass Lewis will, however, recommend voting against the chair of the governance committee if the company has a combined CEO and chairman without an independent lead director.

Institutional Shareholders Services (ISS) similarly favors separating the CEO and chairman positions in most situations. Prior to the 2015 proxy season, ISS generally recommended voting in favor of shareholder proposals requiring an independent chairman, unless the company counterbalanced the combined chairman/CEO structure through *all* of six enumerated governance features. ISS's revised policy, updated for the 2015 proxy season, adds new governance, board leadership, and performance factors to the analytic framework and now looks at all the relevant factors in a "holistic manner." Among the many factors ISS will consider is whether the board has designated a lead director role. ISS considers a lead director role to be robust if the lead independent director is elected by and from the independent members of the board, serves for at least one year, and has "clearly delineated and comprehensive duties" similar to those described earlier.

Notwithstanding the preferences of the proxy advisory firms, each company should determine which board leadership structure is in the best interest of the company and its shareholders at any given time, in light of the company's particular circumstances.

Key Questions

When considering the company's board leadership structure, some important questions directors should consider asking include the following:

- ❑ Is the company's current board leadership structure providing an appropriate balance of the powers of the CEO and those of the independent directors?
- ❑ Does the company's board leadership structure allow independent directors to perform their roles effectively?
- ❑ Does the company's performance suggest that a change in the company's board leadership structure may be necessary or advisable?
- ❑ What are the pros and cons of separating/combining the roles of CEO and chairman? Would separating the roles create a leadership vacuum in times of crisis? Would a combined CEO/chairman exert a dominant influence over the board?

- ❑ What are the views of the company's large shareholders regarding the company's board leadership structure?
- ❑ Is the company's current leadership structure likely to lead to a negative vote recommendation from the proxy advisory firms against our directors? If so, what steps should the company take, if any, to reduce the chances of a negative ISS vote recommendation?

Additional Reading

1. *Commission on Public Trust and Private Enterprise: Findings and Recommendations*, The Conference Board (2003)
https://www.conference-Board.org/pdf_free/SR-03-04.pdf
2. *Lead Directors: A Study of Their Growing Influence and Importance*, PricewaterhouseCoopers (2010)
https://www.thecorporatecounsel.net/member/FAQ/LeadDirectors/05_10_PwC.pdf

Notes

2.3 BOARD MEMBER INDEPENDENCE

CONTRIBUTED BY
Bruce Dravis
Downey Brand LLP[1]

Even the strongest corporate governance practices cannot guarantee the quality of corporate results. Thus, governance focuses on the decision-making processes within a company to limit the likelihood boards and executives will misuse corporate assets or make ill-considered choices. The independence of directors is a proxy for the real objective: Ensure that decision-makers act with integrity and form judgments on behalf of shareholders after thoughtful and fair consideration of the salient facts, untainted by favoritism.

No rule or regulation can ensure that an individual will make a virtuous choice at a critical moment. Instead, independence standards measure potential conflicts of interest, in the expectation that independence from conflicts will produce independence in judgment.

For securities law purposes, director independence is defined primarily by the NYSE and NASDAQ, rather than by the SEC, although the SEC specifies minimum elements of independence for audit committee members. Key factors include whether a director has

1. Bruce Dravis acts of counsel to Downey Brand LLP, specializing in securities, corporate governance, and corporate finance matters.

employment, family, or other significant economic or personal connections to the corporation other than serving as a director.

The term "independent director" is often used interchangeably with the state corporate law term "disinterested director," which means a director who does not have an economic or personal interest in a particular transaction or arrangement requiring board approval. Appointment of special committees of the board, or approval of transactions between the company and insiders, can generate state law questions of independence.

There are also separate IRS and SEC independence measurements connected to the approval of some executive compensation. Measures of independence of outside advisors, such as auditors or compensation advisors, have separate standards.

Independence is usually considered in terms of a director's independence from corporate management. Government and exchange independence rules surround corporate managers with individuals both inside and outside the corporation who are in a position to influence management's decisions and actions, but who can (i) form judgments independent of management and (ii) act as a check on management.

It is important to measure independence *before* electing directors or appointing them to critical committees. If a problem arises later, the company may not be able to cure the failure to meet the independence requirement.

Key Questions

In thinking about board independence, some issues to be considered include the following:

- ❑ Is the particular matter one where independence needs to be considered (related party transaction, special committee, etc.)?
- ❑ Does independence have to be determined before any other action can be taken?
- ❑ What are the elements of the independence standard that must be applied?
- ❑ Are the independence standards written in a governmental or exchange rule, or must they be determined based on a reading of case law?
- ❑ Has the board adopted a committee charter or internal policy that includes additional independence requirements or processes?
- ❑ Can the board's advisors provide a checklist of factors that must be considered in making an independence determination?
- ❑ Has the board been advised about what happens if there is a failure of independence?
- ❑ Are any board members considered "affiliates" under the specific standard?
- ❑ Has the board asked each member to disclose the existence of a potential conflict or fact that could affect a determination of independence?
- ❑ Has the board documented the information it had available in making an independence determination?

Additional Reading

1. *Board Independence and Corporate Governance: Evidence from Director Resignations*
   http://onlinelibrary.wiley.com/doi/10.1111/j.1468-5957.2008.02113.x/full
2. *Board Independence: Striking the Right Balance*
   http://www.longwoods.com/content/18136
3. *The Role of Independent Directors in Corporate Governance* (2nd ed.)
   http://shop.americanbar.org/eBus/Default.aspx?TabID=1537&productId=184948006&ct=3a25aa8b64cbc4b95f815d217905944c2ac619363d1225f63b7b28fbf76def61ba77c8ceb71182630303976a3bbd3c1cc1624c02154928af389142a124b61d96

Notes

___

___

___

___

___

2.4 CLASSIFIED OR STAGGERED BOARDS

CONTRIBUTED BY
Holly J. Gregory, Rebecca Grapsas, and Christine Duque
Sidley Austin LLP[1]

A classified or staggered board divides its directors into classes, each with a term of service of more than one year. A typical classified board structure consists of three classes of directors who are elected for three-year terms, with one-third of the board standing for election each year. A classified board can be contrasted with a declassified or destaggered board, where each director is up for election annually.

Board classification is permitted by Section 141(d) of the Delaware General Corporation Law (the DGCL), which provides that directors may be divided into one, two, or three classes in the certificate of incorporation, an initial bylaw, or a bylaw adopted by the shareholders. Similar statutes exist in most other states. Each class of directors is typically comprised of a similar number of directors, but this is not required by law. Board classification is typically set forth in the certificate of incorporation, which requires approval of the board *and* shareholders to amend, pursuant to Section 242 of the DGCL.

A classified board is a powerful takeover defense for a public company. A classified board structure prevents a hostile bidder from gaining control of a majority of the board

1. Holly J. Gregory is a partner and co-chair of the Global Corporate Governance & Executive Compensation Practice of Sidley Austin LLP and practices in its New York office. Rebecca Grapsas is counsel and Christine Duque is an associate in the Corporate Governance & Executive Compensation Practice of Sidley Austin LLP.

in a single year—instead, two election cycles are required for a hostile bidder to gain control of the board, which can then dismantle a shareholder rights plan (or "poison pill") that may have been adopted to try to thwart the bid. This defensive measure is made even more potent by the legal requirement that directors who serve on a classified board can only be removed *with cause*, pursuant to Section 141(k) of the DGCL (and therefore cannot be removed without cause).

Advocates of classified boards argue that the structure provides leadership stability, improved long-term strategic planning, and enhances the board's ability to negotiate with potential bidders in accordance with the directors' fiduciary duties. Critics, including many institutional investors and proxy advisory firms, view the classified board structure primarily as a mechanism for board entrenchment. Some claim that its most significant effect is to deter bids for the company, thereby depressing shareholder value. There is robust academic debate around the impact of classified boards on firm value.

Classified boards were prevalent among large public companies until relatively recently. A movement to declassify boards using the shareholder proposal process, led by Harvard Law School's Shareholder Rights Project (SRP) and supported by institutional investors and their proxy advisors, has led to a dramatic decline in the number of large companies with a classified board. Classified boards were in place at 8 percent of S&P 500 companies in 2016, compared with 44 percent in 2006 and 24 percent in 2011 (per the Spencer Stuart Board Index 2016).

Classified boards continue to be adopted by many IPO companies (controlled and non-controlled) as this is the only real chance that a company has of adopting such a defensive measure. However, board classification at an IPO company can result in negative recommendations against directors by proxy advisory firms, unless the company includes a reasonable sunset provision.

Shareholder proposals to declassify the board typically receive strong shareholder support. In 2016, out of six proposals voted on, average support was 79 percent and all but one proposal received majority support. In 2012, the first proxy season targeted by the SRP, out of 48 proposals voted on, average support was 80 percent and all but five proposals received majority support (data per Institional Shareholder Services 2016 United States Proxy Season Review—Governance Proposals and Governance Analytics).

Companies that have a classified board should be aware that any shareholder proposal to declassify is likely to receive high support, which then puts pressure on the board to respond. For example, some companies decide to declassify the board in one step, by seeking shareholder approval to amend the certificate of incorporation to provide for annual elections of all directors. Other companies seek shareholder approval to amend the certificate of incorporation to provide that each class of directors will be elected annually after the conclusion of its current term, resulting in complete declassification over several election cycles.

Key Questions

In considering whether a classified board makes sense, some questions a board may wish to consider include the following:

- ❑ Are we currently dealing with a hostile bidder or activist approach, or do we anticipate such a threat in the near future?
- ❑ What is our defensive profile currently and how will it be impacted if we declassify the board?
- ❑ How should we respond if we receive a shareholder proposal to declassify the board?
- ❑ Should we initiate board declassification, without receiving a shareholder proposal?
- ❑ If we decide to declassify the board, should we completely declassify in one step (i.e., provide for annual elections of all directors), or stagger the declassification so it takes effect over several election cycles?
- ❑ For an IPO company—What is our defensive profile? Should we classify the board?
- ❑ For an IPO company—If we decide to classify the board, how many classes will we have and how many directors will there be in each class?
- ❑ For an IPO company—If we classify the board, what impact will this have on our valuation?

Additional Reading

1. Cremers, Martijn, Lubomir P. Litov, and Simone M. Sepe. *Staggered Boards and Long Term Firm Value, Revisited* (November 1, 2016)
   https://papers.ssrn.com/sol3/papers.cfm?abstract_id=2364165
2. Cohen, Alma and Charles C.Y. Wang. *The Value-Decreasing Effect of Staggered Boards* (June 7, 2016)
   https://corpgov.law.harvard.edu/2016/06/07/the-value-decreasing-effect-of-staggered-Boards/
3. Equilar, Fewer Classified Boards Could Mean Higher Director Turnover (March 7, 2016)
   http://www.equilar.com/blogs/84-fewer-classified-boards.html
4. Bebchuk, Lucian A., John C. Coates, IV, and Guhan Subramanian. "The Powerful Antitakeover Force of Staggered Boards: Theory, Evidence, and Policy," *Stanford Law Review* 54 (2002) 887–951
   http://ssrn.com/abstract=304388
5. Harvard Law School Shareholder Rights Project
   http://www.srp.law.harvard.edu/

Notes

2.5 BOARD EVALUATION PROGRAMS

CONTRIBUTED BY
Holly J. Gregory
Sidley Austin LLP[1]

Board and committee evaluations have been considered a component of best practice for almost two decades. Board evaluation programs are designed to obtain feedback from directors regarding the performance of the board, its committees, and/or individual directors, with the goal of enhancing the board's overall effectiveness. Topics that are often addressed in evaluations, in addition to compliance with guidelines and committee charters, include the appropriateness, quality of, and/or efficiency of practices relating to board focus, agendas, and information flow; board size, composition, independence and culture; board accountability; standards of board conduct; relations between directors, between the board and management, and between the board and shareholders; board discussions; board refreshment mechanisms; board committee functions, composition, and leadership; and governance structures and guidelines.

Evaluations provide the board, its committees, and/or individual directors with an opportunity to consider how group culture, cohesiveness, composition, leadership, and meeting and information processes and governance policies influence performance. They

1. Holly J. Gregory is a partner and co-chair of the Global Corporate Governance & Executive Compensation Practice of Sidley Austin LLP and practices in its New York office.

also provide an opportunity to remind directors of their fiduciary duties and the importance of group dynamics and effective board and committee processes in fulfilling those responsibilities. Self-evaluations help identify board practices that may have originated from habit, best practices theories, or obsolete business models or assumptions and assesses them against actual results.

Companies listed on the New York Stock Exchange (NYSE) are required to adopt and disclose corporate governance guidelines, and those guidelines must address, among other topics, board evaluations, which should be conducted at least annually to determine whether the board and its committees are functioning effectively. Key committee charters for NYSE companies are also required to provide for annual evaluations of committee operations. NASDAQ companies do not have similar requirements, but many engage in board evaluations as a matter of good governance. Many private company boards and nonprofit boards also engage in regular board self-evaluation. In addition, independent auditors inquire into the board's evaluation of the audit committee as part of the auditor's assessment of the internal control environment.

It is increasingly common to evaluate individual directors in addition to the full board and its key committees; one-third of S&P 500 companies disclosed in 2016 that they conducted evaluations of the full board, committees, and individual directors, compared to 29 percent in 2011 (per the Spencer Stuart Board Index 2016). Individual director evaluations are likely to become more prevalent, given heightened investor and proxy advisory firm focus on board refreshment mechanisms. Individual director evaluations can help underscore performance expectations, help directors consider their own contributions, and provide directors with feedback that they can use to improve performance. Since individual directors bring very different experiences and competencies to the board, these evaluations tend to be based on fairly general and observable criteria, recognizing that directors contribute in varying ways in board meetings, committee meetings, and outside of the boardroom.

A company's board evaluation program should be customized to reflect the company's particular governance structures, policies, participants, and circumstances. Boards should avoid a "check-the-box" or rote compliance-focused approach to board evaluations. Each year, the board should review the design of the evaluation process and make adjustments as needed to keep the process meaningful and encourage candor. The board needs to determine who will lead the process (such as the governance committee, independent chair, lead director, or outside lawyer or consultant), the participants, the tools (such as a survey, interviews, and/or facilitated discussion), and the timeline and how to analyze and discuss the results. The board should identify any action items that may arise from the evaluation results and determine the timeline for following up on those items.

Some boards find it helpful to engage an outside lawyer or consultant each year—or periodically—to help refresh and facilitate the evaluation process. A third party can serve as a neutral and confidential conduit for the receipt, compilation, and summary of evaluation results. A trusted third party may be particularly helpful if the evaluation process has come to feel "stale" or the evaluation process is otherwise not effective due to distrust or some other issue.

Shareholders are increasingly calling for enhanced disclosure of board evaluation processes, particularly in circumstances where shareholders have concerns around board refreshment or governance failures. Such disclosure typically describes the mechanics of the evaluation process, including the method of evaluation and who facilitates it. Some companies also discuss the key takeaways from the most recent evaluation, although this type of disclosure is relatively uncommon among U.S. companies. The Council of Institutional Investors (CII) 2014 report "Best Disclosure: Board Evaluation" includes examples of what CII considers to be "best in class" disclosures relating to board evaluation. Establishing and disclosing that the board has an evaluation process signals the board's commitment to its governance responsibilities to shareholders.

Key Questions

When considering board evaluation issues, some key questions for the board should include the following:

- ❑ Who will participate in the board evaluation—the full board, its committees, and/or individual directors?
- ❑ Who will take the lead in designing the evaluation process and facilitate its execution?
- ❑ Are there any lessons learned from prior evaluations that should be taken into account in designing and executing this year's evaluation?
- ❑ What issues warrant particular attention in the evaluation process?
- ❑ Is it anticipated that any particular director(s) will be identified as underperforming? How should that be dealt with?
- ❑ What tools will be used to gather information (for example, paper or online survey, interviews)?
- ❑ What is our timeline for conducting the evaluation and reporting back?
- ❑ How do we expect the results to be reported back (for example, a written summary report or facilitated discussion)?
- ❑ What disclosure will we include in our proxy statement relating to our board evaluation process and/or results?

Additional Reading

1. National Association of Corporate Directors, Report of the Blue Ribbon Commission on Building the Strategic-Asset Board (2016)
   http://www.nacdonline.org/resources/blueribbon.cfm?itemnumber=35170

2. EY Center for Board Matters, Accelerating Board Performance Through Assessments (December 2015)

   http://www.ey.com/gl/en/issues/governance-and-reporting/ey-does-an-exceptional-Board-have-to-take-exception-with-itself

3. Gregory, Holly J., "Rethinking Board Evaluation," *Practical Law: The Journal* (March 2015)

   http://www.sidley.com/~/media/publications/march15_thegovernancecounselor.pdf

4. Council of Institutional Investors, Best Disclosure: Board Evaluation (September 2014)

   http://www.cii.org/files/publications/governance_basics/08_18_14_Best_Disclosure_Board_Evaluation_FINAL.pdf

5. National Association of Corporate Directors, Report of the Blue Ribbon Commission on Board Evaluation (2001, most recently reissued in 2010)

Notes

2.6 REMOVING AN UNPRODUCTIVE DIRECTOR

CONTRIBUTED BY
Jayne E. Juvan and Ashley E. Gault
Roetzel & Andress, LPA[1]

Individual directors who are unproductive are at risk for violating the fiduciary duties owed to the corporation. While not all unproductive behavior rises to the level of a breach of fiduciary duty, the following are circumstances in which directors' unproductive behavior may be harmful to the board or the corporation:

- When they fail to prepare for, attend, or meaningfully participate in board or committee meetings
- When they are disruptive in the boardroom or fail to be respectful of other members of the board
- When they fail to properly comply with policies adopted by the corporation

1. Jayne E. Juvan is a partner in the corporate and securities practice group at Roetzel & Andress, LPA. She focuses her practice principally on corporate governance, risk management, and compliance. She currently serves as the co-chair of the ABA's Joint Task Force on the Handbook for the Conduct of Shareholder Meetings. She also serves as the co-chair of the Corporate Governance Committee's (CGC) Task Force on Dealing with Director Misconduct and the co-chair of the ABA CGC Publications Subcommittee, which produces CGC In Sight, the official corporate governance publication of the ABA. Ashley E. Gault is an associate in the law firm of Roetzel & Andress, LPA, where she practices corporate law and regulatory compliance. Ms. Gault is a member of the ABA's Corporate Governance Committee and has presented on corporate governance in an ABA seminar.

- When they fail to bring relevant information to the attention of directors
- When they engage in self-interested transactions
- When they fail to retain the confidentiality of sensitive information

Though a board with an unproductive director may desire to remove that director, many states and the Model Act vest the power of removal of corporate directors solely in the corporation's stockholders, not the board of directors.

When removal is necessary mid-term, stockholders must act at a special meeting or act by written consent to remove a director.

Additionally, although many jurisdictions allow a corporation to petition a court to remove a director for fraudulent or dishonest acts, gross abuse of authority, or breach of duty, court proceedings are often disruptive, costly, and inconclusive.

To address unproductivity, boards should consider appropriate training, education, director evaluations, and policies governing the conduct of directors. If these actions are not sufficiently effective, in some instances, it may be appropriate for the chairman of the board or the lead director to engage the problematic director so that the director understands his or her missteps and has an opportunity to cure it.

In the most egregious circumstances, though the board cannot remove a director on its own, the board may request that the director resign. If the director refuses to resign, the board may adopt resolutions creating one or more committees that exclude(s) a director from participation when the board is dissatisfied with the individual director's conduct, though the board must still ensure that it does not violate the director's legal rights to receive information regarding the board's activities.

Key Questions

In considering the performance and productivity of an individual board member, some questions to be considered include the following:

- ❑ Is the director regularly attending and actively participating in meetings, or is the director consistently absent?
- ❑ Is the director paying attention, asking questions and acting diligently in order to become and remain fully informed?
- ❑ Does the director bring relevant information to the attention of the other directors?
- ❑ Is the director knowledgeable about the corporation and the businesses it operates?
- ❑ Has the director conducted appropriate due diligence concerning matters before the board?
- ❑ Is the director intentionally making meetings unproductive with frivolous debate or conduct that is disrespectful to other board members?
- ❑ Has the director violated a policy adopted by the board or failed to properly disclose a conflict of interest?
- ❑ Has the director inappropriately disclosed confidential information?
- ❑ Does the director have "an agenda" that is personal or otherwise differs from that of the balance of the board?

- ❑ Does the director have the appropriate training and education to know how to act effectively?
- ❑ Would performance evaluations solve the problem of unproductiveness?
- ❑ Has the chairman of the board or the lead director confronted the director about the unproductive behavior and corrective action? How should that occur?
- ❑ Is the conduct sufficiently egregious that the board should request that the unproductive director resign? Be privately censored?
- ❑ If the unproductive director refuses to resign, should the board form one or more special committees that exclude the unproductive director?

Additional Reading

1. Conscious Chief Executives e-Zine, Issue #005: How Do We Remove Unproductive Board Members?
   http://consciousgovernance.com/the-conscious-chief-executive
2. Reclaiming Board Effectiveness
   http://www.christianleadershipalliance.org/?boardeffectiveness
3. "Overcoming the Challenge of Director Misconduct," *Business Law Today* (July 2015)
   http://www.ralaw.com/resources/documents/files/overcoming%20the%20challenge%20of%20director%20misconduct.pdf
4. Charles E. Elson et al. "Director Ownership, Corporate Performance, and Management Turnover," *The Business Lawyer* (May 1999)
   http://www.jstor.org/stable/40687870
5. Director Performance, Corporate Ownership and Management Turnover
   http://heinonline.org/HOL/LandingPage?handle=hein.journals/ucinlr63&div=28&id=&page

Notes

____

____

____

____

____

2.7 DIRECTOR MISCONDUCT

CONTRIBUTED BY
Holly J. Gregory
Sidley Austin LLP[1]

For a board to be effective as a decision-making body in which a variety of views can be raised, explored, and debated, directors need to respect, trust, and rely on one another. The board culture should encourage directors to engage in healthy skepticism and cultivate a supportive atmosphere where dissent and disagreement can be expressed and resolved. Director misconduct damages the culture of boardroom trust that is necessary for directors to air different viewpoints and efficiently reach consensus, and is highly disruptive to the board's efforts to provide direction and oversight. However, the board often has limited ability to take meaningful action against a director who has engaged in misconduct.

Director misconduct takes a wide variety of forms and can be intentional or inadvertent. Examples include fiduciary duty breaches, unauthorized disclosure of confidential information, failure to disclose a conflict of interest, competing against the company, insider trading, other legal violations, disregard of company and board policies, and disruptive or inappropriate behavior in the boardroom or with management or employees.

1. Holly J. Gregory is a partner and co-chair of the Global Corporate Governance & Executive Compensation Practice of Sidley Austin LLP and practices in its New York office.

Breaches of the duty of confidentiality in particular are highly damaging as information leakage severely impacts the development of trust and cooperation among directors, impedes the free exchange of ideas and rigorous discussion, hinders consensus formation, and undermines the board's ability to make timely decisions. Direct harm to the company also occurs in cases where confidential proprietary and strategic information about the company is inappropriately disclosed.

The best tools for avoiding director misconduct are a healthy board culture and agreed expectations for director behavior. Such behaviors generally include maintaining boardroom confidentiality, committing to work towards consensus after an informed and deliberative process, respecting the limits of board discussion time, listening to the viewpoints of others, and using self-control so as to not dominate discussions. Boards can also discourage director misconduct by conducting regular training relating to fiduciary duties and company and board policies, conducting individual director evaluations, and setting clear expectations around how the board would address director misconduct.

When misconduct occurs, the board must determine appropriate remedial action, which may include coaching/education, reprimand, isolation from key decision-making, request to resign, refusal to re-nominate the director, and/or application for judicial order to remove. Boards generally have limited options for removing directors, which will depend on applicable state law and the company's organizational documents; for example, boards of Delaware companies cannot remove a director but could call a meeting and seek shareholder approval to remove. Boards may wish to consider reviewing with counsel the potential merits and risks of instituting contractual means of requiring director resignation in instances of intentional breach of company or board policies or a breach of fiduciary duties (for example, through irrevocable contingent resignation letters). Some companies include in CEO employment agreements a provision requiring the CEO to resign from the board upon his or her departure from the company.

If the misconduct would constitute a breach of the company's code of business conduct and ethics, failure to address it could constitute a waiver of the code, thereby triggering a disclosure obligation.

Having candid discussions about these issues from time to time may assist the board to coalesce around a plan of action for the rare instances of director misconduct. Boards and their counsel should anticipate in advance how director misconduct might be handled and discuss expectations about director conduct and potential remedies.

Key Questions

In evaluating a director's conduct, some questions a board may wish to consider include the following:

- ❑ Do directors receive regular training in relation to fiduciary duties, confidentiality obligations, and company and board policies that apply to them?
- ❑ Have we effectively communicated our expected norms of director behavior?
- ❑ Do we have a protocol in place in case of director misconduct? Do we know what options are available under state law and our organizational documents?

- ❑ Do we require directors to provide irrevocable contingent resignation letters? If not, should we?
- ❑ Do our organizational documents include director qualifications that could potentially be utilized in the event of director misconduct? If not, should they?
- ❑ In the event of director misconduct—What is the appropriate remedial action?
- ❑ In the event of director misconduct—Does the misconduct breach the code of business conduct and ethics? Has there been a waiver of the code of business conduct and ethics that requires disclosure?
- ❑ Does the problem director realize that his or her conduct is inappropriate?
- ❑ What is the best way to approach the problem director? Which of the other directors is best positioned to communicate the issues?
- ❑ If a legal matter is involved, can/should the general counsel or outside counsel play a role?
- ❑ What will we do if the intervention does not produce a solution?
- ❑ If the misconduct involves revelation of material nonpublic information, what are our disclosure or other legal obligations?

Additional Reading

1. Gregory, Holly J., "The Challenge of Director Misconduct," *The Handbook of Board Governance* (edited by Richard LeBlanc) (May 2016).
2. Dunshee, Elizabeth M., Jayne E. Juvan, and Christian Douglas Wright, "Overcoming the Challenge of Director Misconduct," *Business Law Today* (July 2015)
   http://www.americanbar.org/publications/blt/2015/07/02_juvan.html
3. Gregory, Holly J., "The Challenge of Director Misconduct," *Practical Law: The Journal* (October 2013)
   http://us.practicallaw.com/2-543-3846 (subscription required)

Notes

____

____

____

____

____

SECTION THREE

PROTECTING THE BOARD

3.1 STRUCTURAL INDEMNITY AND EXCULPATION PROVISIONS

CONTRIBUTED BY
John Mark Zeberkiewicz and Stephanie Norman
Richards, Layton and Finger, P.A.[1]

There are three principal structural protections afforded to corporate directors: exculpation, advancement of expenses, and indemnification. While each of these measures covers different aspects of liability and exposure, directors are well advised to view the provisions implementing them in combination. In addition to the foregoing protections, many corporations purchase directors' and officers' liability insurance, which is addressed in Chapter 3.2 of this Handbook. Such insurance should also be viewed in combination with the rights to exculpation, advancement of expenses, and indemnification afforded to directors.

Exculpation operates to release directors from monetary liability for breaches of the duty of care, while advancement and indemnification provide for payments to directors for expenses and losses incurred or threatened in connection with their service. There is a further distinction between advancement and indemnification. Rights to advancement operate to pay on behalf of directors' expenses they would otherwise incur before

1. John Mark Zeberkiewicz is a director of Richards, Layton and Finger, P.A., where he practices in the Corporate Advisory group. Stephanie Norman is an associate of Richards, Layton and Finger, P.A. where she practices in the Corporate Advisory group.

the final disposition of a proceeding. By contrast, rights to indemnification are retrospective; they provide coverage for losses, damages, and other liabilities that a director incurs after the final disposition of a proceeding. In many jurisdictions, the extension of rights to "indemnification," without reference to rights to "advancement of expenses," will provide only rights to indemnification. As a practical matter, a director should seek to ensure that, in addition to mandatory indemnification, the corporation's certificate of incorporation or bylaws or the other applicable indemnity arrangements provide mandatory rights to advancement to avoid initially shouldering the costs of litigation or other proceedings relating to the director's service.

Ensuring that the corporation has appropriate structural protections in place serves multiple goals. The existence of the protections promotes prudent risk-taking on the part of corporate directors, without unduly limiting stockholders' rights to hold directors accountable for severe fiduciary misconduct (e.g., breaches of the duty of loyalty). Without assurances that they would be protected from undue liability, directors may be discouraged from taking risks that would otherwise be value-maximizing and serve the long-term best interests of the stockholders. The existence of strong structural protections also serves to assist in recruiting and retaining the most qualified director candidates, recognizing that the individuals who may be the most qualified to serve would be unwilling to do so without adequate assurances that they will be protected against "second-guessing" and other challenges to their good faith business judgments.

Rights to advancement of expenses and indemnification may be provided in the certificate or articles of incorporation or bylaws, or by an agreement between the corporation and one or more of its directors. While the rights afforded to directors under the certificate or articles of incorporation or bylaws are generally viewed as contract rights, directors may seek the additional protection offered by a separate agreement, either because the rights set forth in the certificate or articles of incorporation and/or bylaws are insufficient, or to guard against any risk that the protections offered in those documents, even if robust, could be amended in a manner that would diminish the scope of protection.

As rights to advancement of expenses and indemnification are contractual in nature, directors should be careful to ensure that the protection extends to both current and former directors. Some state statutes provide that a right to advancement or indemnification in the certificate or articles of incorporation or bylaws may not be eliminated or impaired by an amendment after the occurrence of the act or omission that is the subject of the underlying action, suit, or proceeding, unless the provision in effect at the time authorizes such elimination or impairment after the action or omission has occurred. In states that expressly so provide, the protection that directors enjoy while serving will continue—and may not be eliminated or impaired by subsequent amendment—to claims brought against them after they have ceased to be directors in respect of actions or omissions while they were directors, unless the provision in effect at the time of the action or omission authorizes the elimination or impairment after the action or omission has occurred. Nevertheless, directors should take care to confirm that the protection afforded expressly extends to both current and former directors and that the instrument providing such protection does not allow for subsequent amendments that would diminish such protection.

Exculpation

Most state corporation law statutes permit corporations to eliminate or limit the personal liability of directors to the corporation or its stockholders for monetary damages for certain breaches of fiduciary duty through the adoption of so-called exculpatory clauses. In many jurisdictions, the exculpatory clause must be included in the certificate or articles of incorporation to be effective; if included in any other corporate instrument—such as the bylaws, an agreement between the corporation and one or more directors, or a corporate policy—it will be deemed null and void and will have no force or effect.

The scope of any exculpatory clause will be defined and limited, in the first instance, by statute. An exculpatory clause generally will provide that a director cannot be held liable for monetary damages for claims alleging solely a breach of the fiduciary duty of care. In most jurisdictions, a director may not be exculpated from personal liability for monetary damages for, among other things, breach of the director's duty of loyalty, bad faith, intentional misconduct, knowing violations of law or unlawful dividends, stock redemptions, or repurchases. An exculpatory clause may be designed to limit the scope of protection; however, in most instances, the provisions are drafted so as to provide directors the maximum protection afforded under applicable law. Some provisions will also expressly provide that, if the underlying statute is amended to provide directors with greater protection, the scope of protection provided will be construed to provide such greater protection. In addition, many exculpatory clauses will provide that if the clause is amended or repealed, the amendment or repeal will not apply to actions or omissions occurring prior to the time of the amendment or repeal.

While an exculpatory clause shields directors from monetary liability for breaches of the duty of care, it does not limit or eliminate the directors' duty of care. Thus, even if the corporation has a valid exculpatory clause, a court may grant injunctive relief for a breach of the duty of care. Nevertheless, whether the claim against directors is equitable or legal, if the damages for a breach of the directors' duty of care are solely monetary, the claim will be barred by the exculpatory clause, even if the plaintiff has alleged claims for gross negligence.

Advancement

In general, corporations have the power to advance expenses incurred by current or former directors in defense of civil, criminal, administrative, and investigative actions, suits, or proceedings prior to the final disposition of the action, suit, or proceeding. Rights to advancement of expenses generally may be provided through the certificate or articles of incorporation or bylaws, or by a separate agreement between the corporation and one or more of its directors. Corporation law statutes generally provide that rights to advancement of expenses are permissive; that is, the corporation may, but is not required by the relevant corporation law statute to, advance expenses incurred by its current and former directors. Nevertheless, corporations generally may make the directors' rights to advancement mandatory. From a drafting standpoint, the distinction between mandatory and permissive rights frequently comes down to the use of the word "shall" (connoting a mandatory obligation) instead of "may" (connoting an option rather than an obligation).

The directors' adoption of mandatory advancement provisions on a proverbial "clear day"—that is, at a time when no action, suit, or proceeding for which advanced amounts would be sought—should be within the purview of the directors' business judgment. Providing mandatory advancement rights promotes the basic policy that directors should be afforded the funds necessary to defend against claims of fiduciary misconduct. If the rights are adopted at a time when an action, suit, or proceeding is threatened or pending—or if the directors are, by virtue of a "permissive" advancement bylaw, required to make the decision to advance their own expenses—the directors' decision to adopt the mandatory advancement provision or to extend the advanced amounts to themselves may not be reviewed under the deferential business judgment standard but may instead be subject to review for entire fairness (or some other heightened scrutiny).

Rights to advancement of expenses, even when they initially appear to be mandatory, may be made subject to conditions, whether by statute or by the instrument or agreement creating the rights. These conditions, such as evidence of the director's ability to repay amounts ultimately determined to be ineligible for indemnity, could curtail the availability of the rights. It is not uncommon for advancement rights for directors to be made subject to a condition that the director seeking the advanced amounts provide an undertaking to repay the amounts so advanced if it is ultimately determined that he or she is not entitled to indemnification for the underlying claims. (As discussed further on, demonstrating an entitlement to indemnification requires a finding that the director met the applicable "standard of conduct.") In fact, some jurisdictions, like Delaware, require by statute that *current* directors of the corporation provide such an undertaking as a condition to receiving an advancement of their expenses. In several other jurisdictions, the right to an advancement of expenses is made subject to additional statutory conditions, including a written affirmation by the director of the director's good faith belief that such director has met the standard of conduct necessary for indemnification by the corporation.

Even if not required by statute, the corporation may, in the instrument creating the rights to advancement, impose additional conditions upon the directors' rights. For example, the corporation could require that directors post a bond or provide some other form of secured undertaking to repay the amounts so advanced. The corporation could also limit its obligation to advance expenses on some preliminary finding that the director seeking advancement acted in a manner that was in or not opposed to the best interests of the corporation. Such conditions are inconsistent with the basic notion that advancement rights are designed to afford directors the opportunity to mount the best defense possible to vindicate themselves against claims of fiduciary misconduct.

Where the directors' rights to advancement are not mandatory but are merely permissive, the decision to advance expenses is generally left to the discretion of the board of directors. As discussed previously, because a director seeking advancement will have an interest in the decision as to whether his or her expenses are advanced, it is prudent to have such decision approved by disinterested and independent directors. As a general matter, it is unlikely that a director who does not have mandatory rights to advancement could successfully challenge a good-faith decision of the board to deny the director's request for an advancement of expenses.

Indemnification

The corporation's power to indemnify its directors is established by, and subject to the restrictions of, the law of the corporation's state of incorporation. In general, a corporation has the power to indemnify any director who is or was a party to an action, suit or proceeding by reason of the fact that he or she is or was a director of the corporation (or is or was serving another entity in such capacity at the request of the corporation), subject to certain limitations. The corporation's power to indemnify directors is typically divided into two parts: (i) indemnification in respect of third-party actions and (ii) indemnification for actions brought by or in the name of the corporation, including derivative suits.

In general, the corporation's power to indemnify directors in third-party actions extends to expenses, judgments, fines, and amounts paid in settlement. In actions brought by or on behalf of the corporation, however, the corporation's power to indemnify directors is limited to expenses actually and reasonably incurred in connection with the proceedings, but does not extend to judgments, fines, or amounts paid in settlement. The rationale for the distinction is based upon the public policy that, where the corporation has been harmed by an act or omission of one of its directors, the corporation should not be held ultimately liable (through indemnification) for such harm. Moreover, permitting the corporation to indemnify directors for judgments, fines, and amounts paid in settlement of derivative suits would encourage settlement of indefensible claims, thereby potentially removing the important policing power of fiduciary duty claims. It would also encourage frivolous "strike suits," since plaintiffs might perceive corporate directors as more inclined to settle suits (even if such suits were without merit) if they knew the corporation would be footing the bill.

Except in the limited cases where indemnification is required by statute, as described next, a director is not automatically entitled to indemnification under the provisions of the certificate or articles of incorporation, bylaws, or other instrument mandating the indemnification. In many jurisdictions, including Delaware, a determination that a director has met the applicable "standard of conduct" necessary to establish an entitlement to indemnification must be made. Most corporation law statutes will set forth the procedures by which the determination will be made. Depending on the circumstances, the determination will be made by (i) a majority of the directors who are not parties to the action, (ii) a committee of directors designated by a majority of such directors, (iii) if there are no such disinterested directors, or if the disinterested directors so direct, independent counsel, or (iv) the stockholders.

In some circumstances, a state's corporation law statute may require the corporation to indemnify its directors. In Delaware, for example, the corporation is required to indemnify its current and former directors for expenses incurred in connection with actions, suits, or proceedings as to which they are successful on the merits or otherwise. Where indemnification is mandated by statute, there is generally no requirement that the directors be found to have met the standard of conduct otherwise necessary to support the provision of indemnification.

Key Questions

In considering whether to accept a position on the board of directors, or when reviewing the corporation's organizational documents, directors should consider the following:

- ❑ Does the certificate or articles of incorporation contain an exculpatory provision that eliminates liability to the maximum extent of the law?
- ❑ Are the rights to advancement in the certificate or articles of incorporation or bylaws? Are they mandatory? What are the conditions, either by statute or under the instrument providing the rights, to advancement? Is an undertaking required? If so, must the undertaking be secured? Must the director provide an affirmation of his or her good faith belief? What are the implications of providing such an affirmation?
- ❑ If the corporation is required to advance expenses, whether under the certificate or articles of incorporation, the bylaws or by agreement, is there a time period (e.g., 20 days or 30 days after receipt of the request) by which the corporation must provide the requested advances?
- ❑ Are the rights to indemnification in the certificate or articles of incorporation or bylaws? Are they mandatory? What are the conditions, either by statute or under the instrument providing the rights, to indemnification?
- ❑ Which party is entitled to make the determination as to whether the director met the applicable standard of conduct necessary to establish an entitlement to indemnification?
- ❑ Are the protections in the certificate or articles of incorporation or bylaws sufficiently robust? Should the director seek a separate agreement providing different or additional rights? Even if the protections are currently robust, should the director nevertheless seek a separate agreement to guard against a potential diminution in the protection afforded under the certificate or articles of incorporation or bylaws?

Additional Reading

1. Wing, James D., "Corporate Internal Investigations and the Fifth Amendment." *Business Law Today* (ABA September 2014).
2. Wing, James D., "Training for Tomorrow: Corporate Counsel Checklist for a D&O Protection Program." *Business Law Today* (ABA August 2012).
3. Zeberkiewicz, John Mark, and Stephanie Norman, "Recent Delaware Court of Chancery Opinion Provides Guidance on Advancement and Indemnification." *Insights: The Corporate and Securities Law Advisor* 29, no. 10 (October 2015).

4. Zeberkiewicz, John Mark, and Blake Rohrbacher, "The Right Protection: More on Advancement and Indemnification." *The Review of Securities and Commodities Regulation* 41, no. 21 (December 2008).
5. Zeberkiewicz, John Mark, and Blake Rohrbacher, *No Surprises: The Mandatory Nature of Mandatory Advancement and Indemnification*, Corp. Governance Advisor, Nov./Dec. 2007.

Notes

3.2 DIRECTORS AND OFFICERS LIABILITY INSURANCE AND OTHER RISK MANAGEMENT CONSIDERATIONS

CONTRIBUTED BY
Mary Craig Calkins
Kilpatrick Townsend & Stockton LLP[1]

Claims against corporate directors and officers are alive and well. In addition to evolving corporate governance obligations and the ever-watchful class action plaintiffs' bar, corporate America now has additional considerations, such as the whistleblower issues, compliance with a variety of regulations and statutes, inquiries into potential securities violations, requirements of the Sarbanes-Oxley Act of 2002, the Foreign Corrupt Practices Act, the Private Securities Litigation Reform Act (PSLRA), and other inquiries into potential breach of fiduciary duties by board members or other claims of self-dealing. As a result, developing a comprehensive insurance portfolio continues to be a critical vehicle through which a company can protect its management and board. This chapter presents a brief overview of the important issues relating to insurance coverage for board members and corporate executives, followed by a list of questions to assist in the placement of broad coverage to protect against claims.

1. Mary Craig Calkins is a partner in Kilpatrick Townsend & Stockton LLP, where she practices in the firm's Beverly Hills office and heads the firm's West Coast insurance group.

Directors and Officers/Management Liability Policies

Directors and officers liability (D&O) policies typically protect against claims for alleged "wrongful acts" committed by an "insured person" acting on behalf of the organization—while acting "in the capacity as such"—subject to the defined terms, conditions, and exclusions in the policy. D&O policies also commonly provide coverage for the company for "securities claims," as defined by the policies. These policies typically provide coverage for claims arising from perceived failures of general governance decisions, fiduciary liability claims, including allegations of alleged fraud or improper financial oversight, and allegations of personal profit or gain. Because of the diverse nature of these potential claims, it is important that any D&O policy affords broad coverage for a variety of external claims, investigations, and regulatory oversight.

Coverage Parts

D&O policies typically have coverage parts commonly referred to as "Side A," "Side B," and "Side C" coverage. Side A affords coverage directly to individual directors and officers, sometimes called "insured persons," to nonindemnified or nonindemnifiable loss. Side A comes into play if a corporate insured is insolvent or has declared bankruptcy, meaning that it has no assets to fund the defense of its directors and officers. Side A also responds when the law precludes a company from payment of a judgment or settlement, such as a shareholder derivative where paying a settlement effectively would be like the company paying itself. Some insurance policies will afford pure Side A coverage (sometimes called Side A only or Side A Difference in Conditions (DIC) policies), increasing the limits that are dedicated solely to the individual directors and officers who qualify as "insureds."

Side B coverage typically provides reimbursement to the insured company for amounts it has paid to indemnify its directors and officers acting for the company. While Side A provisions typically do not have a retention (the equivalent of a deductible under other forms of insurance coverage), Side B coverage is triggered after the insured entity has paid defense costs or other covered claims to satisfy a per-claim "self-insured retention." Notably, some policies contain presumptive indemnification provisions, which state that a claim will be "presumed" or "deemed" to be indemnified to the full extent of the law, even if the company does not wish to indemnify its director or officer who is believed to be a wrongdoer acting outside of his or her authority or for his or her own personal profits.

Side C provides public companies with "entity" coverage. That portion of the policy provides coverage for claims against the insured company as an entity, as opposed to (or in addition to) claims against the company's directors and officers. The Side C coverage typically issued to public companies provides entity coverage for "securities claims," which in turn is defined by the policy as any actual or alleged violation of federal or state securities laws or regulations, or investigations into such violations, for claims of an actual or alleged act, error, or omission in connection with the purchase or sale, or offer to purchase or sell, of securities issued by the insured company. If negotiated, Side C coverage can also extend to regulatory or administrative investigations or proceedings against the company if the investigations also are focused on, and maintained against, an insured person. Some D&O policies also provide additional coverages, such as crisis management coverage or other provisions that provide predetermined assistance to insureds.

Trustees of nonprofit entities need similar protections, such as claims against nonprofits, including service or relief organizations operating internationally, including the following:

- Investigations by the Office of the Inspector General or other governmental entities
- Improper fundraising allegations
- Improper reporting of revenue
- Allegations of employee or independent contractor frauds, especially where a nonprofit is operating or providing assistance in a third-world country context
- Mishandling of donations and endowments, including funds that were earmarked for certain purposes but used for nondesignated activities
- Failure to report or pay payroll taxes
- Alleged mismanagement of employment benefit plans

Exclusions

The insurance coverage provided by D&O policies is subject to various exclusions and conditions. These limitations on coverage are often raised by insurers in "coverage letters" after a claim is made to eliminate or minimize coverage. It is therefore important to have an understanding of these additional potential hurdles to coverage.

Some exclusions are intended to exclude coverage that likely would be afforded by other policies purchased by the company, like bodily injury claims that typically would be covered by commercial general liability coverage, exclusions for professional services that typically would be covered by errors and omissions insurance, and ERISA-based claims that commonly fall under fiduciary liability insurance. Other exclusions provide limitations on coverage, such as exclusions for "prior and pending" litigation, which would presumably be covered under earlier policies issued to the company, or prior acts that date back well before the inception date of a particular policy or as otherwise required by the policy.

A significant number of coverage position letters focus on the so-called dishonesty exclusions, which purport to eliminate coverage for fraud, knowing criminal conduct or violations of the law, illegal personal profits or gain, or other similar conduct.

In addition, many D&O policies contain a so-called bump-up exclusion, which insurers might seek to characterize too broadly to preclude even claims of breach of fiduciary duty if shareholders allege that a merger or acquisition did not result in a sufficient payment to shareholders. A careful insured will therefore take steps to have a policy audited before purchase, confirming that the language provided in the exclusions, and throughout the entire policy, reflects the best language available in the industry to preserve coverage.

Conditions and Other Limitations to Coverage

Most policies also have a series of conditions to coverage, which sometimes are identified by the policy as "conditions precedent" to coverage (unless those terms are removed before binding the policy through careful negotiation with the insurer). The policy may contain other requirements that an insured must satisfy to preserve its rights to coverage.

One of the more important conditions is that of timely notice, both of the initial action and for later activities that could change the nature of the covered risk.

Most D&O policies are "claims made" or "claims made and reported" policies, requiring that a claim first be made against the insured, or made against the insured and reported to the insurer, within the contractual policy period or during an extended report period (or ERP), if purchased or otherwise available and depending on the particular terms of that policy. If a claim is denied because of a perceived late notice defense, a broker or coverage attorney should be consulted promptly to address that issue due to the potential loss of coverage.

Most policies also include some form of consent requirement. Many D&O policies issued to public companies are "duty to advance" or "duty to pay" policies, instead of the "duty to defend" policy. Where duty to defend policies will allow an insurer to select counsel and control the defense, a duty to pay or duty to advance policy will allow an insured to maintain greater control over its own defense. However, these policies typically condition the insurer's payment of benefits on its prior consent to any material action regarding the claim for which coverage is sought. This will include the selection of defense counsel by an insured and the payment of certain defense costs (including negotiations regarding the hourly rates that might be reimbursed or the number of attorney staffing a particular case).

Like most other forms of insurance, D&O policies also commonly impose a duty to cooperate with the insurer. This means that an insured must share information with its insurer and provide sufficient information at all stages of litigation so that the insurer can make an informed decision about participation in settlements and the defense. Notably, these policies commonly require an insurer's written consent to settlement, even if the insured contractually retains the right to settle claims. A careful prepurchase audit will confirm that insurer consent is not to be withheld unreasonably.

Public Policy Limitations

Some matters are not insurable as a matter of law. For example, in many jurisdictions punitive or exemplary damages are not insurable, nor are claims for conduct that are not covered under the common law, or matters against public policy, such as actions seeking purely injunctive relief or pure disgorgement or restitution of ill-gotten gains, although there are significant arguments that can be raised to ensure coverage. In addition, many states prohibit coverage for intentional acts.

There are also numerous other issues that can catch an insured unaware, such as the requirement that an individual insured person was acting in an insured capacity. D&O policies provide coverage for alleged "wrongful acts" when the person committing the alleged act was "acting in [his or her] capacity as . . . such as on behalf of the insured Organization." As a result, insurers typically look to reserve rights or deny coverage if there is an allegation that the insured person was not acting "solely" in the capacity as a "director, officer, general partner, manager or equivalent executive" of the insured person at the time of the incident. Thus, an insurer might reserve rights or deny coverage if there is an allegation that a document was executed by a corporate officer in his personal capacity, as for example on a loan guarantee, although there are arguments to the contrary. In addition, some cases suggest that officers sitting by designation on the boards of other companies might lose coverage.

Other Conditions and Defenses

Unfortunately, not all limitations on coverage are found in the Exclusions or Conditions sections of D&O policies. Limitations can be lurking in a variety of other policy provisions. For example, if an insured has not negotiated broad coverage before it purchases the property, an insurer can contend that the policy does not state a "claim" as defined by the policy. Alternatively, an insurer can point to other definitions or conditions in the policy as supporting a limitation on coverage. Other insurers will raise an issue as to whether satisfaction of a contractual obligation alleged in a plaintiffs' breach of contract claim can be covered because an insurance policy is not intended to guarantee corporate obligations.

Similarly, case law in various states can differ as to whether a claim, as pled by a plaintiff against the insured company or the insured persons, properly falls within the definition of "loss," which is typically defined by the policy as "damages, judgments, settlements or other amounts (including punitive or exemplary damages where insurance by law) and Defense Costs in excess of the Retention that the Insured is legally obligated to pay." Some insurers will contend that a claim seeking "disgorgement" or "restitution" of ill-gotten gains is not a covered claim. There are often coverage disputes as to whether a claim seeking civil "fines or penalties" can state a claim for "loss," and there is case law that a savvy insured can use to preserve coverage against such arguments. As another example, some insurers question whether "loss" can include the award of attorneys' fees.

Similarly, most D&O policies contain a so-called insured versus insured exclusion, which works to preclude coverage for claims brought or maintained by, or on behalf of, one or more "insureds" against one or more other individuals or companies that also qualify as insureds under the policy. While presumably present to prevent collusion between insureds to access coverage, they operate more broadly. These exclusions came into play after some financial institutions sued their own directors or officers for alleged "wrongful acts" or malfeasance, and then sought to recover from the bank's own D&O insurers. After rulings in favor of coverage, the insurers incorporated the "insured vs. insured" exclusions to prevent against a risk of collusive conduct among insiders, and to prevent coverage for boardroom disputes and in-fighting. However, this exclusion is being limited in some newer policies to apply to claims brought against its former director or officer, or by an insured person who has not qualified as an insured person for at least two or three years (depending on negotiations), or claims brought by a bankruptcy trustee, receiver or creditor committee. In addition, a new form of this exclusion will preclude coverage only where there is a claim brought by the insured entity itself against former officers or directors—called the "entity vs. insured" provision.

Severability clauses and endorsements are also essential. There are significant protections afforded to an insured through severability clauses, which state that the knowledge of, or acts and activities by, one insured are not imputed to other individual insureds. Typically, insurers will seek to impute knowledge or acts of the CEO, CFO, risk manager, and sometimes the general counsel to the company. Policyholders should be wary of such provisions, especially as the question of what knowledge a general counsel might have can invade significant issues of privilege. In addition, policyholders often attempt to limit this provision to the "Top Two," the CEO and CFO. As a result, any time an insurance company reserves rights, or elects not to provide coverage after proper notice, an insurer must consult with knowledgeable coverage counsel to raise a proper basis for coverage and keep that information in the insurer's file.

Other Important Insurance Considerations

The focus of this chapter is on D&O insurance policies to protect the board, but there are numerous other insurance considerations that the board should consider as part of its analysis. For example, officers and managers are often named individually in employment-related lawsuits. In addition, "privacy" and "security breach" coverage, including defense and indemnity coverage for claims arising out of data breach, and professional errors and omissions coverage must be considered as part of a comprehensive insurance package, because D&O policies often attempt to exclude coverage for lawsuits implicating these additional coverage provisions.

The nature of an insured's business will also affect the coverage that should be in place to protect the company. For example, a manufacturing company or pharmaceutical company will likely wish to consider products liability coverage, including recall insurance. A company embarking on an initial public offering or IPO might seek representations and warranties coverage, and a board must consider "run off" insurance if there is a merger or acquisition, spin-off, stock drop concerns, and other potential claims. Financial technology or "FinTech" companies, for example, might need to protect against regulatory investigations as well as cyber intrusions. Technology and entertainment companies are often faced with expensive intellectual property disputes, including patent, copyright and trademark infringement claims that can be excluded from coverage, as well as specialized production issues.

Finally, a company should arrange a prepurchase audit by coverage counsel in addition to reliance on well-qualified brokers. Brokers can have a different focus, because they look at what the market will do or what underwriters at a particular insurer might offer in exchange for the premium. Coverage counsel, on the other hand, are experienced in handling coverage disputes at the time of claims and will address the language of a policy in the context of coverage denials, proposing enhancements to preserve coverage. A careful board will seek annual reviews by its brokers working with coverage counsel to ensure the best policy language available to assure adequate insurance coverage and appropriate limits to protect against loss.

Key Questions

When considering D&O insurance coverage, the board should ask key questions at the time an insurance policy is purchased, when a "claim" is made, and during the course of litigation, including the following:

Selection of Insurers and Policies

- ❑ Does the proposed insurer have a strong reputation for supporting its insureds if claims are filed?
- ❑ Would paying an increased premium provide broader coverage?

- ❑ Have you purchased enough primary and excess coverage to protect against anticipated losses?
- ❑ Do your excess policies "follow form," or will you have to deal with forum selection, choice of law, and different policy terms and conditions?
- ❑ Does your policy cover every party that you would want to be covered as an "additional insured," such as a vendor, subsidiary, joint venturer, or affiliated company, or will that coverage deplete limits from those you want to be covered?
- ❑ Is part of the policy reserved for outside directors (Side A only) to add protections to the individuals sitting on your board?
- ❑ Are insureds sitting on an outside board at the company's request covered?
- ❑ Does your D&O program minimize risk from an insurer's insolvency, and will your policy protect individual directors and officers if the company becomes insolvent?
- ❑ Does your application adequately disclose all potential issues and answer the questions? Have you reviewed it?
- ❑ Do you need other commonly held commercial policies, such as product liability, third-party products, recall coverage, professional indemnity, industrial special risks, cyber coverage, employment practices, first-party property, business interruption, or stand-alone commercial liability policies?
- ❑ Does your broker have the knowledge and market share ability to negotiate enhancements to coverage?
- ❑ Does your team include knowledgeable insurance coverage counsel who can suggest additional language or revisions based on claims experience and case law?

Broad Policy Terms

- ❑ Does the term "claim" include written demands as well as criminal or administrative proceedings, investigations, regulatory, and preclaim inquiries?
- ❑ Is the definition of "insured" broad enough to protect management, including audit or special committees, general counsel, and in-house legal staff?
- ❑ Do your endorsements and definitions extend coverage to subsidiaries and affiliated or related companies?
- ❑ Does the policy contain the broadest definition of "loss"?
- ❑ Do the so-called dishonesty exclusions require a "final, nonappealable adjudication" in the underlying case?
- ❑ Is there a carve-back allowing coverage for defense costs for dishonesty exclusions?
- ❑ Does the policy cover all prior acts or continuing conduct?
- ❑ Is there a severability provision, or will the knowledge or conduct by one director or officer be imputed to destroy coverage for other individuals or the company, both in the application and for exclusions?
- ❑ Have you limited, or eliminated, the insurer's right to rescind the policy?
- ❑ Will prior and pending litigation exclusions eliminate coverage?
- ❑ Is the "insured vs. insured" exclusion limited in time, and does it contain important carve-outs (e.g., whistleblower claims, bankruptcies, cross-claims, derivative suits)? Can those carve-outs be achieved through negotiation?
- ❑ Does the policy cover worldwide activities, or is it limited in territory?

- ❑ Will the change of ownership or acquisition provisions eliminate coverage?
- ❑ Will an allocation provision eliminate coverage for a large percentage of your defense costs?
- ❑ Can you select your own counsel, or do you need to accept panel counsel?
- ❑ Is the insurer obligated to pay or advance defense costs on a timely basis?
- ❑ Has coverage been bound unconditionally, or are there outstanding items or "subjectivities" to be accepted by the insurers before binding?
- ❑ Does your board have other policies to cover claims that are excluded by your D&O policies?
- ❑ Are there broader or different policy terms available in the market that will broaden your coverage?

After Receipt of a "Claim"

- ❑ Have you provided notice of a "claim" as soon as reasonably practicable, or in accordance with the policy terms?
- ❑ Did you give notice of preliminary inquiries, such as claims for appraisals, Section 220 Books and Records demand, or administrative prerequisites to suit (such as EEOC filings, informal SEC inquiries, requests for informal meetings with key individuals, or other preclaim inquiries)?
- ❑ Is there an earlier written demand, request for monetary or nonmonetary relief, notice of investigation, or other demand that might qualify as a "claim" under the policy definition or provide a coverage problem?
- ❑ Has your insurer consented to the retention of counsel, consultants, or vendors that are going to be used? If not, why?
- ❑ Have you provided enough information for the insurer to issue a coverage position?
- ❑ After receipt of a reservation of rights letter or declination of coverage from an insurer, has your coverage counsel reserved your rights and contested the insurer's coverage positions to protect your rights?
- ❑ Can coverage counsel negotiate better reimbursement rates so the insured does not have to fill a gap in "reasonable and necessary" defense fees?
- ❑ Have you pushed back on any allocation provision that would allow less than full reimbursement of defense fees?
- ❑ Has coverage counsel negotiated a confidentiality agreement with your insurers, so that information shared with insurers is not subject to disclosure to your opponent or to third parties?
- ❑ Have you protected your privileges in connection with dealings with your insurers?

During an Investigation, Lawsuit, or Arbitration and in Preparation for Settlement

- ❑ Has your defense counsel complied with the insurers' litigation guidelines, or advised the insurer why it cannot comply with certain requests?
- ❑ Has your defense counsel provided regular status reports and copies of bills in a format that will allow full reimbursement?
- ❑ Can coverage counsel negotiate a greater contribution to defense and, ultimately, to indemnity (settlement or judgment) payments?

- ❑ Have you provided sufficient information to support a settlement funded by your insurer?
- ❑ Did you provide information regarding key testimony, deposition transcriptions, and motion practice?
- ❑ Have you advised of changes in allegations, such as allegations of intentional conduct or claims for punitive damages that might affect coverage?
- ❑ Rather than advising that the case is fully defensible, did your defense counsel advise the insurer of the risks involved and the significant costs that could attach if a jury or trier of fact rules against the defenses?
- ❑ Can you advise the insurer of additional issues or potentially adverse rulings (including motion practice or in limine motions) that might increase a verdict against the insureds and support settlement?
- ❑ Did you notify your insurer of important dates to give sufficient time and information to prepare for mediations or settlement discussions?
- ❑ Have you notified your insurer of settlement opportunities or demands in time for it to analyze the benefits?
- ❑ Did you seek approval of potential mediators or settlement officers and put the insurer on notice of its duty to attend and protect its insureds?
- ❑ If there is a demand within limits, did you advise the insurer of the need to settle to protect against claims in excess of your insurance?
- ❑ Did you seek the insurer's written consent before making a settlement offer to avoid forfeiting coverage?
- ❑ Have you done everything necessary to avoid a "failure to cooperate" defense?
- ❑ Does the insurer have enough information to open its checkbook and fund a settlement?
- ❑ Have you consulted with coverage counsel to address national trends, case law, and conditions hidden in the fine print of your policy that can eliminate coverage when you most need it?

Additional Reading

1. Calkins, M. "Your Checklist for D&O Insurance Protection," Risk Newsletter, Legal Issues in Insurance Coverage, available from author at mcalkins@kilpatricktownsend.com

2. Calkins, M., and L. Kornfeld, "Recovering More Insurance for SEC and Internal Investigations," Bureau of National Affairs, Inc. (BNA) Corporate Counsel Weekly, Copyright 2012, at https://www.google.com/search?q=BNA+Cor%5Bporate+Counsel+Weekly,+%22Recovering+More+Insurance+for+SEC+and+Internal+Investigations%22&rls=com.microsoft:en-US&ie=UTF-8&oe=UTF-8&startIndex=&startPage=1&gws_rd=ssl, visited October 2016

3. Calkins, M."Gotcha! Top 10 Insurance Traps for Corporate Counsel," American Bar Association Section of Litigation, Committee on Corporate Counsel Annual CLE Seminar, January 01, 2011, available from contributor at mcalkins@kilpatricktownsend.com
4. Masters, L. *Checklist for Renewing D&O Insurance Coverage* www.lexology.com/library/detail.aspx?g=f366d73d-c6a0-4ba8-96fd-f8dc5243db13, visited October 2016
5. Miller & Friel PLLC, "Fighting Back Against the D&O Personal Profit Exclusion—7 Tips for Maximizing Coverage" www.google.com/url?sa=t&rct=j&q=&esrc=s&source=web&cd=1&ved=0ahUKEwjrqYK54uLPAhVPMKHRioAJYQFgggMAA&url=http%3A%2F%2Fwww.millerfriel.com%2Fimages%2FMF_7tips_PersonalProfit.pdf&usg=AFQjCNFpm6R79YYlE4qJlQymBw9TylVLwA, visited October 2016
6. IRMI, "Directors and Officers Liability Coverage Checklist," International Risk Management Institute, Inc. (2013).
7. Calkins, M. "To Renew or Not To Renew: The $64,000,000 Question: An Underwriting Checklist for Policyholders During a Difficult D&O Renewal," American Bar Association Section of Litigation 20th Annual Insurance Coverage Litigation Committee CLE Conference, April 16, 2012.
8. McCutcheon, M. and N. Posner, "D&O Insurance Coverage for Financial Institutions: An Insured's Perspective," American Bar Association Section of Litigation Insurance Coverage Litigation Committee CLE Seminar, Mar. 3, 2012.

Notes

3.3 RELIANCE ON MANAGEMENT AND EXPERT OPINIONS

CONTRIBUTED BY
Gregory V. Varallo
Richards, Layton & Finger, P.A.[1]

The seasoned director will understand that governance of a company presents difficult balancing tasks and the application of mature judgment to often intractable problems. To aid the director in the exercise of his or her judgment, the statutory law of many jurisdictions, including Delaware, provides broad protection to directors who rely, in good faith, on the reports of experts chosen with reasonable care. Under Delaware law, a director is also protected in relying on reports or statements of the corporation's officers, and similar provisions are present in the laws of some other states.

Indeed, the statutory protection for good faith reliance on experts chosen with reasonable care is so broad that well-counseled boards will often be presented with expert reports in order to both add to the substance available for the board's consideration and to help further insulate the board's decision-making from later second guessing. In other words, reliance on experts both adds to the substantive mix available for consideration in decision-making and an important layer of statutory legal protection.

1. Gregory V. Varallo is a director and president of Richards, Layton & Finger, P.A., where he practices in the areas of complex business litigation, ADR, and corporate governance. The author wishes to acknowledge the assistance of his colleague Brian F. Morris in the preparation of this chapter.

As noted, the defense based on reliance on experts contains three elements: (i) the advice is on a matter that the director reasonably believes is within the expert's professional or expert competence, (ii) the expert was selected with reasonable care by or on behalf of the company, and (iii) the reliance is itself in good faith.

Advice Reasonably Believed to Be Within the Expert's Competence

Stated simply, directors receive protection when they rely on experts who are presenting within their field of competence. Stated in the negative, directors do not receive protection by relying on lawyers for accounting advice or for relying on accountants for engineering expertise. Given that reliance must be "reasonable" in the sense that the director "reasonably" believed the advice to be within the expert's competence, it would be best to ensure that where a problem involves multiple disciplines, the director insists on fully credentialed experts in every discipline involved in order to build a record of diligence and reasonableness.

Of course, disciplines often overlap, and while there are individuals who are truly capable of giving advice across disciplines (the lawyer/CPA, for example), the reasonableness of a director's reliance on the lawyer for accounting advice (or the CPA who is also a lawyer for legal advice) may be subject to challenge. What is the principle area of practice of the multi-credentialed expert? What discipline is the expert best known for? The director would be well advised to urge the expert to focus on his or her primary area of expertise and to avoid the temptation to short circuit the record-building exercise by professing satisfaction with just one expert where two might better suit the purpose.

Advice from an Expert Selected with Reasonable Care by or on Behalf of the Company

In order to be entitled to rely on an expert, the director need not personally select the expert. Nor does the expert have to be interviewed by the board prior to being hired—the days of the board level "beauty contest" are over. Instead, the director merely needs to assure him- or herself that the process by which the expert was selected for the board (usually by counsel or senior management) was itself reasonable in nature. This would entail asking how the expert was chosen and by whom, as well as what credentials the expert holds.

Advice from Company Experts

The law does not discriminate in favor of or against internal experts. Thus, the board is equally protected in relying on an in-house expert as it is on an outsider. Reports received from the board by the CFO, for example, would typically qualify as expert reports both in the sense that the CFO is a financial and/or accounting expert, and as corporate information presented by the corporation's officers. Just as with outside experts, however, the board must be satisfied in the expertise of the person making the presentation. Thus, a carefully selected CFO reporting on accounting issues is likely to earn the board protection for reliance.

A board should beware, however, of the second-hand presentation of expert advice through a corporate officer, especially where that advice is not within the core competence of the presenting officer. Thus, the presentation of complicated engineering findings on why a plant failed by the chief legal officer of the company likely would not be preferable to the same presentation delivered by the outside engineering expert hired by counsel. The latter presentation allows the board to both become comfortable with the expert's competence and to ask questions the technical expert will be better equipped to respond to.

Good Faith Reliance

Finally, to qualify for the protection of the law, the director's reliance must be in "good faith." Good faith in this context calls for a pragmatic assessment: Does the expert make sense (even if the director is not sufficiently well versed in the nuances of the technical advice being given)? If not, why not? Did the expert's response to questions make sense? If not, why not?

An early 20th-century case presents an easy to understand paradigm of when advice may not be relied upon in good faith. A company in the shipbuilding business unfortunately lost money building ships. During a board meeting, the directors were advised that the company was projected to lose money on every ship it currently was contracted to build.

Later in the same meeting, the board was asked to declare a dividend. The chief financial officer reported to the board that it could declare the dividend because it was likely to generate "surplus" (in fact, profits) sufficient to do so from the completion of one or more ships currently under construction.

Relying on the advice of the CFO, the board voted to pass the dividend. When the company later ran into financial trouble, the board was sued for declaring the dividend. It defended itself by relying on the CFO's report that it would have surplus sufficient to declare the dividend.

The court held that the board's reliance could not have been "in good faith" in the circumstances presented, since the board received a report at the same meeting that it lost money on every ship it completed. Thus, advice that it would make profits from which a dividend could be paid could not have been relied upon in good faith. The directors were held to have breached their duties by not asking questions about the obvious contradiction between the two reports.

While circumstances of "bad faith" reliance are truly rare, and the specific case of directly contradictory advice in the same meeting is not likely to occur in any well-managed meeting, the point is that the director, in order to be able to rely on the projections offered by the statute for reliance on experts, must ask questions where the advice seems suspect or where it runs counter to everyday common sense.

Key Questions

In considering the advice of those retained as "experts" some relevant questions include the following:

- ❑ What are the presenter's professional qualifications and experience? Who hired him or her and how many other firms were contacted? Why did management hire this expert or firm rather than the others it identified?
- ❑ Is the advice being given within the core competence of this expert? If not, is it sufficiently outside that core competence that I should have advice from another expert to "fill in the gaps" left in this person's expertise?

- ❑ Why am I hearing a report about what an actual expert would say rather than hearing from the expert himself? Are there privilege or other concerns? Can these be dealt with?
- ❑ Does the expert's report make sense? What are the key assumptions that the expert is relying on? Are those assumptions contradicted by information I know about the company? Would I rely on this person for advice if I were the client?

Additional Reading

1. Kitchen, J. S., G. V. Varallo, and M. F. Alicks, "Selectica, Inc. v. Versata Enterprises, Inc: A Case Study on the Use (and Usefulness) of Experts in Delaware Corporate Litigation" (ABA Aug. 2010)
   http://www.rlf.com/files/Entire%20Article.pdf
2. Varallo, Gregory V., Daniel Dreisbach, & Blake Rohrbacher, *Fundamentals of Corporate Governance: A Guide for Directors and Corporate Counsel*, (ABA 2nd Ed. 2009)
3. Thomas Uebler, "Reinterpreting Section 141(e) of Delaware's General Corporation Law: Why Interested Directors Should be 'Fully Protected' in Relying on Expert Advice," 65 *The Business Lawyer*, 1023 (2010)
   http://www.rlf.com/files/TBL%2065-4%2001Uebler%20original.pdf
4. John Zeberkiewicz and Blake Rohrbacher, "Prediction Protection: The Delaware Supreme Court's Amylin Footnote," 23 *Insights: The Corporate and Securities Law Advisor* 21 (2009)
   http://www.rlf.com/files/Insight_1109_Zeberkiewicz.pdf
5. Balotti, Franklin R. and Megan W. Shaner, "Safe Harbor for Officer Reliance: Comparing the Approaches of the Model Business Corporation Act and the Delaware General Corporation Law," 74 *Law and Contemporary Problems* 161 (2011)
   http://scholarship.law.duke.edu/cgi/viewcontent.cgi?article=1617&context=lcp

Notes

3.4 RETENTION OF SPECIFIC BOARD OR COMMITTEE COUNSEL

CONTRIBUTED BY
John Mark Zeberkiewicz and Stephanie Norman
Richards, Layton and Finger, P.A.[1]

As covered in the immediately preceding Chapter 3.3 of this Handbook, state corporation law statutes generally recognize that directors, in discharging their fiduciary duties, will need to rely upon the advice of experts and advisors, including legal counsel. To demonstrate their entitlement to reliance, however, the directors must reasonably believe that the advisors they select are competent and capable of advising as to the matters under consideration. While the directors may rely on the corporation's general counsel and regular outside counsel as to legal matters arising in the ordinary course of business, there are certain circumstances, such as an internal investigation, a response to a derivative demand, or the review and negotiation of a related-party transaction, in which members of senior management or specific directors may have divergent interests and where the board (or, in many cases, a committee of the board) is well advised to retain its own (and independent) counsel.

1. John Mark Zeberkiewicz is a director of Richards, Layton and Finger, P.A., where he practices in the Corporate Advisory group. Stephanie Norman is an associate of Richards, Layton and Finger, P.A. where she practices in the Corporate Advisory group.

Managing the Process of Identifying Specific Board or Committee Counsel

As the board's or committee's determination that it requires specific board or committee counsel generally arises by virtue of a transaction or set of circumstances involving an actual or potential conflict of interest vis-à-vis a controlling stockholder or control group, members of management, specific directors, the board, or committee should, in most cases, take steps to ensure that the counsel it selects is independent of the corporation, the controlling stockholder or control group, members of management, or specific directors, as the case may be. Given intense focus on independence in these circumstances, the general counsel or regular outside counsel who regularly advises the directors might not be in the best position to advise the board or committee, due to their relationships with potentially interested parties. Indeed, given the potential for divergent interests, the board or committee should be mindful of its reliance on the general counsel or regular outside counsel in the process of selecting and retaining its own independent counsel.

When initiating the process of selecting and retaining its own counsel, the board or committee, often led by its lead independent director or chairperson, should abide by protocols that ensure the board or committee maintains control over the key decisions. Nevertheless, there are various matters in the selection process as to which the board or committee may (and in fact would be well advised to) seek guidance and input from the general counsel or regular outside counsel. These matters include, but are not necessarily limited to, the following:

- *Advising as to the Standards and Criteria for Evaluating Counsel.* The board or committee may seek input from the general counsel or regular outside counsel as to the criteria it should use in selecting independent counsel, including the standards that the board or committee should use in assessing the reputation, skill, experience, expertise, and independence of specific firms or attorneys. The general counsel or regular outside counsel may assist the board or committee in preparing, among other things, a list of questions that it should pose to its prospective counsel in the course of an interview.
- *Offering Recommendations of Potential Counsel.* The general counsel or regular outside counsel may provide the board or committee recommendations as to potential firms or attorneys that would be qualified to serve as counsel. Where the general counsel or regular outside counsel provides such recommendations, the board or committee should probe the criteria used to identify such firms or attorneys. The board or committee should also consider asking the general counsel or regular outside counsel to furnish materials regarding the qualifications and expertise of the firms or attorneys so identified, and to disclose any known prior relationships or engagements with the corporation or other potentially interested parties.
- *Making Introductions to and Scheduling Interviews with Counsel.* The general counsel (or, less frequently, regular outside counsel) may also assist in scheduling and coordinating meetings at which the board or committee conducts interviews of its prospective counsel.

- *Reviewing and Negotiating Engagement Letters*. The board or committee will generally also require the assistance of the general counsel or outside regular counsel in reviewing and negotiating the terms of the engagement letter between the prospective counsel and the board or committee.

While it may seek guidance or assistance from the general counsel or regular outside counsel as to the foregoing and other matters, the board or committee should be prepared to question and test the advice it receives. Moreover, the board or committee is not (and should not consider itself to be) constrained by any recommendations or suggestions it receives from in-house counsel or regular outside counsel. In particular, it should not necessarily limit its search of prospective counsel to any firms or attorneys that the general counsel or regular outside counsel has identified. Directors should use their own business judgment in assessing whether any list of prospective counsel furnished to them is satisfactory, or whether they should pursue other avenues for referrals for independent counsel. If directors have worked with particular firms or attorneys in connection with other engagements and have had positive experiences, or if they have other sources or referral networks for identifying counsel, they should propose those firms or attorneys to their fellow board or committee members for consideration. In addition, although the board or committee should seek assistance from the general counsel or regular outside counsel to negotiate the terms of the engagement letter with its independent counsel, it should make clear that the decision to retain counsel, and the terms of the engagement, are in the sole discretion of the board or committee.

Assessing the Independence of Specific Board or Committee Counsel

In most cases, a key inquiry for the board or committee when seeking specific counsel is whether counsel is independent from the company and any potentially interested parties, including any controlling stockholder or control group, members of management, or specific directors. Given the heightened focus on independence, both from courts and institutional and other investors, the board or committee should not limit its inquiry to whether its prospective counsel has a conflict of interest under the applicable ethical rules. Rather, it should broaden its inquiry to assess whether the prospective firms, or any member of the prospective firms (particularly those who would be principally responsible for the engagement), have interests or relationships that would (or would reasonably be expected to) affect their ability to provide impartial advice. The independence inquiry involves not only whether the prospective firm or specific attorney had a previous attorney–client relationship with the corporation, a controlling stockholder or control group, members of management or specific directors, but extends to other dealings that they have had with those parties or other persons or entities with which those parties are affiliated or associated. That said, the existence of tangential relationships or immaterial prior engagements with the corporation or other potentially interested parties may not necessarily be disabling. The board or committee should assess the nature, scope, and extent of the relationships or prior engagements and evaluate them in light of the benefits of retaining a specific firm or attorney.

Assessing the Qualifications, Expertise, and Capacity of Specific Board or Committee Counsel

In addition to evaluating the independence of its counsel, the board or committee should be satisfied that the counsel it retains has the requisite expertise and experience to handle the transaction or matter under consideration. As noted earlier, the board or committee, with advance input from the corporation's in-house counsel or regular outside counsel, can establish criteria for assessing expertise. Chief among the factors that the board or committee should consider are the reputation of the prospective firm or attorneys and the depth of experience in the relevant practice area. Most firms will make available to prospective clients pitch books that describe the firm's prior engagements. Boards or committees may also consult reports of third parties that conduct research on, and provide descriptions and assessments of, law firms and attorneys.

The board's or committee's inquiry, however, should not be limited to the firm's or particular attorney's expertise. The board or committee should also attempt to assess whether the firm or specific attorneys have the capacity to undertake the engagement. If the board or committee is selecting a particular firm due to the reputation or strengths of a particular attorney or set of attorneys, the board or committee may wish to seek assurances that the particular attorney or set of attorneys will be principally responsible for managing and undertaking the engagement.

Understanding and Managing the Role of Specific Board or Committee Counsel

While in a broad sense independent counsel to the board or committee represents the corporation, as the board or committee acts for and on behalf of the corporation, it should be clear that independent counsel answers to no party at the corporation other than the board or the committee. While the directors may continue to rely on the general counsel or the corporation's regular outside counsel for matters arising in the ordinary course that are unrelated to the assignment or particular work for which independent counsel was retained, the board or committee should ensure that the general counsel and regular outside counsel, on the one hand, and the independent counsel, on the other, recognize, understand, and respect their separate roles. Where the board or committee has retained independent counsel for a specific matter or transaction, for instance, independent counsel should be the board's or committee's primary resource, rather than the general counsel or regular outside counsel, for seeking advice at meetings of the board or committee that relate to the transaction or matter, as well as advice on the terms of transaction or other documents relating to the transaction or matter. Except at the invitation of the board or committee, the general counsel or regular outside counsel should not participate in meetings of the board or committee relating to matters or transactions as to which independent counsel is advising. In addition, as to transaction or other documents, the board or committee should rely on independent counsel to review and advise as to the terms of the documents, and to coordinate, as appropriate, with the general counsel or regular outside counsel.

Protocols for Managing Legal Fees and Invoices

Where the board or committee has determined to retain independent legal counsel, special protocols should be established for the submission and approval of that counsel's fees and expenses. Invoices that detail the activities of outside counsel are desirable, but may reflect privileged communications, reveal the scope or nature of counsel's activities, or imply counsel's mental impressions of the matter.

Thus, it is often not appropriate or desirable for this information to become known to the company's officers, including its general counsel or accounting staff. Moreover, once these invoices become part of the company's business records, they may be more susceptible to discovery in a legal proceeding.

Accordingly, counsel will often suggest that two versions of each invoice be prepared. The first invoice reflecting detailed descriptions of counsel's activities will be delivered to the chair of the committee, lead director, or other person appointed to receive, review, and approve counsel's fees. The second invoice generally stating only "For Legal Services Rendered" (or statement to that effect) will be submitted to the company for payment. Once the detailed invoice has been approved, the company will be advised of that fact and then pay based upon the summary invoice.

This protocol also protects the independence of counsel, who will be looking to the board or committee, and not the company's general counsel staff, to approve legal fees and expenses.

Key Questions

In considering the selection and retention of specific board or committee counsel, members of the board or committee, as applicable, should consider the following:

- ❑ What was the process by which the list of prospective counsel had been identified? If the general counsel or regular outside counsel was the sole source of the list, has the board or committee asked sufficient questions to understand the process by which the list had been generated? Should the board consider broadening the scope of its search to firms not included on any such list?
- ❑ Has the board or committee sought disclosure of all past, present, and future connections and relationships between the prospective counsel, on the one hand, and other relevant parties, including, depending on the circumstances, the corporation and its affiliates and its and their officers and directors, as well as any actual or potential counterparty, on the other?
- ❑ Has the board or committee received advice and guidance from its independent counsel regarding the appropriate roles of the general counsel and regular outside counsel, on the one hand, and the board's or committee's counsel, on the other?
- ❑ What special protocols for communication, payment of legal fees, or other matters should be established?

Additional Reading

1. Wing, James D., "Corporate Internal Investigations and the Fifth Amendment," *Business Law Today* (ABA September 2014).
2. Rokas, Alexandros N., *Reliance on Experts from a Corporate Law Perspective*, 2 Am. U. Bus. L. Rev. 323 (2012–13).
3. Varallo, Gregory V., Srinivas M. Raju, and Michael D. Allen, *Special Committees: Law and Practice* (2011).
4. Landefeld, Stewart M., David F. Tayor, and Elizabeth D. Oliphant, "The Board of Directors in the Age of Investigation." *Insights: The Corporate & Securities Law Advisor* 21, no. 2 (February 2015).
5. Hazard, Geoffrey C. Jr., and Edward B. Rock, "A New Player in the Boardroom: The Emergence of the Independent Directors' Counsel" 59 *Bus. Law.* 1389 (2003–04).

Notes

SECTION FOUR

OVERSIGHT OF MANAGEMENT

4.1 SELECTING A CEO

CONTRIBUTED BY
Robert Bostrom
Abercrombie & Fitch Co.[1]
Aaron A. Seamon
Squire Patton Boggs (US) LLP[2]

Selecting a CEO can be a time consuming and lengthy process, particularly if the selection is not occurring as part of a well-designed and natural selection plan. A thoughtful approach to selecting a CEO can set up a company for long-term success while a process that is rushed or less than careful can result in wasting time and resources, or hiring a CEO whose vision for the organization is not in line with the board's. CEO selection and succession planning is a key element of a director's fiduciary duties.

Boards should undertake a deliberate and careful process that should dovetail with the board's overall approach to succession planning for management. The CEO succession plan in particular should be one that is fully developed and well documented.

The selection of a CEO begins with establishing the process by which the board will undertake the search. Typically compensation committees are tasked with a CEO search,

1. Robert Bostrom is the senior vice president and general counsel of Abercrombie & Fitch Co.
2. Aaron Seamon is a partner in the corporate finance practice of Squire Patton Boggs (US) LLP where he practices in the Columbus office.

although it is also common for boards to create a special committee of directors who are charged with presenting the board with candidates for consideration. The board should consider identifying a key member of senior management, usually within human resources or similar function, to assist and serve as a project manager in the process.

Once the process for conducting a search is established, it is prudent to have a complete assessment of what skill sets are considered important for the organization's CEO and how those skills relate to the company's long-term strategic and business plan. Having an established skill set matrix or other process to develop CEO characteristics (through a "scorecard" or 360-degree survey) can help to facilitate CEO selection.

The selection process can take a significant amount of time. Relevant decisions the board (or search committee) needs to consider are the pool of candidates from which to choose, how that pool of candidates will be identified (through internal search, national search with the assistance of a search firm, etc.), and how those candidates are assessed. Another key consideration is the role that any key shareholders may play in the process, and how the CEO selection process relates to the company's broader shareholder engagement efforts if there are large investors who may have questions regarding long-term CEO succession.

The selection process varies significantly if the search is in the wake of a crisis, dismissal, or other disruptive event that requires a CEO succession. In those circumstances, having an established short-term management succession plan and process for selecting an interim CEO is critical, and it helps to demonstrate that the organization has effective oversight and risk management in place to address such contingencies.

Developing a strategy for succession planning for both the long-term and short-term can allow for a thoughtful, deliberative process in selecting a CEO.

Key Questions

When considering the selection of a CEO and the process that the board will undertake for CEO succession, some questions to consider are as follows:

- ❑ How does the CEO search relate to the company's existing management succession plan?
- ❑ Does the board have an ongoing succession planning process in place?
- ❑ What subset of the board will be responsible for coordinating the CEO candidate search? What is the mechanism and process that they will undertake? Under what time frame?
- ❑ How will the board develop the characteristics to be considered in selecting a new CEO? What role will diversity play in the selection of possible candidates?
- ❑ Will the board retain a national search firm to conduct a search for candidates?
- ❑ Does the company have any internal candidates for CEO succession?
- ❑ What role will any key stakeholders (stockholders, employees, etc.) play in the evaluation process?
- ❑ Is it necessary to evaluate comparative CEO compensation packages to assess whether the company's approach to compensation, by both amount and compensation mix, is appropriate?

- ❑ Does the company anticipate a transition period between the current CEO and any new CEO? What will that transition look like?
- ❑ In the event of unplanned CEO transition, what are the company's contingency plans regarding succession and how regularly are those plans evaluated?

Additional Reading

1. Board Strategies for Overcoming the Most Common Succession Planning Obstacles, *Spencer Stuart* (2014)
   https://www.spencerstuart.com/research-and-insight/board-strategies-for-overcoming-the-most-common-succession-planning-obstacles
2. Overcoming the Obstacles to CEO Succession Planning, *Nadler Advisory Services* (2014)
   http://nadler-leadership-advisory.com/NAS-White-Papers/5_Overcoming-the-Obstacles-to-CEO-Succession-Planning.pdf
3. A Practical Guide to CEO Succession Planning, *Russell Reynolds Associates* (2008)
   http://www.russellreynolds.com/en/Newsroom/Documents/practical-guide-ceo-succession-planning.pdf
4. Plank, Willa. "The Do's and Don'ts of CEO Succession Planning." *Wall Street Journal* (2014)
   http://www.wsj.com/articles/SB10001424052702303987004579479680859042214
5. The Question of CEO Succession. *The Corporate Board* XXXV, no. 208 (September/October 2014)
6. CEO Succession Practices, *The Conference Board* (2014)
7. Building the Bench: Strategic Planning for CEO and Executive Succession, *Price Waterhouse Coopers* (2015)
   http://www.pwc.com/us/en/people-management/assets/building-bench-strategic-planning-ceos-executive-succession.pdf

Notes

4.2 EVALUATING CEO PERFORMANCE

CONTRIBUTED BY
Robert Bostrom
Abercrombie & Fitch Co.[1]
Aaron A. Seamon
Squire Patton Boggs (US) LLP[2]

The CEO evaluation process can be a powerful resource for boards to engage with the CEO on critical issues affecting the organization. A thoughtful and formal approach to CEO evaluation can also have a downstream effect on the evaluation process utilized for other members of senior management.

The regular, ongoing evaluation of the CEO requires boards to have in place a robust process that establishes clear performance objectives, allows for measurement, and incentivizes the CEO to pursue and achieve those objectives.

At the outset, the board (or relevant committee, such as the compensation committee or the lead independent director or nonexecutive committee chair) should work with the CEO to develop workable performance objectives, which should include fostering an ethical culture that aligns to the board's broad strategic vision for the organization. The

1. Robert Bostrom is the senior vice president and general counsel of Abercrombie & Fitch Co.
2. Aaron Seamon is a partner in the corporate finance practice of Squire Patton Boggs (US) LLP where he practices in the Columbus office.

performance objectives should be focused, measurable, and should allow for meeting various operational and leadership goals. Developing a "scorecard" or 360-degree survey to establish and evaluate performance objectives can also be useful. The use of a balanced scorecard to evaluate the CEO on an individual performance basis, as well as a corporate performance metric is key.

Once established and implemented, of critical importance is the process by which the board will undertake the review of the performance objectives against actual performance. The evaluation process should be balanced, with meaningful dialogue with the CEO as well as a level of objectivity on the part of the board in considering its overall evaluation of CEO performance.

Providing meaningful feedback as to the CEO's performance is another critical component in the CEO performance evaluation loop. Having a candid discussion is important, and determining how that message will be delivered and by whom (e.g., the lead independent director, chair, etc.) is also critical.

Key Questions

When considering CEO performance, some questions to consider are as follows:

- ❑ Does the board have a formal process for the evaluation of CEO performance?
- ❑ What committee of the board will consider CEO performance? How will the performance objectives be developed? Does the board need any third-party consultants to assist in developing performance objectives?
- ❑ Does the board use a 360-degree approach and get the evaluations of the C-Suite team?
- ❑ How will CEO individual performance and use of a balanced scorecard align to the company's overall incentive compensation philosophy for management?
- ❑ Are there any unique factors given the company's industry, geographic footprint, end-markets, or other considerations that should be considered as part of the CEO evaluation?
- ❑ Is there flexibility within the evaluation of CEO performance for both qualitative and quantitative factors? What is the relative weight assigned to such measures?
- ❑ How should corporate culture and establishing "tone at the top" be accounted for when assessing CEO performance? How does compliance and ethics of the organization get measured relative to CEO performance?
- ❑ Are there significant shareholders who should be consulted to gather feedback as to areas that are believed to be of importance in CEO performance assessment that the board should consider?
- ❑ What role will management and employee surveys and feedback play in the board's consideration of the CEO's performance?

Additional Reading

1. "Blueprint for a Better CEO Evaluation Process: Unlocking Real Value," *Mercer* (2013)
   http://www.mercer.com/content/dam/mercer/attachments/global/Talent/executive-reward-perspectives/2013/blueprint-for-a-better-ceo-evaluation-process-us-issue-100-march-2013mercer.pdf
2. Kaufman, Stephen P. "Evaluating the CEO." *Harvard Business Review* (2008)
   https://hbr.org/2008/10/evaluating-the-ceo
3. Larcker, David F., Stephen Miles, Brian Tayan, and Michelle E. Gutman, *CEO Performance Evaluation Survey, Stanford Graduate School of Business* (2013)
   https://www.gsb.stanford.edu/sites/gsb/files/publication-pdf/cgri-survey-2013-ceo-performance.pdf
4. Why Governance Evaluations Fail, *The Corporate Board* XXXVI, no. 214 (September/October 2015)
5. Trammell, J., "How Do You Evaluate CEO Performance? 6 Ways to Grade the Chief," *Forbes*, 2013
   http://www.forbes.com/sites/joeltrammell/2013/08/18/how-do-you-evaluate-ceo-performance-6-ways-to-grade-the-chief/print/

Notes

___

___

___

___

___

4.3 MANAGEMENT SUCCESSION PLANNING

CONTRIBUTED BY
Holly J. Gregory
Sidley Austin LLP[1]

Developing and implementing succession plans for the CEO and senior executives is one of the board's key roles. Effective succession planning requires regular, ongoing attention so that the board is positioned to select from among strong candidates when a change in leadership is needed. Succession planning should involve both a plan for who will step in if the CEO leaves suddenly or is incapacitated and a plan for the orderly transfer of leadership at some appropriate future time in the normal course. Both aspects of succession planning require an understanding of the depth and breadth of the potential available talent, both within and outside the company.

Management succession is often a difficult topic for the CEO, who must face his or her own career ending or mortality. This natural hesitancy can be overcome by linking succession planning to management development. Management development is closely related to succession planning, since it enables the company to look internally in the first instance for potential succession candidates. Succession planning is assisted when the company is an organization that attracts and develops talent with appropriate leadership and

1. Holly J. Gregory is a partner and co-chair of the Global Corporate Governance & Executive Compensation Practice of Sidley Austin LLP and practices in its New York office.

management skills. Addressing these topics in corporate governance guidelines (which is required for New York Stock Exchange companies) provides the board an opportunity to consider its approach to this sensitive issue as a policy matter distinct from decisions concerning a particular individual's position.

The board has the flexibility to adopt a succession planning process that best suits the particular needs of the company. It is up to the board to determine how much time and attention to spend on succession planning, and whether or at what point to retain advisors for assistance, consider internal candidates, conduct an external search, and determine that enough information has been obtained to support an informed judgment.

Because succession planning is a central component of the board's role, generally the full board maintains responsibility for, and is involved in, succession decisions. However, boards routinely delegate responsibility for specific tasks to board committees. For example, the nominating and governance committee, or the compensation committee, may be tasked with hiring a search firm to assist in identifying candidates and specifying desirable candidate criteria. Often, given its role in performance evaluations of top executives, the compensation committee is involved on an ongoing basis in assessing potential internal candidates, identifying their leadership capabilities, and pinpointing areas for further development.

Succession planning should involve the board and the CEO in a continuous, collaborative, and iterative process. The CEO often has the best understanding of the company's leadership needs and the talent within the organization. The board's role is to do the following:

- Consider the likely timeframe in which succession will be called for in the normal course of events
- Work with the CEO to identify a pool of potential internal successors and allow the CEO to share some responsibilities and give "stretch assignments"
- Agree with the CEO and HR on the critical attributes of a successful CEO or other senior executive that are linked to the company's strategy (current and under future conditions)
- Take an active role in evaluating the capabilities, potential, and readiness for promotion of possible successors
- Consider where to find ideal external candidates
- Conduct an open and honest annual performance review of the CEO to determine whether he or she should continue in that position
- Have in place a decision process and a crisis management plan in the event of an unexpected CEO transition

Key Questions

When considering management succession planning issues, some key questions for the board should include the following:

- ❑ Has the board delegated to a committee any responsibilities relating to succession planning?
- ❑ Do we have a written succession plan?
- ❑ How often do we review the succession plan?

- ❑ How does the board and its committees work with the current CEO and management to develop the succession plan?
- ❑ Do we have a roadmap for handling an unexpected CEO transition (for example, involving a CEO termination or health issue)?
- ❑ Do we have current executives who could serve as CEO on an interim basis in case of an unexpected vacancy?
- ❑ How long we do expect our current CEO to serve? Do we anticipate leadership transition in the near future?
- ❑ What attributes should we look for in our next CEO given our current and future strategic plans for the company?
- ❑ Do we have current executives who have the potential to be the company's future leaders/candidates for CEO? What is our assessment of our "bench strength"?
- ❑ Do senior managers get adequate time in front of the board?
- ❑ Should we take steps to develop a "deeper bench"? Do we have the resources to do so? Is our long-term compensation program conducive to doing so?
- ❑ Do we need to consider external candidates?
- ❑ What management development processes are in place to nurture future leaders at the company?
- ❑ Does the company have any talent gaps in the context of our current and future strategic business plans? How do we plan to address such gaps?

Additional Reading

1. Gregory, Holly J. "Planning for Leadership Succession and Unexpected CEO Transitions," *Practical Law: The Journal* (March 2016)
   http://www.sidley.com/~/media/publications/mar16_govcounselor.pdf
2. Charan, Ram, "The Secrets of Great CEO Selection," *Harvard Business Review* 52 (December 2016).
3. "Taking the Emergency Out of Emergency CEO Succession," *Heidrick and Struggles* (September 2015)
   http://www.heidrick.com/~/media/Publications%20and%20Reports/HS_taking%20the%20emergency%20out%20of%20emergency%20succession.pdf
4. "CEO Succession Starts with Developing Your Leaders," *McKinsey Quarterly* (May 2015)
   http://www.mckinsey.com/global-themes/leadership/ceo-succession-starts-with-developing-your-leaders
5. CEO Succession Practices: 2015 Edition, *The Conference Board*
6. Larcker, David F., Stephen A. Miles, and Brian Tayan, "Seven Myths of CEO Succession," *Stanford Closer Look Series* (March 19, 2014)
   https://www.gsb.stanford.edu/sites/gsb/files/publication-pdf/cgri-closer-look-39-seven-myths-ceo-succession.pdf

7. Report of the Blue Ribbon Commission on Talent Development, *National Association of Corporate Directors* (2013)
8. "Lessons from the Boardroom: Seven Succession Planning Missteps Boards Should Avoid," *Spencer Stuart* (December 2010)
   https://www.spencerstuart.com/research-and-insight/lessons-from-the-boardroom-seven-succession-planning-missteps-boards-should-avoid

Notes

4.4 THE BOARD'S ROLE IN CORPORATE CULTURE

CONTRIBUTED BY
Robert Bostrom
Abercrombie & Fitch Co.[1]
Aaron A. Seamon
Squire Patton Boggs (US) LLP[2]

Setting the appropriate corporate culture or "tone at the top" is among the board's most important functions in carrying out its oversight responsibilities. A corporate culture that embraces transparency, legal compliance, and high standards of ethics is now expected by key stakeholders (shareholders, customers, suppliers) as well as by state and federal regulators. As demonstrated by recent corporate scandals, a flawed corporate culture can have dire consequences that impede strategic outcomes, have significant negative reputational impact, subject the organization (as well as directors and officers) to civil and criminal liability, and negatively impact company performance.

The concept of corporate culture and tone at the top can be a nebulous one and therefore can be prone to being given short shrift by boards. While described in many

1. Robert Bostrom, is the senior vice president and general counsel of Abercrombie & Fitch Co.
2. Aaron Seamon is a partner in the corporate finance practice of Squire Patton Boggs (US) LLP where he practices in the Columbus office.

ways, corporate culture can be thought of as the shared values, beliefs, and vision of the organization that guide the organization in achieving its business objectives.

While there is no one size fits all approach, key components of virtually all corporate cultures should include a focus on transparency, diversity, ethics and compliance, and long-term value as opposed to short-term results. These are cornerstones of the broader corporate culture that put a premium on compliance and always looking to "do the right thing." Directors should always view decisions through the lens of a well-articulated corporate culture that is defined, implemented throughout all layers of the organization, and measured to ensure compliance. The board should actively and periodically express its strong commitment to ethics, compliance, integrity, and diversity to management the entire company.

Boards should encourage and enforce an ethical corporate culture through the strategic direction set for management, and in particular for the CEO, by incentivizing and by evaluating management on whether they embrace the corporate culture as articulated or are resistant to such policies. Maintaining an open dialogue with management regarding the values and culture of the company is critical.

Hand-in-hand with having an effective corporate culture is maintaining a board comprised of directors who are not afraid to ask tough questions regarding the corporate culture. Having a diverse make-up of independent-minded directors who bring different perspectives and points of view into the boardroom can greatly enhance the development of an effective corporate culture.

Boards should also consider strategies that are hands-on in order to get a sense for the prevailing corporate culture. Scheduling meetings away from headquarters and near operational facilities, developing relationships with members of management, reviewing the results of organizational cultural surveys and cultural assessments, reviewing employee hotline comments, sending clear and powerful messages such as building cultural values into compensation systems, and otherwise gauging how employees view corporate culture can provide useful feedback to directors.

Key Questions

When evaluating corporate culture and the tone at the top, some questions to consider are as follows:

- ❑ Does the company have an articulated corporate culture that includes diversity, transparency, compliance, and ethics, and does it support the company's overall business strategies and goals?
- ❑ What values does the board want to be reflected in the corporate culture?
- ❑ What message is the board sending to the CEO and management regarding the company's corporate culture?
- ❑ Is corporate culture a consideration when hiring, retaining, and compensating management? Is corporate culture a factor in the board's succession planning?
- ❑ Have any recent events within the company revealed a weakness in the corporate culture?

- ❑ How often should the board discuss corporate culture internally and with management?
- ❑ Does the board review the company's code of conduct and do the directors certify they have read and knew of such violations?
- ❑ What is the marketplace saying, or what is the public's perception, about our corporate culture?
- ❑ How active should the board be in obtaining information about its corporate culture?
- ❑ What involvement should internal and external audit have in informing the board of corporate culture issues?
- ❑ How are we measuring the company's outcomes and results as compared to adherence to our corporate culture? Is an employee survey being used? Should we use one?
- ❑ Is our approach enterprise risk management in line with our corporate culture?
- ❑ How is management implementing corporate culture through training, hiring, and compensation throughout the organization?

Additional Reading

1. Committee of Sponsoring Organizations of the Treadway Commission (COSO) in Internal Control—Integrated Framework (2013)
2. What Do Boards Need to Know About Corporate Culture?, *Spencer Stuart* (February 2015)
   https://www.spencerstuart.com/research and-insight/what-do-boards-need-to-know-about-corporate-culture
3. Managing Corporate Cultural Change, *Corporate Executive Board* (2008)
   http://www.peakperformance.com.au/myfiles/Managing-corporate-cultural-change.PDF
4. Visionary Board Leadership: Stewardship for the Long Term, *CFA Institute* (2012)
   http://www.cfapubs.org/doi/pdf/10.2469/ccb.v2012.n3.1
5. White, B. Joseph. *Boards That Excel, Candid Insights & Practical Advice for Directors* (2014).
6. *Corporate Director's Guidebook*, 6th ed., American Bar Association Business Law Section (2011).
7. ICGN Global Corporate Governance Principles: Revised (2009), *International Corporate Governance Network*
   http://www.ecgi.org/codes/documents/icgn_global_corporate_governance_principles_revised_2009.pdf
8. Corporate Culture and the Role of Boards, Report of Observations, *Financial Reporting Council* (2016)

Notes

4.5 MANAGING THE FOUNDER

CONTRIBUTED BY
Trace Blankenship
Bone McAllester Norton PLLC[1]

Directors who serve on a board with a company's founder may find they are expected not only to discharge their ordinary legal duties to the corporation but also to be counselor, coach, peacemaker, and chief reality officer at any point in time. Founders can create enormous value in advancing the company's mission while adding layers of complexity to its governance. When a founder is either at the helm of the company or remains on the board in a nonexecutive role, the other directors must be vigilant about how the founder's interlocking relationships with board and management affect the board's collegiality and its ability to function and govern effectively. It is equally critical that the other directors stay attuned to how the founder is affecting the company's performance—especially if the founder remains the face of the company and its culture. A level-headed, seasoned lead director may be particularly helpful here.

Boards that can harness and engage the unique energy and vision of a company's founder in the service of reasonable performance goals have an opportunity to support and sustain a healthy company culture while driving long-term growth. The challenge for the board, though, is to have the presence of mind to detect when the founder's emotional connection

1. Trace Blankenship is a member and serves as general counsel and secretary of Bone McAllester Norton PLLC in its Nashville, Tennessee office. He also serves on the law firm's board of directors ex officio.

to the company (or ego) is distracting the founder from addressing imminent challenges or even predicting and preparing for headwinds that could cause the company to stumble.

In particular, the board should expect the founder to have the professionalism and fortitude to solicit and accept constructive criticism, hard questions, and recommendations informed by the various skill sets and experiences of the board members. Likewise, the directors may find that effective communication with a founder may have a different tone and delivery from communication with a nonfounder CEO who was initially hired by the board. No matter what, the hallmarks of a founder CEO's communication to the board should be competence, transparency, and thoroughness. As it should with any CEO, the board must have confidence that the founder—and the senior management team surrounding the founder—demonstrates a personal commitment to high ethical standards, principles of fair dealing, and full compliance with legal requirements. In addition to the founder's compensation, any other "insider" transactions benefitting the founder (or family and close associates) should be carefully scrutinized and evaluated by the board. At a minimum, the board should establish a trustworthy process for evaluating the founder's performance as an executive, so that there are routine opportunities for the board (or a smaller committee) to engage with the founder in deeper conversations about quality of leadership, consistency of performance, vision for the future, and challenges ahead.

If the founder is in a nonexecutive role as a fellow director, the board should be able to call upon a founder's unique perspective about the company's culture and its best opportunities to exploit in the marketplace. Hopefully, a founder serving in this more passive role has the personal strength and sensitivity to promote the company's best interests while constructively engaging with a management team that the founder no longer inhabits. However, some directors may be in the unfortunate position of serving with a founder who holds tightly to a seat on the board in order to protect the founder's large equity stake with little or no remaining affection for the company. If the collegiality and/or effectiveness of the board is seriously impaired by this type of founder, the board chair or lead director may need to work informally with the other directors to develop a strategy for either rehabilitating the founder's relationship or neutralizing the founder's negative effect on the board's ability to discharge its duties, assuming the founder will not voluntarily resign to resolve the problem.

Whether the founder is a respected CEO who consistently delivers exceptional results and continues to promote an enviable culture for its employees and customers, or the founder has stalled and can no longer lead the company effectively, the ultimate obligation to evaluate the circumstances and protect the company rests with the board of directors, which should be cognizant of both the benefits and burdens of leading the company with a founder.

Key Questions

To manage the founder (and the founder's relationship with the board), some questions for the board to consider might be the following:

- ❑ During board meetings, does the founder respond to directors' questions and dialogue with appropriate engagement, transparency, and humility, or do ordinary questions and engagement from directors elicit impatience and/or irritation from the founder?

- ❑ Does the board generally trust the founder to provide fulsome disclosure and robust reporting to the board about the company's performance and challenges?
- ❑ Are the founder and senior management personally committed to high ethical standards, principles of fair dealing, and full compliance with legal requirements? Does the board periodically review what the founder (as chief executive) and senior management are doing to set the right example and how they are communicating this to employees and all constituents of the organization?
- ❑ Does the founder have the background, skills, and mindset to lead the company as it moves forward? To scale the company?
- ❑ What, if any, shortcomings in the founder's skill set or management talents exist? Can they be shored up by surrounding the founder with other seasoned senior executives?
- ❑ Is there an expectation for "telling the truth" at board meetings and within the organization? Do the board and other management team members reactively make excuses for the founder's shortcomings (because it's the founder) or proactively ferret out problems and challenges?
- ❑ Do board members receive regular reports from (or have access to) employees other than the founder/chief executive?
- ❑ What is the board's perception of how the founder promotes and protects the company's culture? How are the company's employees, customers, vendors, and shareholders treated every day? Is there a revolving door for employees? Are there recurring complaints/issues arising from other constituencies?
- ❑ Are routine financial transactions benefiting "insiders," such as the founder or relatives and close associates of the founder, carefully reviewed and approved by the board? Are these "sweetheart" deals that would otherwise be hard to justify if they were on an arms-length basis with a non-insider?
- ❑ Does the board have a succession plan in place that will allow the company to survive and thrive in the absence of the founder?
- ❑ Is the founder likely to cooperate with or resist such succession planning? What can be done to secure the founder's cooperation, including involvement in the planning process?
- ❑ Is the founder purposefully or perhaps unknowingly undermining potential successors by failing to allow them to develop and thrive?
- ❑ Does the founder have any unique relationships with key customers, suppliers, employees, or other constituencies that need to be managed or transitioned to ensure that they survive the departure of the founder?
- ❑ Does the founder have any unique technical, market, or other knowledge that should be effectively transferred to others?
- ❑ If the founder is not the optimal CEO for the company as it grows and scales, is there another role for the founder, perhaps in product development or customer relationships? Will the founder accept that role without unduly interfering with the new CEO?

- ❑ Is there a particular director who can be most effective in conveying potentially unwelcome messages to the founder? If not, can such a relationship be developed?
- ❑ Is the board sufficiently independent of the founder, or were all or most of its members chosen by the founder? What, if any, changes should be made to secure the necessary level of independence?
- ❑ Does the founder have any voting or other governance rights that might make it difficult to make a change if it becomes necessary? Can they be dealt with now?
- ❑ What "knowledge transfer" should occur to mitigate risk of the founder's unavailability due to death or disability?
- ❑ How is the founder's health? Does that have any implications regarding succession?
- ❑ Is key employee insurance in place regarding the founder? Should it be?
- ❑ Does the founder still own any of the intellectual property, real estate, or other assets that are important to the company? Should they be transferred to the company now?
- ❑ How would the market (and employee base) react to the sudden departure of the founder? What steps should be taken to avert an overly negative reaction to the founder's unexpected departure?

Additional Reading

1. Wasserman, Noam. "The Founder's Dilemma." *Harvard Business Review* (February 2008)
   https://hbr.org/2008/02/the-founders-dilemma
2. Hoffman, Reid. If, Why, and How Founders Should Hire a "Professional" CEO (January 21, 2013)
   http://reidhoffman.org/if-why-and-how-founders-should-hire-a-professional-ceo/
3. Bergeron, James. "Director Best Practices for Young CEO Companies." *Private Company Director* (April 2016)
   http://www.privatecompanydirector.com/features/board-director-best-practices-young-ceo-companies
4. Damouni, Nadia. "You Can't Just Fire the Founder of a Company." *Reuters* (August 15, 2014)
   http://www.businessinsider.com/r-corporate-founders-battle-boards-to-overturn-forced-exits-2014-15
5. Griffith, Erin. "To Build a Billion Dollar Company, Keep Your Founder in the CEO Spot." *Fortune* (January 22, 2015)
   http://fortune.com/2015/01/22/unicorn-startups-founder-ceo/

6. Markowitz, Eric. "Why Founders Get Fired." *Inc.* (September 2011) http://www.inc.com/articles/201109/why-founders-get-fired.html
7. Founder's Syndrome http://earlystagetechboards.com/3-9-founders-syndrome
8. Solomon, Steven Davidoff. "Pulte Fight Pits Company's Founder Against Its Board." *The New York Times* (May 3, 2016) http://www.nytimes.com/2016/05/04/business/dealbook/pulte-fight-pits-companys-founder-against-its-board.html?_r=0
9. Winkler, Rolfe. "Silicon Valley Looks for Lessons in Theranos." *Wall Street Journal* (July 13, 2016) http://www.wsj.com/articles/silicon-valley-looks-for-lessons-in-theranos-1468402201
10. Simeonov, Simeon. "When to Fire Your Co-Founders." Venture Hacks blog (January 28, 2010) http://venturehacks.com/articles/fire-co-founders

Notes

4.6 MANAGING REPUTATIONAL RISK

CONTRIBUTED BY
Stephen A. Pike
Gowling WLG[1]
Paul Lanois
Credit Suisse[2]

As part of an increasing focus on the responsibility of boards of directors to manage risk on an enterprise-wide basis, during the past decade the task of managing the reputational risk of an enterprise has taken on a new and, some would say, critical priority. Warren Buffett is famously quoted for having said that "it takes 20 years to build a reputation and five minutes to ruin it. If you think about that, you'll do things differently."

The daily business news provides no shortage of examples of businesses battling to maintain their reputations (or what is left of them) after corporate missteps—some successful in their efforts and some not. A well-prepared board no longer views reputational risk as a mere amorphous risk, somehow linked to goodwill on the balance sheet. Rather, boards are recognizing that reputational risk requires their focused attention and that the

1. Stephen A. Pike is a partner in the Toronto office of the Gowling WLG (Canada) LLP law firm where he advises on corporate and business law matters.
2. Paul Lanois is senior legal counsel at Credit Suisse and is admitted to the bars of the District of Columbia, New York, and the Supreme Court of the United States.

structures, strategies, policies, and systems necessary for the effective management of reputational risk are increasingly crucial.

As part of a corporation's enterprise risk management strategy and systems, boards must develop a deep understanding of the corporation's reputational risk profile; the sources and scope of those risks; and the financial, operational, regulatory, and legal impacts that these reputational risks may present. In the exercise of its oversight responsibilities, the board must ensure that management is identifying reputational risks, assessing the impacts just noted, and developing effective plans to mitigate or attenuate these reputational risks. The board must then ensure that proactive, effective, and prudent action and response plans are in place to prevent, manage, and attenuate these reputational risks.

Many corporations are now very active in identifying not only reputational risks generally, but also in determining which areas of the business are the most vulnerable to reputational risk. It is mandatory that management utilize relevant measurements of reputation and monitoring protocols.

Among the many challenges inherent in managing reputational risk are certain governance-specific issues. Boards must determine the roles and, where applicable, the deliverables assigned to the board and management, as well as the reporting required to adequately inform the board. The board must identify who has the primary responsibility to manage reputational risk, assess and approve how it is to be managed, and determine how and when the performance of management in this task will be evaluated.

Key Questions

Some key questions to consider in relation to the management of reputational risks include the following:

- ❑ Has the organization identified potential sources of reputational risk to which it may be exposed, bearing in mind the industry, company size, structure, and corporate culture of the organization?
- ❑ Is the organization actively monitoring its reputation across the markets where it operates?
- ❑ Is risk management integrated into the organization's strategy, operating systems, and business planning?
- ❑ Does the organization have appropriate strategies, procedures, structures, and systems in place to manage key risks?
- ❑ Is the organization taking risks beyond the board's risk appetite and making decisions that may be controversial?
- ❑ Are the board and senior management driving a risk awareness culture within the organization by setting the tone at the top and communicating its values?
- ❑ Is the company encouraging awareness of reputational risk among the employees, for example by including it in their performance management?
- ❑ Does the organization have in place a crisis response plan involving all important stakeholders (including customers, investors, employees, and regulators) to address potential issues that may arise?

- ❑ Has the crisis response plan been rehearsed, periodically reviewed, and updated?
- ❑ What specific risks relate to the nature of the company's operations? Regulatory environment? Geographic footprint?

Additional Reading

1. Serafin, Tatiana. "Reputation Risk Leading Company Concern in 2015," *Forbes* (2015)
   http://www.forbes.com/sites/tatianaserafin/2015/01/05/reputation-risk-leading-company-concern-in-2015
2. "Ten Keys to Managing Reputation Risk," Protiviti Bulletin, Volume 5, Issue 2, 2013
   https://www.protiviti.com/en-US/Documents/Newsletters/Bulletin/The-Bulletin-Vol-5-Issue-2-10-Keys-Managing-Reputation-Risk-Protiviti.pdf
3. Bonime-Blanc, Andrea. "Reputation Risk Is a Strategic Risk: What Are Your Board Plans?" *Ethical Boardroom* (February 10, 2015)
   http://ethicalboardroom.com/risk/reputation/reputation-risk-strategic-risk-board-plans/
4. Managing Reputation Risk, ERM Initiative at North Carolina State University, 2007
   http://www.mgt.ncsu.edu/erm/index.php/articles/entry/managing-reputation-risk/
5. Eccles, Robert G., Scott C. Newquist, and Roland Schatz. "Reputation and Its Risks." *Harvard Business Review* (February 2007)
   https://hbr.org/2007/02/reputation-and-its-risks
6. Neufeld, George. "Managing Reputation Risk: How to Avoid Being Dragged through the Mud." *Risk Management* (2007)
   http://www.thefreelibrary.com/Managing+reputation+risk%3A+how+to+avoid+being+dragged+through+the+mud.-a0168587137

Notes

4.7 GOVERNING THE MULTINATIONAL CORPORATION

CONTRIBUTED BY
Stephen A. Pike
Gowling WLG[1]
Paul Lanois
Credit Suisse[2]

As globalization and emerging markets drive businesses to continue to expand their horizons, boards of directors are increasingly challenged by the growing scope of their oversight responsibilities. Conducting operations in other jurisdictions require boards to not only understand and to manage additional financial and operational risks, but also cultural, political, and reputational risks. The challenge for directors to use their informed business judgment to determine not only where to do business, but also how to successfully do business in those jurisdictions while preserving the long-term sustainability and profitability of their enterprise, should not be underestimated.

1. Stephen A. Pike is a partner in the Toronto office of the Gowling WLG (Canada) LLP law firm where he advises on corporate and business law matters.
2. Paul Lanois is senior legal counsel at Credit Suisse and is admitted to the bars of the District of Columbia, New York, and the Supreme Court of the United States.

Boards must continually evaluate the skills and experience of their directors and management to ensure that they have the appropriate level of expertise to address the governance and operational challenges inherent in multinational operations.

In exercising its powers and fulfilling its obligations, the board must deal with different laws and regulations, legal systems (e.g., common law and civil law), taxation regimes, employment and immigration laws and compliance obligations, and business customs and mores.

For example, in many countries, violations of environmental rules and regulations may result in criminal sanctions, restitution, performance remedies, and civil penalties. Regulators have become more aggressive in ramping up their regulation and enforcement efforts; therefore, it is becoming increasingly important for companies to stay current on emerging issues and risks. Further, boards must be mindful of differing corporate governance regimes that may impact the company and its subsidiaries. For example, the economic interest of shareholders is not necessarily preeminent in every jurisdiction and the importance of the interests of other stakeholders (e.g., employees, community members, and even the customers or suppliers of a company) can vary from jurisdiction to jurisdiction.

A big temptation for multinational companies is to exploit legal environments, which are more lenient than in the company's head office jurisdiction, in order to maximize profits. However, the media spotlight and potential public backlash must be considered as part of the company's reputational risk.

The board's mandate includes the development and implementation of internal governance and management structures to ensure that the company's policies, as well as legal and regulatory compliance are maintained; that the board is monitoring governance of these functions; and that the board is continuing to receive appropriate and accurate information regarding multinational operations and business.

Board interaction and engagement with local management teams and facilitation of greater knowledge of multinational issues has spurred many boards to hold meetings in jurisdictions other than their home jurisdiction and to invite local managers to the board's home jurisdiction for board meetings.

Parent company liability for the actions (or inactions) of subsidiaries and affiliates is another critical issue, especially in light of domestic laws with extra-territorial effect.

Key Questions

Some key questions to consider in relation to the management of multinational companies include the following:

- ❑ Is the company aware of the areas of law that may be applicable to its business model and industry (e.g., employment, taxation, social security, immigration and work permit, anti-corruption and anti-bribery, export controls, environment, intellectual property, data privacy and security, etc.) and their differential impact on the enterprise?
- ❑ If the company is conducting regulated activities (e.g., financial services, healthcare, defense, etc.), are those rules being complied with?

- ❑ Does the company have enough information about the rules and regulations applicable to each country/jurisdiction where the company is, either directly or indirectly, conducting business? If not, should local external counsel be retained?
- ❑ Is the company receiving expert advice on the legal or regulatory requirements applicable in the countries in which the company operates?
- ❑ Is the company receiving expert advice on the political situation in the countries in which the company operates and any related and relevant political risks the company is facing?
- ❑ If the company conducts business on a cross-border basis, does it comply with the applicable rules and regulations for such cross-border activities?
- ❑ Does the company have in place ethics and compliance programs to ensure that the relevant local rules are also being complied with in jurisdictions in which it operates?
- ❑ Has the board discussed what it wants to achieve from a compliance program and what its broad contours should be?
- ❑ Does the board want the company to simply comply with the legal and regulatory baseline or does it want to set more stringent standards (e.g., for use as a competitive advantage)?
- ❑ Does the company have training programs in place to ensure that all local staff is familiar with the applicable local legal requirements as well as those applicable to the parent company's home jurisdiction?
- ❑ Is the company working with vendors/suppliers and third parties who adhere with all applicable legal requirements? Has the company conducted appropriate due diligence on all third parties engaged by the company?
- ❑ Does the company have an insurance program that provides adequate protection to a multinational company?
- ❑ Has any risk assessment and gap analysis been conducted in relation to the company's global compliance program?
- ❑ Does the company have a code of conduct or otherwise similar governance publication?
- ❑ Are the executive team, the business leadership, and the leaders of key departments (e.g., technology, operations, and other support functions) fully engaged in the company's global compliance program?
- ❑ What country-specific risks are associated with a proposed expansion?
- ❑ What is the country's reputation for corruption and where does it rank on recognized corruption indices?

Additional Reading

1. Husisian, Greg. "Compliance Strategies for Multinational Corporations: Implementing an Integrated, Risk-Based Approach." *Corporate Compliance Insights* (June 11, 2010)

   http://www.corporatecomplianceinsights.com/2010/compliance-strategies-for-multinational-corporations-implementing-an-integrated-risk-based-approach/

2. Méan, Jean-Pierre. "The Implementation of Compliance Programmes in Multinational Organizations." In *The Role of Large Enterprises in Democracy and Society* (Palgrave Macmillan, 2010)

   http://www.transparency.ch/de/PDF_files/Divers/JPM_The_Implementation_of_Compliance_Programmes.pdf

3. Developing Effective Compliance Strategies. *Financier Worldwide Magazine* (March 2014)

   http://www.financierworldwide.com/roundtable-developing-effective-compliance-strategies/#.V6NjnuJEnRY

4. Good Practice Guidelines on Conducting Third-Party Due Diligence, *World Economic Forum* (2013)

   http://www3.weforum.org/docs/WEF_PACI_ConductingThirdPartyDueDiligence_Guidelines_2013.pdf

5. Frederick, W. Richard. "FOCUS 13 Challenges in Group Governance: The Governance of Cross-Border Bank Subsidiaries." *IFC International Finance Corporation* (2014)

   https://www.ifc.org/wps/wcm/connect/c9fb560046efba9b9595fd57143498e5/Focus13.pdf?MOD=AJPERES

Notes

____

____

____

____

____

4.8 DEALING WITH THE GENERAL COUNSEL

CONTRIBUTED BY
Robert Bostrom
Abercrombie & Fitch Co.[1]
Aaron A. Seamon
Squire Patton Boggs (US) LLP[2]

The legal and regulatory landscape has undergone a seismic shift in recent years, placing the role of general counsel front and center in the boardroom. Globalization, the rise of shareholder activism, increased regulatory burdens, increased potential for civil and criminal liability, as well as a focus on compliance and ethics, have resulted in the need for boards to have practical and solution-oriented legal advice so that they may make informed decisions and carry out their duties.

The role of the general counsel has expanded over time, and the general counsel now often serves as the senior corporate officer and executive leader. The general counsel must be equipped with strong business acumen to evaluate ethics, compliance, risk management, and governance issues in light of the corporation's business strategy.

1. Robert Bostrom is the Senior Vice President and General Counsel of Abercrombie & Fitch Co.
2. Aaron A. Seamon is a Partner in the Corporate Finance Practice of Squire Patton Boggs (US) LLP where he practices in the Columbus office.

The increased role of the general counsel can cause its own problems, as the general counsel can become stretched too thin while balancing the management of the legal department and serving as a business leader. Furthermore, it is important for the general counsel not to conflate business advice with legal advice. In circumstances in which the general counsel is serving as a business leader, the general counsel must be clear with respect to which role the particular advice is being given.

Directors are well served to focus on the quality and role of the general counsel and related legal function within the organization, to ensure the board and senior management are receiving effective legal advice. Characteristics that many directors have identified as especially important for a general counsel include having skill in presenting legal information to nonlawyers in an effective manner, business acumen, confidence in the advice they are delivering and its relationship to the business objectives of the organization, and the ability to give unvarnished advice even when it may not be what directors would like to hear. In a nutshell, the most basic trait that a director should have in the general counsel is one of trust—trust that the general counsel will bring to the board those items that are of most significance and to give advice that is in the best interests of the organization and the board, which is ultimately the general counsel's client. The general counsel should be a persuasive counselor who is willing to advocate not just doing what is legal, but what is right.

In many organizations, the general counsel has a direct reporting line to the CEO and a strong working relationship with the board's chair or lead independent director. One of the key challenges for the general counsel is never losing sight of who the client is—the corporation or the corporation acting through its board of directors, not executive management. Oftentimes the general counsel is an active participant in key board committee meetings, and is charged with the overall design and function of carrying out the formalities of board and committee minutes and related materials.

Directors should ensure that they have a strong, independent voice in the role of general counsel who can withstand the challenges of handling the various roles, responsibilities, and challenges that go along with the general counsel position. The interaction of the general counsel and the board should allow the board to seek legal advice and understand the obligations that the board faces. The general counsel is part of the management team, but his or her ultimate responsibility is to the corporation and the board, and the board must have confidence that is the case.

Key Questions

When evaluating the role of the general counsel within an organization and interacting with the general counsel, some issues to consider are the following:

- ❑ Does the general counsel instill faith in the board that the advice given is based on the company's best interests?
- ❑ How effective is the general counsel in managing the company's overall legal risk? Is the general counsel proactive or reactive?

- ❑ Does the general counsel have the resources needed in order to oversee the company's legal function in light of the company's industry and business operations?
- ❑ What is the preferred role of the company's general counsel? Will the general counsel be a business leader and/or corporate officer in addition to the legal function?
- ❑ What is the appropriate relationship between the board and the general counsel to enable the general counsel to be effective but ensure that the board receives candid advice?
- ❑ What is the role of compliance and where does the general counsel fit within the company's overall compliance function? Is the general counsel function and compliance function separate? Or combined?
- ❑ What is the general counsel's role in circumstances requiring the use of outside independent counsel by the board?
- ❑ What characteristics does the board value when evaluating candidates for the general counsel role? What value should the board place on prior government/regulatory experience or industry experience?

Additional Reading

1. General Counsel: The Glue Between the CEO and the Board, *The Metropolitan Corporate Counsel* (2007)
   http://www.metrocorpcounsel.com/pdf/2007/July/01.pdf
2. The Rise of the GC: Form Legal Adviser to Strategic Adviser, *NYSE Governance Services* (2016)
   https://www.nyse.com/publicdocs/2016_BarkerGilmore_The_Rise_of_the_GC.pdf
3. The General Counsel's Relationship with the Lead Director and the Board, *Lead Director Network* (2013)
   https://www.nyse.com/publicdocs/2016_BarkerGilmore_The_Rise_of_the_GC.pdf
4. The General Counsel and the Board, *Egon Zehnder International* (2011)
   http://www.egonzehnder.com/files/the_general_counsel_and_the_board.pdf
5. Veasey, E. Norman and Christine T. Di Guglielmo. *Indispensable Counsel: The Chief Legal Officer in the New Reality* (2013)
6. Changing Role of General Counsel, *Wolters Kluwer* (2016)
   https://ct.wolterskluwer.com/sites/default/files/Changing_Role_General_Counsel_0.pdf

Notes

SECTION FIVE

SHAREHOLDER ENGAGEMENT AND COMMUNICATIONS

5.1 THE DIRECTOR'S ROLE IN SHAREHOLDER COMMUNICATION

CONTRIBUTED BY
Christopher J. Gyves
Womble Carlyle Sandridge & Rice, LLP[1]

Traditionally, directors rarely communicated directly with shareholders. Management handled those communications under the authority and direction of the board. However, market dynamics, proxy advisory firms, and regulatory reforms adopted in response to financial crises and corporate scandals have contributed to a relatively recent change in communication patterns among shareholders and between shareholders and their companies.

The evolving corporate governance landscape reflects increased shareholder influence and increased interest on the part of both shareholders and boards in engaging and communicating directly with one another. Boards are finding that direct communication with shareholders can positively inform their decisions. For shareholders, communication with the board provides an opportunity to be heard at the highest level of the corporation, to address matters not properly or sufficiently addressed by management, and to influence board-level decisions. The communication also promotes goodwill, trust, understanding, and support for corporate policies and strategy.

1. Chris Gyves is a partner at Womble Carlyle Sandridge & Rice, LLP, where he serves as chair of the firm's Public Company Advisors Team.

The relationships established through effective communication can be critical in resolving important issues. Shareholders have opportunities to communicate with each other. Because crises are unplanned and activist campaigns are now a year-round occurrence, it is never too early to consider building direct board–shareholder communications channels.

In establishing communication channels, boards need to consider appropriate policies and responses to shareholder communication requests. Securities laws and stock exchange rules require disclosures related to communication policies, and it is helpful to manage expectations of all involved with a clear statement of board–shareholder communication principles, policies, and procedures. Communication with shareholders generally should begin with management—business and operational matters are best handled by management—and that is often the preference of shareholders for communication. However, shareholders do expect an audience with the board to discuss key governance and related matters. The National Association of Corporate Directors (NACD) Blue Ribbon Commission on Board–Shareholder Communication identified six topics as potentially appropriate for communication between directors and shareholders:

- CEO evaluation and succession
- Executive compensation
- Board nomination and election process and criteria
- Governance issues
- Strategic direction
- Emerging issues (e.g., environmental and social issues)

As with so many other features of corporate governance, one size fits all does not work with board–shareholder communication, and NACD has expressed the view that each board must decide [for itself] the appropriateness of any given topic.

Whatever topics are deemed appropriate for direct board–shareholder communication, it is important to avoid mixed messages—the board acts as a unit and should take care to speak with one voice. An appropriate agenda should be established and sufficient time should be taken to prepare a director acting as the board's spokesperson for any meetings with shareholders. In addition to specific topics within the agenda, preparation should take into account Regulation Fair Disclosure (Reg FD) compliance, the corporation's disclosure posture on various issues, and confidentiality requirements. Often, the greatest risk for a director in this context is speaking—remember that listening to shareholders is an important and "safe" aspect of board–shareholder communications. Director training should be considered, as well as a designation of those directors best equipped to perform this vital communication task.

The potential opportunities and benefits of board–shareholder communication should be balanced against its challenges. For example, time and resources operate as restraints on the ability of boards to address all shareholder communication requests; further, today's institutional shareholders are actively engaged in communications with a large number of corporations, and finding the appropriate opportunity and venue for effective director–shareholder communications can sometimes be difficult. As a practical matter, boards will need to be thoughtful and measured in selecting opportunities to communicate with shareholders.

Key Questions

When considering shareholder engagement, including shareholder communication with the board, key questions that a director might ask include the following:

- ❑ How is the company engaging with its shareholders? What is the tone and tenor of that engagement?
- ❑ Does the company have a formal shareholder engagement policy? Who leads shareholder engagement for the board?
- ❑ What topics are appropriate (and what topics are "off the table") for the company's shareholder engagement?
- ❑ Who are the company's significant shareholders? What are their respective investment objectives and strategies? Does the company have a shareholder that has supported or engaged in activist strategies? Is the company in direct contact with the individual who makes voting decisions for institutional shareholders?
- ❑ Does the company need a strategy for retail shareholder engagement?
- ❑ To what extent do shareholders (or any one of them) influence the company's strategies, practices, and processes? Is the company proactive or reactive in that regard?
- ❑ What views have shareholders expressed—either directly to the company or publicly as part of a policy statement—about key governance and other issues? How do those views and the recommendations of proxy advisors influence shareholders and impact voting results?
- ❑ How is the company addressing any perceived deviation between its direction and the views of shareholders and proxy advisors?
- ❑ How often does the board review and evaluate its shareholder engagement practices? Is shareholder engagement a regular agenda item for the board or committee(s)?
- ❑ How does the board receive updates regarding shareholders and their positions on key issues? Does the corporate secretary have sufficient resources to provide information and updates to the board?
- ❑ Do the company's public filings and statements adequately communicate the way the board views the company?
- ❑ Will I be called upon to participate in a shareholder engagement matter? What am I doing to be "communication ready"? What training do I need? Am I well equipped for this task? Are others better equipped?

Additional Reading

1. ABA Business Law Section, Committee on Corporate Laws. *Corporate Director's Guidebook*. 6th ed. (See Section 10.)

2. NACD Report of the Blue Ribbon Commission on Board-Shareholder Communication. *National Association of Corporate Directors* (2008).

3. Council of Institutional Investors: Investor-Company Roundtable, Effective Engagement (December 2015)
http://www.cii.org/files/about_us/press_releases/2015/12_7_15_Investor_Company_Roundtable.pdf
4. Recommendations of the Task Force on Corporate/Investor Engagement. *The Conference Board*
https://www.conference-board.org/publications/publicationdetail.cfm?publicationid=2712&topicid=30&subtopicid=210
5. Society for Corporate Governance—Shareholder Engagement Resources
http://www.governanceprofessionals.org/governanceprofessionals/currenttopiclandingpages/tpshareholderengagement
6. *SDX Protocol* (February 2014)
http://www.sdxprotocol.com/wp-content/uploads/2015/04/SDX_Introduction-and-Protocol.pdf
7. *Commonsense Principles of Corporate Governance*
http://www.governanceprinciples.org/wp-content/uploads/2016/07/GovernancePrinciples_Principles.pdf

Notes

5.2 THE ANNUAL SHAREHOLDERS MEETING

CONTRIBUTED BY
Abby E. Brown
Squire Patton Boggs (US) LLP[1]

Basis for the Annual Shareholders Meeting

The annual shareholders meeting is intended to provide the shareholders with an opportunity to engage with board members and company management and to vote on certain matters, including election of the board members who are responsible for overseeing the management of the company. There may also be other matters proposed by management and/or shareholders on which shareholders will be asked to vote, such as the ratification of auditors; amendments to the company's organizational documents; a merger or sale, dissolution, or adoption of stock option plans; or other executive compensation arrangements, among others.

Annual meetings of shareholders are required by state corporate law, and for public companies, annual meetings of shareholders are also required under the laws of the major national stock exchanges. State law governs many of the procedural requirements of the annual meeting, such as the date, place, and time of the meeting; notice and

1. Abby E. Brown is a partner at Squire Patton Boggs (US) LLP, where she practices in the firm's corporate group.

record date requirements; vote required for a quorum; vote required for approval of certain actions; and adjournment of the meeting. For public companies, regulations adopted by the Securities and Exchange Commission (SEC) establish the framework for soliciting proxies, disclosure requirements for the proxy statement and the annual report, and the timing upon which shareholders must receive proxy materials in advance of the meeting. Each stock exchange also has rules in connection with annual meetings, including requirements related to notice of a record date and quorum for the meeting. Annual meeting requirements will also frequently be contained within the company's own articles of incorporation and bylaws.

Planning for the Annual Shareholders Meeting

Annual meetings can be held at a physical location, held virtually, or a combination of both. Company management will often prepare a detailed time and responsibility checklist in anticipation of the annual shareholders meeting that includes the proxy solicitation process, all events leading up to the annual meeting, and post-meeting agenda items. Preparing a "script" in advance of the annual shareholders meeting will help to manage the flow of the meeting and ensure that management and designated board members cover all necessary subjects and are prepared for possible shareholder questions.

Prior to the annual shareholders meeting for public companies, board members should be refreshed on Regulation FD so that any directors who speak to shareholders during the annual meeting do not inadvertently disclose material, nonpublic information. Board members should also have a clear understanding of the company's policy on investor engagement, which should lay out director expectations regarding shareholder communications at annual meetings.

At the Annual Shareholders Meeting

Depending on the company's shareholder base, annual shareholders meetings may last as little as a few minutes or may be more elaborate. Companies will typically prepare an agenda (to include calling the meeting to order, welcome and introductions, Q&A session, voting on proposals, announcement of preliminary voting results, and adjournment of the meeting) and rules of conduct for the meeting. Companies are also legally required to maintain a written record of the meeting.

Many companies have policies in place encouraging (or even mandating) director attendance at annual shareholders meetings. Public companies are required to disclose in their proxy statements whether any directors were unable to attend the prior year's annual shareholders meeting. Although historically directors rarely have speaking roles at annual meetings, the expectation for shareholder–director communication is growing, largely due to investor demand and shareholder activism, discussed in several other chapters including Chapters 5.1 and 5.6 in this Handbook.

Key Questions

When considering a director's role in the annual meeting process, key questions that a board member might ask include the following:

- ❑ Has the company prepared a detailed time and responsibility checklist, annual meeting script, and/or annual meeting rules/procedures? If so, have I seen a copy?
- ❑ Have I approved, along with my fellow board members, annual meeting resolutions setting forth, among other things, (i) the date, place, and time of the annual meeting; (ii) the directors up for election at the meeting; (iii) the record date; and (iv) the items to be submitted for shareholder approval?
- ❑ Does the company have a policy for director attendance at annual meetings? If so, have I seen a copy so that I am informed of my attendance responsibilities?
- ❑ Has the company received any shareholder proposals? If so, do I need to develop a response plan with fellow board members and management in advance of the annual meeting?
- ❑ Has the board chosen a designated board spokesperson(s) to respond to any questions that may arise from shareholders at the annual meeting?
- ❑ In determining who should be the designated board spokesperson(s), has the board/management anticipated the questions that may be asked by shareholders, grouped them by topic or categories, and assigned the best person(s) to respond in each area?
- ❑ Has the board, in conjunction with management, adequately prepared for potential disruptions and non-agenda events, including floor proposals, emergency scenarios, and meeting rule violations (e.g., disruptive conduct)?
- ❑ Does the company have advance notice bylaws governing director elections or other shareholder proposals? Should it?
- ❑ What are this year's deadlines for the submission by shareholders of director nominations or other proposals?
- ❑ How will our annual meeting likely proceed? Will it be largely a pro forma exercise, or will shareholders attend and expect to engage with management and the board?

Additional Reading

1. Annual Meeting Handbook (2016), RR Donnelly Publication, Copyright (2016) (available from RR Donnelly Financial Printer).
2. Morrison, Randi and Julie Hoffman. Director Attendance at Annual Meetings Handbook, Practice Guide and Tool Kit, Item 407(b) of Regulation S-K. *TheCorporateCounsel.net* (February 2016)

   http://www.thecorporatecounsel.net/GreatGovernance/member/handbook/DirectorAttendance.pdf

3. "Seven Smart Practices for Shareowner Meetings," *Council of Institutional Investors* (September 2010)
http://www.shareholderforum.com/e-mtg/Library/20100917_CII.pdf

4. "10 Tips for a Smooth Annual Meeting," *Computershare*
http://www.computershare.com/us/Documents/10-Tips-For-Smooth-Annual-Meeting.pdf

Notes

5.3 MAJORITY VOTING

CONTRIBUTED BY
Avrohom J. Kess and Yafit Cohn
Simpson Thacher & Bartlett LLP[1]

Under the usual or "default" system of plurality voting in director elections, the nominees with the largest number of "for" votes are elected to the board, regardless of the number of "withheld" votes that they receive. This means that in an uncontested election, where there are the same number of nominees to the board as there are open seats, shareholders' votes do not have much consequence.

In an effort to afford shareholders an opportunity to influence board composition more meaningfully in uncontested elections—sometimes in response to shareholder proposals or other shareholder pressure—a substantial number of public companies have adopted a "majority voting" rule. Such a rule requires that, in uncontested elections, a nominee that garners a plurality but still receives more "withheld" votes than "for" votes will be denied a seat on the board.

Majority voting can generally be implemented in one of two ways: through majority-plus voting or plurality-plus voting. Under a majority-plus voting standard, a new nominee

1. When this chapter was authored, Avrohom J. Kess was a partner at Simpson Thacher & Bartlett LLP, where he headed the Public Company Advisory Practice; he is currently Vice Chairman and Chief Legal Officer of The Travelers Companies, Inc. Yafit Cohn is counsel at Simpson Thacher & Bartlett LLP, where she practices in the Public Company Advisory Practice. The authors would like to thank Nathan Utterback of Columbia Law School for his valuable assistance in preparing this chapter.

will not be elected unless he or she receives a majority of the votes cast. An incumbent director who does not garner a majority of the votes cast, however, will remain in office due to the "holdover rule" under most states' statutes (including the Delaware General Corporation Law), but is required to offer his or her resignation to the board, which can then be accepted or rejected by the remainder of the board. In a plurality-plus regime, on the other hand, both new and incumbent directors are elected by a mere plurality but are required to offer their resignation to the board should they fail to receive a majority of votes cast. Again, this resignation can be either accepted or rejected by the remainder of the board. Thus, at least under Delaware law, the only practical difference between the majority-plus and plurality-plus voting standards is whether a nonincumbent director nominee who fails to garner majority support is appointed to the board before being forced to offer his or her resignation or is simply not given a seat on the board at all.

When a nominee does not receive sufficient "for" votes to be appointed to the board of directors, the election is referred to as a "failed" election. If the failed nominee was an incumbent—or a new director under the plurality-plus system—the failed nominee submits his or her resignation to the board, which generally is given by the company's policy almost complete discretion to determine whether to accept or reject the resignation. The board may rely on an internal committee, such as the nominating committee, to advise on this decision. If the board's decision results in an open seat on the board, the board may leave the seat vacant, decrease the size of the board, appoint a replacement, or hold a special election to fill the seat. Depending on the corporate governance policies and bylaws in place, the board might even appoint the nominee that was subject to the failed election.

Several states forbid having both cumulative and majority voting, while under the laws of most other states, having both systems in place is permitted but could lead to unprecedented and potentially complicated litigation if a failed election occurs. Accordingly, special consideration must be given to adopting majority voting in the event that the company employs cumulative voting.

Over the past ten years, many companies have implemented a majority-voting standard, either via a shareholder-proposed charter amendment or bylaw or through management's own initiative, with or without a corresponding shareholder vote. As of 2016, several sources report that over 80 percent of S&P 500 companies had adopted a majority-voting standard, usually with the near-unanimous support of shareholders when put to a shareholder vote. Because of the additional enfranchisement that such a system affords shareholders, proxy advisory firms, such as Institutional Shareholder Services Inc. (ISS) and Glass Lewis, almost always recommend a vote for proposals seeking to implement majority voting.

Key Questions

In considering whether to adopt a majority-voting policy, a board may wish to consider the following:

- ❑ Has the company engaged with shareholders on the majority voting issue, and is majority voting something that the company's largest shareholders support?

- ❑ From a strategic perspective, should management propose amending its governing documents to adopt a majority-voting standard or wait until a shareholder proponent proposes its adoption?
- ❑ How likely is it that one of the company's directors will fail to receive a majority of votes in an upcoming election? Under what circumstances might that change?
- ❑ What requirements does the company's state of incorporation impose on attempts to adopt a majority-voting standard?
- ❑ Could a failed election potentially cause the board's composition to violate the listing requirements of the stock exchange on which the company is listed?
- ❑ Would adopting majority voting discourage shareholders from nominating their own slate of directors?
- ❑ Assuming the company decides to adopt a majority-voting standard, which type of majority voting is most appropriate for the company? Plurality-plus or majority-plus?
- ❑ Will implementing a majority-voting standard require amendments to the company's charter, bylaws, or both? Does state law impose any additional requirements affecting implementation?
- ❑ If a director fails to receive a majority in an election, what factors should the board consider in deciding whether or not to accept his or her resignation? Which individuals or committees would be best equipped to make this decision?
- ❑ If a failed election results in a vacancy on the board, how should the remaining directors address the open seat? Leave the seat unfilled, decrease the size of the board, hold a special election, or appoint a replacement via board vote?
- ❑ Would a proposed majority voting amendment be in potential conflict with state law (e.g., if the company uses cumulative voting to elect directors) or an existing corporate governance provision?

Additional Reading

1. *Majority Voting in Director Elections: A Look Back and a Look Ahead* http://www.stblaw.com/docs/default-source/cold-fusion-existing-content /publications/pub560.pdf
2. SEC, *Spotlight on Proxy Matters—The Mechanics of Voting* https://www.sec.gov/spotlight/proxymatters/voting_mechanics.shtml
3. Siegel, Mary. "The Holes in Majority Voting." *Columbia Business Law Review* 2 (2011).
4. Sjostrim, William K. Jr. and Young Sang Kim. "Majority Voting for the Election of Directors." *Connecticut Law Review* 40 (December 2007).

Notes

5.4 THE PROXY PROCESS

CONTRIBUTED BY
Fred A. Summer
Squire Patton Boggs (US) LLP[1]

State corporate laws and the rules of securities exchanges require that companies must hold an annual shareholders meeting.

Federal securities regulations require that sufficient information relating to the meeting be delivered to the stockholders to enable them to make an informed decision as to how to vote on the issues before the meeting.

The federal proxy rules are complex and extensive and result in lengthy and elaborate proxy statement disclosure. The proxy statement is sent to stockholders in advance of the meeting, along with a proxy card that can be completed and submitted by mail or, under certain circumstances, electronically instructing the stockholder's proxy (typically employees of the company) how to vote the stockholder's shares on the matters before the meeting. The proxy statement is a form of direct communication from the company to its stockholders. As one SEC commissioner has observed,

> [t]he Commission recognizes that the proxy statement process is a vital means by which shareholders and companies' leadership communicate with one another.

1. Fred A. Summer is senior counsel at Squire Patton Boggs (US) LLP, where he practices corporate and commercial finance law in the firm's Columbus, Ohio office.

> Consistent with this reality, the Commission recognizes that the proxy rules operate on the principle that the proxy process should function, as close as possible, to replicate the rights of a shareholder who attends the annual meeting in person.

The proxy rules require the proxy statement to disclose who is soliciting proxies and, in the case of the company's proxy statement, the board fulfills that role.

In recent years, many companies have reshaped their proxy statements from dry recitations of mandated disclosure into more accessible and persuasive efforts to communicate with shareholders. This has been particularly true in the area of executive compensation. Such "modern" proxy statements are often interdisciplinary efforts of the company's legal, finance, and investor relations teams.

A debate over a shareholder's ability to include nominees in the company's proxy statement continues to rage. Proxy access, as the issue has been dubbed, is dealt with in more detail in Chapter 5.9 of this Handbook.

The role of the board in the proxy process is of critical importance. Although the proxy statement is prepared by management and in-house and outside counsel, the board must carefully review its contents annually for accuracy and to ensure that the proxy statement "sells" to its stockholders its corporate governance process and executive compensation programs. The proxy rules set out the requirements for the proxy statement, which provides the stockholders with information necessary to help them to decide whether to grant, withhold, or revoke a proxy.

As a general overview, the proxy statement

- provides information about the specific matters to be discussed at the annual meeting, the mechanics of voting, and the board's position on the matters to be voted upon;
- provides information about corporate governance, including descriptions of board committees, the nominating process, and board communication policies;
- provides information about compensation of the company's executives and directors, including extensive information, both in tabular and narrative form, that includes a detailed description of the company's compensation policies, objectives, and practices, as well as information about any related party transactions; and
- solicits proxies for the meeting.

In fulfilling their role in connection with the proxy process, directors must pay close attention to the procedures followed in preparing and disseminating the company's proxy statement. It is good practice for each director to review a close-to-final draft of the proxy statement before it is filed with the SEC and distribute to the company's stockholders, particularly biographical information about the director and sections dealing with matters about which the director has personal knowledge or committees on which the director serves.

Key Questions

When considering the nature and exercise of a director's duties, key questions that a board member might ask include the following:

- ❑ Does the proxy statement accurately describe the policies and procedures used by the board to determine the compensation of executive officers?
- ❑ Should the company employ a "modern" proxy statement?
- ❑ Is the procedure used for shareholder communications with the board properly described in the proxy statement?
- ❑ If any directors have conflicts of interest, have those conflicts been properly reviewed by the appropriate committee and accurately described in the proxy statement?
- ❑ How should the board deal with any shareholder proposals that may have been submitted?
- ❑ How should the board respond to the most recent say on pay vote?

Additional Reading

1. ABA Business Law Section, Committee on Corporate Laws. *Corporate Director's Guidebook*, 6th ed.
2. The Proxy Process
   https://www.shareholdereducation.com/proxy_process.asp
3. Proxy Voting Gives Fund Shareholders a Say
   http://www.investopedia.com/articles/basics/04/082704.asp#12922670916802&close
4. *Ensuring the Proxy Process Works for Shareholders*
   https://www.sec.gov/news/statement/021915-psclaa.html

Notes

UNDERSTANDING THE ROLE OF PROXY ADVISORS

5.5

CONTRIBUTED BY
Avrohom J. Kess and Yafit Cohn
Simpson Thacher & Bartlett LLP[1]

Proxy advisory firms provide recommendations to shareholders on how to vote, both in director elections and on shareholder and management-sponsored proposals submitted to a shareholder vote. Many institutional shareholders rely, to varying degrees, on the voting recommendations of the proxy advisory firms with regard to the companies in their portfolios, with some outsourcing their voting decisions altogether by following the guidance of the proxy advisory firms in all cases. Institutional investors often view their reliance on proxy advisory firms as a means to enable them to fulfill their fiduciary duty to vote shares in the interests of their individual shareholders, while accounting for cost considerations. Specifically, because proxy advisory firms represent a large number of clients, they are able to spread the costs involved in analyzing proposals among numerous subscribers.

ISS and Glass Lewis dominate the market for proxy advisory services, with self-reported 61 percent and 37 percent market shares, respectively, as of June 2016. ISS also offers

1. When this chapter was authored, Avrohom J. Kess was a partner at Simpson Thacher & Bartlett LLP, where he headed the Public Company Advisory Practice; he is currently Vice Chairman and Chief Legal Officer of The Travelers Companies, Inc. Yafit Cohn is counsel at Simpson Thacher & Bartlett LLP, where she practices in the Public Company Advisory Practice. The authors would like to thank Oliver Cohen for his valuable assistance in preparing this chapter.

consulting services to public companies that are intended to help companies design and manage their corporate governance and executive compensation programs to align with company goals, reduce risk, and manage the needs of a diverse shareholder base.

As of February 2015, institutional shareholders own over 80 percent of the outstanding shares of the S&P 500. It is widely reported that ISS clients typically are estimated to control 20 to 30 percent of a mid-cap or large-cap corporation's outstanding shares, while Glass Lewis clients typically control 5 to 10 percent of such shares. The percentage of shares that adhere to the firms' recommendations varies by issue. Negative recommendations by the proxy advisory firms can have a meaningful impact, for example, on shareholder support for say-on-pay proposals, as well as in contested vote situations and director elections where the board has failed to respond to shareholder concerns.

Boards of directors now frequently implement changes to compensation and governance policies both in response to unfavorable proxy advisory firm recommendations and, increasingly, preemptively (i.e., in anticipation of such recommendations). For example, in large part due to the influential policies of the proxy advisory firms, as of June 2016, it is believed that only 10 percent of S&P 500 companies have classified boards, and only 3 percent have poison pills, while 89 percent have adopted majority voting provisions.

Some critics argue that proxy advisory firms are dangerous because they wield significant influence without any regulatory oversight. Critics say that proxy advisors assess companies' governance practices using a one-size-fits-all approach based on the proxy firms' governance policies, which might not be correlated to or predictive of long-term performance. Some also argue that proxy advisory firms are not transparent in how they create their policies, and that, by virtue of the fact that ISS provides consulting services to some of the same companies whose proposals it evaluates for investors, ISS has a conflict of interest.

Proponents, however, take the position that investors choose to pay for the firms' services because they offer an alternative to merely following all of management's recommendations. They also argue that some management-sponsored proposals, such as those pertaining to compensation plans, can be difficult for investors to understand, and the proxy advisory firms offer valuable help to investors in evaluating their voting options in such cases.

Key Questions

Some important questions directors might ask regarding proxy advisors include the following:

- ❑ How do the proxy advisory firms view our company's governance structure and compensation practices?
- ❑ Is our shareholder base significantly influenced by the firms' recommendations?
- ❑ How can we act early to understand our shareholder base and its voting policies?
- ❑ How likely is it that the proxy advisory firms will recommend a vote against our directors for any reason? What is the likely impact of a vote against our directors?
- ❑ With respect to each proposal being submitted to a shareholder vote, what are the views of the proxy advisory firms?

- ❑ In the face of a negative recommendation, what steps should we take?
- ❑ Will our company have the opportunity to view the proxy advisory firms' reports before they are published to investors, and if so, when?
- ❑ What are the pros and cons of acting preemptively to conform to the proxy advisory firms' policies?
- ❑ Should we hire a proxy solicitor or corporate governance advisor to advise on our governance structure and compensation practices?
- ❑ Is the proxy advisory firms' recommendation actually aligned with improved performance? Is it in the best interests of our shareholders to adhere to the proxy advisory firms' recommendation on any given issue, or to pursue another path?

Additional Reading

1. Overview of Proxy Advisory Firms
   http://www.shareholdercoalition.com/content/overview-proxy-advisory-firms
2. SEC Roundtable on Proxy Advisory Services (2013)
   http://www.shareholdercoalition.com/content/sec-roundtable-proxy-advisory-services-december-5-2013
3. Director Elections and the Role of the Proxy Advisors
   http://scholarship.law.upenn.edu/cgi/viewcontent.cgi?article=1229&context=faculty_scholarship
4. ISS 2017 Policy Information
   https://www.issgovernance.com/policy-gateway/2017-policy-information/
5. Glass Lewis Policy Guidelines
   http://www.glasslewis.com/guidelines/

Notes

____

____

____

____

____

5.6 DEALING WITH ACTIVIST SHAREHOLDERS

CONTRIBUTED BY
Christina M. Gattuso
Kilpatrick Townsend & Stockton LLP[1]

A review of the results of the past several proxy seasons has demonstrated that boards and management teams should thoughtfully assess their approach to dealing with institutional investors, including large institutions, hedge funds, and other investors that are considered to be "activists." Recent years have proven that any company, small or large, can be a target of shareholder activism.

There is a broad spectrum of activist behaviors that investors increasingly employ to enhance their returns. Trends in corporate governance that favor shareholder involvement together with the changing willingness of even "traditional" institutional investors to embrace activist tactics has made it more difficult to "just say no" to an activist campaign.

At the outset, it is important for companies to understand the makeup of its shareholder base and to stay out in front of those shareholders who are either disgruntled or are activist investors with an agenda. In order to do this, a company needs to know the composition of its shareholder base, needs to monitor changes in its shareholder base, and needs to keep up-to-date on the voting policies and guidelines followed by its

1. Christina M. Gattuso is a partner in the Washington, D.C. office of Kilpatrick Townsend & Stockton LLP. She is a member of the firm's financial institutions team.

institutional shareholders. Attention should also be paid to trading volume and activity in the company's securities, including SEC filings by institutional shareholders. Companies need to be kept apprised of the corporate governance policies of proxy firms such as Institutional Shareholders Services (ISS) and Glass Lewis & Co. and its large shareholders.

It is important for companies to review their own policies on stock repurchases and dividends, their performance as compared to their peer group, the company's business strategy, and their governance policies. In reviewing the company's strategic business strategy, directors should understand how activists may look at (or publicly depict) the company's strategy and short-term results. Charters, bylaws, and applicable state law should also be reviewed to determine whether strategic changes should be made to governance documents that could be useful in the event of shareholder activism.

Shareholder activists are generally looking for changes to be made by a company. Based on recent trends, the types of changes sought by activists cover a range of matters, including sale of the company; return of capital to shareholders (either through special cash dividends or stock repurchases); management changes; appointment to the board of one or more of their representatives or new independent directors; redemption of a shareholder rights plan and/or the dismantling of other takeover management devices; or binding shareholder proposals seeking to compel or pressure the company to take one or more of the foregoing actions. Activists may also focus on governance matters, such as executive pay and performance plans, board composition, "overboarding," board tenure, and succession planning.

In both the 2015 and 2016 proxy season, proxy access, which allows shareholders who meet certain ownership thresholds to nominate directors to the boards of their investee companies and to have their nominees appear in a company's proxy statement and next to management's nominees on the same ballot, was the most popular corporate governance proposal. Other governance-related proposals included the ability of shareholders to call special meetings, majority voting in uncontested elections, independent board leadership, elimination of super-majority voting, and the ability of shareholders to act by written consent.

If a shareholder activist determines to pursue a campaign against the company, the company must be prepared to respond, as may be appropriate. The board of directors should be apprised by management of the public communications by the shareholder or shareholders and determine how to respond. This could include meeting with the activist, making changes to a company's policies or business strategy or adding a representative to the board in an effort to avoid a proxy contest, and/or determining to stay focused on the company's business strategy and fight the shareholder activist.

Given the likelihood that shareholder activism is here to stay, companies should consider developing and implementing a plan to address shareholder activism directed toward the company, including how to handle any public communications in response to such activity.

Key Questions

When dealing with an activist, a director may wish to consider the following questions:

- ❑ Does the board have sufficient information regarding the identity of the company's top shareholders and their advisors (i.e., proxy advisory firms or other)? Is the board aware of the voting policies and governance guidelines of the key proxy advisory firms?
- ❑ Does the company have good relationships with its long-term investors?
- ❑ Has the board received any published reports or proxy advisor policies relating specifically to the company?
- ❑ Is the board aware of the company's vulnerabilities from an investor's perspective? Is the company prepared to address such vulnerabilities?
- ❑ Has the board been apprised and updated on recent trends in shareholder activism in the marketplace and the possible avenues of attack by activists against the company, including how to respond to such possible attacks?
- ❑ Has the company compiled a team of advisors to assist in the event of shareholder activism? Are they prepared and current in their knowledge?
- ❑ Has the board been apprised of trends and developments from the most recent proxy season?
- ❑ Has the company received shareholder proposals and, if so, has it reviewed those proposals in relation to and preparation for the current year's proxy season?
- ❑ Has the company reviewed its charter and bylaws and applicable governing law to determine whether such documents are up to date as well as whether changes should be made to such documents in areas governing shareholder meeting procedures and board policies?
- ❑ Has the board reviewed the company's adherence to its own governance policies?
- ❑ Has the board received an update on trends in corporate governance and board composition?
- ❑ How does the board's composition look to outsiders? Is the board in need of refreshment?
- ❑ Has the board reviewed the composition of the board and the qualifications of its directors and whether changes or new skill sets are necessary?
- ❑ Has the board reviewed the company's performance in relation to its strategic business plan and its peers?
- ❑ Does the company have a shareholder engagement program and policies to address shareholder communications?
- ❑ How recently has the company engaged with its key shareholders? What feedback came from these sessions? What actions has the company taken in response to that feedback?
- ❑ Has the company developed a plan and protocol to address shareholder activism and public communications from activist shareholders?

- ❑ Does the company have a policy on direct engagement by board members with shareholders?
- ❑ Has the company had a recent negative say-on-pay vote result? What actions were taken to deal with that result?
- ❑ Is there any reason to expect a shareholder proposal or "no vote" campaign at the coming annual meeting of shareholders?

Additional Reading

1. Stokdyk, Steven B., Joel H. Trotter, and Patricia Judge, *Boardroom Perspectives: Three Practical Steps to Stay Ahead of Shareholder Activism*
   https://www.lw.com/thoughtLeadership/BoardroomPerspectives-ThreePracticalStepstoStayAheadofShareholderActivism
2. Ross, Donald C., *Responding to Shareholder Directives to Directors*
   https://corpgov.law.harvard.edu/2016/05/10/responding-to-shareholder-directives-to-directors
3. Clark, Hannah, *How to Fight Off Shareholder Activists*
   http://www.forbes.com/2006/07/13/leadership-five-ways-shareholder-cx_hc_0713fendingoffsharholderactivists.html
4. Ten Rules for Dealing with Activist Shareholders
   http://www.kirkland.com/siteFiles/kirkexp/publications/2254/Document1/Ten%20Rules%20for%20Dealing%20with%20Activist%20Shareholders%20(M&A%20Journal)%20Christopher,%20Sheng.pdf

Notes

____

____

____

____

____

5.7 SEC REGULATION FD

CONTRIBUTED BY

Melodie Rose and Elizabeth Dunshee
Fredrikson & Byron, P.A.[1]

Regulation FD (Fair Disclosure) was adopted by the SEC in 2000 to address wrongful trading by investment professionals and their clients based on selective access to important public company information. The rule transformed the way in which public companies interact with analysts and shareholders by promoting simultaneous access to material information by all investors. Regulation FD applies to all companies that have a class of securities registered under Section 12 of the Exchange Act or that are required to file reports under Section 15(d) of the Exchange Act (excluding most investment companies as well as foreign governments and foreign private issuers).

Under Regulation FD, whenever a company (or person acting on its behalf) discloses material nonpublic information to certain persons outside of the company, then, in the absence of a confidentiality duty or agreement, the company must announce the information to the public. Regulation FD applies to communications with market professionals, such as broker dealers, analysts, investment advisors, institutional investment managers and investment companies, and to communications with any shareholder who

1. Melodie Rose is a partner at Fredrikson & Byron, P.A., where she chairs the firm's corporate division and co-chairs the firm's corporate governance practice group with John Stout. Elizabeth Dunshee, a former partner with Fredrikson & Byron, P.A., is Editor at Executive Press, Inc.

is reasonably likely to trade on the basis of the information. If the company is intentional or reckless in sharing the material nonpublic information, such as through prepared remarks, the public announcement must be made simultaneously. If the company inadvertently shares material nonpublic information, such as in response to an inquiry during a Q&A session, the public announcement must be made "promptly," which means as soon as possible, but in no event after the later of (i) 24 hours or (ii) the start of the next day's trading on the New York Stock Exchange. Making an unplanned disclosure pursuant to Regulation FD can be challenging for a company because it lessens the company's ability to time and refine messaging and may implicate sensitive business developments or third-party relationships.

Information is considered material under Regulation FD if it would be important to an investor in making an investment decision. While this analysis is highly fact-dependent, certain information, such as earnings results and guidance, affirmation of prior earnings guidance, and a change in control or management, is usually considered material. Information is considered nonpublic at any time prior to its broad, nonexclusionary release through a "recognized channel" of distribution. News wires and SEC filings are "recognized channels"; websites and social media outlets may also qualify if the company has consistently used those mediums for investor communications.

While Regulation FD does not prohibit directors from speaking privately with shareholders, it does prohibit sharing material nonpublic information, even nonverbally, in the absence of a confidentiality duty or agreement. It is critical for directors to remain informed of the company's communication policies in order to know who is authorized to speak on behalf of the company and what the company's procedures are for ensuring consistent messaging and avoiding Regulation FD violations. Often these procedures include pre-clearing discussion topics or having legal counsel participate in the discussions. In their oversight role, directors should also ensure that the company's communication policies, procedures, and training programs are reflective of company culture and adequate to protect against violations of Regulation FD and that insurance policies and indemnification agreements would cover costs incurred in connection with an SEC investigation into an alleged rule violation.

Key Questions

Effective oversight of a company's Regulation FD compliance should lead a director to ask the following questions:

- ❑ Who is, and who should be, authorized to speak on the company's behalf?
- ❑ What are the company's policies with respect to communications with analysts, institutional investors, shareholders, employees, the media, and business partners?
- ❑ Has the company established earnings guidance and communication policies that are complementary to and consistent with its insider trading policy and its confidentiality policies and agreements?
- ❑ Does the company provide adequate training to directors, senior officers, investor relations personnel, and other employees on how to comply with its policies?

- ❑ What are the processes for deciding whether information is material and monitoring company communications to determine whether such information has been publicly disclosed?
- ❑ Does the company have a process and team in place for responding to potential Regulation FD violations?
- ❑ Are costs incurred in SEC investigations covered under the company's directors' and officers' insurance policy and director and officer indemnification agreements?

Additional Reading

1. *Fast Answers on Fair Disclosure, Regulation FD*
   http://www.sec.gov/answers/regfd.htm
2. *Final Rule: Selective Disclosure and Insider Trading*
   http://www.sec.gov/rules/final/33-7881.htm
3. Regulation FD Compliance and Disclosure Interpretations
   http://www.sec.gov/divisions/corpfin/guidance/regfd-interp.htm
4. *Frequently Asked Questions About Regulation FD*
   http://media.mofo.com/files/Uploads/Images/FAQs-Regulation-FD.pdf
5. Solomon, Steven Davidoff. "As Information Flows, SEC Faces Difficulty Bottling It Up." *New York Times* DealBook (May 27, 2014)
   http://dealbook.nytimes.com/2014/05/27/as-information-flows-s-e-c-faces-difficulty-bottling-it-up/?_r=0
6. Lynn, David. "Happy Anniversary Regulation FD. Is It Time to Revisit Your Regulation FD Policy?," *Inside Counsel* (September 12, 2012)
   http://www.insidecounsel.com/2012/09/12/regulatory-happy-anniversary-regulation-fd

Notes

5.8 REVIEWING CORPORATE PRESS RELEASES

CONTRIBUTED BY
Frank M. Placenti
Squire Patton Boggs (US) LLP
David A. Zagore
Squire Patton Boggs (US) LLP[1]

Public companies are expected and required to make timely public disclosure of material corporate developments. The most common way in which that disclosure occurs is through the issuance of press releases. Releases are often accompanied by the filing of a Form 8-K with the Securities and Exchange Commission, which either contains parallel information required by specific SEC Rules or, in many cases, merely attaches a copy of the press release to the Form 8-K.

For listed public companies, the requirements regarding press releases are set forth in the rules of the relevant stock exchange. New York Stock Exchange Rule 202.05 requires a listed company to "quickly" release to the public any news or information that might be reasonably expected to materially affect the market value of their securities. The rule

1. Frank M. Placenti is a partner in the corporate practice of Squire Patton Boggs (US) LLP, where he leads the firm's U.S. governance practice. David A. Zagore is a partner in the corporate practice of Squire Patton Boggs (US) LLP in the firm's Cleveland, Ohio office.

recites that the imposition of this requirement is one of the most important and fundamental purposes of the company's listing agreement with the Exchange.

NASDAQ Rule 5250(b)(1) requires that, except in unusual circumstances, NASDAQ-listed companies disclose "promptly" to the public any material information that would reasonably be expected to affect the value of their securities or influence investor decisions.

Both the NASDAQ rule and the New York Stock Exchange rule require that the disclosures be made in a manner that is compliant with SEC Regulation FD. (See Chapter 5.7 of this Handbook.) Both rules also discuss the timing of press releases and contain specific procedures for these releases.

In all but the smallest companies, board members are not directly involved in the preparation of ordinary course press releases. They are, however, generally called upon to review certain key press releases, as discussed in more detail later in this chapter.

Even when not directly involved, directors should remain generally aware of the company's press releases. Directors should pay attention to the nature of the information being released, the frequency of press releases, and whether press releases are being used for legitimate communication purposes, or whether they could be seen to be trying to "hype" the company's prospects. The NYSE press release rules specifically caution that releases not be issued with excessive frequency and that they not cover "trivial" matters, for fear that the volume and nature of a company's releases will obscure important information when it is disclosed. Seasoned investors will sense when a company is hyping its story and excessive communications activity can actually be counterproductive.

Moreover, if and when adverse events occur and a company's stock price drops in response, plaintiff's securities lawyers will comb the company's recent press releases for evidence that the company has sought to paint an unduly rosy picture of the company and its prospects. In considering company releases, directors should be mindful that, in hindsight, statements made are clear, complete, and conservative. In this regard, directors can play an important role of providing perspective and objective distance in evaluating management's disclosure.

Timing Issues

While the stock exchange rules call for "quick" or "prompt" release of material information, it is sometimes appropriate to delay the issuance of a press release for a short period of time in order to ensure that the information released is complete and accurate, or that the release does not prematurely reveal confidential information, such as that relating to pending corporate transactions. Such delays require careful judgment regarding whether a delay is defensible under the federal securities laws and exchange listing requirements. When in doubt, a board member should require that the company's legal counsel address the timing issue in order to establish that a thoughtful approach has been taken and that the director is relying upon expert legal advice.

What to Look For

Directors generally review (and should review) quarterly and annual earnings releases, releases regarding significant corporate transactions, releases regarding matters that might be characterized as "crisis" related, and other releases communicating significant corporate events. In particular, members of the audit committee are expected to pay particular attention to the company's financial press releases.

When reviewing a release, a director should seek to be comfortable that it fairly presents the material information and provides as complete a story as is then known. While granular detail is not the norm in a release, the release should not omit material information necessary without which the information disclosed could be misleading. It is important that the information be presented in perspective—good news should not be trumpeted too optimistically and bad news should not be concealed in a cloud of verbiage.

When reviewing financial press releases, directors should be cognizant of the SEC Regulation G regarding the use of non-GAAP financial information signaled by such phrases as "adjusted EBITDA" or "when adjusted for one time charges," and the like. The SEC requirements for the use of non-GAAP financial information should be discussed with management and legal counsel and the board should be comfortable that the non-GAAP information is being used for an informative purpose and is accompanied by any required GAAP information. It is also appropriate to confirm whether the release has been reviewed by the company's independent auditors.

Care should be taken regarding the inclusion of forward-looking statements in press releases, which can often come in the form of predictions or statements of expectation about business or financial results. They should always be accompanied by appropriate disclaimers that are specific and proximate to the predictions or statements of expectation in order to make clear that they are mere expressions of opinion qualified for the protection of the SEC's safe harbor for forward-looking statements. Moreover, any forward-looking or predictive statement should be phrased with the advice of legal counsel to avoid creating a legal duty to update the statement should intervening events or circumstances cause the statement to become untrue.

Corporate directors who are officers of other public companies will often be familiar with press release procedures and requirements and can provide helpful guidance to other directors who are not.

Key Questions

In considering a company's press release policy and individual press releases a director may wish to ask the following questions:

- ❑ Am I comfortable with the volume, content, and tone of my company's press releases?
- ❑ Do they present the relevant information in proper perspective?
- ❑ Is the volume of press releases used by my company appropriate?
- ❑ Are we announcing only those matters of relevance, or have we descended into "trivia"?

- ❑ Are releases published pursuant to a clearly defined communication plan?
- ❑ Are company releases consistent with the activity and initiatives contemplated by the company's approved business plan and budget?
- ❑ Are we consistent over time and the method of calculation with respect to the company performance indices included in company releases?
- ❑ Do I discern any attempt to hype the company's performance in an attempt to influence its stock price?
- ❑ Is the company releasing information in a timely manner?
- ❑ If I am being advised that it is appropriate to delay releasing material information, what is the basis for that advice?
- ❑ Has legal counsel weighed in?
- ❑ Has the stock exchange been consulted regarding the delay?
- ❑ What advice came from the stock exchange with respect to the issue of delay?
- ❑ With respect to quarterly or annual earnings releases, do they contain any non-GAAP financial information?
- ❑ If so, am I comfortable that SEC regulations regarding the use of non-GAAP financial information are being complied with?
- ❑ Is the non-GAAP information necessary and helpful to investors?
- ❑ What outlet for issuance of press releases does my company use?
- ❑ Would others be appropriate?
- ❑ What other means of dissemination besides press releases is the company using?
- ❑ What is being posted on the company's website or in social media?
- ❑ Has the company received legal advice regarding the appropriateness of the use of those alternative means of communication?
- ❑ Are directors receiving all corporate press releases, social media posts, and other public communications? If not, which ones are not being provided to us and why?

Additional Reading

1. New York Stock Exchange Listed Company Manual, Rules 202.01 through 202.07 and Rule 203 (Reporting Financial Information to Shareholders) http://nysemanual.nyse.com/lcm/

2. NASDAQ Stock Market Equity Rules http://nasdaq.cchwallstreet.com/NASDAQTools/PlatformViewer.asp?selectednode=chp_1_1_1_1&manual=%2Fnasdaq%2Fmain%2Fnasdaq-equityrules%2F

3. *Deloitte Audit Committee Resource Guide*, p. 17 https://www2.deloitte.com/us/en/pages/center-for-board-effectiveness/articles/audit-committee-resource-guide.html

4. *The ABA Corporate Director's Guidebook*, 6th ed., 66 Business Lawyer 975 (2011) 36.

Notes

5.9 PROXY ACCESS

CONTRIBUTED BY
Catherine G. Dearlove and Jennifer Veet Barrett
Richards, Layton & Finger, P.A.[1]

Proxy access provisions allow stockholders who satisfy certain criteria to have nominees for director included in the corporation's proxy statement and on the corporation's proxy card, bypassing the cost to such stockholders of sending out their own proxy materials. This can represent multimillion-dollar savings for stockholders seeking to nominate one or more directors.

Proxy access first garnered widespread attention in 2010 when the Securities and Exchange Commission (SEC) adopted proposed rules that would have mandated proxy access for stockholders (holding at least 3 percent of a corporation's voting securities for at least three years, among other criteria). While the SEC's mandatory proxy access rules were vacated following judicial challenge, the issue was taken up by stockholder activists who began pressuring corporations to adopt proxy access on a case-by-case basis through amendments to their certificate of incorporation or bylaws (referred to as "private ordering"). As of this writing, more than 350 public corporations have adopted proxy access provisions, either voluntarily or as a result of pressure from stockholders. To

1. Catherine G. Dearlove is a shareholder and director with Richards, Layton & Finger, P.A., where she practices in the corporate litigation and corporate governance areas. Jennifer Veet Barrett is counsel with Richards, Layton & Finger, P.A., where she practices in the corporate advisory group.

date, however, no stockholder has successfully used a proxy access provision to nominate a director.

In contrast to the SEC's mandatory proxy access proposal, private ordering allows each corporation to decide when (or whether) to adopt proxy access, and to customize the term and conditions of proxy access to the particular circumstances facing the corporation. Nonetheless, the influence of certain institutional holders (who have made a practice of advocating for proxy access) and the proxy advisory firms (who generally will support proxy access proposals) has led to some standardization of key terms. While the terms most common to proxy access provisions have evolved over time (and will likely continue to evolve in the future), many recently adopted proxy access provisions as of the date of this writing include the following terms:

- Ownership requirement of at least 3 percent of the corporation's voting securities
- A holding period of at least three years
- The ability of a group of stockholders (often capped at 20) to aggregate their shares to meet the required ownership percentage
- A requirement that the nominating stockholders be passive investors with no intent to control the corporation
- A limitation on the number of proxy access nominees at an annual meeting (often 20 percent of the board of directors)
- "Ownership," defined as shares of voting securities for which the stockholder possesses both full voting and investment rights and full economic interest

The majority of such proxy access provisions also include provisions specifying the information about director nominees or the nominating stockholder that must be provided to the corporation as a condition to inclusion in the proxy and circumstances under which a potential nominee may be excluded from the proxy.

Proxy access provisions continue to evolve and additional terms that might be considered include terms addressing the following issues among others: the treatment of loaned shares in determining the number of shares owned by nominating stockholder(s); the treatment of incumbent proxy access nominees in determining whether the specified cap on proxy access nominees is met; and whether and in what circumstances the company may exclude a nominee who has previously been nominated but not elected to the board.

While some corporations have adopted proxy access provisions at the initiative of management or the board, in many cases, the timing of a corporation's adoption of a proxy access provision is influenced by receipt of a stockholder proposal seeking a stockholder vote to recommend implementation of proxy access or some other pressure from stockholders. In either event, when implemented, the proxy access provision is typically adopted as a bylaw, rather than included in the certificate of incorporation. If a corporation receives a stockholder proposal seeking to implement proxy access, the corporation may consider responding in one of the following ways:

- Including the proposal in the corporation's proxy materials and soliciting against the proposal

- Including the proposal in the corporation's proxy materials and recommending in favor of the proposal and, if approved by the stockholders, adopting a proxy access provision consistent with the terms set forth in the stockholder proposal
- Adopting its own proxy access provision and seeking the withdrawal of the stockholder proposal
- Adopting its own proxy access provision and seeking to have the stockholder proposal excluded from the corporation's proxy statement as "substantially implemented" under the rules of the Securities Exchange Act of 1934, as amended
- Adopting its own proxy access provision and submitting both proposals to a vote of the stockholders

Key Questions

When a board considers the issue of proxy access, whether in response to a stockholder proposal or otherwise, some issues to consider are the following:

- ❑ Is this the appropriate time to adopt a proxy access provision? Should the corporation adopt a proxy access provision voluntarily or wait until it receives a stockholder proposal seeking to implement proxy access?
- ❑ Will the voluntary adoption of a proxy access provision preempt submission of a stockholder proposal seeking to implement proxy access?
- ❑ If a stockholder proposal seeking to implement proxy access is received, what action should the corporation take?
- ❑ In considering a specific proxy access proposal, what terms are appropriate for the corporation and its stockholders? Do the proposed terms address the particular circumstances facing the corporation?
- ❑ Are the terms of the proposed proxy access provision consistent with the provisions adopted by peer companies and/or those previously recommended by the proxy advisory firms? If the terms proposed vary from those adopted by peer companies or supported by proxy advisory firms, how and why are they different?
- ❑ If the corporation has received a stockholder proposal seeking proxy access but is considering an alternative management proposal, do the terms of the corporation's proposed proxy access provision differ from the terms requested in the stockholder proposal? How do the terms differ? What is the corporation's rationale for the inclusion of any differing terms?
- ❑ Should the corporation discuss proxy access generally (or the specific terms contained in a proxy access proposal) with the corporation's largest investors, proxy advisor groups, and, if applicable, the stockholder who submitted the proposal? When is the appropriate time to do so?
- ❑ What are the advantages to the corporation and its stockholders in adopting proxy access? Is it likely to provide greater incentive for directors or enhanced accountability to stockholders? Is it likely to facilitate removal of underperforming

directors or to shorten average board tenure? Does the board believe that these effects, if any, are likely to benefit the corporation and its stockholders?

- ❑ What are the disadvantages to the corporation and its stockholder in adopting a proxy access provision? Will it open the boardroom to stockholder activists with interests that may be different from the interests of the corporation's long-term stockholders? Will the adoption of a proxy access provision make it more difficult to attract and retain highly qualified directors? Will it circumvent the corporation's established vetting and nomination process for director candidates?
- ❑ If stockholder approval is not otherwise required under applicable law or the corporation's governing documents, should the proxy access provision be submitted to the corporation's stockholders for approval?

Additional Reading

1. Dearlove, Catherine G. and Werrett, A. Jacob. "Proxy Access by Private Ordering: A Review of the 2012 and 2013 Proxy Seasons." *The Business Lawyer* 69 (November 2013).
2. Gregory, Holly J. "Lesson from the 2015 Proxy Access Front." *Practical Law The Journal, Transactions & Business* (May 2015).
3. Proxy Access: It is Catching On! *The Corporate Counsel* XL, no. 5 (September–October 2015).
4. H. Rodgin Cohen, et. al. "Proxy Access Developments and Trends." *The Corporate Governance Advisor* 23, no. 3 (November/December 2015).

Notes

5.10 SHAREHOLDER PROPOSALS

CONTRIBUTED BY
Catherine G. Dearlove and Jennifer Veet Barrett
Richards, Layton & Finger, P.A.[1]

As a general matter, shareholders are entitled to propose business for consideration at a corporation's annual meeting of shareholders. While shareholder proposals can relate to a variety of topics, including social, political, and environmental issues, the increased focus on corporate governance over the past several years has resulted in a significant increase in the number of shareholder proposals relating to corporate governance and even business topics. Although the specific focus of such proposals evolves from year to year, as of this writing, recent shareholder proposals related to corporate governance matters have primarily focused on increasing shareholder rights through proxy access, majority voting, or the ability of shareholders to call special meetings or to act by written consent.

Shareholders may propose business to be considered at a corporation's annual meeting in one of two ways. The first way that a shareholder may propose business is to seek to have its proposed business included in the corporation's proxy statement and on the corporation's proxy card by submitting its proposal in accordance with Rule 14a-8 of the Securities Exchange Act of 1934, as amended (Rule 14a-8). Under Rule 14a-8, a

1. Catherine G. Dearlove is a shareholder and director with Richards, Layton and Finger, P.A., where she practices in the corporate litigation and corporate governance areas. Jennifer Veet Barrett is counsel with Richards, Layton and Finger, P.A., where she practices in the corporate advisory group.

corporation generally must include a shareholder proposal (and a supporting statement from the proposing shareholder) in its proxy materials and submit such proposal to a vote of the shareholders at its annual meeting unless (i) the proposal or the proposing shareholder has not complied with the eligibility and procedural requirements of the rule or (ii) the proposal can be excluded from the corporation's proxy materials on one or more of the substantive bases for exclusion set forth in Rule 14a-8.

The eligibility and procedural requirements of Rule 14a-8 include, among other things, specific ownership and holding requirements for shareholders seeking to submit a proposal (i.e., a shareholder must have continuously held at least $2,000 in market value or 1 percent of the corporation's securities entitled to vote at the meeting on the proposal for at least one year and must hold the securities through the date of the annual meeting) and a specific time period within which such proposal must be received by the corporation. With respect to the substantive bases for exclusion of the proposal, Rule 14a-8 permits a corporation to exclude from its proxy materials shareholder proposals that, among other things, are not a proper subject for stockholder action under applicable state law; relate to the corporation's ordinary business operations; conflict with one of the corporation's proposals to be submitted to the shareholders at the same meeting; or relate to a proposal that has already been substantially implemented by the corporation.

In responding to a shareholder proposal, the corporation may consider the following courses of action:

- seeking a "no action" ruling by the SEC and, if granted, excluding the proposal, if the proposal or proposing shareholder fail to comply with the eligibility and procedural requirements of Rule 14a-8 and/or one of the bases for exclusion of the proposal apply;
- including the proposal in the corporation's proxy materials and soliciting against the proposal;
- including the proposal in the corporation's proxy materials and recommending in favor of the proposal; or
- negotiating with the shareholder concerning the subject matter of the proposal, which may lead to withdrawal of the shareholder proposal if the corporation and the shareholder reach agreement.

The second way that a shareholder may propose business to be considered at the corporation's annual meeting is by notifying the corporation of such proposed business at any time before or at the corporation's annual meeting or, if the corporation's governing documents include an advance notice provision, by complying with the requirements set forth in such advance notice provision. If a shareholder complies with the requirements of its advance notice provision, if any, a corporation generally must submit such proposal to a vote of the shareholders at its annual meeting, but is not required to include such proposal in its proxy materials.

Most public corporations have included advance notice provisions in their governing documents. Such a provision regulates the submission of shareholder proposals by requiring the proposing shareholder to submit prior notice of such proposed business to the corporation within a specified time frame (often a 30-day period that is several months before the anniversary date of the prior year's annual meeting) and to provide the corporation with certain information related to the proposal and the parties submitting the proposal. For example, advance notice provisions often require the proposing shareholder to provide certain information regarding the proposed business, such as the reason for proposing the business and any material interest that the shareholder has in such business, and information regarding the proposing shareholder and any other party on whose behalf the proposal is made, such as the number and class or series of shares of the corporation's stock owned by such parties, the derivative or similar instruments held by such parties with respect to the corporation's securities, and whether the proposing shareholder intends to solicit or be part of a group that solicits proxies with respect to the proposed business.

If a corporation receives a shareholder proposal pursuant to its advance notice provision, the corporation may consider responding in one or more of the following ways:

- If the proposal does not comply with the requirements of the advance notice provision, disregarding such proposal, including not presenting it for consideration at the corporation's annual meeting
- Presenting the proposal at the corporation's annual meeting and recommending that the shareholders vote against the proposal
- Presenting the proposal at the corporation's annual meeting and recommending that the shareholders vote in favor of the proposal
- Negotiating with the shareholder and seeking the withdrawal of the shareholder proposal

Under the requirements of Rule 14a-8 and most advance notice provisions, the proposing shareholder or a qualified representative of the proposing shareholder must appear at the annual meeting to present the proposal. If such requirement is not met, the corporation is not required to present the proposal for a vote at the annual meeting and, in the case of a Rule 14a-8 proposal, may exclude any shareholder proposal submitted by such proposing shareholder from the corporation's proxy materials for the next two annual meetings.

Key Questions

When the corporation receives a shareholder proposal, whether pursuant to the rules of the Securities and Exchange Commission or the corporation's advance notice provision, some issues for the board to consider are the following:

- ❑ Do the shareholder proposal and the proposing shareholder comply with the requirements of Rule 14a-8 or the corporation's advance notice provision, as applicable?
- ❑ If the proposal was submitted under Rule 14a-8, is there a substantive basis to seek exclusion of the proposal from the corporation's proxy materials?
- ❑ Has the SEC issued any no action guidance in the past concerning the subject matter of the shareholder proposal?
- ❑ What do the corporation's governing documents currently provide with respect to the subject matter of the shareholder proposal? Has management or the board previously considered taking any action concerning the subject matter?

- ❑ What have peer companies done with respect to the subject matter of the shareholder proposal? What guidance have proxy advisory firms provided with respect to the subject matter of the shareholder proposal?
- ❑ What information is known about the shareholder who submitted the proposal? Has the shareholder submitted similar shareholder proposals in the past, at the corporation or at other corporations? If so, what was the result?
- ❑ What are the views of the corporation's largest investors with respect to the subject matter of the shareholder proposal?
- ❑ Should the corporation discuss the shareholder proposal with the corporation's largest investors, proxy advisor groups, and/or the shareholder who submitted the proposal? When is the appropriate time to do so?
- ❑ Should the corporation attempt to negotiate with the proposing shareholder to address the concerns of the proposing shareholder in exchange for the shareholder's withdrawal of the proposal?
- ❑ What are the advantages to the corporation and its shareholders in taking the action proposed in the shareholder proposal?
- ❑ What are the disadvantages to the corporation and its shareholders in taking the action proposed in the shareholder proposal?
- ❑ If the shareholder proposal will be submitted to a vote of the shareholders at the annual meeting, should the board recommend a vote for or against the proposal?
- ❑ What are the ramifications to the corporation if the shareholder proposal is approved by the shareholders at the annual meeting and the corporation does not take the action proposed in the shareholder proposal?

Additional Reading

1. Our Rule 14a-8 Off-Season Check-Up Guide, *The Corporate Counsel* XXXIX, no. 3 (May–June 2014).
2. Director Nominations. *Delaware Journal of Corporate Law* 39, no. 1 (2014).
3. Section 240.14a-8 of the Securities Exchange Act of 1934, as amended.

Notes

____

____

____

____

____

SECTION SIX

MANAGEMENT AND OVERSIGHT OF TRANSACTIONS

6.1 MANAGEMENT AND OVERSIGHT OF TRANSACTIONS

CONTRIBUTED BY
Mark Easton
O'Melveny & Myers[1]
Donald Scotten
University of Southern California School of Law[2]

Consistent with its supervisory and oversight roles under most states' corporate laws, the board is not generally involved in ordinary course transactions. Instead, the board delegates to management most dealings with customers, hiring of nonmanagement employees, supplier negotiations, and other aspects of the company's day-to-day operations. Certain transactions, however, rise to a level of materiality or involve the company's strategic plan in a significant way so as to require board approval. When such transactions arise, increased board involvement becomes necessary.

The board's role in managing major transactions begins with the creation of a strategic plan for the company long before a proposed transaction emerges. Ultimately, the board is responsible for the vision for and future of the company. In crafting a strategic plan, the

1. Mark Easton is a partner at O'Melveny & Myers LLP, where he is the regional head of transactions for Southern California. He wishes to acknowledge the assistance of Adam Ackerman in the preparation of these materials.
2. Donald Scotten is a professor of law at the University of Southern California School of Law.

board must consider not only ordinary course revenue-generating activities, but also the company's approach to acquisitions, expansion, and exit opportunities.

The board's oversight role begins with the selection of a management team that will implement and help shape the company's strategic vision and business plans and continues even after any particular transaction has been consummated. Throughout the business cycle, the board should ask questions of management and stay informed of ongoing developments.

Transactions should be evaluated in advance to determine whether they are consistent with the company's strategic vision, as well as after closing to confirm that the value proposition has been realized. An informed board will be better prepared to make decisions and oversee a major transaction when one arises. Some transactions may require the board to act very quickly, but the board must nevertheless discharge its fiduciary duties in considering any proposed transaction.

Ordinarily the board will delegate the day-to-day management of particular transactions to the company's executive officers, with periodic reporting to the board. The board will also often engage and rely on experts and advisors such as lawyers and investment bankers for specific counsel with respect to certain aspects of an important transaction. However, the board members themselves must have a thorough understanding of the key terms of the transaction and how they compare to market standards. Only then will the board be in a position to evaluate the deal.

Key Questions

To exercise its oversight role with respect to transactions, directors should consider seeking the following information:

- ❑ What kinds of reports should we ask to receive from management with respect to transactions, in what detail, and with what frequency? Are these reports helpful in evaluating whether the proposed transaction is consistent with the company's strategic plan?
- ❑ Why is management proposing this transaction? Is it because (i) we lack some bench strength, (ii) the market is getting too difficult for us to compete in, (iii) this transaction fills in geography and/or products we don't currently have, or (iv) it is a "build or buy" decision?
- ❑ What will be the impact on shareholder value? What are the key assumptions behind the projected value of the deal? How important are cost reductions and other synergies? Are the assumptions about synergies realistic?
- ❑ What valuation methods, besides per share cash value, have been considered when evaluating this offer? How would our assessment be different if we relied upon one of the alternative valuation methodologies we explored?
- ❑ Does the projected impact on shareholder value justify the risks associated with the transaction? What are the three to five major things that might go wrong? What are the warning signs? What are you going to do if you start to see these warning signs? At what point will you involve us once you see the warning signs?

- ❑ What are the alternatives to undertaking the proposed transaction? What alternative opportunities, including forgoing any transaction, have been evaluated?
- ❑ What happens if the deal falls through? Will we have become a target for another deal, possibly a hostile one? Does management have its own alternatives in mind? Or would we decide to continue to operate on our own?
- ❑ What procedures are in place to manage disclosures in connection with this transaction? What is the risk of a premature disclosure and what plans are in place to deal with it if it happens? What is being done to avoid selective disclosures?
- ❑ Has everyone who has a potential conflict of interest been screened from negotiating the terms of the transaction? Who needs to be screened from negotiating the terms of the transaction because of a potential conflict of interest?
- ❑ How involved should the full board, or a committee of the board, be with respect to the negotiation of the transaction? Why do they need to be involved, versus letting management and the outside experts handle it?
- ❑ Have we identified the independent and disinterested directors who would serve on a special committee to evaluate and negotiate this transaction? Has a formal charter been written up for the special committee?
- ❑ What has been done to make sure that our financial advisors are independent and disinterested? Will the board retain its own financial advisor to ensure we can reasonably rely on information free from conflicts?

Additional Reading

1. *ABA Business Law Section, Committee on Corporate Laws.* Corporate Director's Guidebook, 6th ed. (See Section 3.)
2. William M., Lisa A. Schmidt, and Donald J. Wolfe, Jr. "A Brief Introduction to the Fiduciary Duties of Directors Under Delaware Law." *Penn State Law Review.*
   http://www.pennstatelawreview.org/116/3/116%20Penn%20St.%20L.%20Rev.%20837.pdf
3. Lajoux, Alexandra R. FAQs on the Role of the Board in M&A, *NACD* (August 14, 2015).
   http://blog.nacdonline.org/2015/08/faqs-on-the-role-of-the-board-in-ma/
4. Gregory, Holly J. "Board's Role in M&A Transactions"
   http://www.sidley.com/~/media/files/newsinsights/publications/2014/05/the-boards-role-in-ma-transactions/files/view-article/fileattachment/the-boards-role-in-ma-transactions--may-2014.pdf
5. Mergers & Acquisitions: A Delaware Checklist, *Morris, Nichols, Arsht & Tunnell LLP*
   http://www.mnat.com/files/ma_checklist.pdf

Notes

62 THE BOARD'S ROLE IN ACQUISITIONS AND BUSINESS COMBINATIONS

CONTRIBUTED BY
Mark Easton
O'Melveny & Myers[1]
Donald Scotten
University of Southern California School of Law[2]

The board's duty to act in the best interests of the company and its shareholders applies to acquisitions and business combinations to the same extent as in any other company context. When such material transactions arise, explicit board approval will be necessary under most states' corporate laws for transactions of any substantial size. The company's shareholders typically rely heavily on the board's judgment in considering whether to approve a transaction presented to the shareholders for their approval.

The board plays an active role throughout the life cycle of a deal, from the decision to pursue an opportunity to the ultimate decision whether to close the deal or walk away. While the extent of the board's involvement in the negotiations may vary, typically the board does not manage the transaction, but should instead engage in "active oversight." The board relies on the management team and outside experts like lawyers and investment

1. Mark Easton is a partner at O'Melveny & Myers LLP, where he is the regional head of transactions for Southern California. He wishes to acknowledge the assistance of Adam Ackerman in the preparation of these materials.
2. Donald Scotten is a professor of law at the University of Southern California School of Law.

bankers to conduct the negotiations and document the transaction. However, the board will receive periodic reports from management and its advisors regarding the progress of the deal. Prior to approving any acquisition or business combination, the board must be fully informed of the key terms of the proposed transaction as well as alternatives.

At the outset, the board's role is in large part a cost-benefit analysis with respect to the proposed transaction. The board wants to assess the impact of the transaction on shareholder value, and the risk that the projected value does not come to pass. The board should assess various types of risks, including financial, regulatory, legal, and cultural risks that may be associated with the proposed transaction.

- *Company Strategy*. The board will want to confirm that the proposed transaction is consistent with the company's strategy. If not, the board will want to know why the transaction makes sense for the company.
- *Impact on Shareholder Value*. The board will want to assess the impact of the proposed transaction on the company's value to shareholders. The board will want to assess the impact of shareholder value from various perspectives using various methodologies to confirm that the valuation analysis is comprehensive. The board will also want to understand the principal assumptions behind the various valuations.
- *Financial Considerations*. In addition to shareholder value, the board will likely consider other financial impacts of the transaction. Does it require the company to take on additional debt to pay for a proposed acquisition? Will the company offer its own equity instead? If so, does the proposed transaction justify dilution of the existing shareholders? Will the company have adequate financial resources available to conduct its business following the acquisition?
- *Regulatory Considerations*. An acquisition or business combination may require regulatory approvals or notifications, such as antitrust filings or approvals from a lead regulatory body such as an insurance commissioner, healthcare regulator, or national security body. A transaction may also trigger additional regulatory requirements, either in connection with the transaction itself or on a going-forward basis for the surviving company. The board will want to consider any regulatory risks associated with a transaction, including whether the company's compliance systems or internal controls are equipped to meet any regulatory burdens.
- *Legal Considerations*. The board will also expect management, with the assistance of the company's lawyers, to assess any material legal considerations associated with the proposed transaction. This may include any third-party approvals that must be obtained as a condition to closing the transaction, as well as any litigation that may have been filed with respect to the proposed transaction. The board will also want to understand whether a target company has ongoing or potential material litigation that should be taken into account in any valuation of the target.

- *Culture and Employees*. Lastly, acquisitions and business combinations may have adverse effects on the company's culture. Amid changing roles and potential internal restructuring, management and other employees could face uncertainty, including on issues such as compensation and the integration of new personnel.

Key Questions

- ❑ Is the board's role to ask questions and monitor progress, or is it to get more deeply involved in the details? Whichever is the answer, is that the right answer with respect to a particular transaction?
- ❑ Does the management team possess the skills necessary to execute this transaction and integrate the businesses?
- ❑ Who are going to be the outside experts (lawyers, investment bankers, accountants, etc.)? Why has management recommended or selected them? Are they the right ones for the deal?
- ❑ To what extent will or should the board interact directly with these outside experts? And when we do, what are we supposed to be looking for?
- ❑ How does this acquisition further the firm's strategic vision?
- ❑ What assumptions have been made when reviewing our strategic vision, evaluating our strengths and weaknesses, and translating those into acquisition criteria?
- ❑ How else might we use the resources required to undertake this deal?
- ❑ What are the other company's major risks? Are we sure we know what they are? Putting aside the experts but just thinking about the business as we directors know it, what's likely wrong with the other company and are we sure we know how they are handling those risks?
- ❑ What reasonable efforts do we need to make to meet the closing conditions? What circumstances would lead to the conditions not being met? The same questions need to be asked with respect to the counterparty: What would happen if the deal failed to close? Does management have a contingency plan?

Additional Reading

1. Halper, Jason M. *Directors' Fiduciary Duties in Approving Mergers* https://corpgov.law.harvard.edu/2016/08/08/directors-fiduciary-duties-in-approving-mergers/
2. Lajoux, Alexandra R. *The M&A Litmus Test: Part 5* (August 9, 2010) http://blog.nacdonline.org/2010/08/the-ma-litmus-test-part-5/

Notes

6.3 DECIDING WHETHER TO SELL THE COMPANY

CONTRIBUTED BY
Mark Easton
O'Melveny & Myers[1]
Donald Scotten
University of Southern California School of Law[2]

The board has a duty to approve only a sale that is in the best interests of the company and its shareholders. But, in deciding whether to sell the company, the board will often consider the interests of many different constituencies. Although board approval will almost certainly be needed, most state corporate laws also require approval of the company's stockholders for major sell-side transactions. Stockholders are not the only interested stakeholders. A sale may trigger accelerated vesting of options or the acceleration of debt under existing financing arrangements. Existing relationships with third parties—including customers, suppliers, and landlords, among others—may need to be addressed to ensure continuity of the business, as sale agreements are often conditioned on the obtaining of material third-party consents. Existing management and other employees may have a strong interest in the status quo unless uncertainty as to continuing employment is

1. Mark Easton is a partner at O'Melveny & Myers LLP, where he is the regional head of transactions for Southern California. He wishes to acknowledge the assistance of Adam Ackerman in the preparation of these materials.
2. Donald Scotten is a professor of law at the University of Southern California School of Law.

addressed or the sale proceeds are widely shared. Even the interests of preferred and common shareholders may diverge, or at least not be fully aligned.

The existence of so many different stakeholders creates the potential for boards to be presented with complex and possibly conflicting considerations. However, Delaware courts have made clear that once a decision to sell has been made, shareholder value maximization is the guiding principle. In a sale of the company triggering *Revlon* duties (named for the decision of the Delaware Supreme Court in *Revlon, Inc. v. MacAndrews & Forbes Holdings, Inc.*, 506 A.2d 173 (Del. 1986)), the board must obtain a price that is reasonably likely to be the best price available for the shareholders. Delaware courts will generally give deference to the board's judgment, but the board should take care to make sure it has obtained the best value possible for the shareholders, including by seeking alternative bidders when possible.

Indeed, in today's landscape, the board should expect litigation to ensue in connection with a sale and factor such litigation into the expected transaction costs. Litigation—especially shareholder derivative litigation alleging breach of fiduciary duty for failure to take reasonable steps to maximize shareholder value—has become ubiquitous. There are some prospective protective measures, however, that the board may take to mitigate some downside litigation risk:

- *Written Records*. Keeping robust written records, including reports of experts and advisors, written board resolutions, and meeting minutes, can document the decision-making process. Such records may be used as evidence that the board satisfied its duty of care and was properly informed before making a decision.
- *Conflicts of Interest*. Conflicts of interest should be addressed at the outset. Courts have applied enhanced scrutiny over board decisions when decisions were made in the face of conflicts. The board should identify actual and potential conflicts of interest and address them early on. If financial advisors are on both sides of the transaction, independent advisors can be engaged. Similarly, where an existing shareholder or director is involved in the proposed transaction, the separate approval of only disinterested directors can be obtained and independent committees formed to investigate and make recommendations. Monitoring the conflicting interests of financial advisors is of increasing importance.
- *Communication with Shareholders*. Open lines of communication with shareholders can facilitate a smoother sale process. The company will likely have an opportunity to present the rationale for a particular transaction in the proxy materials that are distributed to shareholders prior to a shareholder meeting. Companies will often want to have other communications with shareholders to inform them about a proposed transaction. They must take care that any such communications comply with applicable disclosure rules and filing requirements.
- *Market Check*. The board can often conduct a market check to seek and entertain other offers. By making the sale process a competitive one, the board can show that it has done its reasonable due diligence in getting the best price for the shareholders.

Key Questions

When deciding whether or not to sell the company, the board may wish to consider the following:

- ❑ What procedural safeguards are in place to ensure fairness (e.g., such as conditioning the merger on common stockholder approval)? Will we be seeking approval from the majority of disinterested directors or common stockholders?
- ❑ What was the basis for selecting the experts (including lawyers and financial advisors) we have relied upon for this transaction?
- ❑ What was considered when negotiating the transaction terms?
- ❑ What has been done to attract different types of buyers?
- ❑ Does selling at this point in the company's development provide shareholders with the most value? Can we make it alone instead? If so, why are we doing this?
- ❑ Has a market check been done to discover other opportunities?
- ❑ What will be the impact on shareholder value? Which opportunity presents the greatest likelihood of maximizing shareholder value? Is there a reasonable prospect of generating value for the common stockholders? Has the current, economic value of the common stock been assessed?
- ❑ What will be the impact on other stakeholders (note, different companies and different outside experts have strongly differing views on this)? Such as on senior management? Junior management? Front line employees? The communities where our company and the other side have significant operations?
- ❑ Are the protective measures being taken proportional to the threat posed? What supports taking these actions?
- ❑ Do any board members have a personal interest in the transaction (e.g., affiliation with the owners of preferred stock) that merits creation of a special transaction committee?

Additional Reading

1. Vergilii, Jennifer L. "Protection Against Fiduciary Claims in a Sale or Merger Transaction." *abf journal*

   http://www.abfjournal.com/articles/protection-against-fiduciary-claims-in-a-sale-or-merger-transaction/

2. Simpson, Scott V. and Katherine Brody. *The Evolving Role of Special Committees in M&A Transactions: Seeking Business Judgment Rule Protection in the Context of Controlling Shareholder Transactions and Other Corporate Transactions Involving Conflicts of Interest*

   https://www.skadden.com/sites/default/files/publications/The%20Evolving%20Role%20of%20Special%20Committees.pdf

3. Halper, Jason M. *The Ever-Increasing Importance of the Shareholder Vote* https://corpgov.law.harvard.edu/2016/07/11/the-ever-increasing-importance-of-the-shareholder-vote/
4. Delaware Court of Chancery Finds Accepting Tender Offer Has Same Cleansing Effect as Stockholder Vote, *White & Case* (July 11, 2016) http://www.whitecase.com/publications/alert/delaware-court-chancery-finds-accepting-tender-offer-has-same-cleansing-effect?s=mergers

Notes

____

____

____

____

____

PRESIDING OVER THE SALE OF A COMPANY

6.4

CONTRIBUTED BY
Gregory V. Varallo
Richards, Layton & Finger, P.A.[1]

Presiding over the sale of the company presents a number of issues and concerns that do not usually occur in connection with everyday boardroom life. While the board's job in the context of a sale is controlled by the same basic legal duties that operate in other situations, their particular application in the sale context can seem unfamiliar or even foreign.

At the outset, practitioners sometimes obsess over whether the sale is a sale of control of the company or a "merger of equals." Much ink has been spilled over the differences. In truth, however, from the director's standpoint, it really makes little (some would say no) difference whether the transaction at hand is a "sale of control" or "merger of equals." The director should pursue the best interests of the company and all its constituencies with the same vigor, notwithstanding the form of the transaction. The questions are inevitably the same, regardless of form: Does this transaction make sense? Am I comfortable that all of the parties who should have been talked to were?

1. Gregory V. Varallo is a director and president of Richards, Layton & Finger, P.A., where he practices in the areas of complex business litigation, ADR, and corporate governance. The author wishes to acknowledge the assistance of his colleague John R. Fitzgerald in the preparation of this chapter.

Am I leaving shareholders' money on the table? Would I do this deal if I were selling my family's company and my own financial future depended on it? If a director can answer these questions honestly in favor of the deal then it likely will survive scrutiny in court, regardless of its form.

Consideration of the Litigation Reality—You Will Likely Be Sued

Regardless of how objectively "good" a deal can be shown to be, there is a perspective that must be appreciated by every director who prepares to step into the corporate control arena, and that is the perspective of the judiciary. Recent academic studies suggested that well more than 90 percent of public company deals were subject to lawsuits. While recent innovations in the law have lowered the frequency with which deals are challenged in court, any public company director contemplating a control transaction should assume that the deal will be subject to court challenge. Thus the perspective of a reviewing judge is worth careful consideration by directors contemplating a transaction.

Unlike directors, who are paid to consider the substance of transactions, the law freely acknowledges that judges are not necessarily trained in business and usually not best positioned to pass judgment on the substance of the business decisions that face the board in the context of a sale of control. Thus, the law has evolved to require the judge reviewing a corporate transaction to defer to the judgment of the board where the board acts in a considered manner, in good faith, and without conflicting interests.

Put simply, judges often carefully review the process a board followed to achieve a result, as opposed to the strengths or weaknesses of the result itself. Somewhat paradoxically, the law protects even bad business decisions if taken pursuant to a careful process and without conflict. At the same time, the law applies a special and more searching level of scrutiny to even very good business decisions where the process followed by the board to reach the result was either poorly conceived, poorly executed, or tainted by conflict or lack of independence.

Thus, if the director fully comprehends at the outset that the judge who reviews his or her decisions is likely not to be swayed by arguments concerning the brilliance of the result and instead will focus almost exclusively on the presence or absence of flaws in the process, it naturally follows that the director must ensure that the process itself is carefully considered and thorough, designed to achieve the best available result in all cases. That is not to say that a decision to transact with one well-chosen strategic partner to the exclusion of all others will automatically be met with judicial criticism, but it does suggest that such a decision must rest on particularly compelling business logic.

So what are the hallmarks of a well-run process from the point of view of a reviewing judge? The courts acknowledge that there is "no single blueprint" on how a process must be run. But this flexibility does not imply total deference. Judges ask many common-sense questions about the design of a sale. These include the following:

- Who crafted the design?
- Why was the design structured as it was?
- Were strategic buyers in the mix? If not, why not?

- Were financial buyers sought? If not, why not?
- How broad was the search?
- Were there logical buyers that were excluded from the process? If so, why?
- What role did management play in the process and did the board actively oversee that process?
- Were the advisors independent?
- If not, what role did conflicted advisors play in the process?
- Did unanticipated conflicts arise during the process for the advisors and how were these dealt with?

Acknowledging that the judge or judges likely to review a transaction will want common-sense answers to many of the questions just listed, it follows that directors should be asking the same questions before a process runs to completion and be comfortable with the answers and the business logic behind those answers.

Important Junctures in a Process

Consistent with the law's focus on the process by which a decision is made rather than its substance, the most intense focus of sale of control transactions typically is on three separate areas: First, were the right buyers contacted? Second, was the process run without the taint of conflict on the part of the board or its advisors? And third, did the board exercise an appropriate level of oversight of the process? Each area is dealt with in the following sections.

Were the Right Buyers Contacted?

Optimizing the result in any change of control process, at least in a free market, depends on the participation of as many of the most logical buyers as possible. Thus, the court will want to know (and the board should want to know as well) why any logical buyer was excluded or treated differently than others.

Management faced with the sale of a company often is heard to raise concerns about dealing with competitors as part of the sale process, most often on the basis that competitors may only participate in a process in order to learn unfairly about the company, rather than with a bona fide intent to bid. Of course, inviting direct competitors into a sale of control process often presents practical problems. It is also true, however, that, putting antitrust concerns to the side, competitors are often the most logical strategic buyers and might even be the most likely to pay the highest price in a well-run process.

Put bluntly, directors should be cynical about any attempts to tailor the process in a way that eliminates parties likely to be able to participate in the process and enhance the final result. The more such attempts are raised, the more directors should be concerned about the design of the process.

The board will want to ensure that the process involves all of the buyers likely to be able to pay well for the company. Where logical parties are excised from the process, the board should be very comfortable with the business rationale for doing so and that rationale should be contemporaneously and thoughtfully documented.

Was the Process Run without Conflicts?

Perhaps as important as overseeing the design of a rational process is making sure that the parties involved in the process are free of conflicts. To the extent that management may be interested in participating in the process as potential buyers, the conflict question is squarely presented and the need for close board supervision of management presentations to competing buyers and negotiations with third parties is particularly acute.

Likewise, conflicted advisors present acute problems for the process and the board. Where an investment bank seeks to offer (or simply offers) financing to the buyer while simultaneously offering sell-side services to the company (for example, so-called stapled financing), the courts have raised numerous questions about the ability of the board to rely on fairness opinions and advice rendered by that "conflicted" banker. Attempting to catalogue the total universe of potential advisor conflicts is beyond the scope of this chapter, but it is well within the scope to counsel that the board ensures that conflicts are dealt with in advance in advisor retention letters.

Did the Board Exercise Ongoing Oversight of the Process?

Conflicts of interest can be subtle. Take for example the case of the sale to the strategic buyer that is not likely to need the company's existing management team. Does that team treat the strategic buyer fairly in the sense that it receives treatment consistent with other bidders? Does the team exaggerate problems with buyers that it doesn't favor? Does it exaggerate wins with buyers it does favor? More obviously, what rules have been put in place to avoid financial buyers making employment offers to key management officers during the sales process itself?

All of these issues counsel in favor of board oversight of the process that is relatively more intrusive than typical oversight of transactions that are not prone to conflicts. Put simply, the courts expect the board to be aware of the potential for conflicts in the process and to oversee the process to manage or minimize the effect of those conflicts. Thus, at times board members have personally attended due diligence presentations by management where the board is concerned that management has a reason not to present the company fairly to such potential buyers.

Even without in-person appearances in due diligence, however, a board should expect to have frequent meetings during the sale of control process and to be active in the development of that process. The board should expect its advisors to keep it apprised of key developments in the process and to be consulted for strategic direction as the process unfolds. Perhaps most importantly, the board should keep in mind that this is the board's process—not the advisor's—even though it often does not seem so.

Key Questions

In presiding over the sale of a company, questions that a board may wish to pursue include the following:

- ❑ How is the sales process designed? Are all likely buyers contacted? If not, are there good business reasons for not inviting one or more potential buyers?
- ❑ Do any of the participants in the process have obvious conflicts of interest? Have the advisors promised to remain unconflicted as part of their retention? If not, why not?
- ❑ To what extent should the board be directly involved in the process?
- ❑ Are the board's advisors keeping the board adequately informed of key developments in the process, and is the board functioning to give direction with respect to such key developments?
- ❑ Are our advisors independent? How do we know that? Are we instituting a protocol to ensure they will remain independent throughout the process or at least notify us of potential conflicts?
- ❑ Do our minutes tell an accurate and complete story of our process and appropriately depict the care and attention we paid to it?
- ❑ What type of support, including our investment banker's fairness opinion, should we secure to buttress our decision?
- ❑ Are there any elements of our process that may be difficult to explain or cast the process in a bad light? If so, how can they be eliminated or minimized?

Additional Reading

1. Varallo, Gregory V., Daniel Dreisbach, and Blake Rohrbacher, *Fundamentals of Corporate Governance A Guide for Directors and Corporate Counsel*, (ABA 2nd ed. 2009).
2. Zeberkiewicz, John Mark, "Chancery Court Addresses Revlon Duties and Deal Protection Measures in Small-Cap Transaction," *Delaware Business Court Insider* (May 11, 2011).
3. Varallo, Gregory V. and Srinivas M. Raju, "A Process-Based Model for Analyzing Deal Protection Measures," 55 *The Business Lawyer* 1609 (August 2000).
4. Varallo, Gregory V. "Deal Protection Devices Enforced in the Delaware Court of Chancery," *Insights* (March 2010).
5. Reder, B., "The Obligation of a Director of a Delaware Corporation to Act as an Auctioneer," *The Business Lawyer* 275–82 (1989).

Notes

6.5 BASIC M&A CONCEPTS

CONTRIBUTED BY
Gregory V. Varallo
Richards, Layton & Finger, P.A.[1]

For the uninitiated, the world of mergers and acquisitions (M&A) must seem to be a strange place—fast paced and full of industry-specific jargon, not much of which is intuitively obvious. In this chapter, we unpack the concepts lurking behind the jargon with the hope of providing a guide to unfamiliar territory.

The current state of M&A law is a somewhat uneasy middle ground between traditional deference to well-informed, good faith, and unconflicted board decisions on the one hand and the lurking worry that even well-intentioned directors, when faced with an unsolicited offer to buy "their" company, might tend to be influenced by their own best interests, at least to some extent. One case referred to this latter concern as an "omnipresent specter" of self-interest.

Even though the law is clear that directors are not strictly accountable as "trustees," the law pertaining to trustees provides that when selling an asset the trustee must get the highest price for that asset—simple enough, but far too facile a rule in the often extremely complex context of selling a global enterprise. And so, often guided by

1. Gregory V. Varallo is a director and president of Richards, Layton & Finger, P.A., where he practices in the areas of complex business litigation, ADR and corporate governance. The author wishes to acknowledge the assistance of his colleague Anthony M. Calvano in the preparation of this chapter.

economic concepts, the courts have attempted to fashion a series of guidelines that directors can utilize to steer the process.

With an eye over their shoulder at the economists, and with trust law in mind, business lawyers and courts have designed a system that provides directors the flexibility to design a process they believe to be best in the circumstances. But since no process can truly be perfect, there are boundaries that have been constructed around the board's flexibility. In general, one outer boundary seems to be that a board cannot disable itself from considering and, where appropriate, accepting an unsolicited bid that comes forward prior to shareholder approval of a transaction. No rule is universal in application. Lawyers will certainly argue that there could be circumstances that should allow the board to "lock down" a deal without possibility of being preempted. The purpose of this chapter is not to test the outer bounds of the law or to take a position on an academic debate, but instead to help the director identify where the outer bounds may be in order to avoid testing those boundaries inadvertently.

This translates to several specific ideas in the M&A world. First, directors should beware of "preclusive" contracts that purport to make it impossible under any circumstances for the firm to be sold to a higher bidder.

The No Shop Provision

Avoiding the prohibited "preclusion" while still providing a relatively high degree of certainty to M&A contracts is accomplished with several separate but interrelated provisions in the contract. First, the no shop.

The no shop provision is fairly straightforward. It typically says that once a merger agreement is signed, the board is not free to continue to market (or shop) the company. Typically, this prohibition is coupled with an undertaking on behalf of the company to discontinue any then-ongoing discussions with third parties.

The Fiduciary Out Provision

The second provision of note in a merger agreement is the fiduciary out. These provisions come in many different flavors, but they drive to the same end. Specifically, the provision is designed to ameliorate the possibility that an unexpected and unsolicited superior bid might arise that the board would otherwise be prohibited from considering by the no shop. Thus, these provisions typically provide that if an unsolicited bid is made, the board is permitted to consider such bid if certain conditions are met. Typically the key condition that unlocks the ability of the board to consider and discuss such bids (notwithstanding the prohibitions of the no shop) is advice by a recognized investment banker that the unsolicited bid is likely to or could develop into a "superior proposal" (often defined as economically superior and likely to be able to be accomplished) and advice from an outside lawyer to the effect that the board's fiduciary duties require it to consider the unsolicited bid.

Key Notice Provisions

Use of the fiduciary out often comes with certain ancillary obligations. For example, most fiduciary out provisions are coupled with a requirement that the bidder in contract be given "prompt" notice of any action by the board to exercise its rights to consider an unsolicited bid under the fiduciary out provision.

Match Rights

Similarly, where, after engaging with an unsolicited bidder in compliance with the fiduciary out provisions of the contract, the board determines that such bid is indeed a "superior" one and votes to proceed to terminate the merger agreement to take the new bid, most contracts will require notice of that determination to be given to the initial bidder in contract, and that initial bidder will often have a specified period of time, typically three to five days, to "match" the "superior proposal," which returns the parties to their positions prior to the emergence of the unsolicited bid, with the contract showing the new and higher price.

At this juncture, the board is no longer permitted to continue its discussion with the unsolicited bidder, in that it no longer has a bid on the table that is or could reasonably become "superior." Instead, the unsolicited bidder must take action to make a new unsolicited bid, and the process previously described then starts anew.

Break-Up Fee Provisions

Alternatively, the original bidder in contract may choose not to exercise its "match rights." At that point, the board is typically permitted to terminate the initial merger contract upon the payment of a contractually agreed-upon break-up fee (sometimes called a liquidated damages provision). As a general guideline, the courts tend to regard a break-up fee in the realm of 2 to 3 percent of equity value as not unreasonable. While larger amounts have been approved (typically on smaller deals), the idea here is economic—the break-up fee needs to be large enough to compensate the original bidder for the loss of its transaction, but not so large as to prevent a bona fide unsolicited third-party bidder from paying a higher price to all shareholders.

Reverse Break-Up Fee Provisions

In addition to the break-up fee just described, a separate fee is sometimes included in M&A contracts where the parties are expecting some antitrust or other regulatory risk. This fee is often called the reverse break-up fee. The "reverse" break-up fee is typically triggered where a buyer is unable to get regulatory clearance to buy the target, notwithstanding its best efforts to do so. Unlike the "forward" break-up fee, which is designed to compensate the disappointed buyer without precluding the opportunity for all shareholders to enjoy the premium offered by the third party, the reverse break-up fee is designed to compensate the seller for having to hold itself off the market for control for some considerable period of time while the parties deal with the antitrust authorities and the likely market perception that the seller is now "damaged goods." Accordingly, the 2 to 3 percent of equity value guidelines that have grown up around acceptable forward break-up fees do not apply to the reverse break-up fee. Instead, the fee is universally a subject of contentious negotiations, with fees in the 9 to 10 percent range not being unusual, especially where the regulatory risk was well known at the outset.

Crown Jewel Asset Provisions

A corollary to the idea that the board cannot disable itself from selling the company to an unsolicited higher bidder by agreeing to "preclusive" provisions in the contract is the idea that a board cannot agree to strip out and sell the key assets of the company to protect a favorable sale of control contract. The so-called crown jewel option, which was an M&A fixture in the early 1980s before many of the current "rules of the road" were developed, is no longer common. We note it here, however, as a cautionary note for the director faced with an aggressive purchaser.

Conditions to Closing

Finally, the board charged with overseeing the sale of a company will often be required to contend with a mass of "closing conditions," which, if crafted poorly, could make the M&A contract more like a buyer's option than a firm contract, necessitating some degree of diligence by the board to such conditions. In the area of regulated industry M&A, deal lawyers often spend significant periods of time negotiating the conditions that must be met in order for the buyer to be forced to go forward with a deal. Thus, environmental or antitrust conditions might take on special significance in a deal, depending on the unique issues at the company or its marketplace. We leave further discussion of this specialized area of M&A to counsel to the board at the time a deal arises.

But without regard to specialized regulatory provisions, almost every contract for the sale of control of a company provides the buyer with an out for truly unanticipated and significant adverse events. These provisions are known as material adverse change (MAC) or material adverse event (MAE) provisions.

Material Adverse Event or Change (MAE and MAC) Clauses

What happens to a deal that is likely to take six months—or longer—to get from signing to closing? Hopefully, management carries on in the ordinary course, and the company that the buyer negotiated to purchase is in at least as good a condition at closing as during the buyer's diligence. But what if fate intervenes and the company's key refinery burns to the ground during the interim? What if the U.S. (or a foreign) government announces the (very negative) results of an investigation of the company during the period between signing and closing? What if the business simply trends down sharply?

M&A practitioners have developed specific clauses to deal with anticipated potential issues. But sometimes a company's fate can be truly unanticipated. In order to deal with truly unanticipated events, which are likely to impact the company for a long period of time in a material (and negative) way, M&A practitioners have developed the MAC or MAE clause (the two are sometimes discussed interchangeably). Put most simply, the MAC or MAE clause gives the buyer the right to walk away from the deal where an unanticipated, material, and durationally significant change has occurred to the company prior to closing.

Of course, such clauses come in many flavors and may be as specific as the negotiators agree. From the director's point of view, the importance of the provision revolves around the degree to which it imperils certainty of close and the degree to which it deviates from the "traditional" form of clause. In all cases, this is a matter about which well-informed directors will want to ask for counsel from their M&A experts prior to approving a merger agreement.

Key Questions

To enhance their understanding of an M&A transaction under review, a director may wish to ask the following questions:

- ❑ To what degree do the "deal protection" devices in this merger agreement deviate from the "middle-of-the-road" agreement? In whose favor? Why?
- ❑ What is the amount of the break-up fee and how is it calculated? What is counsel's judgment about whether the record of negotiation of that fee is sufficient to withstand judicial inquiry? Is the fee itself in any sense preclusive of a higher unsolicited deal emerging?
- ❑ Is there a reverse break-up fee? If so, what is it and how was it calculated? What is it designed to protect? Does it do so?
- ❑ What are the conditions to closing or other provisions of this agreement that make closing less than certain? Are they necessary? If so, why?
- ❑ Explain the MAE or MAC clause to me. What does it cover and why? How close to standard or unusual is this particular provision?

Additional Reading

1. Varallo, Gregory V., and Rudolph Koch, "Deal Protection Devices Enforced in the Delaware Court of Chancery," *Insights* (March 2010).
2. Varallo, Gregory V., and Blake Rohrbacher, "Lessons from the Meltdown: Material Adverse Effect Clauses," *Deal Lawyers* (Jan.–Feb. 2009).
3. Varallo, Gregory V., and Blake Rohrbacher, "Lessons from the Meltdown: Reverse Termination Fees," *Deal Lawyers* (Nov.–Dec. 2008).
4. Zeberkiewicz, John Mark, "Chancery Court Addresses Revlon Duties and Deal Protection Measures in Small-Cap Transaction," *Delaware Business Court Insider* (May 11, 2011).

Notes

6.6 INDEMNITY IN THE M&A CONTEXT

CONTRIBUTED BY
Fritz Lark and Ryan M. Philp
Bracewell LLP[1]

When a board of directors is asked to consider a significant M&A transaction involving the corporation, the concept of indemnification can arise in two distinct contexts. The first relates to the indemnification obligations that the corporation and its counterparty have to each other for breaches of the transaction agreement. The second relates to the obligations of the corporation (and its successor, if applicable) to indemnify its directors and officers against claims relating to their exercise of duties owed to the corporation. Indemnification issues in both contexts require careful consideration.

Indemnification provisions often are a key feature of transaction agreements relating to M&A transactions. As a general matter, these indemnification provisions require each party to compensate or reimburse the other party after the closing of the transaction for losses arising out of breaches of the transaction agreement, including breaches of a party's representations and warranties made in the agreement. The indemnification provisions

1. Fritz Lark, a partner in the corporate group at the New York City office of Bracewell LLP, represents clients on a broad range of transactions and corporate governance matters, and frequently advises clients on mergers and acquisitions in the energy and utility industries. Ryan M. Philp, a partner in the litigation group at the New York City office of Bracewell LLP, concentrates his practice on litigation and counseling in the areas of corporate governance, securities litigation, and other business disputes.

may provide the parties' sole and exclusive remedies after the closing for breaches of the transaction agreement (such as breaches of representations, warranties, and covenants in the transaction agreement), and the parties may waive their rights to otherwise seek damages in breach of contract, tort, and other claims in favor of the indemnities provided. However, the parties' indemnification obligations also are usually subject to a number of significant limitations, with common limitations including a deductible or threshold level of losses that must be suffered before an indemnity claim may be made; a minimum size of indemnity claim limitation to bar "nuisance" claims; a cap on the aggregate amount of indemnification that a party can be required to provide; limitations on the periods in which claims may be made after closing (often referred to as "survival" periods); and limitations on the types of damages for which a claim may be made in order to exclude consequential, special, and exemplary damages, among others. These various limitations are discussed in greater detail below.

Because indemnity provisions can severely restrict available post-closing remedies, the board of directors of an acquiring corporation should be sure to understand the key terms of those provisions. Conversely, the selling corporation's board should be sure to understand the extent to which the indemnification provisions (including the various limitations previously noted) limit or expand the selling corporation's potential exposure to post-closing claims. In consultation with their respective legal advisors, the boards of directors of both parties to a transaction should evaluate whether the indemnification provisions strike an appropriate balance that gives their respective companies adequate protection should issues arise post-closing; the foregoing overview highlights certain key elements that should be considered in making this assessment.

Common Indemnity Provisions

The selling corporation frequently will seek to cap its aggregate indemnity obligation at some percentage of the transaction price. This will be a highly negotiated provision; the amount of the cap will depend upon the nature and size of the transaction. The cap is frequently established by reference to "market standards" reflected in published reports of comparable transactions. It is customary to exclude certain indemnity obligations from this type of cap, such as liabilities that relate to "fundamental" matters, such as the selling corporation's power and authority to engage in the sale transaction.

The selling corporation also commonly will seek to have a deductible or "basket" applied to its indemnity obligations. As the name suggests, this is intended to protect the target against a series of small claims that ultimately are not material. Once again, the amount of the basket is highly negotiated. Baskets come in two forms—tipping and non-tipping. A non-tipping basket is a true deductible. For example, if the basket were $100,000, the target would not be responsible for claims until they reached that level. With a tipping basket, once the total amount of the claims equal the amount of the basket, the buyer is permitted to recover either on a "first dollar" basis or some portion thereof.

Indemnity provisions sometimes include de minimis exclusions as well. These are sometimes referred to as mini-baskets and are intended to ensure that only significant claims are presented. By way of example, you could have a $100,000,000 transaction, with a $10,000,000 cap, a $100,000 basket, and a $10,000 de minimis threshold, preventing claims below $10,000 from being presented in any fashion.

The selling corporation also will seek to have the indemnity provisions in the agreement be the sole and exclusive remedy available to the buyer after the closing of the transaction. This is intended to prevent the buyer from circumventing the indemnification cap, basket, and other provisions by bringing legal claims under alternative theories, such as tort claims.

The acquiring corporation typically will seek exceptions to some or all of the foregoing limitations, including any exclusivity provisions. Common exceptions relate to fraud, intentional misrepresentation, claims for taxes, claims under certain fundamental representations (such as ownership of the stock or assets being sold), and sometimes claims for environmental or known risks. The nature and extent of the exceptions is highly negotiated in many transactions. In the case of fraud, the selling corporation sometimes seeks to define "fraud" for purposes of the exception to ensure that a broad interpretation of the fraud exception does not end up thwarting the exclusivity of the indemnity remedy.

The process for resolving indemnification claims is another issue that is frequently addressed in the transaction documents. Often, the agreements provide for mediation, arbitration, or resolution of financial claims by independent third-party experts.

Another often included provision limits "survival" of the representations and warranties in the transaction agreement. In order to provide some finality to the process, transaction agreements generally will provide that claims for indemnification must be presented within a defined time period following the closing. Typical survival periods range from one year to three years with respect to general claims, although the nature and extent of exceptions can be a highly negotiated area. The acquiring corporation often will seek to have indemnity claims for taxes, fundamental representations, and environmental matters, among others, survive for a longer time frame.

Depending upon the creditworthiness of the selling corporation, and its anticipated ability to meet its indemnity obligations following the closing, the acquiring corporation may seek some type of assurance that sufficient funds will be available to satisfy the seller's indemnity obligations if a claim is made. This can take the form of a guarantee from a creditworthy affiliate of the seller, a purchase price holdback (in which the acquirer retains a portion of the purchase price), or often, an escrow of some portion of the sale price for some period of time. The terms and conditions of the escrow arrangements are relatively standard, and it is not uncommon to see multiple release provisions in these escrow arrangements, where portions of the escrow funds are released in stages if there are no pending claims against the escrow funds.

A well-informed board of directors will request that counsel provide a reasonably detailed summary of the indemnification provisions included in the transaction agreement. From the selling corporation's perspective, the board will want to assess the risk that indemnification provisions present with respect to whether the full purchase price will be received. Conversely, from the point of view of the acquiring corporation, the board will want to ensure that adequate protection exists.

Finally, in some circumstances, the parties negotiate special indemnification provisions with respect to certain known risks such as litigation and governmental investigations. These special indemnification provisions are commonly not subject to the basket, cap, or other limiting provisions, and essentially represent separate and independent agreements to provide indemnification with respect to a known risk.

Director Indemnity

The second context in which indemnification arises with respect to M&A transactions relates to a corporation's indemnification of its directors and officers. Most corporations indemnify their directors and officers against claims arising out of conduct within the scope of their position. In the context of an M&A transaction, directors—and, in particular, directors of public companies—frequently face claims that they breached their fiduciary duties in approving the transaction. Such claims typically implicate the directors' rights to indemnification and advancement of expenses under the company's organizational documents, which commonly require that indemnification be provided to the fullest extent permitted by applicable law. A corporation also may enter into stand-alone indemnification agreements with its directors to provide them with greater comfort and certainty that their rights to indemnification cannot be modified without their consent. In addition, a corporation may be required under certain circumstances to provide indemnification to its directors under the state corporation statute of the corporation's jurisdiction of incorporation. The state corporation statute also generally provides the circumstances under which the corporation is permitted (as opposed to required) to indemnify its directors, and limitations on the corporation's right to provide indemnification—for example, if a director is found not to have acted in good faith or has improperly received a personal benefit from the transaction. In light of these indemnification obligations, corporations often purchase insurance to cover the costs associated with these obligations (referred to as D&O insurance), which provides the indemnified directors comfort that the corporation's obligations will be met in the event that the indemnification is called upon at a time when the corporation is unwilling or unable to make the necessary funds available.

In the context of a significant M&A transaction, the directors of a corporation that will be undergoing a change of control may be subject to a heightened risk of breach of fiduciary duty claims yet also face uncertainty regarding available indemnification after the change of control occurs. This is because the availability of indemnification typically is assessed at the time a claim is made rather than when the underlying conduct at issue took place. As such, directors of a corporation in this position may be concerned that the new owner of the corporation may elect not to provide indemnification that is permitted, but not required, by statute, or may amend the corporation's organizational documents to otherwise reduce the corporation's indemnification obligations. These concerns are often addressed in a special post-closing covenant in the M&A transaction agreement that (i) prohibits the corporation from amending its organizational documents after the closing in a way that would impair its indemnification obligations, and/or (ii) provides for the purchase of a D&O insurance "tail policy" which provides continuing D&O coverage to the acquired corporation's directors with respect to claims relating to pre-closing actions. In addition, the corporation being acquired may seek releases in the transaction agreement from the acquirer with regard to post-closing claims against the acquired corporation's directors to ensure that they are not subject to claims individually. These types of provisions, ideally coupled with a stand-alone indemnification agreement that has continuing effect after the closing of the transaction, offer the most comprehensive protection to the acquired corporation's directors.

Key Questions

To better understand indemnity issues, a director may wish to ask the following questions:

- ❑ Does the transaction agreement provide for indemnities or any other post-closing remedies for the corporation?
- ❑ Is the party providing the indemnity creditworthy? If not, has a guarantee or other credit support been provided?
- ❑ What are the limitations on the corporation's ability to make indemnification claims? Are there limits as to the amount that can be claimed, the timing of making a claim, or the types of claims that can be brought?
- ❑ Have any special indemnities been included with respect to particular concerns that were identified in due diligence?
- ❑ Is indemnification the exclusive remedy available to the corporation after closing? Are there exceptions that would permit additional recovery?
- ❑ Is the corporation being asked to provide indemnification after the closing to the counterparty? If so, what limitations have been negotiated? What is the likelihood that an indemnification claim will be made? Have the corporation's management and advisors carefully reviewed the corporation's representations in the transaction agreement to ensure their accuracy?
- ❑ What indemnification is available to directors in connection with the transaction? Does state law mandate or permit director indemnification?
- ❑ What are the statutory limitations on director indemnification?
- ❑ Do the corporation's organizational documents provide for indemnification of directors? If so, what are the restrictions on amending those provisions?
- ❑ Has the corporation entered into individual indemnification agreements with directors? If not, have they been considered?
- ❑ Is the corporation obligated to advance funds to directors to cover expenses prior to final resolution of a claim? If so, are there any circumstances in which advances would not be available?
- ❑ Has management or an outside advisor provided an overview of the indemnification available to the corporation's directors, the corporation's D&O insurance coverage, and the process for accessing indemnification and insurance in the event of a claim?
- ❑ Has legal counsel reviewed the applicable obligations and duties of directors in connection with the transaction?
- ❑ Will the corporation's financial advisor provide a fairness opinion with respect to the transaction? If not, was a fairness opinion considered? If so, did the board consider any potential conflicts of interest? Was a second fairness opinion considered?
- ❑ Will any of the corporation's other advisors provide opinions or reports to the board with respect to the transaction?
- ❑ For a director of an acquired corporation, does the transaction agreement include provisions preserving the directors' rights to indemnification? Will a D&O insurance "tail policy" be purchased for the benefit of directors?

Additional Reading

1. *Not Just Belt and Suspenders: Indemnification Agreements and State Corporate Law*
   http://www.alston.com/Files/Publication/0f8ccedc-31f1-4b4a-8d26-3ba9b160adba/Presentation/PublicationAttachment/559ea044-8264-4841-a265-03d664b25a3f/Sawicki-07_05_09.pdf
2. *Trends in M&A Provisions: Indemnification as an Exclusive Remedy*
   http://www.bna.com/trends-in-ma-provisions-indemnification-as-an-exclusive-remedy/
3. *Top Ten Indemnification Concerns in M&A Transactions*
   http://www.acc.com/legalresources/publications/topten/top-ten-indemnification-concerns.cfm
4. *Indemnification in Delaware: Balancing Policy Goals and Liabilities*
   http://www.djcl.org/wp-content/uploads/2014/08/INDEMNIFICATION-IN-DELAWARE-BALANCING-POLICY-GOALS-AND-LIABILITIES.pdf
5. *Executive Protection: D&O Insurance—The Insuring Agreement*
   http://www.dandodiary.com/2010/08/articles/d-o-insurance/executive-protection-do-insurance-the-insuring-agreement/

Notes

6.7 MANAGING A FAILED BUSINESS COMBINATION

CONTRIBUTED BY
Frank M. Placenti
Squire Patton Boggs (US) LLP[1]

When a business combination fails, both the erstwhile buyer and seller can be presented with difficult strategic, management, and operational choices.

The extent of the challenges facing the seller's board will be dependent upon the circumstances. If the transaction was being pursued by the seller to provide liquidity for investors, alternatives will need to be considered, and the willingness of the investors to remain patient for another exit opportunity needs to be discerned.

If the sale was being pursued because the company simply could not independently compete in the current market conditions and more fundamental challenges were presented, alternative business strategies may be required. In some cases, a sale was being pursued because the company was facing imminent debt payment obligations that could not be refinanced or met. In such situations, a financial restructuring (outside or within the bankruptcy process) may need to be considered.

Depending upon how far along down the line the transaction had proceeded, the seller's management team may be fatigued and demoralized. In some cases, managers

1. Frank M. Placenti is a partner in the corporate practice of Squire Patton Boggs (US) LLP, where he leads the firm's U.S. governance practice.

who were looking at a substantive liquidity event may have difficulty refocusing and getting their "head in the game." The board may need to reshape and refresh the management team, particularly where hiring decisions had been deferred pending potential sale, or the process revealed weaknesses. The board may need to also consider re-evaluating and reconfiguring management incentive compensation.

In certain circumstances, the seller's board may perceive that the management team simply did not present the company well in the sales process. That may present issues of training and/or motivation, or it may suggest an absence of aligned incentives.

The Buyer's Perspective

From the buyer's perspective, the nature of the issues presented to the board will be dependent upon the rational for the acquisition. If the target was being pursued as part of a "build or buy" decision, the board, in conjunction with management, will need to determine whether now to proceed with the "build" alternative or whether a different target can be pursued to meet the buyer's needs.

If the transaction failed for other reasons, including a substandard process, that will need to be evaluated, particularly if the buyer is a serial acquirer.

If the target was purchased by a competitor, the buyer may be facing new strategic threats that may require reconfiguration of product offerings, outreach communications with customers, or other activities to shore up its competitive position.

In the event the transaction had been publicly announced, both the buyer and the seller will need to consider appropriate communications with various constituencies, including customers, suppliers, and employees. Unrest may need to be quelled.

Transactions fail for as many reasons as there are types of transactions. When they do fail, however, the board should be alert for the contributing causes, as well as the activities that need to be undertaken in order to minimize the fallout.

Key Questions

When a transaction fails, a board may wish to consider the following:

- ❑ What strategic initiatives should be considered as an alternative to the transaction?
- ❑ What communication plans may need to be undertaken with respect to the company's customers, suppliers, or employees who are aware of the transaction?
- ❑ What changes in the seller's management team are to be undertaken, if any?
- ❑ Is any refreshing of the management's incentive compensation plan appropriate? If the seller is now going to "hunker down for the long haul" are there any changes in the board composition that are required?
- ❑ Will the failed seller now need additional capital in order to successfully compete in the marketplace? What will be the sources of that capital?
- ❑ From the buyer's perspective, what competitive threats are presented by the failure of the transaction, if any? How would they be dealt with?

- ❑ Were there any flaws in the process? For a serial acquirer, what does that suggest about process changes?
- ❑ Should the buyer actually view the failure of the transaction as a success, in that it demonstrated price discipline or other appropriate discernment by management?

Additional Reading

1. Michel, Allen and Israel Shaked, "Lessons from Failed Corporate Marriages." *Strategy and Business* (October 1, 1996)
   http://www.strategy-business.com/article/12321?gko=51b520

Notes

6.8 RELATED PARTY TRANSACTIONS

CONTRIBUTED BY
Katayun I. Jaffari and Zachary Gorman
Ballard Spahr LLP[1]

Related party transactions appear in many corporate contexts: a director may be an executive officer of a large customer of the company; the company might seek to sell a subsidiary to a significant shareholder; or the CEO's daughter might be employed by or doing business with the company. Directors must be able to identify related party transactions and ensure proper procedures are in place to review, negotiate, and, where appropriate, disclose such transactions. This chapter provides a brief introduction to related party transactions, including disclosure requirements and suggested corporate policies and procedures addressing such transactions.

As mentioned throughout this Handbook, directors owe fiduciary duties (the duty of care and loyalty) to the corporation. Related party transactions—that is, those transactions involving the company on one hand and its directors, executive officers, significant shareholders and their respective immediate family members on the other hand—implicate the duty of loyalty. Specifically, such transactions call into question the director's ability to make decisions based on the company's best interest rather than her own interests.

1. Katayun I. Jaffari is a partner and Zachary Gorman is an associate in the Business and Finance Department of Ballard Spahr LLP, where they practice in the firm's Philadelphia office.

The duty of care is also implicated even for nonconflicted directors, as they must sufficiently inform themselves about the transactions and any available alternatives in order to act upon them appropriately.

Related party transactions trigger disclosure obligations under federal securities laws and are regulated under public company listing regulations. Companies are required to disclose information about related party transactions as well as company policies and procedures regarding such transactions in their annual proxy statements on Schedule 14A and in their annual reports on Form 10-K. In addition, companies are required to disclose such information in 1933 Act and 1934 Act registration statements when selling and registering securities.

Under Item 404(a) of Regulation S-K, a company must disclose any transaction since the beginning of the company's last fiscal year, or any currently proposed transaction in which (i) the company was (or will be) a participant, (ii) the amount involved exceeds $120,000, and (iii) any related person had (or will have) a direct or indirect material interest. A "related person" includes any director or executive officer of the company, any director nominee or a 5 percent shareholder, and immediate family members of these individuals. In the event a related party transaction must be disclosed, the company must disclose the person's name and relationship to the company, such person's interest in the transaction, the approximate dollar amount involved, and other information that is material to investors under the circumstances.

There are a number of exceptions to Item 404(a) where disclosure is not required. Compensation to named executive officers or directors disclosed under Item 402 of Regulation S-K is not required to be disclosed under Item 404. Compensation of executive officers other than named executive officers does not need to be disclosed under Item 404(a) provided that the executive officer is not an immediate family member of another executive officer or director of the company, the compensation would be reported in the proxy statement if the executive officer was a "named executive officer," and the company's compensation committee approved such compensation. Additionally, a person who has a position or relationship with an entity that engages in a transaction with the company does not have an indirect material interest where the interest arises only from (i) the person's position as a director of another company that is a party to the transaction or (ii) the ownership by such person and all other related persons in the aggregate of less than a 10 percent equity interest in another person who is a party to the transaction. Moreover, disclosure is not necessary where rates charged in the transaction with a related party are determined by competitive bids.

In addition to disclosing the specific transaction, Item 404(b) of Regulation S-K requires companies to describe their policies and procedures for the review and approval or ratification of any transaction required to be reported under Item 404(a). Specifically, companies should describe the types of transactions covered by such policies and procedures, the standards used in connection with such policies, and the board members who are responsible for administering such policies and procedures. Item 404(b)(2) requires companies to identify any transaction required to be reported under Item 404(a) since the beginning of the company's last fiscal year where such policies and procedures did not require review, approval, or ratification, or where such policies and procedures were not followed.

Item 404 of Regulation S-K overlaps with regulations addressing conflicts of interest under stock exchange rules. Under Section 314 of the NYSE Listed Company Manual, each related party transaction is required to be reviewed and evaluated by an appropriate group (such as the audit committee) within the company to determine whether the particular relationship serves the best interest of the company and its shareholders. Under NASDAQ Rule 5630, either the company's audit committee or another independent body of the board of directors is required to conduct an appropriate review and oversight of all related party transactions for potential conflict of interest situations on an ongoing basis. Directors must also keep in mind that related party transactions involving a director implicates that director's independence under NYSE, NASDAQ, and SEC rules. In addition, proper treatment of such transactions is critical to good investor relations.

Related party transactions are also subject to exacting review from independent auditors. In 2015, the Public Company Accounting Oversight Board adopted Auditing Standard No. 18, *Related Parties* (ASC No. 18), to address the increased risks of material misstatements in company financial statements resulting from related party transactions. Under ASC No. 18, auditors are required to perform procedures and conduct diligence to obtain an understanding of the company's relationships and transactions with its related parties that might reasonably be expected to affect the risks of material misstatements of financial statements. Among other requirements of ASC No. 18, auditors are required to evaluate whether the company has identified its relationships and transactions with all related parties and followed specific procedures regarding each related party transaction required to be disclosed in the financial statements or determined to be a significant risk. Auditors are also required to discuss with the audit committee its understanding of related party transactions that are significant to the issuer and whether any member of the committee has concerns regarding such transactions.

The following questions are intended to help directors identify related party transactions and ensure that the board has appropriate policies and procedures in place for the review and, where required, disclosure of such transactions.

Key Questions

Key questions in identifying related party transactions that companies include in director and officer questionnaires include the following:

- ❑ Have there been any transactions (or series of similar transactions) since the beginning of the last fiscal year (or any proposed transactions) to which the company or any subsidiary was a participant in which the amount involved exceeds $120,000 and in which a director, director nominee, executive officer, a 5 percent shareholder, or an immediate family member of one of these individuals has a (or will have) a direct or indirect material interest?
- ❑ Is any director, director nominee, executive officer, 5 percent shareholder, or immediate family member of one of these individuals indebted to the company or any of its subsidiaries in an aggregate amount in excess of $120,000?
- ❑ Have any family members of a director, director nominee, executive officer, or 5% shareholder been employed by or acted as consultant to the company or

any subsidiary at any time since the beginning of the company's last fiscal year and is such family member expected to receive annual compensation in excess of $120,000?

- ❑ Since the beginning of the company's last fiscal year, has the director or director nominee been an executive officer of or owned more than 10 percent equity interest in any business
  - that has made payments to the company or any of its subsidiaries for property or services during the last fiscal year?
  - to which the company or any of its subsidiaries has made payments for property or services during the last fiscal year?
  - that proposes to make payments to the company or any of its subsidiaries for property or services during the upcoming fiscal year?
  - to which the company or any of its subsidiaries proposes to make payments for property or services during the upcoming fiscal year?
  - to which the company or any of its subsidiaries was indebted?
- ❑ Since the beginning of the company's last fiscal year, has the director or director nominee been a member of, or counsel to, a law firm that the company has retained in the last fiscal year or intends to retain during the upcoming fiscal year?
- ❑ Since the beginning of the company's last fiscal year, has the director or director nominee been a partner or executive officer of any investment banking firm that has performed services for the company (other than as a participating underwriter in a syndicate) during the last fiscal year or that the company proposes to have perform services during the upcoming fiscal year?

Key questions regarding related party policies and procedures may include the following:

- ❑ Does the company have a related party transactions policy? Code of conduct?
- ❑ Has the board delegated administration and enforcement of said policy to the appropriate committee, typically the audit committee or corporate governance committee?
- ❑ Are the appropriate types of transactions pre-approved under the policy for ease of administration purposes?
- ❑ Does the related party transactions policy (and, if applicable, the company code of conduct) establish adequate procedures for reporting potential related person transactions?
- ❑ Does the policy provide for adequate procedures for the review of related party transactions by the appropriate independent committee of the board?
- ❑ How does the related party transaction policy fit with the company's code of conduct and other company policies addressing conflicts of interest?
- ❑ Does the policy require the board or committee to assess ongoing related party transactions on a recurring basis (such as annually)?
- ❑ Does the D&O questionnaire adequately address the related party disclosure requirements?
- ❑ Has the director fully and accurately completed the D&O questionnaire?

Additional Reading

1. Item 404 of Regulation S-K—Transactions with Related Persons, Promoters and Certain Control Persons, *Securities and Exchange Commission Compliance and Disclosure Interpretations*
   https://www.sec.gov/divisions/corpfin/guidance/execcomp404interp.htm
2. *Auditing Standard No. 18 (Related Parties)*
   https://pcaobus.org/Standards/Auditing/Pages/Auditing_Standard_18.aspx
3. *NASDAQ Listing Rules*
   http://nasdaq.cchwallstreet.com/NASDAQTools/PlatformViewer.asp?selectednode=chp_1_1_1_1&manual=%2Fnasdaq%2Fmain%2Fnasdaq-equityrules%2F
4. *NYSE Listed Company Manual*
   http://nysemanual.nyse.com/LCM/Sections/
5. *Related Party Transactions Disclosure Checklist*, The Corporate Counsel
   http://www.thecorporatecounsel.net/member/FAQ/Checklists/RelatedPartyTransactions.pdf
6. *Related Party Transactions Disclosure Handbook*, The Corporate Counsel
   http://www.thecorporatecounsel.net/GreatGovernance/member/handbook/Related.pdf
7. *Sample Related Party Transactions Policies and Procedures*, The Corporate Counsel
   http://www.thecorporatecounsel.net/member/FAQ/RPTransactions/policies.htm

Notes

___

___

___

___

___

6.9 LOAN AGREEMENTS AND FINANCING TRANSACTIONS

CONTRIBUTED BY
Vikas Varma
Crush & Varma Law Group P.C.[1]

Serving on a corporate board can present challenging issues, particularly when the company's activities require external financing. Yet, at some time during their life cycle, most companies will need to secure debt financing to maintain an adequate amount of cash to fund their operations. If financings are not thoughtfully done, tremendous value can be destroyed for existing equity holders.

In addition to traditional term loan arrangements, a company can resort to various other types of financing transactions, such as factoring of receivables, credit line, letters of credit, or overdraft agreements, to meet its cash flow needs. Although loan and other financing documents are reviewed and negotiated by executives, counsel for the company, and third-party experts, a board member should, as required by the duty of care, review such documents (or summaries thereof) and conduct appropriate due diligence of

1. Vikas Varma is a partner at the law firm of Crush & Varma Law Group P.C., where he practices in the areas of commercial transactions and business finance. Mr. Varma has been the lead counsel in numerous acquisition, joint venture, and financing transactions for various U.S., Indian, and multinational corporations. He has extensive experience in structuring and negotiating share-purchase agreements, joint ventures, and cross-border business transactions, with emphasis on investment in and from South Asia. Mr. Varma received his Masters of Laws (LL.M.) degree, with concentration in International Business Practice, from Boston University School of Law, where he was the recipient of the Sebastian Horsten Prize for Academic Achievement.

the transaction. It is a collective duty of the board to provide oversight and direction to the executives negotiating the transaction.

The board should request company counsel to negotiate all reasonable changes necessary to achieve the objectives of the company. Needless to say, the extent of negotiations and bargaining power of the company to command changes in the lender's "standard" documentation will depend on factors like size of the loan, relationship with the lender and size of the lender to parties' respective leverage, and the borrower's financial condition.

While reviewing and deliberating upon any loan or financing transaction, and requesting any changes to the draft documentation, the board member should keep the following key objectives of the transaction in mind:

- Procure sufficient financing to meet the short-term and long-term needs of the company.
- Procure financing at the most beneficial terms then available to the company.
- Ensure that the proposed transaction or the terms of the loan or financing documents do not adversely affect the business of the company or restrict its ability to thrive.

Key Questions

The following provides a non-exhaustive list of questions a board member may wish to consider in reviewing a loan agreement or other financing transaction:

Corporate Governance Issues

- ❑ Do I have enough information to make an informed decision? If not, what additional information do I need?
- ❑ What is the purpose of the loan or financing transaction? Is it within the strategic plan and/or advance-approved goals and objectives?
- ❑ If the purpose of the loan is to finance an acquisition, has appropriate due diligence been completed for the acquisition?
- ❑ Is the transaction recommended by required committees of the company, for example, the executive committee or finance committee?
- ❑ Is the transaction recommended by independent third parties' advisors and experts?
- ❑ Are there any conflict of interest issues? Do I, or any of my fellow board members, have (or appear to have) a personal interest in the transaction? Should that director participate in our deliberations? Abstain from voting?
- ❑ Do any of the other board members, officers, or third-party financial advisors have any personal interest in the transaction?
- ❑ What are the alternative financing mechanisms available to the company besides the proposed financing transaction? Have those alternatives been explored and evaluated by the company? Am I in agreement with the choice being recommended?
- ❑ What will be the effect of the transaction on the market image of the company? Could it be perceived negatively (e.g., the company is having financial troubles)?
- ❑ Are there reasonably available alternatives?

Transaction Specific Issues

- ❑ What are the different types of financing arrangements (revolving credit line, letters of credit, term loan, etc.) available to the company?
- ❑ What will be the annual cost of servicing the debt? How will that affect the projected financials of the company? Can the company service that level of debt? What sensitivity analysis has been performed?
- ❑ Is the debt secured or unsecured? What assets of the company are being collateralized under the transaction?
- ❑ What will be the effect of debt on earnings per share?
- ❑ If the purpose of the loan or financial transaction is to finance a capital acquisition, what will be the return on investment and is it reasonable?
- ❑ Will the proposed loan or financial transaction, together with other collateralized debt obligations of the company, violate any financial covenants of the company under any agreement to which the company is a party?
- ❑ Is the execution of the loan agreement or any other financing document in violation of any law applicable to the company or any contractual obligation of the company?
- ❑ What will be the tax effects of the proposed financing? Will the proposed transaction lead to tax benefits or tax impositions?
- ❑ Are the terms of the loan agreement or financing documents consistent with the term sheet or commitment letter approved by the board?
- ❑ What will be the closing costs for the loan or the financing transaction? Have all "soft" costs been accounted for?
- ❑ Are there any regulatory issues to be considered? Are there any disclosures or reporting requirements pursuant to securities laws that the company must comply with?
- ❑ Are operating covenants being imposed on the company under the loan agreement and other financing documents? Are they reasonable? What is the likelihood the company will be able to comply? What sensitivity analysis has been performed?
- ❑ Are there any financial reporting obligations or compliance tests that the company would have difficulty meeting? Are the standards for testing reasonably objective?
- ❑ If there are financial covenants, have they been reviewed and approved by the chief financial officer of the company (and tested with the effect of the new loan or other financial transaction included)?
- ❑ Is there any covenant in the loan agreement or other financing documents that may interfere with the business operations of the company or impede the ability of the company to adhere to its long-term growth plans?
- ❑ Which executives are managing the transaction? Do they have sufficient experience to manage this type and size transaction? Is there a need to retain expertise of third-party professionals?
- ❑ Does the loan agreement provide an express right of prepayment by the company? If yes, is there any penalty or premium associated with the prepayment of the loan?

- ❑ Do the loan agreement and other financing documents provide adequate grace periods and provide adequate opportunity to cure any breach?
- ❑ What are the "events of default" provisions? Are they carefully negotiated and reasonable?
- ❑ What will be the consequences and effect on the company if the lender accelerates loan repayment or other defaults occur?
- ❑ Do the loan agreement or other financing documents contain anti-debt restrictions? If yes, are there appropriate exceptions to the anti-debt restrictions allowing the company to incur unsecured debt in ordinary course of business, such as purchase money debt and capital leases?
- ❑ In the case of a syndicated loan, are the decisions taken by the lead lender or by majority vote of the lenders?
- ❑ Will the loan be resold? Would loss of a relationship with the original lender change the comfort level with the loan or transaction?
- ❑ If the company is proposing to undergo a merger, acquisition, or any other form of corporate reorganization, does any loan agreement or financing documentation currently in place require approval of the lender or financing entity?

Additional Reading

1. ABA Business Law Section, Committee on Corporate Laws. *Corporate Director's Guidebook*, 6th ed.
2. Oest, John N. "Negotiating the Loan Commitment—The Borrower's Perspective." *Business Law Today* 19 no. 3 (Jan./Feb. 2010).
3. Oest, John N. "Negotiating the Loan Agreement—The Borrower's Perspective Part II." *Business Law Today* (May 2011).

Notes

____

____

____

____

____

SECTION SEVEN

COMPENSATION MATTERS

7.1 THE ROLE OF THE COMPENSATION COMMITTEE

CONTRIBUTED BY
Melodie Rose and Elizabeth Dunshee
Fredrikson & Byron, P.A.[1]

U.S. stock exchanges require almost all listed companies to maintain a compensation committee of independent directors to oversee executive compensation and related matters. The duties of the compensation committee are specified in a written charter.

The committee's role, and thus its charter, will vary somewhat based on the company's circumstances and its board dynamics. Some boards prefer to remain involved in considering compensation arrangements for the CEO and other executives, whereas others prefer to simply receive a committee report on final actions. The desired level of committee involvement in non-officer compensation decisions also varies, as does a board's tendency to delegate additional responsibilities that applicable rules do not expressly require, such as responsibility for executive succession planning. Moreover, companies listed on the New York Stock Exchange are subject to detailed, express requirements for compensation committees, including the requirement to conduct an annual self-evaluation. Committees

1. Melodie Rose is a partner at Fredrikson & Byron, P.A., where she chairs the firm's corporate division and co-chairs the firm's corporate governance practice group with John Stout. Elizabeth Dunshee, a former partner with Fredrikson & Byron, P.A., is Editor at Executive Press, Inc.

for NASDAQ-listed companies are subject to less specific listing standards but are generally charged with similar duties via their charters.

While compensation committee duties are company-specific, many similarities exist. The role of the vast majority of compensation committees is described in the following sections.

Structuring Executive Compensation and Conducting Performance Evaluations

Structuring executive compensation arrangements and evaluating executive performance are fundamental to the compensation committee's existence. The compensation committee should oversee negotiation of executive employment, severance, and change of control agreements, as well as other compensatory matters such as perquisite programs and clawback policies. The committee typically conducts an annual review of executive compensation arrangements, during which it considers adjustments to base salaries, establishes performance goals and payout levels for incentive programs, reviews benefits, and calculates target total compensation for each executive officer for the upcoming fiscal year. With respect to a completed fiscal year, the committee must evaluate company and executive performance in order to determine payout levels under applicable incentive programs. For NASDAQ issuers, voting and deliberations on CEO compensation must occur outside of the CEO's presence. For NYSE issuers, the full board is permitted to discuss CEO compensation but only independent directors are permitted to vote on such matters.

Designing an effective executive compensation program requires balancing the interests of key executives with the interests and perceptions of employees, investors, and other stakeholders. Compensation committees should focus on establishing performance goals that link pay to company strategies and performance, with particular attention to the outcomes and risks that the programs incentivize as well as the company's articulated compensation philosophy and messaging on matters such as internal pay equity. Committees should gather adequate data, engage in a robust decision-making process, and be mindful of potential conflicts of interest in order to satisfy their fiduciary duties of care and loyalty and avoid liability for decisions that are questioned with the benefit of hindsight.

Communicating Compensation Strategies and Decisions

Effective communication underlies all of the compensation committee's responsibilities. SEC and exchange rules require accelerated and large accelerated filers to publish a Compensation Discussion and Analysis (CD&A) on an annual basis, which the compensation committee must review. In addition, all public companies must annually publish detailed executive compensation information, as well as information about compensation committee members and committee activities. Throughout the year, approving material compensatory agreements or non-routine grants to named executive officers may require an announcement within four business days of committee action.

While the CD&A and related proxy statement disclosures are the primary means to communicate with shareholders, it is critical that members of the compensation committee maintain a dialogue with the executive team regarding strategy, goals, performance, and value. In order to encourage positive opinions among employees, investors, and other constituents, compensation committees must explain compensation in a way that highlights its alignment with the company's key philosophies and goals. Finally, proactive communications with legal counsel and compensation consultants can help the committee remain aware of trends and avoid pitfalls that may arise from the complex regulatory and competitive landscape of executive compensation.

Approving Equity Grants and Related Policies

In order to ensure awards are exempt from short-swing trading restrictions and qualify as "performance-based compensation" under tax rules, and to create proper legal and accounting records, it is a best practice to require compensation committee approval of all equity grants to executives and of all management share pools for employee grants. All grants should be made in accordance with the company's equity incentive plan and any equity grant policies, and should ideally be documented in form resolutions that establish all necessary grant information. The committee generally also oversees equity plans, ensuring that adequate shares remain available for grants, that the shares are registered for issuance with the SEC, and that shareholder approval of new or amended plans is obtained in a timely manner.

Evaluating Significant Nonexecutive Compensation Matters and Policies

It is important for the compensation committee to understand whether employee incentive programs and practices motivate the appropriate level of risk-taking within the company, either via direct assessment of such matters or by overseeing management's assessment process. Whether the compensation committee also oversees administration of company-wide compensatory programs, policies, and plans is determined by the board, typically in consultation with the committee, and depends on circumstances such as company size, the number and complexity of company-wide programs, director time constraints, the magnitude and probability of risks relating to nonexecutive compensation programs, and the company's compensation philosophy. If the company maintains plans that are subject to the Employment Retirement Income Security Act of 1974 (ERISA), as amended, it is usually advisable for the committee's role with respect to such plans to be clearly limited to appointment and oversight of an employee or third-party fiduciary in order to avoid incurring significant duties to plan participants.

Retaining and Overseeing Consultants and Advisors

Compensation committees of listed companies are required to have direct responsibility for retaining, compensating, and overseeing compensation consultants, legal counsel, or other advisors, at the committee's discretion. Although the committee is permitted to retain advisors who are not independent, the committee must, prior to retaining or receiving advice from an advisor, consider factors that may affect the provider's independence from the company, executive officers, and compensation committee members.

Further, with respect to compensation consultants, the company's proxy statement must indicate the consultant's name and role and, for consultants who advise the company or its affiliates on matters in addition to executive and director compensation, quantify the consultant's fees, describe the role of management and the board in retaining the consultant, and discuss how the company is addressing any conflict of interest.

Conducting a Regular Charter Review

In light of evolving rules and circumstances applicable to compensation committees and in order to minimize the risk that charter requirements will be overlooked, every compensation committee should regularly review and recommend updates to its charter. A compensation committee's failure to observe its enumerated responsibilities may lead to a violation of listing standards for the company or evidence a lack of due care by the committee.

Key Questions

Questions a board member may wish to consider when participating on a compensation committee include the following:

- ❑ Is the committee's charter reflective of applicable listing standards, SEC rules, preferences of the full board, and actual practices?
- ❑ Have the committee and the board recently discussed the committee's role and responsibilities?
- ❑ Does the committee receive timely updates on developing legal requirements and the company's processes for ensuring compliance?
- ❑ Has the committee recently reviewed the company's compensation philosophy?
- ❑ Are the company's executive compensation programs aligned with its compensation philosophy, strategies, performance, and risk tolerance, and does the company's proxy statement clearly explain this?
- ❑ Does the committee receive assessments from management regarding risk-taking incentives that may result from employee compensation policies and practices?
- ❑ Does the committee oversee risk management practices with respect to compensation policies and practices that are reasonably likely to have a material adverse effect on the company?
- ❑ Do/will the payouts under the company's executive compensation programs correlate with the company's performance and return to shareholders?
- ❑ Does the committee engage in an ongoing dialogue with executive officers regarding establishing and achieving performance goals and other matters that may affect compensation?
- ❑ Does the committee's performance evaluation process for executives provide insight into both quantitative and qualitative factors that will contribute to company success?

- ❑ Does the committee have access to adequate company and market data regarding compensation and related trends?
- ❑ Do any relationships or processes involving the committee and the company's executives or the committee's outside advisors create actual or perceived conflicts of interest, and if so, how has the committee addressed those?
- ❑ Does the company maintain an equity grant policy?
- ❑ Does the committee maintain a governance calendar or other processes to ensure that it is executing all of its responsibilities and work with management to develop meeting agendas?

Additional Reading

1. NYSE, Rule 303A.05 Compensation Committee, New York Stock Exchange Listed Company Manual
   http://nysemanual.nyse.com/lcm/Help/mapContent.asp?sec=lcm-sections&title=sx-ruling-nyse-policymanual_303A.04&id=chp_1_4_3_6 (last visited July 5, 2016)
2. NASDAQ, Rule 5605(d) Compensation Committee Requirements, *Equity Rules*
   http://nasdaq.cchwallstreet.com/NASDAQTools/bookmark.asp?id=nasdaq-rule_5605&manual=/nasdaq/main/nasdaq-equityrules/ (last visited July 5, 2016)
3. Arora, Puneet, et al., "Dodd-Frank's Executive Compensation Provisions: A Progress Report," *Willis Towers Watson* (Nov. 16, 2015)
   https://www.towerswatson.com/en-US/Insights/Newsletters/Americas/insider/2015/11/dodd-frank-executive-compensation-provisions-a-progress-report
4. Dunshee, Elizabeth M., "5 Tips for Successfully Chairing a Public Company Compensation Committee," *Fredrikson & Byron, P.A.* (Jan. 5, 2016)
   http://www.fredlaw.com/news__media/2016/01/05/1096/5_tips_for_successfully_chairing_a_public_company_compensation_committee
5. "Pay Governance, Compensation Committee Responsibilities and Best Practices," *Executive Pay at a Turning Point: Demonstrating Pay For Performance and Other Best Practices in Corporate Governance* (Ira T. Kay ed., 2012) (ebook)
   http://paygovernance.com/chapter-6-compensation-committee-responsibilities-and-best-practices/
6. Wachtell, Lipton, Rosen & Katz, *Compensation Committee Guide* (March 2016)
   http://www.wlrk.com/files/2016/CompensationCommitteeGuide.pdf
7. Skadden, Arps, Slate, Meagher & Flom LLP, *2016 Compensation Committee Handbook* (2nd ed. 2015)
   https://www.skadden.com/insights/2016-compensation-committee-handbook

Notes

7.2 COMPENSATION COMMITTEE COMPOSITION

CONTRIBUTED BY
Melodie Rose and Elizabeth Dunshee
Fredrikson & Byron, P.A.[1]

When appointing directors to the compensation committee, the board must consider the directors' relevant skills, availability, and independence. Overseeing executive compensation can be a demanding, time consuming, and (at times) stressful job. It is therefore essential that committee members are interested in serving and can be available for regular and special committee meetings that may arise if unexpected circumstances require consideration of changes to the compensation programs.

It is beneficial for committee members to have knowledge and experience in compensation and human resource issues. Awareness of evolving investor and public perceptions of compensation issues is also useful.

Committee members should be strong communicators and possess a thorough understanding of the company's strategy and financial performance. Committee members must evaluate recommendations for compensatory programs, approve the company's Compensation Discussion and Analysis (CD&A) and explain compensation decisions to investors. Moreover, it is important for the committee to regularly communicate with the full board

1. Melodie Rose and Elizabeth Dunshee are partners at Fredrikson & Byron, P.A., where they practice in the firm's Minneapolis office. Ms. Rose chairs the firm's corporate division and Ms. Dunshee co-chairs the firm's corporate governance and executive compensation practice groups.

and the corporate secretary, and to be capable of collaborating with management while also being willing to negotiate on the company's behalf and deliver constructive feedback and difficult messages.

In order to avoid stalemate votes and allow the committee to easily convene meetings, most compensation committee charters provide that the committee will consist of three members. Consistent with state corporate law, U.S. stock exchanges generally require that all directors who sit on a listed company's compensation committee be independent from management and the company.

Under NYSE and NASDAQ listing standards, directors qualify as independent only if the board affirmatively determines, based on all relevant circumstances, that they have no relationship with the company that would interfere with their exercise of independent judgment. For example, directors are not considered independent if they or their immediate family members have recently served as executive officers of the company or receive or make significant payments to the company, either directly or through companies with which they are affiliated.

In determining the independence of compensation committee members, listing standards also require boards to consider whether the individual received consulting, advisory, or compensatory fees (other than directors' fees), in any amount and from any person or entity, that would impair his or her ability to make independent judgments about the company's executive compensation. Further, the board must consider whether compensation committee members have any "affiliate" relationships with the company or any of its subsidiaries, such as a significant ownership interest in the company, relationships with company management, or other indications that the individual controls, is controlled by, or is under common control with the company or its subsidiaries.

Although listing standards do not expressly prohibit committee members' consulting and affiliate relationships, companies whose shareholder base includes institutional investors must closely monitor such matters. Proxy advisory firms and many institutional investors discourage any family relationships between committee members and the company's employees, the delivery by a committee member of any professional services to the company, and other relationships between a committee member and the company or its executives. Such organizations may recommend a vote against a committee member's election to the board even when a relatively immaterial relationship exists.

Using an independent compensation committee also allows the company to receive favorable tax treatment for executive awards, ensures that grants do not negatively impact executives' ability to engage in market transactions, and demonstrates that the committee is acting in the best interests of the company. A company's ability to take tax deductions for "performance-based" compensation, which is useful if any executives earn in excess of $1 million per year, and its officers' and directors' ability to sell shares within six months of an equity grant, depends on whether the relevant awards were approved by a committee consisting solely of two or more directors who satisfy enhanced independence criteria. It is typical for the committee's charter to require all committee members to satisfy these criteria, but in the event that is not the case, the charter may permit the committee to form a subcommittee to approve incentive and equity awards.

In order to properly approve performance-based compensation, the directors involved should not be current or former company employees or receive any compensation directly or indirectly from the company other than in their capacity as a director. This would include fees that were paid within the last two years to an entity in which the director has a more than 5 percent ownership interest or is employed or performs significant services. In order to ensure that equity awards do not affect an officer's ability to trade, unless the awards are approved by the full board, the voting directors must not be current employees of the company or any of its parents or subsidiaries or have any interest in transactions involving the company with a value of greater than $120,000 that would require disclosure in the company's proxy statement.

Key Questions

When considering the composition of the compensation committee, directors may want to consider the following:

- ❑ Do the committee's members have the interest and availability to serve on this company's compensation committee?
- ❑ What experience, qualifications, and skills will make committee members well suited to serve on this company's compensation committee?
- ❑ Are the membership requirements imposed by the committee's charter reflective of applicable listing standards, SEC rules, relevant tax code provisions, and actual committee practices?
- ❑ Is it desirable for elements of the company's executive compensation program to qualify as "performance-based" under Section 162(m) of the Internal Revenue Code?
- ❑ What procedures do the board and committee have in place to monitor the existence of any consulting, familial, or other relationships that would affect a director's ability to serve on the compensation committee?
- ❑ What criteria do the company's investors apply when determining whether to elect directors who serve on the compensation committee, and do the committee's current members satisfy that criteria?
- ❑ Do any relationships or processes involving the committee and the company's executives or the committee's outside advisors create actual or perceived conflicts of interest, and if so, how has the committee addressed those?
- ❑ Does the board annually evaluate the committee's composition and the independence of committee members?

Additional Reading

1. NYSE, Rules 303A.02 and 303A.05 Compensation Committee, New York Stock Exchange Listed Company Manual

   http://nasdaq.cchwallstreet.com/NASDAQTools/PlatformViewer.asp?selectednode=chp%5F1%5F1%5F4%5F3&manual=%2Fnasdaq%2Fmain%2Fnasdaq%2Dequityrules%2F (last visited July 9, 2016)

2. **NASDAQ,** Rule 5605 Independence and Compensation Committee Requirements, *Equity Rules*
http://nasdaq.cchwallstreet.com/NASDAQTools/bookmark.asp?id=nasdaq-rule_5605&manual=/nasdaq/main/nasdaq-equityrules/ (last visited July 9, 2016)
3. Institutional Shareholder Services Inc., *United States 2016 Summary Proxy Voting Guidelines* (Nov. 20, 2016)
https://www.issgovernance.com/file/policy/2016-us-summary-voting-guidelines-23-feb-2016.pdf
4. Reiter, Barry J., "The Role of Compensation Committees in Corporate Governance," *FindLaw.com*
http://corporate.findlaw.com/finance/the-role-of-compensation-committees-in-corporate-governance.html (last visited July 9, 2016)
5. Regina Olshan et al., Section 162(m): Limit on Compensation, *Practical Law Company* (2011)
https://www.skadden.com/sites/default/files/publications/Publications2574_0.pdf (last visited July 9, 2016)
6. Transactions between an Issuer and Its Officers or Directors, 17 C.F.R. § 240.16b-3 (1996).
7. Wachtell, Lipton, Rosen & Katz, *Compensation Committee Guide* (March 2016)
http://www.wlrk.com/files/2016/CompensationCommitteeGuide.pdf
8. Skadden, Arps, Slate, Meagher & Flom LLP, *2016 Compensation Committee Handbook* (2nd ed. 2015)
https://www.skadden.com/insights/2016-compensation-committee-handbook

Notes

73 RETAINING AN INDEPENDENT COMPENSATION CONSULTANT

CONTRIBUTED BY
Julia M. Tosi
Squire Patton Boggs (US) LLP[1]

Public company executive compensation programs and the work of the compensation committee have become increasingly complex. Decisions are made against a backdrop of recent (and ongoing) changes in pay-related laws and regulations, tax and accounting implications, robust public disclosure, shareholder advisory say-on-pay voting and enhanced scrutiny by investors, proxy advisors, and the public. Although practices and needs vary from company to company, most public company compensation committees find it valuable to retain outside compensation consulting firms or other advisors to ensure that they have the necessary expertise, support, and information when making executive compensation decisions and fulfilling their other responsibilities.

It is important that committees have access to separate compensation consultants to provide independent expert advice on executive compensation matters. This principle has been formalized for U.S.-listed companies through the Dodd-Frank Act (Dodd-Frank) and the SEC and stock exchange listing rules implementing Dodd-Frank. Under these laws and regulations, compensation committees of U.S.-listed companies must have the

1. Julia M. Tosi is a partner at Squire Patton Boggs (US) LLP, where she is a member of the firm's corporate group, practicing in its Cleveland, Ohio office.

authority to hire compensation advisors and to commit company funding for compensation advisors. In particular, under U.S.-listing standards adopted under Dodd-Frank, the compensation committee

- may, in its sole discretion, retain or obtain the advice of a compensation advisor;
- is directly responsible for the appointment, compensation, and oversight of compensation advisors; and
- must be appropriately funded by the listed company.

It also is important that compensation committees use sound processes to select, retain, and evaluate compensation consultants. This can help protect the committee when relying on information provided by the consultant and can enable the committee to demonstrate the reasonableness of its choice, if needed. Committees will want to consider a variety of factors in engaging a compensation consultant, some of which are covered in the Key Questions section. In addition, committees should be attune to the fact that the recent and ongoing broader public discussion and scrutiny of executive pay has resulted in a heightened focus on how compensation consultants are used and potential independence or conflicts of interest issues. This focus has resulted in additional disclosure requirements and listing standards designed to help improve transparency and to require certain independence factors be considered as part of the compensation consultant selection process.

Examples of compensation consultant information that public companies must disclose include the role of compensation consultants in determining or recommending executive and director compensation, which consultant(s) were engaged and by whom, the scope of the consultants' engagement, fee details where consultants receive fees for other services in excess of specific amounts, and conflicts of interest concerns. In terms of the selection process, compensation committees of U.S.-listed companies may select a compensation consultant, legal counsel. or other advisor, other than in-house legal counsel, only after considering the following six independence factors:

- Whether the compensation consulting company employing the compensation advisor is providing any other services to the company
- How much the compensation consulting company who employs the compensation advisor has received in fees from the company, as a percentage of that person's total revenue
- What policies and procedures have been adopted by the compensation consulting company employing the compensation advisor to prevent conflicts of interest
- Whether the compensation advisor has any business or personal relationship with a member of the compensation committee
- Whether the compensation advisor owns any stock of the company
- Whether the compensation advisor or the person employing the advisor has any business or personal relationship with an executive officer of the issuer

The stock exchanges may impose additional factors or interpretations on these requirements. For example, the NYSE rules require a compensation committee to take into consideration "all factors relevant to that person's independence from management," including the six factors just listed. Consultants are accustomed to providing information for these assessments, and independence questionnaires are completed for new potential engagements and periodically for existing clients (often annually as part of a performance review and re-approval of an engagement). Companies also expect consultants to provide updates to this information at appropriate times when new circumstances arise.

The statute and implementing rules do not require a compensation advisor to be independent, but most committees choose to hire one who is. Consultants who are not independent, and other situations that may be perceived to create a conflict of interest, generally will be viewed with suspicion by investors and proxy advisory firms. For example, significant fees for other services can give rise to questions about objectivity or conflicts of interest under investor or proxy advisory firm policies.

Key Questions

When considering the selection, retention, and use of an independent compensation consultant, key questions that a board member might ask include the following:

- ❑ Does my company have any specific guidelines or policies in place regarding the compensation committee's selection and use of a compensation consultant or conflicts of interest that we should consider in addition to the listing rules?
- ❑ What process should we follow to identify a pool of potential compensation advisors to interview and consider?
- ❑ Should we conduct a formal request for proposal (RFP) process or only interviews? Who do we want to lead and participate in that process? Who should reach out to the consultants' references and report back to the committee? Have we taken care to appropriately limit management's involvement in the selection?
- ❑ What specific services would we, as a committee, want our compensation consultant to provide? Have potential consultants under consideration offered useful suggestions for services they would recommend based on our company's current program, circumstances, and disclosures?
- ❑ Are there protocols we should implement or other ways we can set expectations for working relationships and interactions between the consultant, committee, committee chair, and management/HR teams? Do I think this consultant will be successful in balancing these relationships?
- ❑ What are the consulting firm's, individual lead consultant's, and proposed team members' qualifications, experience, and credentials? Do they have tax, accounting, securities, industry, say-on-pay, proxy advisory firm, and shareholder engagement experience?
- ❑ What is the consultant's relationship to management or any other board members, and how independent are they? Have we given due consideration to the independence factors that we are required to assess? Are there circumstances that could be perceived by investors, proxy advisors, or others to

involve a conflict of interest or affect the consultant's independence, even if the committee does not think there is an actual conflict or issue?

- ❑ Will this consultant's and team's personalities work well with our committee, chair, and others involved in our compensation process? Are they professional, creative, objective, candid, and able to raise and consider alternative viewpoints?
- ❑ What is their proposed cost/fee structure? Is their compensation structured to create any bias that I should consider?
- ❑ What resources do they have available, including value-added resources for clients, such as alerts and publications?
- ❑ How should we document our advisor retention process, decision, and engagement agreement?
- ❑ When and how will we review the advisor's performance, update our independence review, and re-approve the engagement?

Additional Reading

1. American Bar Association Committee on Corporate Laws, *Corporate Director's Guidebook*, 6th ed. (See Section 8.D.).
2. "A Practical Guide to Compensation Committee Service: Lessons from the Field," *Compensation Advisory Partners* (2015), Chapter 7. External Advisors https://theknowledgegroup.org/wp-content/uploads/2016/01/CAP-A_Practical_Guide_to_Compensation-Lessons_White-Paper-Listing_Matt-Vnuk.pdf
3. Compensation Consultant Market Share Rankings 2015, *Equilar* (January 13, 2016) http://www.equilar.com/reports/30-2015-compensation-consultant-market-share-rankings.html
4. Longnecker, Brent, Kevin Kuschel, and Josh Whittaker. "Choosing a Strategic Compensation Consultant." *Longnecker & Associates* (June 21, 2016) http://longnecker.com/choosing-strategic-compensation-consultant/
5. Seelig, Steve. *Myths and Realities of the New SEC "Independence" Rules: Some Frequently Asked Questions (Part One)* (September 2012) https://www.towerswatson.com/en-US/Insights/Newsletters/Global/executive-pay-matters/2012/Myths-and-Realities-of-the-New-SEC-Independence-Rules-Some-Frequently-Asked-Questions-Part-1
6. Fact Sheet—Listing Standards for Compensation Committees and Compensation Advisers, *Securities and Exchange Commission* (Modified July 28, 2014) https://www.sec.gov/News/Article/Detail/Article/1365171586172

(See also the applicable listing standards of the specific exchange on which your company is listed and your company's corporate governance guidelines or any other relevant policies.)

7. 2016 Compensation Committee Handbook, *Skadden, Arps, Slate, Meagher & Flom LLP and Affiliates*, Chapter 3. The Use of Advisors by the Compensation Committee https://www.skadden.com/eimages/Skadden_2016CompensationCommitteeHandbook_120715_web.pdf

8. "Compensation Consultants and Conflicts of Interest: Two Different Views" (April 16, 2008), copyright of the Wharton School of the University of Pennsylvania, available through Knowledge@Wharton http://knowledge.wharton.upenn.edu/article/compensation-consultants-and-conflicts-of-interest-two-different-views/

9. Executive Compensation Principles and Commentary, *Business Roundtable* (January 30, 2007), Principle 5 and related commentary http://businessroundtable.org/resources/executive-compensation

Notes

14 STRUCTURING EXECUTIVE COMPENSATION PLANS

CONTRIBUTED BY
Toby D. Merchant
Squire Patton Boggs (US) LLP[1]

The board of a well-managed public company will want to establish an executive compensation plan that not only attracts and retains the talent needed by the company, but also incentivizes that talent to achieve the company's specific strategy and business objectives. Often, that latter objective is accomplished by tying a significant portion of an executive's compensation to the achievement of those business objectives. This goal must be accomplished in an environment where the compensation practices of public companies experience increased scrutiny from shareholders and proxy advisory firms, such as Institutional Shareholder Services (ISS) and Glass-Lewis & Co. (Glass Lewis), as well as changing regulatory and taxation requirements.

An executive compensation plan typically consists of four elements: (i) annual base salary, (ii) incentives tied to short-term performance, (iii) incentives tied to long-term performance of the company (usually in the form of equity, such as stock options, restricted stock, restricted stock units, and stock appreciation rights), and (iv) benefit plans. The challenge for boards is to design a plan that achieves the right combination of these four

1. Toby D. Merchant is a partner at Squire Patton Boggs (US) LLP, where he is a member of the corporate and financial institutions practice groups practicing in its Cincinnati, Ohio office.

elements for the company yet remains sufficiently flexible to evolve with the company and the ever-changing expectations and requirements of executive compensation.

A board, generally acting through its compensation committee comprised of independent directors, should design an executive compensation plan with the company's unique circumstances, strategy, and objectives in mind while also considering the expectations of its shareholders (which would typically include the policies and expectations of the various proxy advisory firms, such as ISS and Glass Lewis, as well as institutional investors who may have their own unique policies and expectations), employees, consumers, and other stakeholders. Due to the multiple complexities involved in designing an executive compensation plan, boards should also consider involving an independent compensation consultant early in the process. Benchmarking to the compensation practices of a company's peers can also be helpful in informing the board about "market" compensation practices, but boards should also be careful to not simply match or otherwise blindly follow the executive compensation practices of its peers. Once a compensation plan has been designed and implemented, periodic reviews of the plan, ideally involving an independent compensation consultant, will also be helpful to ensure that the plan continues to be appropriately designed and structured.

The structure of executive compensation plans varies across industries and companies. Further, a board should be mindful of current trends in executive compensation; tax implications, such as Internal Revenue Code (IRC) Sections 162(m) and 409A; and other factors that continue to shape the current executive compensation landscape. For example, shareholders have increasingly desired that compensation plans be more closely linked to long-term, sustained performance. The various tax implications of IRC Section 162(m), which prohibits public companies from deducting more than $1 million per year in compensation paid to certain covered employees unless specified requirements are satisfied, and IRC Section 409A, which imposes complicated rules on the deferral and payment of nonqualified deferred compensation, should also be reviewed and considered in detail when structuring an executive compensation plan.

The SEC disclosure rules require that virtually all aspects of a company's executive compensation plan be disclosed to the public, which typically occurs in a company's proxy statement or annual report on Form 10-K. In addition, a board should consider the implications of a number of reforms to the compensation practices of public companies under the Dodd-Frank Wall Street Reform and Consumer Protection Act of 2010 following the global financial crisis. Among these reforms are requirements that companies (i) implement policies to clawback incentive based compensation that was paid based on inaccurate financial statements that do not comply with applicable accounting standards, (ii) provide narrative disclosure regarding "pay versus performance," (iii) provide pay ratio disclosure that compares the compensation of the chief executive officer to the median compensation of its employees, and (iv) hold an advisory vote on executive compensation and "golden parachutes" (commonly referred to as a say-on-pay vote). Of the foregoing reforms, the rules and regulations regarding pay ratio disclosure and the say-on-pay vote have been formalized by the SEC rules, while rules and regulations regarding pay versus performance and clawback policies have been proposed but not yet formally adopted.

In short, there is no one-size-fits-all approach to structuring an executive compensation plan for any public company. The executive compensation landscape is dynamic, and developments in the SEC disclosure rules, as well as a number of regulatory developments and other factors, are sure to keep the topic of executive compensation in the spotlight for years to come. Boards will need to devote a significant amount of time, resources, and attention to the process in order to design an executive compensation plan that satisfies the company's unique strategy and business objectives, attracts and retains top talent, is able to withstand scrutiny from the public-eye, and meets the various regulatory requirements.

Key Questions

In structuring compensation plans, some questions a director may wish to consider include the following:

- ❑ Should the company engage an independent compensation consultant? If so, which one?
- ❑ What are the specific business objectives and strategy that should be tied to the executive compensation plan?
- ❑ What is the right balance of short- and long-term incentives? What about the mix of cash and equity incentives? In regards to equity incentives, should the company use stock options, restricted stock, restricted stock units, stock appreciation rights, or something else? Does the company's incentive plan contemplate the issuance of such equity incentives?
- ❑ Has the company performed any benchmarking against the executive compensation plans of its peers? If so, how do the company's executive compensation plans compare to its peers' plans?
- ❑ Has the interplay among the various components of the executive compensation plan been considered such that any unintended or disproportionate benefits to any senior executives can be identified?
- ❑ Has the company complied with all applicable SEC regulations relating to the issuance of equity incentives? For example, will any shares issued pursuant to such equity incentives be registered under the Securities Act using a Form S-8?
- ❑ Has the company considered the tax implications of an executive compensation plan? For example, has the company considered whether it will be able to satisfy the requirements of Section 162(m) of the Internal Revenue Code in order to deduct certain compensation paid to its executives? Has the company considered any effects of Internal Revenue Code Section 409A, which concerns deferred compensation?
- ❑ Is the executive compensation plan flexible such that it can evolve with the ever-changing shareholder, employee, and other stakeholder expectations of compensation plans and scrutiny?
- ❑ How will the executive compensation plan be viewed by the company's stakeholders, such as shareholders and employees?
- ❑ How will shareholder interest groups, such as ISS and Glass Lewis, view the executive compensation plan?

❑ What about institutional shareholders that have their own policies and expectations? Does the company expect that these groups and/or shareholders will recommend that shareholders approve such plans in connection with an upcoming say-on-pay vote?

Additional Reading

1. CFO Insights: Executive Compensation: Plan, Perform and Pay, *Deloitte LLP* (2010)
   http://www2.deloitte.com/content/dam/Deloitte/us/Documents/financial-services/us-fsi-cfo-exec-comp-070710.pdf
2. 2016 U.S. Equity Plan Scorecard, Frequently Asked Questions, *Institutional Shareholder Services*
   https://www.issgovernance.com/file/policy/faq-on-iss-us-equity-plan-scorecard-methodology.pdf
3. 2016 Trends and Developments in Executive Compensation, *Meridian Compensation Partners, LLC* (May 2016)
   http://www.meridiancp.com/wp-content/uploads/2016-Trends-and-Developments-in-Executive-Compensation.pdf
4. American Bar Association Committee on Corporate Laws, *Corporate Director's Guidebook*, 6th ed., Section 7.

Notes

____

____

____

____

____

7.5 SETTING THE BOARD'S COMPENSATION

CONTRIBUTED BY
Rebecca C. Grapsas
Sidley Austin LLP[1]

Director compensation programs are generally designed to compensate directors for the significant time they are expected to devote to board service and to align their interests with those of shareholders. Director compensation programs have been subject to heightened scrutiny in recent years.

Director compensation is typically recommended to the full board for approval by either the compensation committee or the nominating/corporate governance committee. Compensation consultants are sometimes used to assist in benchmarking. The elements and total amount of director compensation must be disclosed in a public company's proxy statement each year. The elements typically include an annual retainer in cash, an equity award (in the form of common stock, restricted stock, and/or stock options), and additional annual retainers for serving in a board or committee leadership role and/or on a committee. Stock ownership by directors is generally favored as a way of aligning directors' interests with those of shareholders, although in recent years the use of stock options as a component of director compensation has been called into question,

1. Rebecca C. Grapsas is counsel in Corporate Governance & Executive Compensation Practice of Sidley Austin LLP, where she practices in the firm's New York and Sydney offices.

especially if the options are exercisable within a short period or other option conditions provide undue incentives for directors to support management and continue their position on the board.

The Spencer Stuart Board Index 2016 reports that board meeting fees are becoming less common; they were paid by just 16 percent of S&P 500 companies in 2016 compared with 37 percent in 2011 and 57 percent in 2006. Some companies also offer other benefits, such as charitable matching grants. Employee directors, including the CEO, typically do not receive additional compensation for board service.

Companies listed on the New York Stock Exchange are required to adopt and disclose corporate governance guidelines, and those guidelines must address, among other topics, director compensation. NYSE commentary provides that director compensation guidelines should include general principles for determining the form and amount of director compensation (and for reviewing those principles, as appropriate). The NYSE commentary further provides that when determining the form and amount of director compensation and director independence, the board should critically evaluate whether directors' fees and emoluments exceed what is customary, whether the company makes substantial charitable contributions to organizations in which a director is affiliated, or enters into consulting contracts with (or provides other indirect forms of compensation to) a director.

The National Association of Corporate Directors described the following principles and procedures for boards to consider in implementing or revising nonemployee director compensation policies, in a report first issued in 1995:

- Director compensation should be determined by the board and fully disclosed to shareholders.
- Director compensation should be aligned with the long-term interests of shareholders.
- Compensation should be used to motivate director behavior.
- Directors should be adequately compensated for their time and effort.
- Compensation should be approached on an overall basis, rather than as an array of separate elements.
- Boards should establish a transparent process by which directors can determine the compensation program in a deliberate and objective way.
- Boards should set and disclose a substantial target for stock ownership by each director and a time period during which this target is to be met.
- Boards should define a desirable total value of all forms of director compensation.
- Boards should pay directors solely in the form of equity and cash—with equity representing 50 to 100 percent of the total, dismantle the existing benefit programs, and avoid creating new ones.
- Boards should adopt a policy stating that a company should not hire a director or a director's firm to provide professional services to the company.
- Boards should disclose fully in the proxy statement the philosophy and process used in determining director compensation and the value of all elements of compensation.

- Boards should also exercise caution when approving compensation plans that permit equity awards to be made to nonemployee directors. Such plans should include meaningful limits on the amount of equity that directors can award themselves, and those limits should be approved by shareholders to ensure that awards made under the plan are entitled to business judgment rule protection under Delaware law, where applicable, instead of the more demanding "entire fairness" standard.

There is not currently a say-on-director-pay vote in the United States, although such votes (advisory or binding) are required in some countries.

Finally, if nonemployee directors are paid for services provided other than as a director (i.e., for consulting fees or professional services), issues of independence as well as disclosure can be implicated.

Key Questions

When setting the board's compensation, questions to consider include the following:

- ❑ Which board committee is responsible for recommending director compensation for approval by the full board?
- ❑ Do we need the assistance of a consultant to advise on the amount and form of director compensation and, if so, how will we select that consultant?
- ❑ How much should total director compensation be per year?
- ❑ What are the different elements of director compensation that we should include in our program and what should be the amount of each element? For example, annual retainer for directors, board leaders, committee chairs and/or committee members; equity grants (such as common stock, restricted stock units or stock options); and/or other benefits? Should we pay additional fees per meeting attended and, if so, should such fees be payable beginning with the first meeting or only after a certain number of meetings (such as six)?
- ❑ Do we need to adjust our stock ownership guidelines in light of any changes to director compensation?
- ❑ Who are our peer companies for purposes of determining director compensation? Have we reviewed appropriate survey data?
- ❑ Does our director compensation exceed what is customary or reasonable?
- ❑ What is the risk that a proxy advisory firm could determine that our directors are not independent or otherwise raise concerns on the basis of our director compensation program?
- ❑ Does our compensation plan applicable to nonemployee directors include a meaningful limit on equity grants and/or cash payments to directors? Have shareholders approved that limit in accordance with corporate formalities? How do we expect proxy advisory firms to evaluate a proposal seeking shareholder approval of our plan?
- ❑ What will our proxy statement disclosure relating to director compensation look like?

Additional Reading

1. Willis Towers Watson, Executive Compensation Bulletin: New Analysis Reveals Moderate Increases in Fortune 500 Outside Director Pay (July 2016)

   https://www.towerswatson.com/en-US/Insights/Newsletters/Global/executive-pay-matters/2016/Executive-Compensation-Bulletin-New-analysis-moderate-increases-Fortune500-director-pay
2. Lentz, Alec, and Ken Sparling. "Scrutiny and Standardization of Director Pay." *The Corporate Board* (May/June 2016)

   http://www.fwcook.com/content/documents/publications/05-16_Scrutiny_And_Standardization_of_Director_Pay.pdf
3. National Association of Corporate Directors, 2015–2016 Director Compensation Report (March 2016)
4. Sidley Austin LLP, Delaware Courts Tighten Their Scrutiny of Non-Employee Director Compensation Awards (May 2015)

   http://www.sidley.com/~/media/update-pdfs/2015/05/20150529-corporate-governance-update.pdf
5. National Association of Corporate Directors, Report of the Blue Ribbon Commission on Director Compensation (1995, most recently revised 2006)

Notes

---

76 COMPENSATION FOR SPECIAL COMMITTEE SERVICE

CONTRIBUTED BY
Gregory V. Varallo
Richards, Layton & Finger, P.A.[1]

Special committee work is time consuming, generally challenging, and often uncomfortable. The question often faced at the outset of a special committee assignment is: What is fair compensation for this unusual and often extraordinary work?

The answer is context specific. What is the committee tasked with doing, how long is it likely to take, and what is the size of the transaction or matter being investigated? The more complex the task, the longer the committee is likely to have to work and the more it should be paid. Conversely, in a comparatively small deal (for example, a $5 million transaction in a $500 million company), an otherwise defensible fee might well be scaled back in light of the small size of the transaction.

Likewise, where a committee is formed to conduct an investigation (rather than negotiate a transaction) the committee will want counsel's help in estimating the likely length and scope of the investigation to assist it in setting a reasonable fee.

1. Gregory V. Varallo is a director and president of Richards, Layton & Finger, P.A., where he practices in the areas of complex business litigation, ADR, and corporate governance. The author wishes to acknowledge the assistance of his colleague John R. Fitzgerald in the preparation of this chapter.

Fee Structures to Avoid

Before we get into specifics of fee structuring and sizing, there are a number of things that should *not* be done in the context of compensation for committee work.

First, special committee fees should *never* be made contingent on an outcome. Recall that most special committees are set up to deal with conflicts of interest. Where a fee is paid based on a favorable outcome, especially in the context of a transaction with a controller, the work of the committee automatically becomes suspect.

Second, the timing of when a fee is agreed upon is important. The committee's fee should be set at the outset of an assignment, immediately after the appointment of the committee and the hiring of its counsel. Under no circumstances should the committee be put in the position of negotiating a fee after it has done its work. To many, this paradigm would seem to be little different from an independence point of view than the contingent fee structure.

Third, in a going private transaction or other conflicted transaction with a controlling stockholder, the committee should reject the controller's invitation to "negotiate" its fee. If a record is inadvertently made of the committee "giving in" to demands of the "controller" of the transaction at the outset and on the question of its fee, the ordinary level of suspicion of a reviewing court will likely increase, perhaps materially. Indeed the invitation to negotiate the fee is a wonderful first opportunity for the committee to begin building its record of independence. Such an invitation should be met with a polite but firm "no" in almost all circumstances.

Structuring and Sizing the Fee

Having hopefully avoided the forgoing pitfalls, the question then becomes: What is the appropriate fee structure and size for special committee work? In general, committees have followed four separate approaches, with many variations within each approach.

The first is to set a flat fee per committee member: No matter how many times the committee meets or how long the process takes, and especially no matter what the result, the committee's fee is "X." Variations on this theme include a premium for the committee chair and a flat fee that refreshes after so many months of effort. The additional reading list includes the author's treatise on special committees where extensive data is collected from many special committees about the size of their fees.

The second prevalent fee structure is a per meeting charge, usually in the range of fees paid for other committee meetings. It is not unusual to see per meeting fees in the range of $1,000 to $2,500 per meeting, often with a slight premium for the chair.

This structure tends to be perceived as a fair one in transactional or other contexts where the committee is expected to meet frequently. Depending upon the scope of the committee's work, this structure could lead to a greater "all-in" fee than a simple flat fee structure. It is not unusual, for example, for a deal committee to have to meet several dozen times during the evolution and negotiation of a transaction. In addition, this fee structure has the benefit of matching the work required of the committee with its fee, since the more the committee is called upon to meet, the more it is paid.

The third common structure is a monthly stipend during the pendency of the committee's work.

A fourth, hybrid approach is also used. This approach starts with an attempt to guess how long the committee's work is likely to go on, and then to compare and pay for that work on the same basis that the board is paid annually. Thus, where a board is paid $100,000 a year, if it is anticipated that the committee's work will continue for six months, the committee fee would be $50,000 per member. Of course, there are always variations that may be contextually specific and useful, but the approaches previously described tend, in the view of the author, to be the most prevalent.

Finally, it is not uncommon that the committee's chair will receive additional compensation for the incremental administration burden of chairing the committee.

Key Questions

In setting compensation for special committee service, issues to consider include the following:

- ❑ Is the fee that the committee will be paid in any way conditional? Does it depend in any way on the outcome of the committee's work?
- ❑ When does counsel anticipate addressing the topic of the committee's fee, given that the committee believes that the subject should be addressed prior to commencement of the committee's work?
- ❑ Have inside counsel or representatives of the controlling party (where there is one) suggested a fee structure or approach? If so, what should the committee's response be where the objective of the response is to begin to set the record of arm's-length dealing and independence in fact?
- ❑ How long do the committee's advisors believe will be required for the committee to complete its work? How often is the committee expected to meet?
- ❑ Are the committee's advisors aware of recent market-based comparability data for similar committee assignments? If so, what does that data suggest?
- ❑ Should the committee's chair receive additional compensation? How much should that be?

Additional Reading

1. Varallo, Gregory V., Srinivas M. Raju, and Michael D. Allen. *Special Committees: Law and Practice* (Appendix 3F) (2014) (showing all recent special committee fees publicly reported as of the time of publication of the treatise).

2. Zeberkiewicz, John Mark. "Revisiting the Special Committee Process: In re Southern Peru Copper Corporation." *BNA's Corp. Counsel Weekly*, November 2011.

3. Conyon, M. J., and S. I. Peck. "Board Control, Remuneration Committees, and Top Management Compensation." *Academy of Management Journal* 41 no. 2 (1998) 146–57.
4. Engel, E., R. M. Hayes, and X. Wang. "Audit Committee Compensation and the Demand for Monitoring of the Financial Reporting Process." *Journal of Accounting and Economics* 49 no. 1 (2010) 136–54.

Notes

---

7 EXECUTIVE EMPLOYMENT AGREEMENTS

CONTRIBUTED BY
Ellen Canan Grady
Cozen O'Connor[1]

All companies must attract and retain top talent in order to compete successfully, and employment agreements are one tool to effectively recruit and keep experienced senior executives. Employment agreements protect both the company and the executive by specifying the material terms upon which the executive will be employed and offer the employee a sense of job security and minimum agreed compensation for a period of time. It is customary for public companies to have employment agreements with their most senior executive officers, particularly the CEO and the CFO, but large public or private companies also may enter into agreements with other key employees who contribute significantly to their business and who are not easily replaced.

Although agreements vary among companies and across industries, the principal terms and conditions generally addressed in executive employment agreements include the following:

- The term of employment, which generally is three years or less, and whether the term will automatically renew for successive terms unless terminated;

1. Ellen Canan Grady is a member of the Corporate Law Practice and Privacy Data Security and Cybersecurity Industry team at Cozen O'Connor, located in the firm's Philadelphia office.

alternatively, an employment agreement may provide that the executive is employed "at will," which means that the executive is terminable by the company "at will," but is entitled to specified severance pay and continuing benefits for an agreed period

- The title, duties, and responsibilities of the executive, which is important because a breach of the specified duties or responsibilities by the executive or a change in title that is a demotion may give rise to a right to terminate the agreement
- The compensation to be paid to the executive officer, including the base salary, short-term bonus, long-term incentive compensation, and equity-based compensation, including the type of equity award and any vesting conditions (which should be consistent with the company's equity incentive compensation plan under which the award is made)
- The health, wellness, and vacation benefits to which the executive is entitled annually, which are generally consistent with the benefits offered by the company to other executives at a similar level of seniority
- The circumstances under which the executive can be terminated or demoted, or under which the executive may resign for "good reason," and the consequences of termination, resignation for "good reason," or demotion, which generally include an obligation on the part of the company to pay severance to the executive
- The confidentiality provisions to which the executive is subject to ensure that confidential company information, such as financial information and technological innovations, is not divulged by the executive (these provisions are sometimes set forth in a separate agreement)
- An assignment of inventions provision under which the executive agrees that any inventions or ideas that are related to the business of the company and conceived by the executive during the term of employment are assigned to and owned by the company (again, these provisions are sometimes set forth in a separate agreement)
- The consequences of the death, disability, or retirement of the executive during the term of the employment agreement, including how "disability" is defined for purposes of the agreement, and whether the vesting of any outstanding equity awards will be accelerated upon such an event
- Whether the executive is subject to any post-employment covenants, such as a nonsolicitation of employees clause and/or a noncompetition clause, including the time during which any such clause is enforceable and, in the case of a noncompetition clause, the geographic area to which it extends (directors should be aware that noncompetition clauses are not enforceable in all jurisdictions and, in certain jurisdictions, the executive must receive specific consideration for his or her agreement not to compete)
- What happens in the event of a change in control of the company during the term of the executive's employment agreement, including whether such an event gives rise to the executive's right to terminate the employment agreement for "good reason" and receive severance, and whether the vesting of the

executive's equity awards accelerate upon such an event (so-called single-trigger acceleration), or whether the executive also must be demoted or terminated within an agreed period following the change in control in order for the awards to vest (so-called double-trigger acceleration)

- The state's laws that will govern the terms and enforceability of the employment agreement, which should be a state with which the company has a nexus (i.e., the state in which the company has its principal office or its jurisdiction of incorporation, or the state in which the executive will be performing services for the company)
- Whether there is an agreed arbitration clause in the event of a dispute arising out of the employment agreement and, if so, where the arbitration will take place and which rules of arbitration will be applicable

The terms and conditions of an employment agreement with a new officer may be subject to significant negotiation between the company and the incoming executive. Newly recruited senior executive officers are often represented by their own legal counsel. Generally, senior officers within the company or competent in-house or external legal counsel take the lead role in negotiating and drafting specific terms and conditions, but any employment agreement with a senior executive officer should be reviewed with and approved by the company's compensation committee (or the full board of directors if there is no compensation committee) prior to being executed.

The corporate governance rules of the NYSE and the NASDAQ Stock Market provide that, with certain limited exceptions, companies with securities listed on such exchanges must have a compensation committee comprised of at least two independent directors, and it must have responsibility for determining, or recommending to the full board of directors for its determination, the compensation of the CEO and the other executive officers of the company. This requirement generally is reflected in the charter of the compensation committee. Thus, the compensation committee must approve employment agreements with the company's senior executive officers. In the case of particularly visible or high-ranking executives, such as the CEO, compensation committee members also may be involved in negotiating the agreements.

In considering whether to approve executive employment agreements, the compensation committee (or full board of directors if there is no compensation committee) should have the benefit of a summary of the material terms and conditions of the agreement and, in certain circumstances, also may be presented with guidance from an outside compensation consultant about the compensation types and levels paid at comparable and competitive peer companies. For executives with less seniority, but for whom employment agreements are determined to be in the best interests of the company, the compensation committee may delegate to the CEO, the COO, or another senior officer the authority to negotiate and approve the terms of such employment agreements, perhaps within specified parameters.

Public companies also need to consider how the terms and conditions of employment agreements with senior executive officers will be viewed by the company's shareholders, the public, and proxy advisory firms. Compensation committees advised by outside compensation consultants, which provide metrics about the types and levels of compensation for a particular executive position compared with that of peer companies, may also ask the consultant to provide insight into how the executive's employment agreement may be viewed by the company's shareholders. Shareholders in public companies today are focused on "pay for performance," and it may be important for the compensation committee (or full board of directors) to consider whether the short-term and long-term incentive compensation opportunities are tied to appropriate performance-based measures. Similarly, proxy advisory firms today have specific compensation-related concerns that, if ignored, may trigger a proxy advisory firm negative vote recommendation for compensation committee chairs, members, or the entire board of directors. Some specific provisions in executive employment agreements that may cause concern for proxy advisory firms include "golden parachute" gross up payments on excise taxes; the alignment between CEO pay and company performance; problematic pay practices, including option repricing or backdating; change in control or severance payments that could result in payments greater than three times annual base salary; termination or severance payments without involuntary job loss or substantial diminution of duties; single trigger change in control provisions; and excessive perquisites.

Directors of public companies also should be aware that executive employment agreements for the company's most senior officers are required to be publicly disclosed by the company in a Current Report on Form 8-K filed with the SEC within four business days, and the agreement will be filed with and publicly available from the SEC. The material terms and conditions of executive employment agreements also will be described annually in the public company's proxy statement relating to its annual meeting of shareholders. Directors should be knowledgeable about the terms and conditions of these agreements; be sensitive to how they will be perceived by their shareholders, employees, and other constituencies; and have undertaken a thoughtful, considered process in negotiating and approving the agreements.

Key Questions

When considering executive compensation agreements, questions to consider include the following:

- ❑ What are the key components of our company's compensation package and benefits offered to senior executive officers?
- ❑ What are the key terms of the employment agreements that the company offers its executives, other than compensation and benefits?
- ❑ What is the role of the compensation committee in negotiating and approving executive employment agreements? Does the compensation committee have an independent compensation consultant advising it on competitive compensation metrics and current market trends?
- ❑ How will our company's particular elements of compensation and benefits likely be perceived by our shareholders, institutional shareholders, and shareholder proxy advisory groups?
- ❑ How does our company's compensation package compare with that offered by our key competitors and peer companies?

- ❑ Will we offer the executive a signing bonus and, if so, will it be paid in cash or equity?
- ❑ What circumstances should constitute "cause" in this executive's employment agreement, under which the company may terminate this executive without having to pay severance? What is the appropriate period for severance for this executive and should severance be payable over time or in a lump sum?
- ❑ What is the company obligated to pay the executive (or his or her estate) in the event of the executive's death, disability, or retirement during the term of the employment agreement?
- ❑ What are the appropriate vesting provisions applicable to the equity component of the executive's compensation? If the vesting provisions include performance-based conditions, what are the appropriate performance metrics for our company, and to what extent should these performance-based metrics relate to individual performance and company performance?
- ❑ Will a "change in control" of the company or a change in a specified percentage ownership of the company trigger a termination event under the executive's employment agreement? Will change of control payments for executives be subject to a "single trigger" or a "double trigger" change of control provision?
- ❑ What post-employment obligations of confidentiality should be imposed on the executive in the employment agreement? What restrictive covenants (nonsolicitation of employees and noncompete agreements) should be included in the employment agreement and, if any are included, what is the appropriate term for the restrictions? Are the restrictions reasonable and legally enforceable?
- ❑ What post-termination indemnification provisions should the company provide, consistent with its certificate of incorporation and bylaws, and the provisions of its directors' and officers' insurance policies?

Additional Reading

1. Sherrod, Andrew. "5 Key Considerations When Negotiating an Employment Agreement." *Corporate Compliance Insights*
   http://corporatecomplianceinsights.com/5-key-considerations-negotiating-executive-employment-agreement/

2. Harroch, Richard. "Negotiating Employment Agreements: Checklist of 14 Key Issues." *Forbes* (November 11, 2013)
   http://www.forbes.com/sites/allbusiness/2013/11/11/negotiating-employment-agreements-checklist-of-14-key-issues/#6c4c468f475f

3. Woolf, David J. "Ten Considerations in Drafting Executive Employment Agreements." *LaborSphere* (March 24, 2014)
   http://laborsphere.com/ten-considerations-drafting-executive-employment-agreements/

4. Lazar, Wendi S., and Katherine Blostein. "Executive Employment Agreements." *BNA's Executive Compensation Library On the Web* (September 12, 2009) http://www.americanbar.org/content/dam/aba/administrative/labor_law/meetings/2010/am/lazar1.authcheckdam.pdf

5. Schwab, Stewart J., and Randall S. Thomas. "An Empirical Analysis of CEO Employment Contracts: What Do Top Executives Bargain For?" 63 *Wash. & Lee L. Rev.* 231 (2006) http://law2.wlu.edu/deptimages/Law%20Review/Schwab-ThomasPublished.pdf

Notes

78 COMPENSATION CLAWBACKS AND FORFEITURES

CONTRIBUTED BY
Julia M. Tosi
Squire Patton Boggs (US) LLP[1]

Compensation clawback and forfeiture policies and provisions allow companies to require executives and employees to return compensation that was not earned or is later determined to have been awarded in error, or prevent compensation from being paid in the first place. Use of these mechanisms as ways to enhance accountability, mitigate risk, improve the quality of financial reporting, and drive other behaviors has become commonplace for public companies. This has been driven by the business case for these mechanisms, shareholder and proxy advisory firm pressure and voting policies, governance best practices, and statutory clawback requirements.

Companies' clawback and forfeiture mechanisms may mirror one or more statutory clawback requirements, or may go beyond the statutory minimums (e.g., by covering more officers or employees or other conduct or time frames). There are many different ways in which companies have structured their policies and provisions, as illustrated by the market studies cited in the Additional Reading section at the end of the chapter.

1. Julia M. Tosi is a partner in Squire Patton Boggs (US) LLP, where she is a member of the firm's corporate group, practicing in its Cleveland, Ohio office.

Decision points in establishing a compensation clawback or forfeiture mechanism include determining the following:

- Who the policy or provision should cover
- What circumstances and events should trigger compensation clawback or forfeiture
- What kinds of compensation should be covered
- Whether there would be a lookback period
- How the amount to be recovered would be determined
- How the clawback or recovery would be enforced
- What level of discretion is desirable

U.S. public companies already are subject to statutory clawback provisions under the Sarbanes-Oxley Act of 2002. As a result of the Dodd-Frank Act, U.S.-listed companies also will be required to adopt, implement, and comply with compensation recovery policies that satisfy SEC and stock exchange rules and provide certain related disclosures (once those requirements are finalized). As of the date of this writing, the SEC has published proposed but not final rules. The final rules may differ from the proposals, and the stock exchanges will need to propose and implement their listing requirements after final SEC rules are adopted. Companies may need to revise existing policies and agreements in order to ensure that they are in compliance with and able to enforce policies they put in place to satisfy the final rules.

Key Questions

With respect to compensation clawback and forfeiture policies, and in anticipation of the forthcoming final Dodd-Frank clawback rules, key questions that a board member might ask include the following.

To assess existing agreements and policies:

- ❑ Does my company currently have any compensation clawback or forfeiture agreements or policies in place?

If *not*:

- ❑ Should the company voluntarily adopt a clawback policy now, recognizing that we may need to revise it in short order depending on the final rules?
- ❑ Have our investors or proxy advisory firms taken issue with the company not having a clawback in place?
- ❑ Are we planning to enter into new executive employment agreements or to adopt any new incentive plans or agreements? Have we included appropriate clawback provisions in them?

If so:

- ❑ Has a review been undertaken to determine how our current policies and provisions compare to the proposed Dodd-Frank clawback rules? How do our provisions compare to market practices?

- ❑ Recognizing that the final Dodd-Frank rules may differ from the proposals, how might our company agreements and policies need to be updated if the rules become final as proposed?

When establishing or updating clawbacks and forfeiture mechanisms:

- ❑ What behaviors should we seek to incentivize, for what actions should we seek to hold employees accountable, and what risks would we seek to mitigate through such a policy or provisions?
- ❑ What should the scope and details be? Would those details have accounting implications or an impact to the perceived value of any awards under our executive compensation program?

In anticipation of final Dodd-Frank rules:

- ❑ Which of our executives and former executives would be covered under the proposed rules, and how will the company track that?
- ❑ Which of our incentive plans and outstanding awards would be subject to the required clawback policy if the proposed rules become final? Could any of those pose difficulties in a clawback situation? Does this impact how we view the design of our program or any elements of it?
- ❑ Will we be able to enforce the clawback requirements with respect to employment, award, or other agreements that we already have in place? Should we, or will we, need to make any updates to those agreements?

Additional Reading

1. SEC Proposes Rules Requiring Companies to Adopt Clawback Policies on Executive Compensation—Proposed Rules Designed to Improve Quality of Financial Reporting and Enhance Accountability Benefiting Investors, *SEC Press Release 2015-136 and Fact Sheet* (July 1, 2015)

   https://www.sec.gov/news/pressrelease/2015-136.html

2. "SEC Proposes Rules to Implement Compensation Recovery ('Clawback') Requirement," *Compensia Thoughtful Pay Alert* (July 10, 2015), short version (and link to detailed version)

   http://www.compensia.com/tpa_0715_sec_proposes_section954_short.html

3. SEC Proposes Clawback Rules, *ClearBridge Compensation Group Market Update* (July 2, 2015)

   http://www.clearbridgecomp.com/wp-content/uploads/SEC-Proposes-Clawback-Rules.pdf

4. SEC Proposes Rules on Clawback Policies—Broad Sweeping, No Fault Recoupment of Incentive Compensation Based on Financials, Stock Price, or TSR, *Pearl Meyer and Partners Client Alert* (July 7, 2015)

   https://www.pearlmeyer.com/pearl/media/pearlmeyer/clientalerts/pmp-ca-sec-proposes-rules-on-clawback-policies-7-2015.pdf

5. Corporate Governance Study, *Frederic W. Cook & Co., Inc.* (December 2015)
http://www.fwcook.com/content/Documents/Publications/FWC_2015_Corp_Gov_Study_Final.pdf
6. Executive Compensation: Clawbacks (2014 Proxy Disclosure Study), *PwC* (January 2015)
http://www.pwc.com/us/en/hr-management/publications/assets/pwc-executive-compensation-clawbacks-2014.pdf?_ga=1.131568652.207660596.1439215529
7. Whitehouse, Tammy. "Study: Companies Taking Own Action on Clawbacks." *Compliance Week* (February 10, 2015)
https://www.complianceweek.com/blogs/accounting-auditing-update/study-companies-taking-own-action-on-clawbacks#.V5_0yGX2YdU
8. Gerek, Bill, Suzanne Barrow, and Paul Hudson, Hay Group. "Clawbacks: Getting Ready for the Spotlight." *Compensation Focus from WorldatWork* (August 2013)
http://www.haygroup.com/downloads/us/clawbacks_getting%20ready%20for%20the%20spotlight_gerek.pdf
9. Policies on Corporate Governance, *Council of Institutional Investors (CII)* (April 1, 2015), Section 5.5d
http://www.cii.org/corp_gov_policies

Notes

____

____

____

____

____

19 DISCLOSURE CONSIDERATIONS IN STRUCTURING EXECUTIVE COMPENSATION

CONTRIBUTED BY
John P. Kelsh
Sidley Austin LLP[1]

Compensation of public company executive officers is a topic that continues to be of significant interest to investors, institutional investor advisory services, and the media. In response to this interest, the SEC has adopted extensive rules pertaining to the disclosure of executive officer compensation. The disclosure required by these rules is complex, and for many companies, extremely lengthy. It is not uncommon for a company's compensation disclosures to rival or even exceed in length its disclosures relating to the company's financial performance.

These disclosures receive considerable attention, particularly following the advent of say-on-pay. ISS bases its recommendations regarding say-on-pay and, to some extent, director re-election on its review of an issuer's compensation program. The media each year run articles on executive compensation generally and on individual companies in particular.

1. Mr. Kelsh is a partner at Sidley Austin LLP, where he is a co-chair of the Corporate Governance and Executive Compensation practice.

Given this level of attention, directors who review and approve proposed executive compensation arrangements are well advised to understand how such arrangements will be disclosed.

Key Questions

In considering your company's disclosures about executive compensation, issues to consider include the following:

- ❑ Do ISS, Glass Lewis, or any of our large shareholders have a policy with regard to any particular item of compensation that is under consideration? Will our policy produce resistance from these organizations?
- ❑ In the context of new programs or arrangements, has management or an outside advisor explained to me how the program or arrangement will be disclosed, if at all, in (i) a Form 8-K and/or (ii) the company's proxy statement? Have I seen a draft of such disclosure?
- ❑ Also in the context of new programs or arrangements, what rationale will be provided in the Compensation Discussion and Analysis (CD&A) regarding the reasons for the change?
- ❑ If the compensation item in question contains performance targets, do I know whether those targets will have to be disclosed or whether there might be a basis for excluding such disclosure (as could be the case if disclosure of the target would cause competitive harm)?
- ❑ Is the company's disclosure regarding its compensation program in the proxy and elsewhere consistent, particularly with regard to questions of corporate strategy and results, with other disclosures the company has made on these points?
- ❑ When will each element of compensation that is under consideration be included in the Summary Compensation Table? In the year of grant (as would generally be the case in terms of equity), in the year in which performance is attained (as would generally be the case with cash incentive programs), or something else?
- ❑ In the context of cash incentive programs, will amounts paid under the program, if any, be disclosed in the Summary Compensation Table as "bonus" or "non-equity incentive plan compensation"?
- ❑ If the compensation arrangement that I am being asked to approve is an agreement with a new executive or a departing executive, is it clear when disclosure regarding the executive transition will be required?
- ❑ Also in the context of an employment or separation agreement, will the agreement itself have to be filed and, if so, when?
- ❑ Given the company's current circumstance, will the level of executive compensation create resentment or morale issues within the company?

Additional Reading

1. SEC Adopting Release re 2006 Changes to Executive Compensation Disclosure Rules
   https://www.sec.gov/rules/final/2006/33-8732a.pdf
2. ISS U.S. Executive Compensation Policies: Frequently Asked Questions (March 2016)
   https://www.issgovernance.com/file/policy/us-executive-compensation-policies-faq-16-march-2016.pdf

Notes

7.10 LOANS TO DIRECTORS AND EXECUTIVE OFFICERS

CONTRIBUTED BY
Toby D. Merchant
Squire Patton Boggs (US) LLP[1]

Subject to limited exceptions that primarily apply to financial institutions or companies otherwise in the business of consumer lending, public companies are prohibited from making, or arranging for any third party to make, personal loans to their directors and executive officers. This prohibition, contained in Section 402 of the Sarbanes-Oxley Act of 2002, is broad and encompasses many circumstances that would not ordinarily be thought of as a "personal loan" in the general sense. The key reason for such uncertainty is that the term "personal loan" is not defined and there is little, if any, formal guidance issued by the SEC on the subject. Due to the absence of regulatory or legislative guidance, on October 15, 2002, a group of 25 major law firms issued a memorandum titled "Sarbanes-Oxley Act: Interpretive Issues under § 402—Prohibition of Certain Insider Loans," which provides a blueprint for a consensus among practitioners as to a variety of interpretive issues under Section 402 of the Sarbanes-Oxley Act. Violations of the loan prohibitions of Section 402 of the Sarbanes-Oxley Act are potentially severe and could subject a company to the civil and criminal penalties applicable to violations of the Securities Exchange Act of 1934.

1. Toby D. Merchant is a partner at Squire Patton Boggs (US) LLP, where he is a member of the Corporate and Financial Institutions practice groups.

The prohibition on personal loans is generally considered by practitioners to apply not only to directors and executive officers but also to their family members and affiliated entities as a result of the prohibition applying to personal loans made "to" or "for" any director or executive officer. Consequently, boards should be aware of the general prohibition and consider, in detail, whether a particular transaction could be encompassed by the prohibition.

Personal loans to public company employees other than directors and executive officers are not prohibited. Importantly, however, loans made to such employees will need to be repaid or forgiven in the event such person becomes a director or executive officer. For example, a loan made to a promising employee who is later promoted to an executive officer position will become problematic for the company—especially in light of the fact that it is often difficult to terminate a loan without unwanted consequences to either of the parties or replace a loan without the company running afoul of the prohibition on the company from arranging for any third party to make a replacement loan.

Private (i.e., nonpublic) companies are not subject to the prohibitions of Section 402 of the Sarbanes-Oxley Act and, consequently, are not prohibited from making personal loans to their directors and executive officers. In the event, however, a private company becomes a public company, all such loans will be prohibited. Accordingly, private companies considering becoming public in the future should carefully consider the potential consequences of making personal loans to directors and executive officers and provide for the repayment or termination of such loans in the event the company desires to become a public company.

Public companies (and private companies considering becoming public companies) should steer clear of any activities that could be encompassed by the prohibitions on loans to directors and executive officers. Moreover, boards should keep in mind that the prohibition on loans to directors and executive officers is broad and encompasses a variety of arrangements that would not ordinarily be thought of as falling within the prohibition.

Key Questions

To ensure that a company does not make a loan in violation of Section 402 of the Sarbanes-Oxley Act, some questions might be as follows:

- ❑ Even though the transaction or arrangement on its face may not appear to be a "loan," could the transaction or arrangement nevertheless be interpreted to be a "loan"?
- ❑ Is the borrower a director or executive officer of the company?
- ❑ Is the borrower a family member of, or otherwise affiliated with, a director or executive officer of the company?
- ❑ If the borrower is not a director or executive officer of the company, is the borrower expected to become a director or executive officer in the future?
- ❑ If the company is private, is it contemplating becoming a public company?

Additional Reading

1. Section 402 of Sarbanes-Oxley
   https://www.sec.gov/about/laws/soa2002.pdf
2. SEC Issues SOX 402 Guidance, *Harvard Law School Forum on Corporate Governance and Financial Regulation* (April 18, 2013)
   https://corpgov.law.harvard.edu/2013/04/18/sec-issues-sox-402-guidance/
3. Interpretive Issues under Section 402 of the Sarbanes-Oxley Act of 2002 (Oct. 17, 2002)
   http://www.thecorporatecounsel.net/member/FAQ/Section402/25_firms.pdf

Notes

SECTION EIGHT

AUDIT COMMITTEE MATTERS

8.1 THE ROLE OF THE AUDIT COMMITTEE

CONTRIBUTED BY
Katherine J. Blair and Suwani Karki
Manatt, Phelps & Phillips, LLP[1]

In 1987, the Report of the National Commission on Fraudulent Financial Reporting, more commonly referred to as the Treadway Commission Report, recommended that audit committees should be "informed, vigilant, and effective overseers of the financial reporting process and the company's internal controls." Nearly 29 years later, this principle still stands true today.

Although a company's management team holds primary responsibility for the company's financial reporting, a company's board of directors oversees the process. The audit committee is a standing committee of the board of directors, which is given authority to help the board of directors carry out its oversight responsibility. In particular, the audit committee is tasked with providing accountability with regard to a company's financial report process. The expectations are high with regard to what an audit committee is going to report and what its standards will be. Ultimately, a company places a lot of

1. Katherine J. Blair is a partner in the Capital Markets group at Manatt, Phelps & Phillips, LLP, where she practices in the firm's Los Angeles office. Suwani Karki is an associate in the Corporate and Finance group, where she practices in the firm's Washington, D.C. office.

faith and confidence in its audit committee, and, as a result, the audit committee may be required to make difficult decisions.

The role of the audit committee does not relieve the other directors of their responsibility with regard to oversight of the company's financials. Rather, the audit committee's smaller size allows it to carry out its responsibilities in a more concentrated manner because its principal focus is overseeing the financial reporting process and being aware of the company's overall financial well-being.

The responsibilities of the audit committee are governed by rules of the SEC, the stock exchanges, and the Public Company Accounting Oversight Board (PCAOB). The audit committee has responsibility for, and provides oversight in, the following general areas:

- Accounting and financial reporting processes, including internal controls and financial risks
- Appointment and oversight of independent auditor and audit services
- Financial statement and disclosure matters

The audit committee is a fundamental pillar in building a structurally sound company with strong internal controls and financial integrity.

SEC and Stock Exchange Requirements

A public company is not, directly as a result of filing reports with the SEC, required to establish an audit committee. In fact, an audit committee is only required if the company is listed on a stock exchange. In 1999, based on the Blue Ribbon Committee on Improving the Effectiveness of Corporate Audit Committees, which was sponsored by the NYSE and NASD (the parent of NASDAQ), the stock exchanges revised their listing rules regarding the requirements and responsibilities of audit committees. Then, in 2003, as directed by Section 301 of SOX, the SEC adopted rules directing the national exchanges to prohibit listing of any security of any company that does not comply with the exchange's audit committee requirements, which includes the responsibilities of the audit committee.

The table on the next page sets forth a summary of the responsibilities of an audit committee as required by the NYSE and NASDAQ (and through SEC rules).

The SEC's rules (Section 10A and Rule 10A-3 of the Exchange Act) not only require the stock exchanges to prohibit listing if certain substantive requirements are not satisfied by public companies (see table), but they also require disclosure of the composition and effectiveness of audit committees. The company's proxy statement (per Item 407(d) of Regulation S-K) must disclose whether (i) an audit committee has been established, (ii) there is a charter for the audit committee, and (iii) the members of the committee satisfy certain qualifications. (See Chapter 8.2, Audit Committee Composition.)

Accounting and Financial Reporting Processes, Internal Controls, Financial Risks

Generally. The integrity of its financial statements is paramount to a public company. The audit committee is required to review and understand the company's financial statements, accounting procedures, and internal controls and assess the related risks. Its members

Item	NYSE (Rule 303A.07)	NASDAQ (Rule 5605(c))
Financial Statements and Accounting Procedures	Assist board oversight of (i) the integrity of the listed company's financial statements, (ii) the listed company's compliance with legal and regulatory requirements, (iii) the independent auditor's qualifications and independence, and (iv) the performance of the listed company's internal audit function and independent auditors	Oversee the accounting and financial reporting processes of the company and the audits of the financial statements of the company
Audit Committee Report	Prepare the Audit Committee Report to be included in the company's proxy statement pursuant to Item 407(d)(3)(i) of Regulation S-K	**Although not specifically required by NASDAQ rules, an audit committee is required to provide an Audit Committee Report in the company's proxy statement per SEC rules.
Evaluation	Perform an annual performance evaluation	Assess charter annually
Auditor Report/ Independence	Obtain and review annually an auditor report describing the firm's internal quality-control procedures; any material issues raised by such review, and any steps taken to deal with any such issues; and the auditor's independence	Ensure receipt from the outside auditors of a formal written statement delineating all relationships between the auditor and the company and independence of the auditor
Related Party Transactions	Recommended to review and evaluate related party transactions and determine whether or not a particular relationship serves the best interest of the company and its shareholders and whether the relationship should be continued or eliminated (Rule 314)	Conduct an appropriate review and oversight of all related party transactions for potential conflict of interest situations on an ongoing basis (Rule 5630)
Auditor Oversight	Be directly responsible for the appointment, compensation, retention, and oversight of the independent auditor (Rule 10A-3(b)(2))	
Whistleblower Procedures	Establish procedures for confidential, anonymous submission by employees of and the receipt, retention, and treatment of complaints regarding auditing matters (Rule 10A-3(b)(3))	
Advisors	Possess authority to independent counsel and advisors (Rule 10A-3(b)(4))	
Funding	Possess funding for the payment of the auditor and any advisor (Rule 10A-3(b)(5))	

must understand, at an appropriate level, how the company's management develops and handles internal financial information so that the audit committee will be in a position to assess the overall approach, process, and quality of the financial statements. Accordingly, SEC and stock exchange rules mandate specific skills and competencies for audit committee members, including at least one "audit committee financial expert." (See Chapter 8.2, Audit Committee Composition.)

For example, to ensure that the audit committee satisfies its oversight responsibilities, Rule 303A.07 of the NYSE Listed Company Guide specifically requires that the audit committee meet to review and discuss the company's annual and quarterly financial statements with management and the independent auditor. In its discussions with management, the audit committee should review recurring issues related to financial reporting, including significant accounting policies, estimates, and judgments. As discussed in the following paragraphs, this type of information is also reviewed with the auditor.

Internal Controls. The audit committee must be familiar with the financial processes and controls (commonly referred to as "internal controls") management has put in place and understand whether they were designed effectively. This can be performed in conjunction with the required certification requirements for the principal executive officer and the principal financial officer in the company's annual and quarterly reports. (See Item 307 of Regulation S-K.) Internal controls, most importantly, help companies detect fraud in its business and financial reporting. The audit committee should be able to assess internal controls, evaluate whether adequate controls are in place, which includes whether there are any significant deficiencies or materials weaknesses, and what can be done to improve such controls. The 2013 COSO framework provides a more formal structure for the design and evaluation of the effectiveness of internal controls. The COSO framework emphasizes the role of the audit committee (via delegation from the board) in overseeing internal controls. The adequacy of internal controls is especially important because the lack or inadequacy of internal controls can make the task of financially auditing the company exceptionally difficult. (See Chapter 8.6, Internal Controls, and Chapter 8.7, Deficiencies and Material Weaknesses in Internal Controls.)

Risk. In connection with overseeing the financial reporting process and understanding internal controls, the audit committee must also evaluate the risks of the company and understand its financial risk management policies and processes. The audit committee should stay current in economic and business trends and changes in the company's operations and accounting standards to ensure that they understand potential risks. It should understand how the company documents and assesses identified risks. (See Chapter 8.5, Critical Accounting Policies, and Chapter 8.10, Enterprise Risk Management.)

Corporate Governance—Whistleblower Procedures, Code of Ethics, Related Party Transactions. Overseeing and being involved in certain aspects of corporate governance allows the audit committee to assess the company's controls and risks. As previously noted, the SEC's rules require that the audit committee establish procedures for receiving, retaining, and addressing complaints regarding accounting, internal accounting controls, or auditing matters, whether from internal or external sources, as well as reporting a range of compliance matters, including violations of the code of conduct, and the confidential, anonymous submission of employee concerns regarding questionable accounting or auditing matters. These whistleblower policies provide another tool for the audit committee to assess potential risks and deficiencies in internal controls and to ensure the integrity of the company's financial statements. (See Chapter 9.9, Dealing with a Whistleblower.)

The audit committee is required to review and approve related party transactions and, in connection with its role to oversee compliance with legal and regulatory requirements, it may also be involved with the company's code of ethics. The audit committee should have a thorough understanding of any related party transactions and issues related to the code of ethics, including the waiver processes and disclosure requirements. (See Chapter 6.8, Related Party Transactions; Chapter 9.2, The Director's Role in Corporate Ethics and Compliance Programs; and Chapter 9.3, Code of Conduct Waivers.)

Overall, to ensure that it understands the financial process, the audit committee should not only have an existing understanding of financial statements and the accounting process, but it should also meet separately with management, including internal auditors, to further collect and analyze information and ask questions.

Oversight of Independent Auditor and Audit Services

Based on SEC and stock exchange rules, audit committees are directly responsible for engaging and overseeing the company's independent auditor. Such responsibility encompasses everything from selecting the independent auditor to reviewing the independent auditor's deliverables. Section 10A of the Exchange Act as well as Article 2 of Regulation S-X provide requirements for the audit of financial statements by an independent auditor and reports to management. (See Chapter 8.8, Management Representation Letters.)

The rules of the SEC and PCAOB require auditors to be independent of their audit clients, and therefore, audit committees must take this into consideration when choosing the company's auditor. The SEC (Rule 2-01 of Regulation S-X) and PCAOB (Auditing Standards No. 3500) independence rules address relationships between the auditor and the company arising from financial interests, employment, certain business dealings, nonaudit services, contingent fees and commissions, partner rotation, the audit committee's administration of the audit engagement (preapproval policies), and compensation of audit partners. For example, the auditor is absolutely prohibited from providing certain services to the company, such as designing financial information systems and providing internal audit services. The audit committee must pre-approve both audit and nonaudit services (those that are not specifically prohibited) from the auditor. However, certain nonaudit services do not require approval if they are de minimis. (See Chapter 8.3, Retaining and Changing an Audit Firm, and Chapter 8.4, Managing the Company's Relationship with Its Auditors.)

In its oversight of the auditor, the audit committee should set expectations regarding communication with the auditor, such as quarterly meetings. Plus, private meetings with the auditor and without management allow the audit committee to have open communication and identify concerns.

SEC and PCAOB rules (See Section 10A(k) of the Exchange Act, Rule 2-07 of Regulation S-X, and PCAOB Auditing Standard No. 3500 et al.) require that the auditor report to the audit committee on various matters, including the following:

- Critical accounting policies and practices
- Alternative treatments of financial information within generally accepted accounting principles that have been discussed with management officials of the issuer, ramifications of the use of such alternative disclosures, and treatments
- The treatment preferred by the registered public accounting firm
- Other material written communications between the registered public accounting firm and the management of the issuer, such as any management letter or schedule of unadjusted differences
- Terms of the annual audit engagement, objective of the audit, and responsibilities of the auditor and management
- Whether the auditor is aware of violations of law and regulations
- Significant and critical accounting policies and practices and estimates
- Significant unusual transactions
- Schedule of uncorrected misstatements related to accounts and disclosures
- Disagreements with management

Financial Statement and Disclosure Matters

As part of its role in overseeing financial statements, the audit committee also has responsibility with respect to the company's disclosures related to the oversight of the financial statements and auditor.

MD&A, Earnings Releases, Non-GAAP. The audit committee should schedule to meet and discuss the company's quarterly and annual financial statements, as well as the MD&A and earnings releases and guidance. The audit committee should confirm that an appropriate legal review has been completed to verify the accuracy and completeness of disclosures, including any obligation to report on trends. Pursuant to Rule 303A.07 of the NYSE Company Guide, the audit committee is required to review with management and the auditors the specific disclosures in "Management's Discussion and Analysis of Financial Condition and Results of Operations" and discuss the company's earnings press releases, as well as financial information and earnings guidance. The NYSE's guidance provides that the review may be done generally (i.e., discussion of the types of information to be disclosed and the type of presentation to be made). The NYSE guidance also states that the audit committee need not discuss in advance each earnings release or each instance in which a listed company may provide earnings guidance. The NYSE commentary also provides that the committee should pay particular attention to any use of "pro forma," or "adjusted" non-GAAP, information. Accordingly, the committee should be familiar with the SEC's rules regarding the use of non-GAAP financial measures in Regulation G and Item 10(e) of Regulation S-K.

Audit Committee Report. Item 407(d)(3) of Regulation S-K requires a company to include an audit committee report in its proxy statement. The audit committee report must state whether it has

- reviewed and discussed the audited financial statements with management;
- discussed with the auditors the matters required to be discussed pursuant to PCAOB Auditing Standard Rule 1301, which includes terms and results of the audit, quality of the company's financial reporting, misstatements, and disagreements with management;
- received the written disclosures and letter from the auditor regarding the independent accountant's; and
- based on the review of such information, it has recommended to the board of directors of the company that the audited financial statements be included in the Form 10-K.

Auditor Fees and Services. The company's Form 10-K and proxy statement are required to disclose fees paid to the auditor during the previous two fiscal years, as well as a description of the nature of the services. The categories are (i) audit fees, (ii) audit-related fees, (iii) tax fees, and (iv) all other fees (Item 9(e) of Schedule 14A and Section 10A-3(i) of the Exchange Act). Furthermore, the company is required to disclose the audit committee's pre-approval policies and procedures and the percentage of nonaudit fees (audit-related, tax, and all other fees) that were not pre-approved but later approved based on the de minis exception (i.e., the fees in the aggregate did not constitute more than 5 percent of the company's revenues).

Risk Oversight. The company's proxy statement is required to disclose the extent of the board's role in the risk oversight of the company, such as how the board administers its oversight function and the effect that this has on the board's leadership structure (Item 407(h) of Regulation S-K). The SEC stated that disclosure about the board's approach to risk oversight might address questions such as whether the persons who oversee risk management report directly to the board as a whole, to a committee, such as the audit committee, and how it monitors risk. To the extent that in connection with its role, the audit committee oversees risks that could relate to financial disclosures, this would be disclosed as well.

Related Party Transactions. The company is required to disclose its policies and procedures for the review, approval, or ratification of any related party transaction and the material features—for example, the types of transactions that are covered, the standards applied, the persons on the board of directors or otherwise who are responsible for applying such policies and procedures, which may be the audit committee, and whether such policies and procedures are in writing and, if not, how are they evidenced. Plus, it is required to report whether any disclosed related party transaction did not require review, approval, or ratification or where the policies and procedures were not followed. These required disclosures should be kept in mind by the audit committee when it reviews any related party disclosures.

Key Questions

In considering the role and function of the audit committee, issues to consider include the following:

- ❑ How often should the audit committee meet?
- ❑ Does the audit committee charter comply with applicable SEC and stock exchange rules?
- ❑ How will the audit committee evaluate itself?
- ❑ How does the audit committee educate itself about the company's accounting and financial reporting process?
- ❑ Does the audit committee have a regular schedule to meet with management to review the company's financial reporting process?
- ❑ Has management provided information about the company's internal controls and do any significant deficient or material weaknesses exist? If so, how does the company plan to address and mitigate internal control issues?
- ❑ What business and operational risks does the company face? What role will the company take in overseeing the company's risk profile?
- ❑ How does the audit committee receive complaints under the whistleblower policy and how does the committee plan to address any complaints?
- ❑ How does the company identify and track related party transactions? How will the audit committee review and assess related party transactions?
- ❑ Does the audit committee have oversight of the company's code of ethics? And, if so, what are the committee's responsibilities? Who reports to the committee regarding corporate governance issues?
- ❑ Does the audit committee have a regular meeting schedule with the independent auditors and do the auditors provide an agenda and materials for meetings?
- ❑ What is the committee's pre-approval policy with respect to services provided by the auditor? Has the committee complied with the policy?
- ❑ What services have the auditors provided to the company during the past two years?
- ❑ Does the audit committee need to engage any advisors to assist with its responsibilities?
- ❑ Does MD&A sufficiently describe the company's performance and trends in its reports?
- ❑ What is the company's process in preparing earnings releases? How is the audit committee involved?
- ❑ Does the company issue guidance? What is management's process to develop guidance? What are the assumptions?
- ❑ Does the company provide non-GAAP financial information in its disclosures, and, if so, what are the related internal controls and are the required disclosures included?
- ❑ Has the audit committee reviewed and approved the audit committee report for the company's proxy statement?

Additional Reading

1. Section 10A (Audit Requirements) Rule 10A-3 (Listing Standards relating to audit committees) of the Exchange Act

   https://www.law.cornell.edu/uscode/text/15/78j-1 and https://www.law.cornell.edu/cfr/text/17/240.10A-3

2. Audit Committee Back to Basics, Powerpoint Presentation, The SEC Speaks, Paul Beswick, Chief Accountant, Office of the Chief Accountant of the Securities and Exchange Commission, February 22, 2014

   https://www.sec.gov/News/Speech/Detail/Speech/1370540846980

3. PCAOB Information for Audit Committees

   https://pcaobus.org//Information/Pages/AuditCommitteeMembers.aspx

4. The Committee of Sponsoring Organizations of the Treadway Commission (COSO)

   http://www.coso.org/

5. NYSE Listed Company Manual; Rule 303A.07 Audit Committee Additional Requirements

   http://nysemanual.nyse.com/LCMTools/PlatformViewer.asp?selectednode=chp%5F1%5F4%5F3&manual=%2Flcm%2Fsections%2Flcm%2Dsections%2F

6. NASDAQ Listing Rules; Rule 5605-3(c) Audit Committee Requirements

   http://nasdaq.cchwallstreet.com/NASDAQTools/PlatformViewer.asp?selectednode=chp%5F1%5F1%5F4%5F3&manual=%2Fnasdaq%2Fmain%2Fnasdaq%2Dequityrules%2F

7. Ernst & Young Audit Committee Resources

   http://www.ey.com/gl/en/issues/governance-and-reporting/ey-center-for-board-matters#audit-committee

8. PWC Audit Committee Resources

   http://www.pwc.com/us/en/governance-insights-center/audit-committee-resources.html

9. Deloitte Audit Committee Resource Guide

   http://www2.deloitte.com/us/en/pages/center-for-board-effectiveness/topics/audit-committee.html?icid=nav2_audit-committee

10. KPMG Audit Committee Guide

    https://boardleadership.kpmg.us/relevant-topics/articles/2015/09/audit-committee-guide.html

Notes

8.2 AUDIT COMMITTEE COMPOSITION

CONTRIBUTED BY
Katherine J. Blair and Suwani Karki
Manatt, Phelps & Phillips, LLP[1]

A company's audit committee plays a critical role in ensuring the integrity of the company's financial reporting. An effective audit committee should be comprised of individuals who understand the financial reporting process, have the experience necessary to oversee the company's financial reporting function, and possess the integrity to ensure that the company's financial reports fairly present its financial condition. An effective audit committee will also include members who will be able to assist management in assessing and reporting on risk management issues. However, the specific composition of the audit committee will depend on the nature of the company, the scope of its operations, and the industry in which it operates.

An audit committee is comprised entirely of members of the board of directors and generally consists of three to eight members. Companies listed on the NYSE or NASDAQ are required to have at least three directors on their audit committees. Sufficient

1. Katherine J. Blair is a partner in the Capital Markets group at Manatt, Phelps & Phillips, LLP, where she practices in the firm's Los Angeles office. Suwani Karki is an associate in the Corporate and Finance group, where she practices in the firm's Washington, D.C. office.

membership on an audit committee helps to ensure that there is an adequate mix of skills and experience to effectively carry out the functions of the committee.

Enhanced Independence Requirements

In order to maintain objectivity for the financial reporting process, members of an audit committee must be independent directors. Section 10A(m) and Rule 10A-3 of the Exchange Act require stock exchanges to adopt strict independence tests for audit committee members. These enhanced independence requirements are in addition to the general independence qualifications for directors. (See Chapter 2.3, Board Member Independence.) In order to be independent, an audit committee member may neither

- accept any consulting, advisory, or other compensatory fee, directly or indirectly, from the company or its subsidiaries (other than fees for board service), nor
- be affiliated with the company or its subsidiaries.

Consulting and Advisory Fees. Unlike other stock exchange independence requirements for directors that have de minimis exceptions, the prohibition on consulting and advisory fees for audit committee members is absolute. For example, a general independence requirement of the NYSE requires that the director must not have received, during a 12-month period within the last three years, more than $120,000 in direct compensation from the issuer. The audit committee requirement, on the other hand, prohibits *any* payment for consulting and advisory services.

The prohibition on consulting and advisory fees also includes *indirect payments*. Per guidance from the SEC, this includes the following indirect payments to family members and entities in which a director holds a certain position:

- Payments to spouses, minor children or stepchildren, or children or stepchildren sharing a home with the member
- Payments to an entity

  in which the director is a partner or member (except for limited partners, non-managing members and those occupying similar positions who, in each case, have no active role in providing services to the entity), an officer such as a managing director occupying a comparable position, an executive officer (to address organizations that do not have partners or members), or occupies a similar position

  and

  which provides accounting, consulting, legal, investment banking, or financial advisory services to the issuer or any subsidiary.

In its adopting release, the SEC clarified that the restriction on indirect payments also includes payments to persons such as partners or members in professional services organizations whose compensation could be directly affected by the prohibited fees, even if they are not the primary service provider to the issuer and do not control the service provider. The SEC also noted that the term "principal" is not included in its list as they believe that the reference to "those occupying similar positions" covers entities such as professional corporations that use the "principal" designation for positions similar to a partner in a partnership. The prohibition on indirect payments does *not* include a mere employee of an entity providing services to the issuer.

Prohibited compensatory fees *do not include* the following:

- The receipt of fixed amounts of compensation under a retirement plan (including deferred compensation) for prior service with the issuer (provided that such compensation is not contingent in any way on continued service)
- Payments for nonadvisory financial services such as lending, check clearing, maintaining customer accounts, stock brokerage services, or custodial and cash management services
- If the audit committee member is also a shareholder of the issuer, the prohibition does not include payments made to all shareholders of that class generally, such as dividends

Affiliations. A director that is an "affiliate" of the company does not qualify for service on the audit committee. The determination of whether a director is an "affiliated person" requires a factual determination based on a consideration of all relevant facts and circumstances. The terms "affiliate" and "affiliated person" have the same meanings as used in Rule 144 of the Securities Act and Rule 12b-2 of the Exchange Act. The term "control" is also consistent with other definitions under the Exchange Act as "the possession, direct or indirect, of the power to direct or cause the direction of the management and policies of a person, whether through the ownership of voting securities, by contract, or otherwise."

To assist with the determination of whether a director is deemed an affiliate, the SEC has provided a *safe harbor*. Under the safe harbor, a director will not be deemed to control the issuer (and, thus, not be presumed an affiliate) if

- the director is not an executive officer, and
- does not own 10 percent or more of any class of voting equity securities of such entity, based on ownership of any class of voting equity securities.

The safe harbor is designed to identify a group of directors who are not affiliates so as to provide comfort to those individuals or entities that no additional facts and circumstances analysis is necessary. The safe harbor does not in any way specify or imply that a certain level of share ownership automatically presumes that a person is an affiliate. It only creates a safe harbor position for determining nonaffiliate status; failing to meet the 10 percent ownership threshold has no bearing on whether a director is an affiliate based on an evaluation of other facts and circumstances. An instruction to the SEC rule provides that calculations of beneficial ownership are to be made consistent with Rule 13d-3 of the Exchange Act. (See Chapter 11.4, The SEC's Beneficial Ownership Reporting Regime.)

With regards to relationships with entities that are already deemed affiliates of the issuer, directors will be deemed affiliates of the issuer if they are also executive officers, or directors who are also employees, or general partners, or managing members of an affiliate. Passive, noncontrol positions, such as limited partners, and those who do not have policy-making functions, are not covered. In other words, a director would not be deemed an affiliate solely based on a noncontrol position with an affiliate of the issuer. Note that this list is narrower than the formulation of covered positions for indirect payments under consulting and advisory fees.

Other NASDAQ Requirements. NASDAQ also requires that each audit committee member has not participated in the preparation of the financial statements of the company or any current subsidiary at any time during the past three years and be able to read and understand fundamental financial statements, including a balance sheet, income statement, and cash flow statement.

No Look Back

Unlike the general stock exchange director independence requirements discussed in Chapter 2.3 of this Handbook, the enhanced audit committee independence requirements under Rule 10A-3 only extend to *current* relationships; they do not have a "look back" period. However, note that NASDAQ's rules do contain a three-year look back with respect to the participation in the preparation of the company's financial statements.

Exemptions (Rule 10A-3(c)) and Exceptional and Limited Circumstances

The audit committee independence requirements provide exemptions for new issuers and directorships at affiliates of the issuer. However, unlike the general stock exchange director independence standards, the SEC audit committee requirements do not contain any exemptions based on "exceptional and limited circumstances." Plus, the SEC specifically notes that it does not entertain exemptions or waivers for particular relationships on a case-by-case basis.

IPO Transition. New issuers (i.e., those who are filing an initial registration statement) have a grace period in that they are required to have at least one fully independent member at the time of the issuer's initial listing, a majority of independent members within 90 days, and a fully independent committee within one year.

Affiliate Director. An audit committee member may sit on the board of directors of an issuer and any affiliate so long as, except for being a director on each such board of directors, the director otherwise meets the independence requirements for both the issuer and the affiliated entity, including the receipt of only ordinary-course compensation for serving as a member of the board of directors, audit committee, or any other board committee of each such entity. Under this exemption, audit committee members will still be required to be independent of the issuer and its affiliate, but the exemption will apply regardless of the source of control.

Exceptional and Limited Circumstances. NASDAQ rules allow for the appointment of a non-independent director for exceptional and limited circumstances (Rule 5605(c)(2)(B)). If a director does not qualify under the general director independence standards but satisfies the independence requirements under Rule 10A-3 and is not (nor is a family member) an executive officer of the company, then such director may be appointed to the audit committee if the board, under exceptional and limited circumstances, determines that membership on the committee by the director is required by the best interests of the company and its shareholders. A company that relies on this exception must comply with the disclosure requirements set forth in Item 407(d)(2) of Regulation S-K (see Disclosure section in this chapter). A member appointed under this exception may not serve longer than two years and may not chair the audit committee.

Financial Literacy Requirements; Audit Committee Financial Expert

Being a member of the audit committee also comes with the expectation that that individual is capable of understanding the financial reporting process and what it entails. The NYSE rules require all members of the audit committee to be financially literate, as such qualification is interpreted by the company's board in its business judgment, while NASDAQ rules require each member to be able to read and understand financial statements.

The NYSE, NASDAQ, and SEC rules each require that at least one individual on the audit committee possess financial expertise, although each defines such expertise slightly differently. The SEC requires (Item 407(d) of Regulation S-K) disclosure of the "audit committee financial expert." The audit committee financial expert, among other qualifications, understands generally accepted accounting principles and financial statements, has experience with preparing, analyzing, and evaluating financial statements, understands procedures and internal controls for financial reporting, and understands the audit committee's role and responsibilities. Such an audit committee financial expert must have acquired the necessary skills through experience as a principal financial officer, controller, public accountant, auditor, or other relevant experience, such as supervising or overseeing individuals in those capacities or supervising or overseeing the preparation, auditing, or evaluations of financial statements. If a company does not have an audit committee financial expert it must disclose its reason for not having one.

The NYSE requires that at least one individual on the audit committee have related accounting or financial management expertise. While the NYSE does not require that a company's audit committee include an audit committee financial expert, if a person satisfies the definition, then the board may presume that such person has accounting or related financial management expertise. NASDAQ also requires at least one member to be financially sophisticated and presumes that a person qualifies as such if they satisfy the criteria of the audit committee financial expert.

Ultimately, a company's board of directors will determine in its business judgment what attributes are necessary to be an effective member of the audit committee and draw upon those needs in choosing the members of the company's audit committee who have the desired skills and experiences to help the company thrive.

Disclosure

SEC rules require the company's proxy statement to identify each member of the audit committee. If a company relies on any exemption provided in Rule 10A-3, it must disclose in its proxy statement its reliance on the exemption and its assessment of whether, and if so, how, such reliance would materially and adversely affect the ability of the audit committee to act independently and to satisfy the other requirements of Rule 10A-3.

Furthermore, if, apart from the requirements of Rule 10A-3, a company includes a non-independent member on its audit committee as a result of stock exchange exceptions to its independence requirements (such as exceptional and limited circumstances), Item 407(d) of Regulation S-K requires the company to disclose the relationship that causes the member's disqualification as independent and the reasons for the board's determination.

NYSE rules require that if an audit committee member simultaneously serves on the audit committees of more than three public companies, the board must determine that such simultaneous service would not impair the ability of such member to effectively serve on the company's audit committee and must disclose such determination either on or through the company's website or in its annual proxy statement or, if the company does not file an annual proxy statement, in its annual report on Form 10-K filed with the SEC. If this disclosure is made on or through the company's website, the company must disclose that fact in its proxy statement or annual report, as applicable, and provide the website address.

NASDAQ recommends that a company disclose in its annual proxy statement (or, if the company does not file a proxy statement, in its Form 10-K) if any director is deemed eligible to serve on the audit committee but falls outside the safe harbor provisions of the meaning of control of an affiliate (does not own more than 10 percent of voting securities and not an executive officer) set forth in Rule 10A-3(e)(1)(ii) of the Exchange Act.

Cure

If the composition of a company's audit committee does not comply with the SEC and stock exchange enhanced independence requirements, the company may be able to rely on a cure or transition period. Rule 10A-3 provides that companies must have an opportunity to cure defects and that the stock exchange may provide that if a member of an audit committee ceases to be independent for reasons outside the member's reasonable control, that person may remain an audit committee member of the listed issuer until the earlier of the next annual shareholders meeting of the listed issuer or one year from the occurrence of the event that caused the member to be no longer independent.

NASDAQ specifically followed the SEC's rules. Under NASDAQ Rule 5605(c)(4), if an audit committee member resigns or an audit committee member ceases to be independent for reasons outside the member's reasonable control, the company has until the earlier of the next annual shareholders meeting or one year from the date of the occurrence to regain compliance. If the annual shareholders meeting occurs no later than 180 days following the resignation, the company will instead have 180 days from such resignation to regain compliance. A company relying on this cure period must provide notice to NASDAQ immediately.

The NYSE provides a more broad cure in that its commentary states that the stock exchange will provide companies the opportunity to cure defects provided in Rule 10A-3(a)(3) under the Exchange Act.

Key Questions

The following questions pertain to the composition of an audit committee:

- ❑ How many members are required for the audit committee to be an effective decision-making body for the company?
- ❑ What skills and experience (including industry experience) will be necessary to understand the company's purposes and financial reporting obligations and serve as a member or chair of the audit committee?
- ❑ Who should be chair of the committee? Is there a clear succession plan in place for leadership within the committee?
- ❑ What process will be used to evaluate and vet potential audit committee members?
- ❑ Does the company include in its D&O questionnaires audit committee member questions that address SEC and stock exchange requirements, such as affiliations and advisory fees?
- ❑ Does the company ensure compliance with independence requirements for its audit committee members on a periodic basis?
- ❑ Does the company rely on an exemption or exception or transition period for audit committee composition?
- ❑ How will the performance of current audit committee members be evaluated?
- ❑ Does the audit committee have at least one financial expert who satisfies the requirements of the SEC rules and stock exchange?
- ❑ Do the members of the audit committee understand the company's accounting principles and risks?
- ❑ Does the company provide in its proxy statement or annual report the required disclosure about its audit committee members and reliance on an exemption, exception, or cure?

Additional Reading

1. Section 10A (Audit Requirements) of the Exchange Act
   https://www.law.cornell.edu/uscode/text/15/78j-1
2. Rule 10A-3 (Listing Standards relating to audit committees) of the Exchange Act
   https://www.law.cornell.edu/cfr/text/17/240.10A-3
3. NYSE Listed Company Manual Sections 303A.06 (Audit Committee) and 303A.07 (Audit Committee Additional Requirements)
   http://nysemanual.nyse.com/LCMTools/PlatformViewer.asp?selectednode=chp%5F1%5F4%5F3%5F3&manual=%2Flcm%2Fsections%2Flcm%2Dsections%2F

4. NASDAQ Listing Rules; Rule 5605(c) and IM-5604-4 (Audit Committee Composition)
http://nasdaq.cchwallstreet.com/NASDAQTools/PlatformViewer.asp?selectednode=chp%5F1%5F1%5F4%5F3&manual=%2Fnasdaq%2Fmain%2Fnasdaq%2Dequityrules%2F
5. NASDAQ FAQs re: Audit Committee Requirements
https://listingcenter.nasdaq.com/Material_Search.aspx?cid=108&mcd=LQ

Notes

8.3 RETAINING AND CHANGING AN AUDIT FIRM

CONTRIBUTED BY
Lori Zyskowski, Elizabeth A. Ising, and Michael Scanlon
Gibson, Dunn & Crutcher LLP[1]

Among the most important roles of the audit committee is retaining the audit firm and then considering whether that firm should continue in its role. Audit committees need to develop a process not only for the initial retention of the audit firm, but also for the annual review and evaluation of the audit firm's performance.

In its initial hiring of an audit firm, the audit committee should first review whether or not the audit firm is independent of the company. Audit committee members should be aware of independence requirements for auditors, which include the SEC's auditor independence rules and the ethics and independence rules of the Public Company Accounting Oversight Board (PCAOB). Under these rules, the auditor is required to advise the audit committee of any services or relationships that reasonably can affect the audit firm's independence, and the audit committee has to consider whether the audit firm is capable of exercising objectivity and professional skepticism.

The audit committee should also consider whether the audit firm brings to bear the capability and expertise necessary to handle the breadth and complexity of the company's

1. Lori Zykowski, Elizabeth A. Ising, and Michael Scanlon are all partners in the Securities Regulation and Corporate Governance practice group at Gibson, Dunn & Crutcher LLP.

operations, particularly if the company operates globally. The firm's familiarity with the company's industry and any specialized accounting issues in that industry is crucial. The audit committee should further review external data on audit quality and performance, including recent PCAOB reports on the audit firm and its peer firms. In addition, the audit committee should review and analyze the audit firm's known legal risks and any significant legal or regulatory proceedings in which the audit firm is involved.

On an annual basis, when the audit committee is deciding whether to retain the company's current audit firm or consider engaging another firm as the independent auditor, the audit committee should review the same matters just noted: the audit firm's independence, the firm's capability and expertise, and the firm's known legal risks and legal or regulatory proceedings (updated annually). In particular, the audit committee, as part of its annual process, should evaluate the performance of the lead engagement partner and other key partners on the audit engagement team. In addition, the audit committee should review the audit firm's performance on the company's audit. This can be accomplished through surveys regarding the audit firm's service and quality. A survey would ask company personnel who have had substantial contact with the audit firm to answer questions regarding the quality of services provided by the audit firm; the sufficiency of audit firm resources; communication and interaction with the audit firm; and the audit firm's independence, objectivity, and professional skepticism. The survey process can be led by the company's internal audit team, and results should be reported to the audit committee before it considers whether or not to retain the audit firm for the coming audit year. Care should be taken to separate valid complaints from simple objections to the firm's rigor.

The audit committee also should annually discuss with the audit firm the independence controls that it has in place. Since the audit committee is tasked with approving the compensation of the audit firm, it should also review a report on the audit firm's fees for audit and non-audit services. It is important that the audit committee look at the fees both on an absolute basis and, to the extent possible, by comparing them to the fees of other audit firms.

When the audit committee is considering changing the audit firm, it should also take into account the significant time and resource commitment that is required to bring on a new auditor. There are, of course, situations where changing the auditor is warranted, but it is important for the audit committee to consider the potential distraction and impact on management's focus on financial reporting and internal controls that could result from a change.

The audit committee should also be aware that the cooperation of the former firm will be needed for a minimum of three years as the financial statements audited by the former firm will be included within the company's SEC reports for that time period. The former firm must consent to the inclusion of the prior years' financial statements in the company's reports and a consent fee will be charged. The grace with which the transition is handled may have an effect on the relationship, which may influence the attitude of the former firm and the size of the consent fee it charges. In some instances, it may be possible to negotiate the size of the consent fee (or at least a range in which the fee will fall) as part of the review process if the former firm remained under consideration. In other cases, it may be possible to do so once the decision to make the change has been made.

Key Questions

In evaluating whether to retain or change the audit firm, the audit committee should consider the following questions:

- ❑ Does the lead engagement partner and audit team have the necessary knowledge and skills to meet the company's audit requirements?
- ❑ Will/has the audit firm dedicated appropriate resources to the audit?
- ❑ Has the audit firm provided an explanation of its quality control processes?
- ❑ Did the audit firm meet the agreed upon performance criteria as set forth in the engagement letter and scope of the audit?
- ❑ Did the lead engagement partner advise the audit committee of the results of consultations with the firm's national professional practice office in a timely manner?
- ❑ If the company's audit was subject to inspection by the PCAOB or other regulators, did the auditor advise the audit committee of the selection of the audit, findings, and the impact, if any, on the audit results in a timely manner?
- ❑ Was the cost of the audit reasonable for the size, complexity, and risks of the company?
- ❑ Does the audit firm have the necessary industry expertise and geographical reach required to serve the company?
- ❑ Did the audit engagement partner maintain a professional and open dialogue with the audit committee and its chair?
- ❑ Did the auditor adequately discuss the quality of the company's financial reporting, including the reasonableness of accounting estimates and judgments?
- ❑ In executive sessions, did the auditor discuss sensitive issues candidly and professionally?
- ❑ Did the auditor take steps to help ensure that the audit committee was informed of current developments in accounting principles and auditing standards relevant to the company's financial statements and potential impact on the audit?
- ❑ Did the audit firm report to the audit committee all matters that might reasonably be thought to bear on the firm's independence, including exceptions to its compliance with independence requirements?
- ❑ What safeguards does the audit firm have in place to detect independence issues?
- ❑ If there was a significant difference in views between management and the auditor, did the auditor present a clear point of view on accounting issues where management's initial perspective differed? Was the process of reconciling views timely and professional?
- ❑ If the audit firm is placing reliance on management and internal audit testing, did the audit committee agree with the extent of such reliance?
- ❑ In obtaining pre-approval from the audit committee for all non-audit services, did the lead engagement partner discuss safeguards in place to protect the independence, objectivity, and professional skepticism of the auditor?

- ❑ Were the results of company personnel surveys on the audit firm's performance satisfactory? Does the audit firm have a process in place to address any concerns in the coming year?
- ❑ What are the approximate aggregate costs of effecting a change in auditors? Are those costs justifiable?

Additional Reading

1. External Auditor Assessment Tool
   http://www.thecaq.org/file/162/download?token=-NF7SRc_
2. Statutes and Regulations Governing Auditor Independence
   http://www.aicpa.org/InterestAreas/CenterForAuditQuality/Resources/CAQAuditLibrary/Pages/Ethics%20and%20Independence.aspx
3. Information for Audit Committees about the PCAOB Inspection Process
   https://pcaobus.org/Inspections/Documents/Inspection_Information_for_Audit_Commitees.pdf

Notes

____

____

____

____

____

84 MANAGING THE COMPANY'S RELATIONSHIP WITH ITS AUDITORS

CONTRIBUTED BY
Kevin A. Burke
Sidley Austin LLP[1]

External auditors are required to exercise professional skepticism in their evaluation of the company's financial statements. Moreover, the auditors' collection of sufficient, competent audit evidence at times can impose inconvenience upon a company. These factors can present challenges in managing the company's relationship with the external auditors. However, by establishing clear expectations, engaging in regular and open communications, and constantly evaluating the performance of auditors and management, the audit committee will be better able to effectively manage the relationship.

At the outset of an engagement, the audit committee should establish with the external auditor clear expectations based on the unique circumstances of the company. Issues to address include the audit requirements, communications procedures, audit team resources (including with respect to foreign locations), issue resolution, and progress reporting. The committee should also address the reasonableness of audit fees, procedures for lead audit partner rotation, and procedures for the approval of non-audit services, which bear on the auditor's requisite independence.

1. Kevin Burke is a partner in Sidley Austin's New York office and practices in the areas of regulatory enforcement, professional liability, and corporate governance, among others.

Thereafter, the audit committee should have regular and open communications with the external auditor to discuss significant developments as they occur. Such discussions should address, for example, issuance and implementation of new accounting principles, judgments regarding unusual transactions, budgeting or scheduling issues, and disagreements with management regarding control assessments or otherwise.

It is particularly useful for the audit committee chair to hold private meetings with the lead audit partner. Doing so can help build a constructive and respectful working relationship. Likewise, given the increasing extent to which audit firms engage in consultations with their national offices regarding complex accounting and auditing issues, the audit committee, or its chair, also may want to meet directly with national office representatives to establish familiarity with the consultation process and available resources.

Regulators and stock exchange listing requirements specifically identify a number of matters about which auditors are required to communicate with audit committees throughout the audit process. In particular, pursuant to PCAOB Auditing Standard No. 16, the auditor is required to communicate regarding, for example, the audit strategy, timing and significant risks (16.9-11), critical accounting policies and critical accounting estimates (16.12), difficult or contentious matters for which the auditor consulted (16.15), uncorrected and corrected misstatements (16.18), and disagreements with management (16.22).

Notably, the PCAOB recently proposed (actually, re-proposed) a new standard to enhance the external auditor's report on the financial statements. If adopted, the standard would require the auditor to convey in its audit report any "critical audit matters" (CAM), that is, matters communicated or required to be communicated to the audit committee that relate to material accounts or disclosures in the financial statements or involve especially challenging, subjective, or complex judgment. Regular and open discussions with the auditor could minimize the extent to which CAM become the subjects of miscommunication or inordinate concern.

While the audit committee should hold executive sessions with the external auditor, there are circumstances in which the committee will want to involve management in discussions with the auditor as well. For example, because management has primary responsibility for establishing the company's accounting principles, involving management in discussions regarding judgments concerning the quality of the company's accounting principles will likely be productive.

Throughout the audit process, the audit committee should evaluate the auditor's performance. While more formal assessments may be appropriate to address specific aspects of performance, such as the auditor's skepticism in evaluating unusual transactions or the audit firm's controls around the quality and performance of audit personnel in foreign locations, informal assessments can be made throughout the variety of interactions had with the audit team.

Ultimately, the nature and quality of communications with the auditor provide the audit committee with a valuable basis upon which to assess the auditor's performance. Among the relevant considerations are whether the auditor is able to explain accounting and auditing issues in an understandable manner; whether the auditor informs the committee of current developments in accounting principles and auditing standards relevant to the company's financial statements and the potential impact on the audit; whether the auditor discusses sensitive issues candidly and professionally; whether the auditor promptly notifies the committee if management fails to provide appropriate cooperation or disagrees with the auditor's judgments; and, whether the auditor seeks feedback regarding the quality of services provided.

Key Questions

In managing the company's relationship with the external auditor, the audit committee should consider asking the following:

- ❑ What compliance procedures does the external audit firm have in place with respect to independence? Were any relationships between the auditor and the company not disclosed to the audit committee because they were deemed not material?
- ❑ Are appropriate procedures for the approval of non-audit services by the external audit firm in place?
- ❑ What technical skills, knowledge, and experience do the lead audit partner, review partner, tax partner, and audit managers have that make them qualified to conduct the audit (company/industry-specific, accounting, auditing)?
- ❑ If portions of the audit are to be performed by teams in foreign locations within the auditor's global network or from other audit firms, what technical skills, knowledge, and experience do those auditors have that make them qualified to conduct the audit? How does the lead audit partner exercise appropriate supervision over those auditors?
- ❑ How are changes or rotations of lead audit partner and senior audit team personnel handled and managed, including monitoring compliance with applicable requirements?
- ❑ Does the audit team have sufficient access to specialized expertise to the extent necessary during the audit?
- ❑ How does the audit plan address company/industry-specific areas of accounting and audit risk, including fraud risk? How, if at all, did the auditor adjust the audit plan to respond to changing circumstances?
- ❑ To what extent does the external auditor intend to rely on or otherwise leverage the work of internal audit? How will that impact the external audit fees?
- ❑ What are the auditor's views regarding the aggressiveness or conservatism—or appropriateness versus mere acceptability—of management's accounting judgments? What is the auditor's reasoning in accepting or questioning the significant estimates made by management?
- ❑ Were disagreements regarding accounting or control issues, if any, between management and the auditor promptly raised with the audit committee?
- ❑ What consultations took place by the audit team with the audit firm's national office or leadership regarding audit quality, standards, methodology, or other technical resources on accounting or auditing matters?
- ❑ If the audit was subject to inspection by regulators, what were the findings and what was the impact, if any, on the audit results? How does the auditor plan to

respond to the inspection findings and to internal findings regarding its quality control program?

- ❑ How is our company rated (regarded) by our auditor in its evaluation of the company as an audit risk? If not well-rated or regarded, why? What, if any, remedial actions (including changes to our internal controls or accounting policies) should be taken to mitigate the risks perceived by the auditor?

Additional Reading

1. KPMG's Audit Committee Institute, The Audit Committee Guide, Chapter 4 and Appendix F (2015)
   https://kpmg-blc.adobecqms.net/content/dam/blc/pdfs/2015/kpmg-audit-committee-guide-2015.pdf
2. Deloitte Audit Committee Resource Guide, Section Four (February 2015)
   http://www2.deloitte.com/content/dam/Deloitte/us/Documents/center-for-corporate-governance/us-aers-audit-committee-resource-guide-2015-032615.pdf
3. PCAOB Auditing Standard No. 16, Communications with Audit Committees.
   https://pcaobus.org/Standards/Auditing/pages/auditing_standard_16.aspx
4. External Auditor Assessment Tool: A Reference for Audit Committees Worldwide, *The Center for Audit Quality* (June 2, 2015)
   http://www.thecaq.org/docs/default-source/reports-and-publications/auditor_assessment_tool_worldwide.pdf?sfvrsn=2/external-auditor-assessment-tool-a-reference-for-audit-committees-worldwide
5. Fact Sheet: Auditor's Reporting Model Reproposal, *PCAOB* (May 11, 2016)
   https://pcaobus.org/News/Releases/Pages/Fact-Sheet-Reproposal-Auditors-Report-051116.aspx

Notes

8.5 CRITICAL ACCOUNTING POLICIES

CONTRIBUTED BY

Elizabeth A. Ising, Eric Scarazzo, and Michael J. Scanlon

Gibson, Dunn & Crutcher LLP[1]

Critical accounting policies are a subset of the accounting policies that companies use in preparing their financial reports. Specifically, critical accounting policies are those policies that are important to the presentation and understanding of the company's financial condition, and applications of these policies often require management to make the most difficult, subjective, or complex judgments.

U.S. Generally Accepted Accounting Principles (GAAP) requires companies to report all accounting policies in the financial statement footnotes, focusing on the method used to apply them. In the wake of the financial failures at Enron and other companies, the Securities and Exchange Commission (SEC) became concerned that greater disclosure about accounting policies was needed, specifically the "need for greater investor awareness of the sensitivity of financial statements to the methods, assumptions, and estimates underlying their preparation." As a result, the SEC staff reminded companies of their duty to provide, as part of Management's Discussion and Analysis (MD&A), "plain English" explanations of their critical accounting policies, the judgments and uncertainties affecting the

1. Elizabeth A. Ising, partner; Eric Scarazzo, of counsel; and Michael J. Scanlon, partner, are all members of the Securities Regulation and Corporate Governance practice group at Gibson, Dunn & Crutcher LLP.

application of those policies, and the likelihood that materially different amounts would be reported under different conditions or using different assumptions.

When selecting a company's critical accounting policies for disclosure in MD&A, management should consider which estimates or assumptions (i) are material due to the subjectivity and judgment needed to account for highly uncertain matters or the susceptibility of those matters to change, and (ii) would have a material impact on the company's financial condition or operating performance.

The SEC believes that the disclosure of critical accounting policies in MD&A should supplement the description of accounting policies that typically appears separately in the financial statement notes with analysis of the uncertainties involved in applying the accounting policies or variability that is reasonably likely to result from its application over time. The SEC proposed rules in May 2002 to broaden the scope of required disclosures regarding critical accounting policies. While those rules were not adopted, companies in practice provide the disclosures contemplated by the proposed rules when discussing critical accounting policies in SEC filings. They include the following:

- A discussion of the critical accounting estimate, the methodology used to determine it, any underlying assumption that is about highly uncertain matters and any other underlying assumption that is material, any known trends, demands, commitments, events, or uncertainties that are reasonably likely to occur and materially affect the methodology or the assumptions described, if applicable, why different estimates that would have had a material impact on the company's financial presentation could have been used in the current period, and, if applicable, why the accounting estimate is reasonably likely to change from period to period with a material impact on the financial presentation
- An explanation of the significance of the accounting estimate to the company's financial condition, changes in financial condition and results of operations and, where material, an identification of the line items in the company's financial statements affected by the accounting estimate
- A quantitative discussion of changes in overall financial performance and, to the extent material, line items in the financial statements if the company were to assume that the accounting estimate were changed
- A quantitative and qualitative discussion of any material changes made to the accounting estimate in the past three years, the reasons for the changes, and the effect on line items in the financial statements and overall financial performance
- A statement of whether or not the company's senior management has discussed the development and selection of the accounting estimate, and the MD&A disclosure regarding it, with the audit committee of the company's board of directors
- A discussion of matters related to the impact of the estimate on the company's segments

The SEC also expects that there will be board oversight of management's selection of and disclosure regarding a company's critical accounting policies. This oversight most often occurs within the company's audit committee. The SEC staff has stated that the independent auditors should understand the audited company's critical accounting policies; management must be able to defend their selection of these policies; and the audit committee must review the selection, application, and disclosure regarding these policies.

Key Questions

In evaluating disclosure of a company's critical accounting policies, the audit committee should consider the following questions:

- ❑ What criteria did management use to select the critical accounting criteria disclosed in MD&A?
- ❑ Are there other accounting policies that require management to make difficult, subjective, or complex judgments?
- ❑ Do the critical accounting policies supplement instead of duplicate the accounting policies described in the financial footnotes?
- ❑ Does the description of the critical accounting policies provide greater insight into the quality and variability of information regarding financial condition and operating performance?
- ❑ Is management able to defend the quality and reasonableness of the critical accounting policies?

Additional Reading

1. Cautionary Advice Regarding Disclosure About Critical Accounting Policies, SEC Release No. 33-8040 (December 12, 2001)
   https://www.sec.gov/rules/other/33-8040.htm
2. Proposed Rule: Disclosure in Management's Discussion and Analysis about the Application of Critical Accounting Policies, SEC Release No. 33-8098 (May 10, 2002)
   https://www.sec.gov/rules/proposed/33-8098.htm
3. Interpretation: Commission Guidance Regarding Management's Discussion and Analysis of Financial Condition and Results of Operations, SEC Release Nos. 33-8350; 34-48960 (December 29, 2003)
   https://www.sec.gov/rules/interp/33-8350.htm
4. FASB Accounting Standard Codification 235, Notes to Financial Statements (providing that "[d]isclosure is preferred in a separate summary of significant accounting policies preceding the notes to the financial statements, or as the initial note, under the same or a similar title.")

Notes

8.6 INTERNAL CONTROLS

CONTRIBUTED BY
Kevin A. Burke
Sidley Austin LLP[1]

For most boards, the audit committee is tasked with overseeing management's implementation and maintenance of effective "internal controls." Internal control generally consists of those processes and procedures that management establishes to provide "reasonable assurance" that the company (i) achieves its operational, reporting, and compliance objectives in accordance with applicable policies; and (ii) can provide timely and accurate financial reports in accordance with applicable regulations and accounting principles.

Reasonable assurance, of course, does not mean absolute assurance. The likelihood of a company achieving its objectives is affected by limitations intrinsic to all practical control systems. These include human error and the uncertainty inherent in judgment. Internal control also can be circumvented by collusion and fraud. An effective system of control should be designed to address such possibilities, taking into consideration the particular circumstances of the company.

As applicable to U.S. public corporations, internal control over financial reporting (ICFR) consists of those processes and procedures designed to provide reasonable assurance that

1. Kevin Burke is a partner in Sidley Austin's New York office and practices in the areas of Regulatory Enforcement, Professional Liability, and Corporate Governance, among others.

transactions are recorded as necessary to permit preparation of financial statements in accordance with generally accepted accounting principles (GAAP). See SEC Rule 13a-15(f). The SEC and PCAOB increasingly are focused on ICFR, including in their enforcement initiatives.

Section 404 of Sarbanes-Oxley requires most U.S. public companies annually to assess and report on the effectiveness of ICFR. Management also must evaluate any change in ICFR that occurs during a fiscal quarter that materially affected, or is reasonably likely to materially affect, the company's ICFR. Likewise, Section 302 requires responsible officers to make quarterly certifications regarding the effectiveness of internal control as well as the company's disclosure controls and procedures (the SEC has recommended that companies have a management-level disclosure committee).

Section 404 further requires most U.S. public companies to engage external auditors to express opinions, based on their own audit procedures, regarding the effectiveness of the company's ICFR. Under PCAOB standards, the ICFR and financial statement audits are "integrated," that is, performed as a single, mutually reinforcing process. (See PCAOB AS 5.)

Beyond ICFR, there are other implementations of internal control with which audit committees should be familiar to the extent applicable. For example, pursuant to a recent SEC rule amendment, regulated broker-dealers annually must assess and report on the effectiveness of internal control over compliance (ICOC) with respect to certain financial responsibility rules. (See SEC Rule 17a-5(d)(3).) Here, too, broker-dealers must engage external auditors to express opinions, based on the auditors' own examination procedures, regarding the effectiveness of ICOC. Management assertions, and auditor opinions, regarding ICOC are reported to the SEC and other regulators where applicable, but not to the public.

Management's internal control assessment generally should follow a top-down, risk-based approach that considers the entire system of control. The assessment should focus greater attention on entity-level controls pertinent to areas most susceptible to material misstatement, error, or noncompliance. Internal audit should play a central role in testing the design and operating effectiveness of key controls.

The 2013 updated *Internal Control—Integrated Framework* from the Committee of Sponsoring Organizations of the Treadway Commission (COSO) both refines the principles for evaluating internal control and emphasizes the role of the board, and audit committee, in overseeing internal control. The 2013 framework continues to set forth five basic components of internal control: control environment, risk assessment, control activities, information and communication, and monitoring activities.

The control environment, in particular, consists of the standards, processes, and structure that provide the basis for carrying out internal control. In this context, the board and audit committee play an essential role in establishing an appropriate tone at the top, emphasizing the importance of internal control.

Management, internal audit, and the external auditor must keep the audit committee apprised of the assessments of internal control, including with respect to the identification of any possible deficiencies. To state what may be obvious, timely identification of potential deficiencies is important, because deficiencies can impact the company's ability to achieve its operations, reporting, or compliance objectives. In addition, certain types of deficiencies must be disclosed (discussed further later in the chapter).

Lastly, given that control assessments require judgment, and reasonable minds can differ, disagreements may arise between management and the external auditor regarding the effectiveness of controls. The audit committee promptly should be apprised of any such disagreements so that it is in a position to take appropriate action to resolve the issue.

Key Questions

In exercising oversight with respect to internal control, the audit committee should consider asking the following:

- ❑ Beyond ICFR, what internal control evaluation and reporting requirements exist based on the company's business?
- ❑ Has management adopted a plan to assess the effectiveness of internal control using the current COSO framework?
- ❑ What involvement has internal audit had in identifying key controls and testing the design and effectiveness of such controls?
- ❑ Is it appropriate to engage an accounting firm, or another professional services firm, to assist in control assessment?
- ❑ What are the key risks identified by management (or internal audit) and the external auditor regarding the effectiveness of internal control? What are the key controls designed to address those risks?
- ❑ What sub-certifications will support the Section 302 certifications? What are the processes pursuant to which sub-certifications are provided?
- ❑ What factors (e.g., staffing issues, system changes) have had an impact on the effectiveness of internal control? What factors are anticipated to have an impact in the future?
- ❑ What, if any, changes have been made to internal control in the reporting period, and why?
- ❑ What reliance does the external auditor place on ICFR in planning its financial statement audit procedures?
- ❑ What recommendations, if any, does the external auditor have with respect to enhancing internal control, regardless of whether any deficiency has been raised with the audit committee?
- ❑ What, if any, disagreements initially occurred between management and the external auditor regarding the effectiveness of internal control, regardless of whether the disagreements were resolved?
- ❑ How is our company rated (regarded) by our auditor in its evaluation of the company as an audit risk? If not well-rated or regarded, why? What, if any, remedial actions (including changes to our internal controls or accounting policies) should be taken to mitigate the risks perceived by the auditor?

Additional Reading

1. Internal Control—Integrated Framework, Executive Summary, *Committee of Sponsoring Organizations of the Treadway Commission* (May 2013)
   http://www.coso.org/documents/990025P_Executive_Summary_final_may20_e.pdf
2. The Center for Audit Quality, Guide to Internal Control Over Financial Reporting
   http://www.thecaq.org/guide-internal-control-over-financial-reporting
3. KPMG's Audit Committee Institute, The Audit Committee Guide, Chapter 3 (2015)
   https://boardleadership.kpmg.us/content/dam/blc/pdfs/2015/kpmg-audit-committee-guide-2015.pdf
4. Audit Committee Resource Guide, Section Three, *Deloitte* (February 2015).
   https://www2.deloitte.com/us/en/pages/center-for-board-effectiveness/articles/audit-committee-resource-guide.html
5. 17 CFR 240.13a-15—Controls and Procedures
   https://www.law.cornell.edu/cfr/text/17/240.13a-15

Notes

8.7 DEFICIENCIES AND MATERIAL WEAKNESSES IN INTERNAL CONTROLS

CONTRIBUTED BY
Kevin A. Burke
Sidley Austin LLP[1]

As a general matter, a deficiency in internal control exists when the design or operation of a control does not allow management or employees, in the normal course of performing their duties, to prevent or timely detect misstatements, errors, or noncompliance. Such deficiencies can give rise to disclosure and reporting obligations and otherwise can impact a company's ability to achieve its objectives.

In the context of internal controls over financial reporting (ICFR), a "material weakness" is a deficiency or the aggregate of individual deficiencies creating "a reasonable possibility that a material misstatement of the company's annual or interim financial statements will not be prevented or detected on a timely basis" (PCAOB AS 5, Appendix A, A7). By comparison, PCAOB AS 5, Appendix A, A11 states a "significant deficiency" is "less severe than a material weakness, yet important enough to merit attention by those responsible for oversight of the company's financial reporting." Neither a significant deficiency nor a material weakness necessarily means the financial statements are misstated. Yet, both material weaknesses and significant deficiencies should be brought—by the

1. Kevin Burke is a partner in Sidley Austin's New York office and practices in the areas of Regulatory Enforcement, Professional Liability, and Corporate Governance, among others.

external auditor if not by management—to the attention of the audit committee. And, pursuant to appropriate disclosure controls and procedures, the company must describe in its financial statements any material weaknesses that exist.

There are other contexts in which control deficiencies must be disclosed. For example, with respect to registered broker-dealers, the definition of material weakness in ICOC has two prongs. It is a deficiency or aggregate of deficiencies creating a reasonable possibility that (i) noncompliance with certain financial responsibility rules (regarding net capital and reserves) will not be prevented or detected on a timely basis, or (ii) noncompliance "to a material extent" with other financial responsibility rules (for example, customer protection) will not be prevented or detected on a timely basis. With respect to the latter prong, the SEC has not defined the phrase "to a material extent," leaving the determination to considerable judgment.

If a material weakness in ICOC is deemed to exist, either by management or the external auditor, the broker-dealer must notify the SEC within a specific time frame and report on what it is doing, or has done, to correct the situation. (See SEC Rule 17a-11(e).) In addition, the broker-dealer in its annual compliance report, and the external auditor in its corresponding compliance opinion, must describe the material weakness and indicate whether it persisted at the end of the reporting period. (See SEC Rule 17a-5(d)(3).) The broker-dealer also must provide notice to its customers of the existence of the material weakness. (See SEC Rule 17a-5(c)(2)(iv).)

While identification of a material weakness is not typically considered a positive development, appropriate disclosure can be beneficial to the company. Disclosing what the problem is, where, when, and why it occurred, and how it will be fixed helps puts the weakness in perspective. In addition, disclosure demonstrates that management understands the issue and, presumably, has adopted an appropriate plan to remedy the issue.

Thus, in addition to ensuring that the company meets disclosure and reporting obligations, the audit committee should ensure that management takes appropriate action to remediate any significant control weaknesses. While the wisdom of prompt remediation may seem clear, there are possible consequences of failing to do so that are not necessarily so. For example, there are indications that companies failing to remediate material weaknesses experience larger increases in audit fees and a higher likelihood of auditor resignation as the number of material weaknesses increase. In addition, when entity-level material weaknesses exist, non-remediating companies are more likely to miss filing deadlines and experience increased cost of debt capital due to poorer credit ratings and higher interest rates.

Ultimately, the audit committee should obtain a clear understanding of management's remediation plan and ensure its satisfactory completion. Any such plan should identify, among other information, the specific enhancements necessary to accomplish the remediation, the members of management who will be responsible for directly overseeing implementation, and the estimated time to complete implementation, including, where applicable, the estimated times to complete component stages of implementation.

Key Questions

With respect to weaknesses in internal control, the audit committee should consider asking the following:

- ❑ What reporting and disclosure obligations apply if a deficiency in internal control is deemed to exist?
- ❑ Was the material weakness assessed with respect to the current COSO framework?
- ❑ Why are management and the external auditor confident that the material weakness is not broader—or narrower—than described?
- ❑ Has management identified, analyzed, and corrected all instances of errors in the company's records? If not, what efforts are still required to do so?
- ❑ What has management done to be confident that, notwithstanding a deficiency in ICFR, the financial statements are fairly stated?
- ❑ What remediation plan has management developed to address the deficiencies identified? Specifically, what new processes, procedures, or controls are necessary to remediate?
- ❑ What members of management were involved in developing the remediation plan, and are they the appropriate participants? What members of management will be responsible for directly overseeing the remediation, and are they the appropriate participants?
- ❑ Is it appropriate to engage an accounting firm, or another professional services firm, to assist in remediation?
- ❑ Is it appropriate to replace any member of the company's accounting and financial reporting staff as part of the remediation?
- ❑ Should the audit committee directly oversee some aspect of the remediation?

Additional Reading

1. Huber, John J., and Joel H. Trotter, Disclosure of Internal Control over Financial Reporting
   http://apps.americanbar.org/abastore/products/books/abstracts/5070471_SampleChWebstore.pdf
2. Hammersley, Jacqueline S., The Failure to Remediate Previously-Disclosed Material Weaknesses in Internal Controls (July 11, 2012)
   http://papers.ssrn.com/sol3/papers.cfm?abstract_id=1327470##
3. KPMG's Audit Committee Institute, The Audit Committee Guide, Chapter 3 (2015)
   https://kpmg-blc.adobecqms.net/content/dam/blc/pdfs/2015/kpmg-audit-committee-guide-2015.pdf

4. Deloitte Audit Committee Resource Guide, Section Three (February 2015) http://www2.deloitte.com/content/dam/Deloitte/us/Documents/center-for-corporate-governance/us-aers-audit-committee-resource-guide-2015-032615.pdf

Notes

8.8 MANAGEMENT REPRESENTATION LETTERS

CONTRIBUTED BY
Sean Sullivan, Elizabeth A. Ising, and Michael J. Scanlon
Gibson, Dunn & Crutcher LLP[1]

A company's independent auditor generally requests that the company's management provide a management representation letter in connection with the completion of a company's annual audit and the quarterly review processes. In addition, management representation letters are requested in connection with the filing of a registration statement (or the filing of a post-effective amendment) pursuant to the Securities Act of 1933, as amended, by the company, which occurs when the company contemplates the public offering of securities (as the financial statements of the company are either included in the filing or incorporated therein by reference). In addition, the delivery of the comfort letter by the auditor to underwriters in connection with a securities offering will typically trigger a request for management to deliver a management representation letter (or an update to a previously delivered letter).

During the financial statement audit and review processes, members of the company's management and others make written and oral representations to the auditor, which constitute evidence used by the auditor in support of its audit. The auditing standard set

1. Sean Sullivan, associate; Elizabeth A. Ising, partner; and Michael J. Scanlon, partner, are all members of the Securities Regulation and Corporate Governance practice group at Gibson, Dunn & Crutcher LLP.

forth in Public Company Accounting Oversight Board Interim Auditing Standard (AU 333) establishes circumstances in which a management representation letter is necessary and sets forth guidance with respect to the scope of the representations to be made by management in the letter. The representations are obtained by the auditor to supplement the audit and review procedures. The preparation of a management representation letter also serves a broader confirmatory purpose in that in the event a representation made by the company's management is not consistent with other audit evidence, the auditors will consider the reliability of that and other representations. If there is such inconsistency, this likely would be a point of interest for members of the board of directors and its audit committee.

The management representation letter is addressed to the auditor and is generally dated as of the date of the auditor's report or at the date of the delivery of financial statements, or in the case of a consent, on or about the date of the consent. The management representation letter is executed by members of management with overall responsibility for financial and operating matters of the company and who are knowledgeable with respect to the matters addressed by the representations, which typically includes the chief executive officer and the chief financial officer (or equivalents thereof). The auditor also may request written representations from other individuals at the company in appropriate circumstances. The representations are made by current management with respect to all applicable periods, even when one or more members of the company's management did not serve in such roles during all periods addressed in the financial statements. Specifically, pursuant to AU 333, the auditor is responsible for obtaining a management representation letter for all financial statements and periods covered in the report to be issued or the consent to be delivered.

The specific representations to be included in the management representation letter depend on the facts and circumstances of the company, the purpose of the auditor's engagement, and the basis of the presentation of the financial statements. Importantly, the representations made by management may be limited to matters that are considered material (individually or collectively) if the company's management and its auditor are in agreement with respect to what constitutes materiality for purposes of certain representations. AU 333 prescribes certain matters that the letter should cover, including, among others, the following:

- Management's responsibility for the fair presentation in the financial statements of the company's financial position, results of operation, and cash flow in conformity with GAAP
- The availability of all financial records and related data, the completeness and availability of all minutes of meetings of stockholders, directors, and committees of directors
- Communications from regulatory agencies concerning noncompliance with or deficiencies in financial reporting
- The absence of unrecorded transactions
- The immateriality of any uncorrected financial statement misstatements
- Management's responsibility for the design and implementation of programs and controls to prevent and detect fraud

- The knowledge of, or allegations of, fraud or suspected fraud and violations or possible violations of law or regulations, the effects of which should be considered for disclosure in the company's financial statements or as a basis for recording a loss contingency
- Plans or intentions that may affect the carrying value or classification of company assets or liabilities
- Information with respect to related-party transactions, guarantees made by the company, and significant estimates and material considerations known to management
- Any unasserted claims that the company's lawyers have advised the company are probable of assertion and require disclosure pursuant to Financial Accounting Standards Board Accounting Standards Codification 450, Contingencies
- Information with respect to events occurring subsequent to the end of the period under review by the auditor

Business and industry-specific representations also may be added, and customary representations may be tailored to address matters that should be disclosed to the auditor. If the company uses a specialist with respect to evaluating certain information, such as an outside tax or valuation expert, management typically will make a representation that it agrees with the findings of such specialist. In addition, representations addressing unaudited interim financial information may be included if such information is included in the SEC filing in which the audit report or auditor consent is included.

It is important to note that a refusal by management to furnish customary representations when requested by the company's auditor constitutes a limitation on the scope of the audit, which alone is sufficient to preclude an unqualified audit opinion and may justify an auditor's decision to disclaim an opinion or withdraw from an engagement entirely. Members of the board of directors and its audit committee should be highly attuned to any suggestion by management that it cannot or will not deliver a customary management representation letter in response to an appropriate request by the company's auditors.

Key Questions

Members of the board of directors should consider a number of issues, including those set forth below, with respect to the delivery of management representation letters:

- ❑ Are the appropriate members of the company's management consulted in the preparation of management representation letters?
- ❑ Should other members of management be consulted with respect to certain of the representations made in the letters (e.g., consultation with the corporate secretary in connection with a representation as to the delivery of all minutes from meetings of the stockholders, the board of directors, and committees thereof)?
- ❑ Do the members of management signing the management representation letters have the necessary knowledge and information to appropriately deliver the letters?

- ❑ Do all financial statements fairly present the financial positions, results of operation, and cash flows of the company in conformity with GAAP?
- ❑ Are all related party transactions appropriately disclosed to the auditors?
- ❑ Has management dedicated appropriate resources to the preparation of management representation letters?
- ❑ Does management have the proper internal controls and processes to help ensure that the representations made by management in the letter are accurate?
- ❑ Does management maintain a professional and open dialogue with the company's auditor throughout the preparation of the SEC filings for which consents are issued?
- ❑ Do management and the company's auditor have a consistent understanding of the meaning of "materiality" in connection with certain representations made in the management representation letter? Is management familiar with the definitions of "fraud" and "related parties" as used in AU 333?
- ❑ If standard representations cannot be delivered, or are delivered in a modified or unusual form, what facts and circumstances resulted in such determinations and are such facts and circumstances expected to reoccur? Has or should management take any steps to change such facts and circumstances in the future?
- ❑ If there has been a recent change in accounting principles by the company, why is the newly adopted accounting principle preferable to the former accounting principle?

Additional Reading

1. Public Company Accounting Oversight Board AU 333, Management Representations
   https://pcaobus.org/Standards/Auditing/Pages/AU333.aspx

Notes

____

____

____

____

____

8.9 ACCOUNTING RESTATEMENTS

CONTRIBUTED BY
Fiona A. Philip
Sidley Austin LLP (Washington, D.C.)[1]

Public companies have an obligation to provide accurate and timely financial reports to their investors. Financial statements must be certified by corporate officers, and an independent auditor must express an opinion as to the fairness of the presentation of those financial statements. The board of directors also has a role in monitoring the financial reporting process. More specifically, the audit committee performs an oversight role in the financial reporting process and the internal control mechanisms of a company. The effective oversight of the financial reporting process and the evaluation of internal controls can lead to the detection of material misstatements or errors.

When misstatements or errors are discovered in a financial statement, the proper way to correct those misstatements or errors turns on an assessment of materiality. In Staff Accounting Bulletin No. 99, a "material" error or misstatement has not been defined per se; however, the U.S. Securities and Exchange Commission (SEC) instructs companies to conduct quantitative and qualitative analyses to determine if the misstatement or error is material to its financial statements. For quantitative materiality, 5 percent of pretax

1. Fiona A. Philip is a partner in the Securities & Derivatives Enforcement and Regulation practice of Sidley Austin LLP, practicing in its Washington, D.C. office. Grady Nye, an associate at Sidley Austin LLP, assisted in drafting this chapter.

income is generally considered the starting point for the materiality analysis. However, the assessment of the quantitative element alone is insufficient. Qualitative materiality also must be considered. The assessment of qualitative materiality includes the consideration of non-exhaustive factors, including the nature of the error, and whether the error or misstatement

- arises from an item capable of precise measurement or whether it arises from an estimate (and if so, the degree of imprecision inherent in the estimate);
- masks a change in earnings or other trends;
- conceals a gap between expected and actual earnings;
- changes a loss into income or vice versa;
- affects an aspect of the company considered to be important for the company's operations or performance;
- affects the company's compliance with loan covenants or other contractual requirements;
- increases management compensation;
- conceals unlawful transactions; and
- is sufficiently important that it would result in a significant positive or negative market reaction.

The materiality of an error or misstatement should be assessed in an "SAB 99 memo" proposed by management and reviewed by the board and the company's auditors. An error or misstatement that is "material" to the relevant quarter or year-end must be corrected through a restatement by filing a Form 10-K/A or Form 10-Q/A, depending on the circumstances. The filing of a restatement raises a rebuttable presumption that the error or misstatement resulted from a material weakness in internal control over financial reporting. As a consequence, a restatement is often accompanied by disclosure of a previously unknown material weakness in internal controls. In addition, the auditor must modify its opinion to reflect the consequences of the restatement. If management reaches the conclusion that prior financial statements should not be relied upon, the company must file a Form 8-K within four business days of drawing that conclusion. In contrast, an immaterial error corrected in a restatement may be reflected in a future 10-K or 10-Q.

When a financial restatement occurs, the board must consider a variety of ancillary issues and consequences. Both an SEC investigation and shareholder litigation are not uncommon in the wake of a significant restatement, particularly if it brings about a reduction in stock price. The company's readiness to deal with that litigation should be evaluated and a preliminary consultation with outside counsel may be advisable.

Since the company's officers and directors are likely to be called to testify in an SEC investigation and to be named in shareholder litigation, the company should be prepared to give notice to the carrier issuing its directors and officers liability insurance. It may be necessary to negotiate with the insurer regarding the selection of legal counsel. In some (but not all) instances, separate counsel for the officers and directors must be arranged. In every case, the company needs to be prepared to address potentially burdensome SEC and plaintiff counsel subpoenas for documents, among other things.

The company should have a well-thought out plan to address the following: (1) a potential SEC investigation; (2) potential shareholder litigation; and (3) investor and market communications relating to the restatement. Although candor and transparency must be balanced with concerns over worsening the company's exposure in litigation, the market and the SEC must, in the end, be given a complete and accurate picture of the reasons for the restatement and the likely impact, if any, upon the company's future operating results if the restatement reflects a change in accounting policy.

Restatements may trigger clawbacks in management compensation agreements or arrangements, even where the need for the restatement does not reflect any misconduct on the part of any particular officer. This can present sensitive management issues where able executives who performed well are adversely impacted due to a financial restatement that is completely unrelated to their activities. This can challenge a board and place strain on the cohesiveness of the team.

Finally, the company should consider whether a restatement reflects any internal weaknesses in controls or deficiencies in staffing and take the opportunity to make necessary changes. Proactively addressing these issues will go a long way to alleviate investor and SEC concerns.

Key Questions

When considering the potential need to issue an accounting restatement, key questions that a board member might ask include the following:

- ❑ What is the nature of the error or misstatement?
- ❑ How was the error or misstatement discovered?
- ❑ Does the company have enough information about the error or misstatement to correct it? If not, what additional information is needed?
- ❑ What effect did the error or misstatements have on past results? What impact might it have on future results?
- ❑ Would it be advisable to seek additional input from independent third parties or experts about the nature of the error or misstatement?
- ❑ Does the error or misstatement raise any issues that an investor might take into consideration when forecasting the future performance of the company?
- ❑ Has the company received appropriate legal advice concerning any potential legal or regulatory implications of the error or misstatement?
- ❑ How should the error or misstatement be corrected?
- ❑ When should the error or misstatement be corrected?
- ❑ When should the SEC be notified?
- ❑ Do any prior SEC filings need to be amended?
- ❑ Before making any announcement of the restatement, is the company certain that the information is verifiably accurate?

Additional Questions

When considering the role of board members in the oversight of accounting controls, additional questions that the board may ask include the following:

- ❑ What was the role of management in the error or misstatement?
- ❑ Was the misstatement a consequence of purposeful conduct? By whom?

- ❑ Is the company communicating clearly and in a timely manner with the auditors and the SEC regarding the restatement?
- ❑ Is the company working with its auditors in connection with this restatement?
- ❑ Is the error or misstatement likely to occur again?
- ❑ Why was the error not discovered prior to issuing the financial statement?
- ❑ What improvements in internal controls are necessary to prevent the error from recurring?
- ❑ What consequences will the restatement have on management's compensation either because of missed performance targets or the trigger of clawback provisions?

Additional Reading

1. SEC Staff Accounting Bulletin No. 99, August 12, 1999
   https://www.sec.gov/interps/account/sab99.htm2
2. Bricker, Wesley R., Remarks Before the 2015 AICPA Conference on Current SEC and PCAOB Developments (December 9, 2015)
   https://www.sec.gov/news/speech/bricker-remarks-2015-aicpa-conference-sec-pcaob-developments.html

Notes

____

____

____

____

____

8.10 ENTERPRISE RISK MANAGEMENT

CONTRIBUTED BY
Stephen A. Pike
Gowling WLG[1]
Paul Lanois
Credit Suisse[2]

Enterprise risk management (ERM) is a comprehensive management framework comprised of protocols and policies designed to provide a structure for businesses to identify, understand, access, and manage risks, and for use by their board to fulfill the organization's obligations in relation to risk management. The task of the board includes aligning the enterprise's risk management strategy with its risk tolerance and implementing monitoring processes and protocols to continually gauge enterprise risk as well as the enterprise's mitigation and management thereof.

The board must accept responsibility for the ownership of ERM and appropriately task management with its adaption and implementation, from strategy to compensation, in order for management to effectively manage risk.

1. Stephen A. Pike is a partner in the Toronto office of the Gowling WLG (Canada) LLP law firm, where he advises on corporate and business law matters.
2. Paul Lanois is senior legal counsel at Credit Suisse and is admitted to the bars of the District of Columbia, New York, and the Supreme Court of the United States.

The initial focus of ERM is to identify and categorize the potential risks facing a business. Experts suggest dividing the risk universe into a number of "buckets." For the purposes of this chapter, we can consider four main categories of risks: operational risks (i.e., internal or inherent risks arising from within the organization, such as business processes, capacity, supplies, health and safety, etc., that are predominantly controllable and ought to be eliminated or avoided), strategic risks (i.e., risks that are not necessarily undesirable but are accepted by the business to generate superior returns from its strategy, such as business, economic, and political conditions, customer preferences, brand perceptions, etc.), financial risks (e.g., foreign exchange, regulatory, compliance, interest rates, legal, tax, etc.), and external risks (i.e., known and unknown, expected and unexpected risks truly arising from events outside the organization and are beyond its influence or control, such as natural disasters, systemic failures, geopolitical turmoil, sabotage, etc.).

Boards must oversee these risks within an ERM framework that recognizes both risk and reward. While it is obvious no vibrant and growing business enterprise or its strategies can be completely risk-free (nor can it choose to be), ERM rather intends to foster a better balance of known risks with anticipated rewards. Boards must, through their reviews and monitoring of the business strategy and results of the organization's operations, continually address management's assessment, strategies to manage risk, and deliver reward, through an ERM framework that is both effective and appropriate for the business. Accordingly, the board is the best placed to ensure that ERM is not simply an afterthought, but is instead an integral part of the organization's goal-setting efforts, as well as its corporate and operational structure, performance management, compensation structure, and reporting systems.

ERM is a dynamic practice, therefore as risks evolve, so must ERM. For example, the Committee of Sponsoring Organizations of the Treadway Commission (COSO) published its widely used ERM framework, "Enterprise Risk Management-Integrated Framework," in 2004 (the Framework). According to COSO, ERM

> [i]s a process, effected by the entity's board of directors, management, and other personnel, applied in strategy setting and across the organization, designed to identify potential events that may affect the entity, and manage the risk to be within the risk appetite, to provide reasonable assurance regarding the achievement of objectives.[3]

This framework has been recently updated to take into account "significant new risks" that require "heightened board awareness and oversight of risk management as well as improved risk reporting." The updated proposed framework, "Enterprise Risk Management—Aligning Risk with Strategy," was published in June 2016 as an exposure draft for public comment until September 30, 2016. The public exposure draft is intended to introduce changes in ERM practices and to provide better guidance as to how ERM can help boards to better carry out their responsibility in fulfilling their risk oversight role, including examining the significance and influence of an organization's culture on its ERM practices; enhancing alignment of ERM to performance and of risk to value; simplifying

---

3. Committee of Sponsoring Organizations of the Treadway Commission (COSO) Enterprise Risk Management Integrated Framework, http://www.theiia.org/media/files/virtual-seminars/COSO_ERM_Integrated_Framework.pdf

the definition of ERM; and focusing on the integration of ERM into all aspects of an organization's operations.

Key Questions

Some key questions to consider in relation to the enterprise risk management include the following:

- ❑ Does the organization have an enterprise risk management framework in place?
- ❑ Does the organization's enterprise risk management framework adequately identify all potential risks it may face (whether internal or external to the organization)?
- ❑ Has the organization assessed the impact of these risks?
- ❑ Does the board review the identification and assessment of risks in its consideration of the organization's business strategy?
- ❑ What actions are taken by management when a new risk is identified or when there is a change in management's assessment of a risk?
- ❑ What is being done in the organization to prevent the occurrence of risks?
- ❑ Can the risks be mitigated or reduced and what are the consequences if the mitigation fails (e.g., counterparty risks)?
- ❑ Is the board satisfied that management has allocated sufficient resources to risk management?
- ❑ Has management kept the board fully informed of the organization's risk management framework and processes?
- ❑ Has responsibility in relation to the risk management framework and processes been assigned?
- ❑ Is there regular reporting of risk management issues to the board or the audit committee?
- ❑ Does the organization possess the required capabilities, experience, and know-how to adequately manage the risks facing the organization? Does the organization have a methodology in place to assess risks?
- ❑ Does the organization have a system in place to monitor risks?
- ❑ Is there a periodic review of the risk monitoring system?

Additional Reading

1. Enterprise Risk Management—Aligning Risk with Strategy and Performance, Frequently Asked Questions, COSO (2016)
   http://erm.coso.org/Documents/COSO-ERM-FAQ.pdf
2. Enterprise Risk Management—Aligning Risk with Strategy and Performance, Executive Summary, COSO (2016)
   http://erm.coso.org/Documents/COSO-ERM-Public-Exposure-Executive-Summary.pdf

3. Enterprise Risk Management—Aligning Risk with Strategy and Performance, Public Exposure Draft, COSO (2016)
   http://erm.coso.org/Documents/COSO-ERM-Public-Exposure.pdf
4. M-16-17, OMB Circular No. A-123, Management's Responsibility for Enterprise Risk Management and Internal Control (July 15, 2016)
   https://www.whitehouse.gov/sites/default/files/omb/memoranda/2016/m-16-17.pdf
5. A Framework for Board Oversight of Enterprise Risk. John E. Caldwell, CPA, CA, Chartered Professional Accountants Canada (2012)
   https://www.cpacanada.ca/en/business-and-accounting-resources/strategy-risk-and-governance/enterprise-risk-management/publications/a-practical-approach-to-board-risk-oversight
6. How Enterprise Risk Management Can Impact a Company's Value, *Smart Business Online* (2016)
   http://www.sbnonline.com/article/how-enterprise-risk-management-can-impact-a-companys-value-2/
7. Boosting Valuation with Enterprise Risk Management, *CFO* (May 31, 2016)
   http://ww2.cfo.com/risk-management/2016/05/boosting-valuation-enterprise-risk-management/

Notes

8.11 GOING CONCERN QUALIFICATIONS

CONTRIBUTED BY
Michael A. Titera, Elizabeth A. Ising, and Michael J. Scanlon
Gibson, Dunn & Crutcher LLP[1]

Under Generally Accepted Accounting Principles (GAAP), a company's ability to continue as a going concern is presumed until its liquidation is deemed imminent. When liquidation *is not imminent*, the company's financial statements are prepared under the going concern basis of accounting. Once the company's liquidation *is imminent*, the financial statements are prepared under the liquidation basis of accounting. However, before liquidation becomes imminent, conditions or events may raise substantial doubts about the company's ability to continue as a going concern. Under such circumstances, financial statements are still prepared under the going concern basis of accounting, but rules applicable to companies and auditors may require public disclosure regarding the substantial doubt about the company's ability to continue as a going concern and related issues.

Going Concern Determinations by Company Management

In 2014, the Financial Accounting Standards Board (FASB) issued Accounting Standards Update No. 2014-15 (Disclosure of Uncertainties about an Entity's Ability to Continue

1. Michael A. Titera, associate; Elizabeth A. Ising, partner; and Michael J. Scanlon, partner, are all members of the Securities Regulation and Corporate Governance practice group at Gibson, Dunn & Crutcher LLP.

as a Going Concern), which modified the steps management has to take in evaluating the company's ability to continue as a going concern and the disclosures that have to be made in the financial statements under certain circumstances. The rules are effective for annual periods ending after December 15, 2016, and interim periods thereafter. Accounting Standards Update No. 2014–15 (which modified ASC 205-40, Presentation of Financial Statements—Going Concern) provides that substantial doubt about an entity's ability to continue as a going concern exists when relevant conditions or events, considered in the aggregate, indicate that it is probable that the entity will be unable to meet its obligations as they become due within one year after the date the financial statements are issued. The FASB update was significant because it provided the foregoing guidance for management about the meaning of substantial doubt. If such conditions or events are identified, management must consider whether its plans for mitigating those conditions and/or events will alleviate the substantial doubt, taking into account the probability that the plans will actually be effectively implemented and will actually mitigate the conditions and/or events.

Regardless of the conclusion reached by management whether its plans will alleviate substantial doubt regarding the company's ability to continue as a going concern, the company must disclose information that will allow users of the financial statements to understand (i) the principal conditions or events that raised the substantial doubt, and (ii) management's evaluation of the significance of those conditions or events. In addition, if the substantial doubt that was raised *is alleviated* by management's plans, the disclosure must address the plans that alleviated the substantial doubt; however, if the substantial doubt *is not alleviated*, the disclosure must address the plans that are intended to mitigate the conditions and events that gave rise to the substantial doubt.

Going Concern Determinations by the Auditor

Under current auditing literature, in connection with its audit, the auditor must evaluate, based on information obtained during the course of the audit, the ability of the company to continue as a going concern. (See PCAOB Interim Auditing Standard, AU Section 341 [The Auditor's Consideration of an Entity's Ability to Continue as a Going Concern].) This evaluation is focused on whether the auditor has identified conditions and events that, in the aggregate, could raise substantial doubt about the company's ability to continue as a going concern for a reasonable time (but not longer than a year) from the date of the financial statements.

If such conditions or events are found to exist, the auditor assesses management's plans for mitigating the effect of those conditions or events, as well as the likelihood that those plans can be effectively implemented. If, after consideration of management's plans, the auditor concludes that *there remains substantial doubt* about the company's ability to continue as a going concern for a reasonable period of time, the auditor must consider the adequacy of the financial statement disclosure relating to the company's possible inability to continue as a going concern and must also "qualify" the audit report by adding an explanatory paragraph disclosing the auditor's conclusion. If, however, the auditor concludes that *substantial doubt does not remain*, the auditor needs only to consider the need for disclosure in the financial statements.

Upon concluding that there is substantial doubt about the company's ability to continue as a going concern, the auditor is responsible for communicating with "those charged with governance" at the company (e.g., the board of directors) information regarding its conclusion. The discussion should cover (i) the nature of the conditions or events that gave rise to the auditor's conclusion, (ii) the possible effect on the financial statements of those conditions or events and the adequacy of the related disclosures in the financial statements, and (iii) the effect that the auditor's conclusion will have on its audit report (i.e., the inclusion of an explanatory paragraph following the auditor's opinion). The auditor typically fulfills its obligation to communicate with those charged with governance by holding a meeting with the audit committee of the board of directors or the entire board.

Key Questions

When issues are raised regarding the company's potential inability to continue as a going concern, key questions that a director might ask include the following:

Questions for Management

- ❑ Is there any additional information beyond what was identified by the auditors that you believe indicates that there could be substantial doubt about the company's ability to continue as a going concern?
- ❑ What plans are currently in place to mitigate the negative effects of the conditions and/or events identified by the auditor that could raise substantial doubt regarding the company's ability to continue as a going concern? What plans do you intend to implement in the future in this respect?
- ❑ Do you believe those plans will be effectively implemented? Why? Do you believe those plans will effectively mitigate the conditions and/or events identified by the auditor? Why?
- ❑ Even if the plans will allow the company to remain viable for the next year (thus avoiding the need for the auditor to qualify its audit report), what consideration have you given to longer-term plans or strategies for the company?
- ❑ Do you believe the financial statements adequately and accurately reflect the impact of the conditions and/or events identified by the auditor (taking into account any mitigating factors, including your plans) on the company's financial position, results of operations, and cash flows?
- ❑ Should the company make any changes to its internal control over financial reporting as a result of these issues?

Questions for the Auditor

- ❑ What was the scope of the audit procedures that were used in auditing the going concern assumption?
- ❑ What information did you obtain and what conditions and/or events did you identify that could raise substantial doubt about the company's ability to continue as a going concern?

- ❑ What is your understanding of management's plans to mitigate the effects of the conditions and/or events identified? Why do you believe that management's plans do (or do not) alleviate the substantial doubt regarding the company's ability to continue as a going concern?
- ❑ Do you believe the financial statements adequately and accurately reflect the impact of the conditions and/or events identified (taking into account any mitigating factors including management's plans) on the company's financial position, results of operations, and cash flows?
- ❑ What disclosures do you intend to make in the explanatory paragraph included in the audit report?
- ❑ Did you encounter any difficulties in carrying out your audit procedures designed to audit the going concern assumption? What was the reaction of management to your inquiries regarding potential going concern issues? Was management cooperative and responsive to your requests? Was there information you sought, but were unable to obtain, with respect to potential going concern issues?

Additional Reading

1. The Going Concern Principle

   http://www.accountingtools.com/going-concern-principle
2. What Is a Going Concern Qualification?

   http://www.accountingtools.com/questions-and-answers/what-is-a-going-concern-qualification.html
3. Requirements Applicable to Company Management. FASB Accounting Standards Update No. 2014-15, Disclosure of Uncertainties about an Entity's Ability to Continue as a Going Concern (August 2014)

   http://www.fasb.org/resources/ccurl/599/128/ASU%202014-15.pdf
4. Accounting Firm Summaries of Accounting Standards Update No. 2014-15

   Detailed summary from Deloitte:

   http://www.iasplus.com/en/publications/us/heads-up/2014/going-concern/file

   Detailed summary from PwC:

   https://www.pwc.com/us/en/cfodirect/assets/pdf/in-depth/us2014-07-going-concern.pdf

   Brief summary from EY:

   http://www.ey.com/publication/vwluassetsdld/tothepoint_bb2823_goingconcern_4september2014/$file/tothepoint_bb2823_goingconcern_4september2014.pdf

5. Requirements Applicable to the Auditor. PCAOB Interim Auditing Standard, AU Section 341, The Auditor's Consideration of an Entity's Ability to Continue as a Going Concern
   https://pcaobus.org/Standards/Auditing/Pages/AU341.aspx

Notes

SECTION NINE

SELECTED LEGAL MATTERS

9.1 REVIEWING SECURITIES FILINGS

CONTRIBUTED BY
Christina M. Gattuso
Kilpatrick Townsend & Stockton LLP[1]

A public company is subject to many legal and regulatory obligations, including (i) the filing of periodic reports on the company's business and financial operations, (ii) dissemination of "material" information to the public concerning the company's business and corporate events, (iii) the obligation to convene shareholder meetings, and (iv) the maintenance of insider trading and other policies and controls. The company's reporting obligations are imposed under the Securities Act of 1933, as amended (the Securities Act); the Securities Exchange Act of 1934, as amended (the Exchange Act); the rules and regulations of the Securities and Exchange Commission (the SEC); and the rules and regulations of the exchange on which the company's stock is traded.

With respect to SEC filings, a public company must file annual and quarterly reports and continue to do so until it becomes eligible to deregister its securities with the SEC and takes the steps to do so. This includes three quarterly financial reports on Form 10-Q and an annual report in Form 10-K. The Form 10-K must be signed by a person on behalf of a company; a majority of the directors of the company; and each of the company's

1. Christina M. Gattuso is a partner in the Washington, D.C. office of Kilpatrick Townsend & Stockton LLP. She is a member of the firm's Financial Institutions team.

principal executive officer, principal financial officer, and controller or principal accounting officer.

Typically, the audit committee will review the financial information in advance of its inclusion in the Form 10-K (and preferably in advance of the release of that information by press release), and the entire board of directors will meet and discuss the Form 10-K before its filing with the SEC. Additionally, the principal executive officer and principal financial officer must certify in writing, among other things, that (i) he/she has reviewed the annual report; (ii) to his/her knowledge, the report does not contain any untrue statement of a material fact or omit to state a material fact necessary to make the statements made, in light of the circumstances under which they were made, not misleading; and (iii) the financial statements, and other financial information included in the report, fairly present in all material respects the financial condition, results of operations, and cash flows of the company.

A Form 10-Q must be signed by the company's principal executive officer and principal financial or principal accounting officer. In the event the report contains material omissions or misstatements that result in litigation, the signatories may be liable (and, with respect to the 10-K Report, all directors, whether or not signatories, may be liable) unless they can demonstrate they were duly diligent with respect to the matter at issue. Penalties include fines and, in situations involving fraud, imprisonment. Sarbanes-Oxley increased the severity of the penalties for violating the fraud provisions of the securities laws and also created penalties for the CEO and the CFO for misstatements in their certifications required thereunder.

Public companies must also file periodic reports on Form 8-K with the SEC within a specified number of days after the occurrence of certain events as are specified in the instructions to the Form 8-K.

Additionally, before any company with a class of securities registered under the Exchange Act may solicit proxies in connection with any shareholder meeting, it must, depending on the matters to be acted upon, file with the SEC preliminary or definitive copies of all proxy materials it intends to send to shareholders. Preliminary proxy materials must be filed before finalizing whereas definitive proxy materials must be sent to the SEC on or before the date they are mailed to shareholders regardless of the matters to be voted upon.

A company that is raising capital through a public offering or acquiring another company and issuing its securities is required to register its securities by filing certain securities documents, including a registration statement and prospectus, with the SEC prior to commencing such an offering or closing an acquisition. Directors are required to sign the registration statement. Each of the directors and each officer who signed the registration statement are liable under Section 11 of the Securities Act to purchasers of the securities registered thereunder for any misstatement or omission of a material fact therein, unless the officer or director can prove he or she was duly diligent with respect to the matters at issue.

A director of a public company has a responsibility to review securities filings made by the company. Adequate time should be given to directors to review and comment on securities disclosure documents prior to filing. In exercising this responsibility, a director should review the filings for accuracy and focus on those areas that may be within a particular director's knowledge or expertise. A director should also understand and be satisfied that the corporate disclosure controls and procedures in place for preparation of company securities filings are adequate to ensure accuracy and completeness of the company's filings. Directors should also understand the significant disclosures made by the company in its securities filings, including risk factors and forward looking statements. If the company uses non-GAAP financial measures in its earnings releases and securities filings, directors should be aware of the practices and policies that could result in SEC scrutiny under new guidance issued by the SEC and ensure they understand the reasons management believes the use of such non-GAAP measures are appropriate and not considered misleading under that new guidance. In particular, audit committees should be familiar with the SEC's new guidance and undertake a review of the company's practices relating to use of non-GAAP measures.

In recent proxy seasons, there has been an increased focus by shareholders on a company's environmental, social, governance and "sustainability" disclosures and the need for transparency with respect to such matters. Directors should ensure that they regularly obtain information from management on any concerns expressed by major shareholders.

For directors, it is important to understand that, while the requirements discussed are primarily corporate obligations, directors have legal responsibilities as well. The courts and the SEC have used principles of conspiracy, as well as aiding and abetting, to impose liability on individual members of management for causing or permitting corporate misconduct. There are also express statutory provisions under the federal securities laws that make a person (such as a director who "controls" an issuer) jointly and severally liable for certain liabilities of the issuer. It is notable that a controlling person can avoid individual liability in certain situations if he or she had no knowledge of, or reasonable grounds to believe, the existence of the facts by reason of which the issuer's liability exists. Therefore, directors and officers have a personal responsibility to ensure that a company complies with its obligations under the federal securities laws and may have liability if they have not undertaken "due diligence" to ensure that the filings are complete, accurate, and truthful.

As a practical matter, an individual director may wish to review past minutes and board materials for significant matters that may be topics for disclosure. This is particularly true with respect to the Management's Discussion and Analysis portion of the company's filings, which is intended to allow investors to see the company "through the eyes of management." Any items not disclosed should be discussed with management, counsel, or both, and a rationale for not disclosing the item should be determined and perhaps documented.

Particular care should be taken to ensure that disclosure of key items is understandable and transparent. Too often, management may seek to conceal bad news in a cloud of words or opaque disclosure. Directors may well be the final gatekeeper to ensure that the company's disclosure is candid and complete.

Key Questions

- ❑ What are the company's internal processes and procedures to ensure that potential disclosure items are identified and properly handled? Are these processes and procedures adequate to ensure compliance with securities disclosure obligations?
- ❑ Does the company provide earnings projections and, if it does, what future periods are covered by the earnings projections? How do the projections compare with current analyst projections?
- ❑ Has the board reviewed the risk factors and other portions of Form 10-K to understand management's view of key risks of the company?
- ❑ Are all material risks disclosed, including cybersecurity and data security risks, enterprise risks, and business and operational risks specific to the company?
- ❑ Does the board's review of the company's financial statements evidence any unusual trends, abnormal losses, or recent accounting policy changes?
- ❑ Does the board have a basic understanding of critical accounting policies applicable to the company?
- ❑ Does the board have an understanding of the significant disclosures contained in the company's securities filings?
- ❑ Has the audit committee reviewed and approved the inclusion of the audited financial statements in the Form 10-K?
- ❑ Does the board receive drafts of material press releases and earnings releases to review prior to public dissemination and have an opportunity to ask questions and comment on such releases?
- ❑ Does management keep the board apprised of current SEC reporting and disclosure issues and trends?
- ❑ Has the company adequately addressed any SEC comments on its securities filings?
- ❑ Does the company have a policy on materiality and has all information that would be material to an investor been adequately disclosed?

Additional Reading

1. ABA Business Law Section, Committee on Corporate Laws *Corporate Director's Guidebook* (see Section 10, Duties under the Federal Securities Laws)
   http://apps.americanbar.org/buslaw/newsletter/0020/materials/book.pdf
2. A Few Things Directors Should Know About the SEC, speech by Mary Jo White, Stanford University Rock Center for Corporate Governance, Twentieth Annual Stanford Directors' College
   https://www.sec.gov/News/Speech/Detail/Speech/1370542148863

3. SEC Comment Letters: A Look at Top Issues in 2016
   http://www.auditanalytics.com/blog/sec-comment-letters-a-look-at-top-issues-in-2016/

Notes

THE DIRECTOR'S ROLE IN CORPORATE ETHICS AND COMPLIANCE PROGRAMS

92

CONTRIBUTED BY
Christopher J. Gyves
Womble Carlyle Sandridge & Rice, LLP[1]

The board of director's role in overseeing the company's business and affairs includes significant responsibilities for the organization's ethics and compliance with applicable laws. Boards are called upon to establish a "tone at the top" of ethics and compliance, and to conduct their business accordingly.

Programs promoting ethics and compliance should be tailored to the organization's culture, history, plans, complexity, geographic scope, and industry. Management is responsible for the design of a corporation's ethics and compliance program. The board's active oversight of management and the objectivity of engaged, independent directors are critically important. Directors should understand how the corporation's ethics and compliance program functions (including how the program is communicated throughout the organization) and the program's effectiveness in identifying and eliminating misconduct.

All company policies create incentives and influence behaviors. The design of an ethics and compliance program should be coordinated and calibrated with policies such as executive compensation, equity ownership, and management evaluations. Directors must

1. Chris Gyves is a partner at Womble Carlyle Sandridge & Rice, LLP, where he serves as chair of the firm's Public Company Advisors Team.

understand the adverse impact a failure of ethics or compliance could have on the corporation and its stakeholders, including the potential that directors may incur personal liability.

Experienced directors are familiar with the Delaware Chancery Court's ruling in the well-known *In re Caremark International Derivative Litigation*, which imposed an affirmative duty on boards to create appropriate compliance mechanisms. The design and implementation of compliance programs have been influenced by several forces, particularly the United States Sentencing Commission's guidelines for sentencing organizations (discussed in Chapter 9.4 of this Handbook), which impose less onerous treatment on corporations with compliance manuals and programs and announce key criteria for effective compliance and ethics programs, summarized as follows:

- A company must establish standards and procedures to prevent and detect criminal conduct.
- A specific senior executive or other high-level person is expected to have responsibility for the compliance and ethics program, and the board must oversee its implementation.
- Due care should be taken in delegating compliance responsibilities—an individual who has engaged in illegal activity or other conduct inconsistent with an effective compliance program should not have supervisory responsibilities in the compliance program.
- Compliance and ethics programs should be implemented through education and practical, relevant training.
- Compliance programs should be audited and monitored, and periodically evaluated regarding implementation and effectiveness. Employees must have effective mechanisms through which to (anonymously or confidentially) report misconduct or seek guidance on compliance matters; and employees should be protected from retaliation.
- A company must promote and enforce its compliance and ethics programs through appropriate incentives that encourage employees to comply with the program. In addition, a company must impose appropriate disciplinary measures when employees engage in misconduct or fail to take reasonable steps to prevent or detect misconduct. The compliance and ethics program must be enforced consistently, or risk losing credibility.
- If misconduct is detected, a company must take reasonable steps—including adjustments to compliance programs—to prevent similar misconduct in the future. In addition, the board must receive regular and meaningful reports on audit results and the status of corrective action.

The rapidly changing business, risk, and legal environment requires sustained attention to ethics and compliance programs. Boards can promote lasting and effective legal and ethical environments by establishing a "tone at the top" and incentivizing, measuring, and rewarding ethical behaviors and compliance with laws.

Key Questions

When considering ethics and compliance, key questions that a director might ask include the following:

- ❑ What are the company's core values and how are they communicated throughout the organization? Is there a tone at the top of ethics and compliance? Am I comfortable that the board understands and is committed to the purpose, values and direction of the company?
- ❑ Which member of management has responsibility for the company's ethics and compliance program? Does that person have sufficient authority, resources, and access to the board to accomplish the company's compliance goals? Does the board have sufficient access to that person and other compliance resources?
- ❑ What is the compliance history of the company and its competitors? How does the company's ethics and compliance program compare to those of its peers?
- ❑ Who are the company's key regulators? What guidance have those regulators provided to the company or its industry? Does the company have a good relationship with key regulators?
- ❑ How are the company's ethics and compliance policies and procedures communicated throughout the organization? Do employees receive regular training?
- ❑ Have employees reported misconduct or potential misconduct? How are such reports made? What steps and corrective actions were taken in response to any such reports?
- ❑ How is the effectiveness of the company's ethics and compliance program measured? Is effectiveness of the program a component of management's annual evaluation?
- ❑ What is the company's business plan? What ethical dilemmas and compliance risks may be faced by management in pursuing the plan? Which aspects of the company's existing and planned business are most vulnerable to ethical and compliance failure? What is being done to measure, monitor, and mitigate those vulnerabilities?
- ❑ Does the company have any risk management assessments? Are they appropriately reflected in the design of the compliance program?

Additional Reading

1. ABA Business Law Section, Committee on Corporate Laws. *Corporate Director's Guidebook*, 6th ed. (See Section 4)
2. Ethics Pays. Ethical Systems
   http://www.ethicalsystems.org/content/ethics-pays
3. Society of Corporate Compliance and Ethics
   http://www.corporatecompliance.org

4. Murphy, Joseph E. Using Incentives in Your Ethics and Compliance Programs. *Society of Corporate Compliance and Ethics* (2011)

   http://www.corporatecompliance.org/Portals/1/PDF/Resources/complimentary/IncentivesCEProgram-Murphy.pdf

5. Director Essentials: Strengthening Compliance and Ethics Oversight. *NACD* (November 2015)

   https://www.nacdonline.org/Resources/Article.cfm?ItemNumber=21600

6. Compliance 360, White Paper: The Seven Elements of an Effective Compliance and Ethics Program

   http://compliance.saiglobal.com/assets/whitepapers/SAI-GLOBAL-whitepaper-seven-elements-effective-compliance-programs.pdf?mtcEmail=aboniface,nacdonline.org

7. NACD Corporate Director's Ethics and Compliance Handbook (2003)

8. Conference Board. The Role of Directors in Risk Oversight

   https://www.conference-board.org/retrievefile.cfm?filename=DN-010-10.pdf&type=subsite

Notes

____

____

____

____

____

9.3 CODE OF CONDUCT WAIVERS

CONTRIBUTED BY
Cheryl Scarboro and Diana Wielocha
Simpson Thacher & Bartlett LLP[1]

Chapter 9.2 of this Handbook addresses the components of corporate ethics and compliance programs. This chapter focuses on one of those elements, the company's code of conduct (referred to interchangeably as the "code of ethics") and, more specifically, on waivers of the code of conduct for directors and executive officers. We begin with an overview of SEC and listing agency rules regarding waivers of the code of ethics and provide guidance on factors to consider in determining whether to grant waivers.

Required Disclosure

Section 406 of the Sarbanes-Oxley Act required the SEC to issue rules requiring issuers to disclose whether they adopted a code of ethics. That mandate also required the SEC to require disclosure of any waivers of the code of ethics for certain senior officers. In response, in 2003, the SEC promulgated Item 406 of Regulation S-K, which requires

1. Cheryl Scarboro, partner, and Diana Wielocha, associate, are members of Simpson Thacher & Bartlett LLP's Government and Internal Investigations practice located in the Washington, D.C. office.

companies to promptly disclose waivers of the code of ethics for the company's principal executive officer, principal financial officer, principal accounting officer, and other persons performing similar functions. Also in 2003, the SEC approved NYSE and NASDAQ rules requiring listed companies to promptly disclose waivers of the code of ethics for all executive officers and directors. In addition to requiring prompt disclosure of waivers, NYSE and NASDAQ rules also require that any waivers of the code of ethics for directors and executive officers must be approved by the company's board of directors or, in the case of NYSE, a committee of the board.

Form 8-K defines a waiver as "the approval by the registrant of a material departure from a provision of the code of ethics." If a company decides to grant a waiver of its code of ethics (either explicitly, or implicitly by failing to take action within a reasonable period of time), then the company must publicly disclose this information to investors.

The disclosure of a waiver must describe the nature of the waiver, the name of the person to whom the waiver was granted, and the date of the waiver. Additionally, the disclosure must be made within four business days after the waiver is granted via a Form 8-K filing or a posting on the company's Internet website. A website posting may be used to disseminate this information only if the company disclosed in its latest annual report its website address and its intent to disclose this type of information on its website. Disclosures of waivers must remain available on the company's website for a period of 12 months. Foreign issuers, unlike domestic issuers, are not subject to the four-day window for disclosures and have a few different options for disclosing waivers. These include a website posting, a press release, or inclusion in the company's next annual report.

Advisable Procedures

While the SEC, NYSE, and NASDAQ rules do not prescribe controls or procedures to be established in connection with granting and disclosing waivers of codes of ethics, companies are advised to clearly set forth the process for requesting waivers and the factors to be considered in entertaining requests for waivers. This information should be readily available to directors and executive officers. Additionally, the company should have controls in place designed to facilitate the timely disclosure of material waivers in an appropriate fashion. After-the-fact waivers are strongly discouraged.

The practice of granting waivers of codes of ethics is fairly infrequent, and understandably so, based on the nature and purpose of codes of ethics—which is to promote things like honesty and a respectful work environment, and to encourage compliance with governmental laws and regulations. In the few instances in which waivers are granted, they are typically in connection with potential conflict of interest situations and related party transactions. Because waivers are not looked upon favorably by investors, it is important for directors to carefully consider whether a waiver is warranted in a particular situation and how to limit the scope of the waiver in order to ensure that the company and shareholders are adequately protected.

Key Questions

Key questions to consider when deciding whether and to what extent to grant a waiver of the code of ethics to an executive officer or director include the following:

- ❑ Does the activity or transaction in question constitute a material departure from the company's code of ethics? What constitutes a material departure? Do I need any additional information to make this determination?
- ❑ What justification has the director or executive officer provided in connection with their request for a waiver? Does this constitute a valid justification for the grant of a waiver? Is the waiver necessary to alleviate any undue hardship or unforeseen circumstances? Is the waiver appropriate based on the facts and circumstances at issue?
- ❑ Does the company's code of ethics articulate any standards under which requests for waivers must be construed or any requirements that must be met before a waiver is granted? Have those requirements been satisfied here? Would granting a waiver be inconsistent with the intent and objectives of the code of ethics?
- ❑ Would granting a waiver lead to a transaction that violates any applicable laws or regulations?
- ❑ How will the waiver impact the company? How will it affect shareholders? Is there any potential for the company or shareholders to be harmed?
- ❑ Is a waiver absolutely necessary? If not, what alternatives should be considered? If a waiver is necessary, is there any way to limit the scope of the waiver to minimize any potentially adverse effects on the company and shareholders? For instance, in a conflict of interest situation, is there a way to limit the interaction that the director or executive officer would have with the entity in question, perhaps by requiring that the director or executive officer recuse themselves from any and all business decisions relating to that entity?
- ❑ Would it be advisable to consult with independent third parties, experts, or outside counsel for advice on whether to grant a waiver?
- ❑ If the decision is made to grant a waiver, how will the waiver be disclosed—via an 8-K filing or website posting? What are the implications, if any, of disclosing in a filing versus posting on the company's website? Can 8-K filings be used by the government as a basis for civil liability?
- ❑ How will the waiver be perceived by shareholders and investors?

Additional Reading

1. 15 U.S.C. § 7264 (2016).
2. Item 406 of Regulation S-K (Code of Ethics), 17 C.F.R. § 229.406 (2016).

3. NYSE, Inc., Listed Company Manual § 303A.10 (2009).
4. NASDAQ, Inc., Listing Rules § 5610 (2009).
5. Form 8-K, Sec. and Exch. Comm'n, Item 5.05.
6. Romanek, Broc and Randi Morrison, *Code of Ethics/Conduct Disclosure Handbook*, TheCorporateCounsel.Net (February 2016).
7. Mori, Madoka. "A Proposal to Revise the SEC Instructions for Reporting Waivers of Corporate Codes of Ethics for Conflicts of Interest." 24 *Yale J. on Reg.* 293 (2007).

Notes

94 FEDERAL SENTENCING GUIDELINES AND THEIR IMPLICATIONS

CONTRIBUTED BY
Paul Lanois
Credit Suisse[1]

The United States Sentencing Commission (the USSC) developed the Sentencing Guidelines in order to increase uniformity and transparency in sentencing. Chapter 8 of the Sentencing Guidelines addresses the sentencing of organizations and Part B.2 of that chapter encourages organizations to develop a compliance program since it provides that organizations that choose to voluntarily disclose misconduct and undertake certain steps (such as implementing an "effective" compliance and ethics program) may alleviate their culpability.

According to the Sentencing Guidelines, an effective compliance and ethics program must aim at preventing and detecting criminal conduct and promote an organizational culture that encourages ethical conduct and a commitment to compliance with the law. This means that such program should include the following seven elements:

1. Standards and procedures to prevent and detect criminal conduct
2. Active leadership and oversight of the compliance and ethics program, including specific duties imposed on various levels of management, including

1. Paul Lanois is senior legal counsel at Credit Suisse. He is admitted to the bars of the District of Columbia, New York, and the Supreme Court of the United States and is a Certified Information Privacy Manager (CIPM) and a Certified Information Privacy Professional for Asia (CIPP/A), the United States (CIPP/US), Europe (CIPP/E), and Canada (CIPP/C).

the company's "governing authority" (i.e., the board of directors), senior management, as well as individuals with operational responsibility over the program
3. Reasonable efforts to avoid delegating substantial authority to individuals who have previously engaged in illegal activities or other behavior inconsistent with an effective compliance and ethics program
4. Periodic communication and training of employees (as well as agents) on the company's compliance and ethics program
5. Periodic evaluation of the effectiveness of the compliance and ethics program through monitoring and auditing, as well as implementing a helpline and whistleblowing mechanism so that employees and agents may report or seek guidance regarding potential or actual breaches of the compliance program without fear of retaliation
6. Consistent enforcement and promotion of the program throughout the company through appropriate incentives, discipline, and enforcement
7. Appropriate response to incidents and steps taken to prevent future incidents

Once the seven elements are in place, the compliance and ethics program must be periodically reassessed and amended where necessary to ensure that it remains current and effective.

In addition to informing the company about potential issues and how to address them, having an effective compliance and ethics program in place may help protect the company in the event that it is investigated for potential misconduct by reducing any penalty that may be imposed.

The Sentencing Guidelines, and in particular the seven elements just listed, have had a significant impact on organizations across and outside the United States, as companies have accordingly created and modeled their compliance and ethics programs. According to the USSC, the Bank of Tokyo, Ltd. declared in 1995 that it has "made the federal [S]entencing [G]uidelines the focal point of its overall compliance effort" since the Sentencing Guidelines have provided a "road map" and a clear picture of what a compliance program should look like and a set of instructions on how to construct a program. The same USSC document indicates that New York-area banks as well as the Canadian Imperial Bank of Commerce (CIBC) have used the Sentencing Guidelines as a foundation for their overall compliance efforts. Thus, the Sentencing Guidelines have had an impact on the creation and implementation of ethics programs, and it seems that they have also been used by the courts in assessing fines and placing companies on probation. The Sentencing Guidelines may also have improved the culture within organizations, since according to a National Business Ethics Survey of the U.S. workforce published in 2014, the observed workplace misconduct has fallen to a historic low, and the percentage of workers who felt pressure to compromise standards fell substantially.

Key Questions

Some key questions to consider in relation to the implementation of a compliance program include the following:

- ❑ Does the organization have a code of conduct or otherwise similar governance publication?
- ❑ Has the board discussed what it wants to achieve from a compliance program and what its broad contours should be?
- ❑ Is the executive team, the line of business leadership, and the leaders of other disciplines fully engaged in the company's compliance program?
- ❑ Is there any training/education in place within the organization to promote within the company an ethical and compliant conduct?
- ❑ Has the organization conducted an assessment of the awareness of its employees in relation to ethical/legal issues that may arise at work?
- ❑ Is there sufficient knowledge within the organization of the applicable legal rules and regulations?
- ❑ Is there a perception that the organization cares as much about ethical and compliant behavior as much as its bottom line?
- ❑ Is there a perception within the organization that unethical behavior would be punished, regardless of the level where such behavior takes place?
- ❑ Is there a perception within the organization that employees may report or seek guidance in relation to potential or actual misconduct, without any reprisal for having made a report in good faith?

Additional Reading

1. 2016 Guidelines Manual, United States Sentencing Commission
   http://www.ussc.gov/guidelines
2. What Can We Learn from the U.S. Federal Sentencing Guidelines for Organizational Ethics? *Journal of Business Ethics*, 17, no. 9/10
   http://library.businessethicsworkshop.com/images/Library/Federal_Sentencing_Guidelines_and_Organizational_Ethics.pdf
3. Corporate Crime in America: Strengthening the "Good Citizen" Corporation, United States Sentencing Commission
   http://www.ussc.gov/corporate-crime-america-strengthening-good-citizen-corporation

4. The Implementation of Compliance Programmes in Multinational Organizations, *The Role of Large Enterprises in Democracy and Society*. Palgrave Macmillan (2010)
   http://www.transparency.ch/de/PDF_files/Divers/JPM_The_Implementation_of_Compliance_Programmes.pdf
5. National Business Ethics Survey of the U.S. Workforce, Ethics Resource Center https://www.ibe.org.uk/userassets/surveys/nbes2013.pdf

Notes

9.5 BOARD OVERSIGHT OF GOVERNMENT INVESTIGATIONS

CONTRIBUTED BY
Philip S. Khinda, Thomas R.L. Best, and Eric J. Lipton
Steptoe & Johnson LLP[1]

In this era of heightened regulatory scrutiny, navigating a government investigation, in which multiple stakeholders often have competing interests, can be a difficult and complicated affair involving many sensitive strategic and governance considerations. When shareholder activism and class action litigation are added to the mix, the stakes become even higher for a public company board. Notwithstanding the many pressures now on public company directors, they can still take comfort in knowing that courts and regulators continue to recognize the importance of business judgment protection. To qualify for that protection, however, it is imperative that directors exercise their oversight responsibilities and business judgment faithfully and on an informed basis, rather than relinquishing that role to management, outside counsel, accountants, or experts. In our experience, ensuring that boards and directors stay involved and informed throughout any inquiry or investigation yields the best results from a legal, business, and practical perspective.

1. Mr. Khinda is a partner at Steptoe & Johnson LLP and leads the firm's corporate governance and crisis management practices. Mr. Best is a partner and Mr. Lipton is an associate at the firm, and they also practice in these areas. The authors are grateful for the assistance of Chelsea Gold, a legislative assistant and summer associate at the firm.

The Regulatory Landscape

The past two decades have seen U.S. public companies subjected to an ever-increasing framework of rules and regulations directed at preventing the latest corporate crisis (or perceived crisis) and its impact on the U.S. economy and investors. The Enron and WorldCom scandals of the early 2000s brought on a wholesale overhaul of governance and compliance standards, in addition to the introduction of new concerns about personal liability for corporate misconduct. With the issuance of SEC audit committee disclosure rules and the passage of the Sarbanes-Oxley Act of 2002 (SOX), the regulation of corporate governance shifted from a market-oriented philosophy to a prescriptive one that in many ways "deputizes" directors as agents of public oversight and disclosure.

More recently, the financial crisis of 2008 sparked calls for significant reform to the country's financial sector, culminating in the passage of the comprehensive Dodd-Frank Wall Street Reform and Consumer Protection Act of 2010 (Dodd-Frank). Like SOX, Dodd-Frank also contained strong whistleblower protections, including significant financial incentives, intended to bring alleged misconduct to the attention of regulators.

Directors' Duties in the Investigations Context

Regulatory developments over the last few decades may have altered the perception of the modern board, but the essential fiduciary duties of corporate directors remain their fundamental duties of care and loyalty. The essence of the duty of care is that directors must make business decisions on an informed basis, based on the material reasonably available to them, after due consideration and deliberation. The duties of loyalty and care go hand in hand with the business judgment rule, pursuant to which courts (and regulators) generally recognize a presumption that shields the decisions of disinterested directors made in good faith after due deliberation. Absent facts demonstrating that board members reached their decision "by a grossly negligent process that includes the failure to consider all material facts reasonably available," the business decisions made by the board should not be second-guessed.

Beyond the duties to exercise care and loyalty in business decisions, directors also have a duty to monitor business operations and employee conduct, which was solidified in the Delaware Supreme Court's landmark *Caremark* decision, *In re Caremark Int'l Inc. Deriv. Litig.* Under *Caremark*, a directors' duty to monitor "includes a duty to attempt in good faith to assure that a corporate information and reporting system, which the board concludes is adequate [] exists . . ." and the "failure to do so under some circumstances may, in theory at least, render a director liable for losses caused by non-compliance with applicable legal standards." Courts have set the bar high for the evidence required to prove such a breach of duty, explaining that the necessary conditions predicate for director oversight liability in the context of failing to set up a corporate compliance program require a showing that (i) the directors utterly failed to implement any reporting or information system or controls; or (ii) having implemented such a system or controls, consciously failed to monitor or oversee its operations, thus disabling themselves from being informed of risks or problems requiring their attention.

Thus, Delaware law effectively recognizes a *scienter* requirement to establish directorial liability for violations of a board's oversight duties, either through direct knowledge or involvement in the underlying problematic conduct, or through deliberate failure to establish the necessary reporting systems to apprise the board of such conduct. To be successful, plaintiffs must prove that the board of directors consciously chose not to discharge its duty to oversee the corporation. As a result, violation of a board of directors' oversight duty has been called "possibly the most difficult theory [of liability] in corporation law" and recent decisions in derivative actions have confirmed that high bar.

When discharging their fiduciary duties, directors are permitted to rely upon and delegate certain board functions to board committees as well as independent advisors under appropriate circumstances. Upon such good faith delegation, a board is still entitled to the presumption that it exercised proper business judgment, including proper reliance on the expert. Directors are not entitled, however, to enjoy a "blind" reliance on the reports of experts and must make a "reasonable inquiry" into reports submitted to the board. Indeed, as a general rule, a board should not and cannot delegate all control of an investigation. Business judgment protection demands adequate information under *Caremark*. Even when not leading investigations, directors must remain informed with periodic updates and reports.

Corporate Governance in Action: Directors Rising to Meet Their Situational Duties

Public companies may face the prospect of an investigation for a variety of reasons—whether arising from a government inquiry or from private claims, such as in connection with shareholder derivative litigation or securities class actions. The press also has increasingly uncovered allegations of wrongdoing in recent years. Notable (but by no means exclusive) examples include the *Wall Street Journal* articles on improper options backdating at corporations such as UnitedHealth Group Inc. and Apple Inc., the *New York Times* investigation into allegations of bribery at Walmart's Mexican subsidiary, and the "Panama Papers" leak of confidential client documents relating to offshore holdings. A number of crucial decisions must be made, often in the initial stages of an investigation, about whether an internal review or investigation is necessary and who should oversee it, whether outside counsel and/or other advisors should be employed, and whether disclosure to regulators is necessary or in the company's interest, among other important early questions.

Who Should Lead the Investigation and Being Sure One Is Necessary

There is no set rule as to when an inquiry or investigation will require board involvement. In some cases, such as an internal inquiry into the misconduct of a single employee, senior management and/or the company's in-house legal department may be able to take the lead. Management-led investigations are only possible, of course, when it is clear that management will retain its independence from the issue being investigated and potential regulatory action is not implicated. Regardless of who is leading the investigation, the board needs to remain informed and ready to escalate its involvement if necessary.

Although anti-corruption laws, for example, increasingly require companies to implement internal controls and compliance systems that review potential breaches (and, in some cases, voluntary disclosure is evaluated as a component of an effective compliance program), companies may not necessarily be under any clear legal obligation to conduct an internal investigation. Management may be reluctant to initiate an investigation under such circumstances, perhaps hoping to avoid incurring substantial investigation costs or uncovering significant legal violations. Management and board directors are well advised to take any shareholder allegations or accounting red flags seriously and address them promptly, showing the courage and will to act when necessary.

Investigations into more serious conduct that might involve company management or financials typically require that some part of the board take control of the process. This may be through the audit committee (which is, by definition, populated by outside directors) or a special committee, if appropriate, in response to a shareholder demand or derivative claims. While not an exhaustive list, the following allegations or perceived misconduct typically require at least some board involvement: (i) widespread misconduct within the organization; (ii) a demand from an aggrieved shareholder; (iii) action or conduct that could reasonably implicate key executive officers or directors; (iv) significant compliance issues discovered through whistleblowers, audits, or other means; (v) action or conduct that calls into question the objectivity of a management-directed investigation; or (vi) action or conduct that subjects the company to regulatory investigation or potential enforcement action.

Management and existing board committees may be able to oversee many investigations, given that many issues will fall naturally under their jurisdiction and may not raise independence concerns. Revenue recognition-related allegations or any of the myriad other accounting and/or internal controls-related risks facing companies today may generally be addressed by the board's audit committee. Special committees, on the other hand, may be necessary in situations where an existing committee lacks apparent jurisdiction, the company is seeking to ensure that the board has sufficient expertise in order to manage a particular type of investigation, or the board requires an additional layer of independence.

Selection of the Investigative Team

Once an investigation is deemed necessary, the investigative team should be assembled promptly and the decision should be made as to whether to engage outside counsel, accountants, or other experts. As a general matter, in-house counsel will rarely be used to conduct investigations that warrant board oversight due to a perceived absence of objectivity and potential conflicts of interest. Thus, where a board-driven investigation is appropriate, it is likely that the board will rely on outside counsel who will report directly to the board or the applicable board committee or special committee thereof.

The use of specially retained outside counsel, as opposed to in-house counsel or the company's regular corporate counsel, can have significant advantages. Outside counsel typically have significant experience with potential regulators and expertise in the area of the law at issue. The use of outside counsel also fosters a view of credibility and independence that may otherwise be lacking. As noted above, retention of outside counsel or auditors does not mean that management or the board can relinquish oversight of the process, but rather should stay involved and informed, such as through the use of periodic reports. Not only will this help to ensure business judgment protection, but companies may also achieve significant efficiencies by working closely with outside counsel.

The Scope of the Investigation

Investigations can continue for years, particularly if not managed properly. It is important for directors not to let outside counsel and advisors get out too far ahead of them in terms of planning and undertaking the investigation. While credible allegations should be investigated thoroughly, investigation costs can quickly outpace potential liability if left unchecked. Thus, a board should apply its business judgment even when defining the scope of the investigation.

The scope of the investigation is necessarily a fact-specific determination. As a general matter, courts in the shareholder derivative context, for example, have suggested that the corporation may be expected to show that the areas and subjects to be examined are reasonably complete and there has been a good-faith pursuit of inquiry into such areas and subjects. For practical purposes, the scope of the investigation should strike a balance between being so narrow that it fails to capture all relevant information and being so broad that it delves into extraneous facets of the corporation's affairs.

Although a company often assumes that regulators expect it to undertake an expansive, global investigation, the top priority is usually to cut to the substance of the allegations at hand in a timely fashion. For example, the DOJ commented in enforcement papers on the scope and size of Avon's internal investigation of FCPA-related matters in 2011. While recognizing that the compliance and internal control improvements at Avon gained through its company-wide review, the DOJ also noted that these efforts were undertaken without Department request or guidance, and at times caused unintended delays in the progress of the Department's narrower investigations. Discussing the scope of a regulator's requests in a subpoena and the focus of its investigation can yield significant benefits and cost savings. Prompt attention to document retention and collection issues is similarly critical for defining the scope of the investigation and keeping investigative costs under control.

Memorializing and Reporting Findings

How a company and its board of directors determine to memorialize and report the investigation's findings, or receive interim updates as the investigation progresses, also needs to be carefully considered. An important threshold decision is whether the interim and final reports a company may receive should be produced in writing or orally.

There has been a trend toward using oral investigation reports for companies and their boards in recent years—particularly in connection with investigations of SEC issuers, where reporting can trigger the SEC's own investigation or shareholder or other collateral litigation in which an investigation report may become admissible evidence. On the one hand, the trend toward oral reporting has been driven by the advantage of not creating documentation that could be discoverable in litigation or in connection with a government investigation. Unlike oral reports, written reports create a document that could be leaked or be required to be produced. Written reports can also be costly and time-consuming to prepare, sometimes delaying the consideration of the investigation's findings longer than the time at which they were first known and presented.

A written report, however, can provide advantages. For independent directors who are overseeing an investigation and who may be less familiar with the inner workings of a particular company, well-prepared written descriptions of the allegations, investigation process, and their context can serve to better inform directors in the short term, and better demonstrate the rigor of the board's diligence and the basis for its judgments in the long term. Of course, the determination as to whether to produce an oral or written report needs to be made in the context of the specific matter at hand, weighing the benefits and drawbacks of each approach. Whether reporting the findings of an investigation internally or to external parties, the information presented must be thorough and complete as a general matter.

Directors' Duties in Addressing Findings of the Investigation

Once the board has received the findings of the investigation, its duty of care requires that it act on them appropriately. Depending on the substance and nature of the findings, subsequent actions may involve any of the following remedial steps discussed below. Board members should ensure, however, that whatever the findings of the investigation, the remedial actions recommended by the board's advisors are followed up on, and any deviation from that advice be explained—and explainable—through contemporaneous notes written to memorialize the fact of the decision, and nothing more.

Compliance and Remediation

Upon receiving the findings of the investigation, the board must decide whether the findings require remedial action, which can include any number of context-specific measures, but most often involve changing business processes or business relationships. Such changes ensure that outside parties, who may have contributed to the conduct, no longer have business relationships with the company, and the business processes that enabled the problematic relationships and/or conduct no longer apply.

Employee discipline can be another important aspect of the company's remedial measures where it is appropriate. Considerations that ought to be weighed when determining the appropriate degree of discipline include the effect on the company's other employees, ongoing operations, the continuing investigations, and the company's relations with regulators and/or law enforcement. Such disciplinary action—if taken appropriately, proportionally, and immediately—can indicate to regulators that the board is taking its duty of oversight seriously. Regulators also are increasingly asserting that employee discipline is another component of their evaluation of whether a company has an effective compliance program, as defined under the U.S. Federal Sentencing Guidelines, in addition to how enforcement officials make their charging decisions in their own right.

The enhancement of the company's compliance program may also be necessary, to the extent that the investigation uncovers weaknesses in the program itself or other failures in a company's control environment. Depending on the areas of law involved, the SEC has taken the position that compliance programs targeted at a particular area of companies' legal risks are part of their legally mandated internal controls.

To Cooperate or Not to Cooperate

Cooperation with government regulators should always be the starting proposition. At various points during the investigation, however, the question must be asked as to whether or not the fact of the investigation itself or investigation findings should be voluntarily disclosed to the prosecutors, law enforcement officials, and/or regulators with jurisdiction over the matter. This calculus can be difficult given that the decision may have significant legal, business, and reputational consequences for a company, its executives, its employees, and its shareholders alike. Management and directors must balance the prospect of an uncertain benefit against the increased likelihood of exposure to an enforcement action and/or civil litigation and then decide how the company's interests are best served. If the decision is made to move forward with disclosing information or materials to a government regulator, steps should still be taken to protect the company as best as possible, such as by pursuing a confidentiality agreement with the government.

Special Investigation Considerations

The 2015 Yates Memorandum

Throughout its involvement in the investigation, the board must consider how recent regulatory and policy pronouncements may affect the company and the ongoing investigation. One such development is the release of the so-called Yates Memorandum. i.e., the Memorandum from Deputy Attorney General Sally Quillian Yates to All United States Attorneys on September 15, 2015. The DOJ sought to strengthen its pursuit of individual accountability for corporate wrongdoing, responding to criticism prevalent after the global financial crisis that it failed to address corporate misconduct at the individual level. In response to those pressures, the Yates Memorandum set forth six key steps to strengthen its pursuit of individual corporate wrongdoing.

Though the steps echo previously enunciated DOJ priorities, the Yates Memorandum presents some new difficulties and challenges for boards of directors. For example, the requirement that corporations disclose "all relevant facts" regarding individuals' misconduct in order to receive cooperation credit will make the voluntary disclosure and cooperation decisions more difficult. In an effort to respond to these concerns, the DOJ has explained that where a company provides the government with the relevant facts and otherwise assists the government in obtaining evidence, the company should still be eligible for cooperation credit, even if it cannot identify culpable individuals. If a board does opt to participate, the board should ensure it has experienced counsel and is committed to gathering all information required, even if that information may lead to key corporate executives. Needless to say, boards will need to conduct a careful cost-benefit analysis before starting down the disclosure road.

The DOJ's FCPA "Pilot Program"

Consistent with the Yates Memorandum, in April 2016, the Fraud Section of the DOJ launched a one-year pilot program intended to encourage companies to disclose FCPA misconduct. The program aims to incentivize corporations to provide cooperation in exchange for "mitigation credit"—which can amount to reduced penalties ranging from reductions in fines to declinations. To qualify for the program, the corporation must (i) make a voluntary self-disclosure, (ii) cooperate fully with the government, and (iii) implement timely and appropriate remediation measures. These requirements inject new uncertainty into the process because the measuring stick used by the DOJ appears to be largely subjective. Because of the subjective nature of the program requirements, corporations should be cautious when deciding whether to make voluntary disclosures under its new pilot program.

Recent Developments in the Law on Individual Director Liability

Public company directors should also be cognizant of the potential for personal liability, particularly in light of recent regulatory focus on holding corporate "gatekeepers" responsible. For example, the SEC has expressed a willingness to take action against directors, who "play a critically important role in overseeing what [their] company is doing, and by preventing, detecting, and stopping violations of the federal securities laws at [their] companies, and responding to any problems that do occur." Indeed, directors have been identified as the "most important gatekeepers" because by law, it is ultimately the fiduciary responsibility of the board of directors to oversee the business and affairs of a company.

More often than not, regulators and litigants will focus on direct, intentional misconduct of directors. Such conduct has ranged from knowingly signing false disclosure documents to actively concealing losses or other pertinent information. Of greater concern are some recent indications of possible director liability for less direct, unintentional conduct.

In one recent action, the SEC entered into a deferred prosecution agreement with the board chairman of public company Uni-Pixel, Inc. after he allegedly became aware that company press releases were inaccurate and apparently failed to take adequate action. The board chairman testified that the company CEO was "basically out of control on press releases" and that he had repeatedly instructed the CEO to stop issuing press releases containing false or misleading information. The chairman, however, "took no affirmative steps to implement any oversight of outgoing press releases or correct misleading press releases after their issuance." Pursuant to the agreement, the chairman agreed to cooperate with the SEC in its case against the company CEO and CFO and be barred from serving as an officer and director for five years.

With a keen eye on the source of recovery provided by directors' and officers' insurance, private litigants also continue to explore new theories of director liability with some success of late. For example, a U.S. district court recently held that directors may be subject to liability under federal whistleblower provisions. The case involved an employee informing senior management and the audit committee of the board of suspicions that the company may be bribing Chinese officials in violation of the FCPA. After conducting an internal investigation, the company concluded there was no wrongdoing and subsequently terminated the employee who reported the concerns after a determination was made by the board of directors. Although noting the "scant case law" on the issue, the court concluded that Congress failed to expressly include directors in the list of those who may be individually liable under Sarbanes-Oxley, thereby undermining the conclusion that it intended to shield directors in retaliatory conduct from individual liability.

Dealing with government investigations is rarely a simple affair. Investigations present companies and their boards and directors with a multitude of procedural, substantive, and tactical issues that require careful consideration. Board members should remain engaged from the outset of any investigation, as their exercise of business judgment and fulfillment of their fiduciary duties to the company demand that they be active and informed—efforts that will not only be most protective for the company in the face of regulators or litigation, but also for each of the directors personally.

Key Questions

When overseeing an investigation, a board may wish to consider the following:

- ❑ Is an investigation necessary? What should be its scope?
- ❑ Can it be conducted internally, or should it be handled by outside counsel?
- ❑ Is the counsel suggested by management appropriately independent?
- ❑ Do they have the right specific experience for this situation? Do they have relationships with the relevant governmental authorities?
- ❑ When and how should we interface with the government?
- ❑ Does any member of the board or management need separate counsel? If so, how should that process be managed?
- ❑ Should the investigation be handled by the board's audit committee or a special committee?
- ❑ Do we have the right kind of experience (and sufficient independence) on our board to conduct this investigation? If not, should board members be added?
- ❑ Do we need a crisis communications consultant or other communications advisor?
- ❑ What should we tell the market? When? How often should we communicate?
- ❑ Does the investigation reveal any deficiencies or shortcomings in our management team? What remediation should be undertaken?
- ❑ Does the investigation reveal any weaknesses in our internal controls over financial reporting or elsewhere at the company? How should any deficiencies be remediated?
- ❑ How and when should we communicate with our auditors regarding the investigation and its causes? Its findings? How do we preserve the attorney–client privilege in doing so?
- ❑ Do we want a written or oral report on the investigation?
- ❑ What should be our plan regarding voluntary disclosure and governmental cooperation?

Additional Reading

1. Ferrara, Ralph C. and Philip S. Khinda. *Deputizing Directors,* Directors and Boards (Summer 2000)
   https://www.directorsandboards.com/article-library
2. Cole, James M. and Philip S. Khinda. *Conducting Investigations Post-Yates Memo*. ABA Presentation (Nov. 12, 2015)
   http://apps.americanbar.org/dch/thedl.cfm?filename=/CL260030/related resources/yates_memo.pdf

3. Ferrara, Ralph C. and Philip S. Khinda. *Board Oversight of SEC Investigations*, Directors and Boards (Spring 2000)
   https://www.directorsandboards.com/article-library
4. Ferrara, Ralph C. and Philip S. Khinda. SEC Enforcement Proceedings: Strategic Considerations for When the Agency Comes Calling. 51 *Admin. L. Rev.* 1143 (Fall 1999)
5. U.S. DOJ and SEC, *A Resource Guide to the U.S. Foreign Corrupt Practices Act*, (November 14, 2012)
   https://www.sec.gov/spotlight/fcpa/fcpa-resource-guide.pdf
6. Memorandum from Deputy Attorney General Sally Quillian Yates to All United States Attorneys (September 15, 2015)
   https://www.justice.gov/dag/file/769036/download
7. U.S. DOJ, *The Fraud Section's Foreign Corrupt Practices Act Enforcement Plan and Guidance* (April 5, 2016)
   https://www.justice.gov/criminal-fraud/file/838416/download

Notes

9.6 INTERNAL INVESTIGATIONS

CONTRIBUTED BY
Colby A. Smith
Debevoise & Plimpton LLP[1]

One of the most vexing problems that can confront any board arises when information of potential corporate misconduct comes to light. Senior enforcement officials at the Securities and Exchange Commission (SEC) and Department of Justice repeatedly have referred to boards as fulfilling a "gatekeeper" function in such circumstances—in which the board is expected to act as an objective and independent bulwark against corporate wrongdoing. A board's failure to appropriately and adequately discharge this responsibility can exacerbate problems, lead to enhanced fines and penalties, harm a corporation's reputation, and, in egregious cases, lead to potential personal liability. More than many other responsibilities of corporate directors, this is an area where mistakes can cost companies real money and do reputational damage that can take years to repair.

Issues that warrant consideration for internal investigation can arise in any number of ways: they may be identified by management, they may be highlighted in an internal audit report or a compliance officer's presentation, they may be raised by a company's auditors during the course of their review, they may come from a whistleblower, they may

1. Colby A. Smith is a partner in the Washington, D.C. office of Debevoise & Plimpton LLP. He is co-chair of the firm's Securities Litigation practice.

arrive in the form of a request for documents or other information from a government regulator, or they may take the form of a letter from a shareholder that raises a derivative demand. Regardless of how an issue comes to the board's attention, the decisions by the board concerning how to handle the issue can mean the difference between a problem that gets vetted and addressed in relative short order and a problem that begins to spin out of control and becomes a corporate crisis. In most cases, the first 48 hours after a board learns of such issues are the most critical, because that is the time when (i) the board has the least information from which to work, (ii) management and other advisors are most likely to be dismissive of the seriousness of any allegations, and (iii) a number of key decisions need to be made about how to respond.

Key Considerations

In many cases, the issues that come before a board will present obvious questions that will make for relatively straightforward decisions. In such circumstances, the board likely can consider the 10 key questions set forth in the following section and make reasonably informed decisions. But in some circumstances, the issues may be unclear, and that lack of clarity could prompt the board to over or under react. It is always worth assessing whether the board is currently in a position to take reasonably informed action—and it if it is not, consider, in the first instance, what more information can be obtained quickly to allow the board to take the next step with more information, while at the same time acting within an appropriate time frame. Experienced boards are normally very good at asking the right questions and gathering as much information as they can when they are asked to make critical decisions. When the issue on the agenda is the conduct of an internal investigation, the need to assertively ask questions and gather information is particularly acute. Critical decisions about internal investigations often are made under circumstances where information is limited (hence the need for the investigation). Boards should be certain, however, that they have as much information as is available to inform their decisions.

The board should bear in mind that even the best corporate management team may decide, consciously or unconsciously, to focus its disclosures to the board on the facts that are known at the time, even while the team works to confirm other potential issues. Directors should inquire what further work is being done and what other potential issues may be out there—again, so the directors can evaluate all available information—even if some of that information may be less than certain. Clearly, if, at the outset, a board can be confident that a small issue will stay small, the issue may warrant a different response than an issue that appears small today but that may grow tomorrow and therefore require a more scalable response.

When considering available options for conducting an investigation, the board should think from the outset about the level of company management that may be implicated in the issues under review. Obviously, an issue that is confined to a single employee or a small group of mid-level managers presents a different profile than an issue that may implicate senior management. The board needs to consider these issues, because they may influence how an investigation gets conducted, how it should be supervised, and what should be its scope. A board should almost always solicit management's views on an appropriate response to an issue that is being considered for investigation. In the end, however, the board should exercise its own independent judgment about the parameters of the response—doing so is part and parcel of the board's gatekeeper role. As it deliberates, the board should consider whether and to what extent the management team members may have interests that undermine their judgment with respect to the issue at hand. Those interests can range from obvious conflicts were management is implicated directly in the issues, to more subtle biases, where, for example, management's judgment may be clouded by loyalty to trusted employees whose conduct may be reviewed.

Many issues that arise within an organization can be reviewed using internal resources. Issues of relatively limited significance that appear to involve a limited group of employees who are not part of senior management can be reviewed by trusted groups within the company, with reporting to the board or a board committee. In-house counsel can tackle many such issues and some companies have developed sophisticated teams that focus exclusively on reviewing issues that arise deep within an organization. Some issues, however, require the use of other resources, including potentially outside counsel or other advisors, such as forensic firms. Normally, the decision about who should conduct the investigation depends on the scope of the review (many companies have limited internal resources) and the levels of management that may be implicated (where senior management's conduct may need to be reviewed, more objective external resources may be appropriate). In some instances, it will be important to ensure that the review is undertaken by truly independent advisors who have no loyalty other than to the board or a board committee. In those cases, wholly new counsel, who have not recently worked for the company, may need to be identified and employed.

Wholly apart from the decision about who should conduct the review, a decision also needs to be made about who should oversee the review. Again, a range of options is available, depending upon the particular circumstances, the scope of the issues, and the level of the organization that my come under scrutiny. Where the issues may implicate the conduct of senior management or systemic misconduct within the organization, review by a board committee may be the most appropriate option. In other circumstances, however, supervision by others, with appropriate periodic reports to the board, may be sufficient to ensure that the review is thorough and complete.

One of the trickiest questions a board must address early in an investigation is the appropriate scope of the review. Investigations are expensive and companies have a natural desire to control the costs by making sure the review is appropriately focused on the real issues. At the same time, investigations are usually begun at a time when knowledge of the underlying facts is limited and the ultimate scope of the problem to be investigated may not be fully known. The board will need to work with those conducting and supervising the review to make sure the scope is right sized to thoroughly assess the situation and ensure that it is not a bigger problem than initially anticipated. At the same time, the board will want to make sure the review does not needlessly spin out of control and become an unnecessary drain on corporate resources.

In the context of an internal investigation, it is never too early to ask the question whether and when disclosure may be appropriate. In many cases, such disclosure may await a further understanding of the issues and whether they may have material implications for the organization, but those questions should be asked early and re-asked frequently as the investigation progresses and matures.

Experienced boards can, in many instances, answer the myriad questions that arise early in an investigation by relying on their own experience and judgment. But in an increasingly complex environment, where regulators look to boards to fulfill a significant gatekeeper function, the early decisions confronting a board may warrant consultation with outside advisors who can help ensure that all the right questions have been asked and that the board's decisions do not run afoul of legal requirements. The early stages of an investigation can be a potential minefield that directors often must navigate when information is limited and the decisions to be made are significant. A board may want to consider whether they should be guided by their own outside advisor who can help them ensure that all of the most important and necessary requirements for an effective and conclusive internal review have been put in place from the outset.

The Importance of Keeping an Open Mind and Not Prejudging the Issues

The board, of course, needs to take serious issues seriously and approach the evaluation of those issues with an open mind. Especially when an allegation is made against senior members of management, a board often will be tempted to view the allegations as unfounded—taking the view that the allegations have been lodged against people the board knows and works with regularly. These are managers the board trusts with the company's business, making it difficult for the board to believe they may have engaged in wrongdoing. The board, however, must not prejudge what an internal investigation will reveal, because any hint of prejudgment risks tainting the board's actions in fulfilling its gatekeeper role. The board must remain an objective observer of the corporation's activities. The response of a member of HealthSouth Corporation's board to allegations of misconduct by the company's CEO is instructive. Soon after the allegations were raised and after the board appropriately appointed a committee of directors to review the issues, a member of the board who was chair of the review committee said the CEO had "absolutely no knowledge" of facts that were a key part of the investigation. When that board's delegation of the investigation to the committee was challenged in Delaware Chancery Court, then Vice Chancellor Strine (who is now Chief Justice of the Delaware Supreme Court) said the committee could not be trusted to act objectively, in part because the chair of the committee had prejudged the outcome. For this reason, Vice Chancellor Strine said he would never be able to "defer to a decision" by the directors who were investigating the issues.

This judicial pronouncement is a reminder that the appropriate conduct of internal investigations can be a minefield for the unwary. The following questions and resources are designed to allow directors to intelligently gauge the seriousness of the underlying issue and make critical early decisions about the best approach to the investigation, including its scope, conduct, oversight, and reporting of results.

Key Questions

- ❑ What is the source of the issue—how did it come to the board's attention? Does that give the board more or less confidence that it has a preliminary understanding of the issue? Or is more preliminary work needed before critical decisions can be made? What more information can be obtained quickly that may better inform key decisions about what actions to take?
- ❑ At what level of the organization does the issue currently appear to reside? Does the issue implicate members of senior management or does it appear to be confined to lower level managers or employees? How confident can the board be that the issue will stay at that level or is there a possibility that senior management may be implicated as more information becomes available? How should this information influence the board's deliberations over the conduct of an internal investigation of the issues?
- ❑ Is the board confident it is hearing the whole story or is management waiting to tell the board more after it understands the issues better? What further work is management doing now to try to understand the full breadth and scope of the issues that are currently known and of other potential issues that may not now be known, but that may be suspected or that may be worrying management?
- ❑ To what extent is it appropriate to follow management's recommendation in this instance? Do members of management have interests (ranging from personal interests to interests in supporting colleagues or friends) that may affect their recommendations and judgment concerning the investigation? How should that influence the board's thinking about management's recommendations?
- ❑ Who should investigate the issue? Should responsibility be given to in-house resources, such as the general counsel or internal audit, or should responsibility be given to outside lawyers and forensic specialists? How reliable will the results of the investigation be if one team or another conducts the review? How will regulators or other interested constituencies view the investigation if it is done one way or another? Are the potential benefits of using outside counsel (such as objectivity and independence) worth the added expense?
- ❑ Who should supervise the investigation? Management? The usual watchdogs within management (e.g., internal audit, compliance, legal)? A committee of the board? Again, how will regulators or other interested constituencies view the investigation if it is supervised in one way or another?
- ❑ How wide and deep should the investigation go? What additional information does the board need to be confident the scope of the review is sufficient to get to the bottom of the issues? How credible will the investigation be in the eyes of interested parties, including regulators, potential legal claimants, and others, if the investigation is narrowly focused on the known issues, or is additional scope needed?
- ❑ Are all of the potentially interested constituencies being considered and is disclosure to those constituencies being appropriately managed? The auditors?

Potential government investigators? Shareholders? Employees? Others? How frequently should these questions be reconsidered?

- ❑ What additional information does the board need to discharge its obligations to the company and to its shareholders? How can the board go about getting that information?
- ❑ Does the board need its own advisors?

Additional Reading

1. "Directors as Gatekeepers: A Few Things Directors Should Know About the SEC," Speech by SEC Chair Mary Jo White, June 23, 2014
   https://www.sec.gov/News/Speech/Detail/Speech/1370542148863
2. *Biondi v. Scrushy*
   http://caselaw.findlaw.com/de-court-of-chancery/1384908.html
3. *Defending Corporations and Individuals in Government Investigations*, Mark P. Goodman and Daniel J. Fetterman, eds., Chapter 3, "Conducting Internal Investigations" (Thomson-Reuters 3rd ed. 2014–2015)
   http://static.legalsolutions.thomsonreuters.com/product_files/relateddocs/189018_2014339_93646.pdf

Notes

____

____

____

____

____

9.7 SHAREHOLDER DERIVATIVE LITIGATION AND SERVING ON A SPECIAL LITIGATION COMMITTEE

CONTRIBUTED BY
Michael D. Blanchard
Morgan, Lewis & Bockius LLP[1]

In Delaware and elsewhere, the business and affairs of every corporation is committed to the management of a board of directors. The corporation's involvement in litigation falls within the business and affairs of the corporation. Thus, the general rule is that the decision to pursue or not to pursue litigation on behalf of the corporation is within the scope of management decisions ultimately committed to the board, although most routine litigation is delegated to management.

One exception to the general rule involves a unique form of corporate litigation referred to as shareholder derivative actions. A shareholder derivative action is a lawsuit commenced by a shareholder of the corporation, purporting to bring claims on behalf of the corporation, frequently naming as defendants some or all of the board and management.

Because the decision to pursue litigation is typically committed to the board, the law has developed special rules governing when a shareholder is permitted to bring litigation on behalf of the corporation, and conversely, when a board may take control over the shareholder's derivative lawsuit. In general, a shareholder is only permitted to pursue a

1. Michael Blanchard is a partner with Morgan Lewis & Bockius LLP, where he specializes in securities and shareholder litigation.

derivative action when a majority of the board lacks the independence and disinterestedness necessary to exercise good faith judgment concerning whether to pursue the claims at issue—that is, make a determination that would be entitled to judicial deference under the business judgment rule. Even when directors are named as defendants in a derivative action, courts will examine the complaint to determine whether the shareholder has sufficiently pleaded specific facts that, if true, would render a majority of the board interested or lacking independence. If the shareholder meets that burden, the derivative action is permitted to proceed. That is not the end of the story, however.

When a majority of the board has a conflict of interest in determining whether pursuit of the claims would be in the best interests of the company, the board may appoint a special litigation committee, consisting of independent and disinterested directors, charged with the authority to investigate the claims asserted by the shareholder and determine if their pursuit would be in the best interests of the corporation. The board similarly may appoint a special litigation committee, with essentially the same mission, when a shareholder demands that the company investigate and pursue claims, as opposed to actually commencing the litigation. In either scenario—provided that the special litigation committee is disinterested and independent, conducts a thorough investigation in good faith, and reaches a rational decision about whether to pursue the litigation—the special litigation committee's decision will typically be respected by the courts.

A special litigation committee must be formed by a resolution of the board in accordance with the laws of the state of incorporation and the corporation's articles of incorporation and bylaws. The resolution should specify the committee's purpose and the extent of its authority—either the full authority to decide whether to pursue the litigation, or in limited circumstances, only to report its recommendation to the full board for decision (the latter typically occurring when there is certainty that a majority of the full board will be found to be disinterested and independent). To permit the committee to conduct a thorough investigation in good faith, the resolution should also specify that the committee is permitted to hire experts, including independent legal counsel, to assist in conducting the investigation.

Special litigation committee investigations typically begin with a meeting between the committee and its counsel, where the key issues are identified and discussed and a plan of investigation is developed. Because the counsel hired to conduct the investigation should be independent—that is, have not previously (or at least extensively) represented the company—counsel will typically have to be educated about the company's organizational structure and key personnel. Determinations must then be made about the categories of information that will be germane to the issues raised by the shareholder's allegations, and whom within the corporation will have it. That list will typically serve as a starting point for directing document collection efforts and, in a later phase, witness interviews. On recommendation of counsel, the committee may invite the derivative plaintiff, and their counsel, to meet with the committee and provide it with any factual or legal material that they believe would be helpful in conducting its investigation. Consideration should also be given to any potential collateral consequences that might arise as a result of the investigation, and the special litigation committee should plan accordingly. For example, if the focus of the investigation concerns the same allegations as are made in a parallel class action lawsuit, there is a risk that the committee's work might ultimately fall into the hands of plaintiff's counsel and serve as a roadmap for prosecuting their case.

Counsel is tasked with collecting, reviewing, and analyzing (in the first instance) all documents relating to the shareholder's allegations. The scope and nature of the document collection and review will be dictated by the alleged wrongdoing, but could include, among other things, contracts, SEC filings, internal reports and presentations, publicly available information, e-mails, financial statements, financial projections, internal and external market data, correspondence with regulators, etc. The volume of documents collected can be expansive—in the hundreds of thousands or even millions of pages. As many of the documents collected may be determined not to be important to the investigation, however, committee members are not required to review them all themselves. The task of culling the documents down to those that are material is delegated to counsel, provided that the committee is kept apprised of all information material to the investigation and is provided with all key documents.

After the relevant documents have been collected and analyzed, counsel will also interview persons with relevant information. Committee members may, but are not necessarily required to, participate in these witness interviews. Counsel typically generates memoranda summarizing the key points from the interviews. As the investigation winds down, counsel prepares a detailed report of the investigation. Oftentimes, the report will later be made public and serve as the basis for establishing that the special litigation committee's decision is entitled to judicial deference. Accordingly, the report typically recounts the board's formation of the committee, the independence and disinterestedness of the committee members, the shareholder's allegations, the facts as determined by the documents reviewed and interviews conducted over the course of the investigation, an explication of the law governing the shareholder's claims, and an analysis of the strengths and weaknesses of the claims under the law and facts. Finally, the report sets forth and explains the committee's decision about a course of action (i.e., pursue the litigation, dismiss the litigation, settle, etc.) and reasoning. In the majority of cases, special litigation committees decide against pursuing the derivative action. In those cases where a committee determines that the litigation should be pursued, the committee may assume control over the litigation and pursue it on behalf of the company.

The special litigation committee's ultimate decision about whether to pursue the litigation should consider all pertinent factors, dictated by the nature of the allegations. That said, typically the committee will consider the strengths and weaknesses of the potential claims, likely defenses, and probable outcomes, and in that light, whether the potential benefit outweighs the costs and potential harm that might result from pursuing the litigation. Just because a valid claim exists does not dictate that the claim should be pursued if the costs outweigh the benefits. That is especially so when other remedial options are available that may benefit the corporation without risking harmful consequences.

Should the special litigation committee determine that the litigation be dismissed, counsel will prepare motion papers to that effect. The committee's report will often be submitted to the court and shareholder derivative plaintiff in connection with the motion to dismiss. In some jurisdictions, so long as the committee was independent, disinterested, conducted its investigation in good faith, and had rational reasons for its decision, the courts will respect that determination. In Delaware, the court may, in its discretion, conduct a second step review to determine whether the litigation ought to be pursued, despite the committee's determination.

In most jurisdictions, there is very little discovery permitted to the shareholder plaintiff who challenges the special litigation committee's decision to dismiss the litigation. Typically, the discovery is limited to examining whether the committee was in fact independent and disinterested and conducted its investigation in good faith. The committee members may be deposed on these subjects, and the court may order the production of limited categories of documents.

Notably, there is great variance among jurisdictions regarding the extent that the attorney–client privilege will shield the committee's communications with counsel, drafts of the report, and so on, depending on the circumstances. When conducting the investigation, committee members are well advised to assume that all of their work and communications with counsel may someday be revealed to plaintiff's counsel, and beyond.

The special litigation committee must proceed with the expectation that the shareholder plaintiff's counsel will challenge any decision to dismiss the litigation on all bases available: the independence of the committee members, the independence of its counsel, the adequacy and good faith prosecution of the investigation; and, if permitted in the jurisdiction, the rationality of the committee's final decision. Every aspect of the special litigation committee's work will be, to the extent permitted, scrutinized under a magnifying glass, and attacked in an effort to negate it. For the committee's work to be respected by the courts, its members must remain faithful to their fiduciary obligations to the corporation, relying on experts as appropriate but never delegating their ultimate authority, and coming to their decision on a fully informed basis. The committee must maintain its independence from the putative defendants and individuals who are the subject of the investigation and can never appear to be simply performing a "white wash." The committee must also remember that, while reliance upon counsel and experts is not only permitted but likely necessary, the committee must be ultimately in charge of directing the investigation.

Key Questions

When serving as a member of a special litigation committee, key questions that a board member might ask include the following:

- ❑ Has the committee been formed properly, meeting all requirements of the law and the corporation's organizational documents?
- ❑ Are the committee members truly disinterested and independent? What process was used to discover potentially debilitating relationships and interests?
- ❑ Has the committee been given sufficient power to conduct a thorough investigation and ferret out all material information such that the committee's decision will be made on a fully informed basis?
- ❑ Is the committee permitted to hire experts? Has the committee in fact hired those experts necessary to provide the committee with a full understanding of the issues?

- ❑ Is the committee's counsel independent from the corporation? How was that determined?
- ❑ Will the committee's investigation potentially have adverse collateral consequences, for instance, with respect to a parallel class action?
- ❑ Should the shareholder derivative plaintiff and his/her counsel be permitted to present their theories to the committee? If so, will the committee be later subject to attack if it fails to investigate every nuance presented?
- ❑ Does counsel expect to ultimately share the committee's final report?
- ❑ Does counsel expect that the attorney client privilege will be waived in any respect?
- ❑ With respect to the committee's final decision, has the committee considered all the costs and benefits to be weighed in making its decision?
- ❑ Has the committee considered potential remedial measures that could be imposed which would benefit the corporation without the potential disruption and cost that a litigation would cause?

Additional Reading

1. ABA Business Law Section, Committee on Corporate Laws. *Corporate Director's Guidebook*. 5th ed. (See Section 3)
2. *Fiduciary Duties and other Responsibilities of Corporate Directors*, RR Donnelly Publication, Copyright (2008) (available from RR Donnelly Financial Printer)
3. Essentials of a Special Litigation Committee (2003)
   http://www.stblaw.com/docs/default-source/cold-fusion-existing-content/publications/pub428.pdf?sfvrsn=2
4. Appointing and Managing the Special Committee of the Board of Directors (2011)
   http://www.robinsonbradshaw.com/media/publication/480_Article_pbuck_BizLawInstitute.pdf
5. What Is a Special Committee of the Board of Directors and When Does Our Company Need One? (2011)
   http://www.haynesboone.com/news-and-events/news/alerts/2011/07/15/what-is-a-special-committee-of-the-Board-of-directors-and-when-does-our-company-need-one
6. Cutting the Cost of Derivative Claims: The Role of the Special Litigation Committee (2009)
   http://www2.mnbar.org/benchandbar/2009/mar09/claims.html
7. Special Litigation Committees in Shareholder Derivative Litigation (2010)
   https://corpgov.law.harvard.edu/2010/04/25/special-litigation-committees-in-shareholder-derivative-litigation/

Notes

9.8 MANAGING SIGNIFICANT LITIGATION

CONTRIBUTED BY
Gregory V. Varallo
Richards, Layton & Finger, P.A.[1]

Litigation (including arbitration, regulatory, or administrative proceedings) is unfortunately a fact of corporate life, and it is almost never inexpensive. Some litigation is or can become critical to the ongoing success of the company. While it is the job of the general counsel to manage litigation and outside counsel in the first instance, in at least the more significant of such cases (measured from the point of view of the potential impact of the litigation on the company), there is a role for the board to oversee that management. Given that many board members are trained in business and not law, this chapter is designed to allow a non-lawyer director to understand the basics of litigation and its effect on the company.

Spotting Important Corporate Litigation

There is no single description of when a particular piece of litigation may be important enough for directors to want to take notice and exercise some degree of oversight. Certainly, a starting point in this regard is the litigation that the company is forced to disclose

1. Gregory V. Varallo is a director and president of Richards, Layton & Finger, P.A., where he practices in the areas of complex business litigation, ADR, and corporate governance.

as part of its financial statements or in its periodic disclosures. But, as we will see, it is not necessarily the high-dollar cases that are the most important or deserving of board attention. Reputational and other interests must be considered.

Not every litigation that must be disclosed merits the careful attention of the board. Even material litigation can be entirely routine, and it is conversely the case that litigation that might not yet need to be disclosed or reported in financial statements (either due to timing or otherwise) could be quite material to the company and deserving of careful board consideration.

Take intellectual property, for example. Many companies have invested millions of dollars protecting their intellectual property, and some are importantly dependent upon the ability to continue to protect their IP for their long-term survival. Litigation that challenges the continuing validity of some or all of that intellectual property protection, even in the absence of a request for monetary relief, could still be critically important to the company.

Finally, litigation relating to noncompliance with corporate policies could also be important, regardless of the amount at issue either for the possibility of embarrassing the company and thus tarnishing its reputation and brand, or for the possibility of pointing out a deficiency in corporate controls, or both.

Identifying the Litigation the Board Should Follow

Given the wide variety of cases that a company could be faced with at any time, directors would do well to regularly question the company's general counsel, or its outside law firm where there is no general counsel, about whether any of the cases facing the company could materially affect its ability to continue to pursue its business in its current form, and if so, why. Likewise, board members should review the litigation disclosures in the company's annual financial statements and public filings, and ask questions about each, so as to determine which cases merit more direct oversight.

Regular Reporting on Key Cases

Once the board identifies cases that are important to the well being of the enterprise, it should make clear that it wants regular reports on developments in such cases and extraordinary reports where extraordinary events have transpired in the case, such as an important judicial opinion.

Overseeing Key Cases

Having identified and called for regular reporting on key cases, the role of the board is then to monitor such cases and, as appropriate, engage with general counsel on the strategy and direction of each such case. While business-trained directors may not be in a position to volunteer legal strategies in every case, they can certainly ensure that they understand what the company's strategy is and become comfortable that it is a well-designed and well thought-out strategy.

Moreover, where either the general counsel or outside counsel does not appear to instill confidence that the company's significant cases are being competently handled, the board ultimately has the power to replace counsel. Although this is unusual and likely to be disruptive to the case itself, no director should allow a significant case to proceed under the direction of lawyers about whom the director has serious questions.

Finally, every director's review of any significant case should include a discussion about whether and how the subject of alternative dispute resolution (ADR) has been broached. For this purpose, ADR includes nonlitigated solutions such as mediation, nonpublic resolution of cases through arbitration, or simply the exploration of a negotiated resolution to the case that is acceptable in substance to the company. Sadly, not every lawyer is attuned to how important it may be for the company to resolve its significant litigation and return to doing business, and so a director may be surprised when he or she learns that even the most important cases have not involved any direct effort at resolution or ADR. Asking the questions and being satisfied that the answers are well thought out and make sense signals counsel in the matter that the board is interested in a fair and expeditious resolution of the litigation, a signal that may be important to send.

A Note on Self Protection

Significant corporate litigation is not necessarily limited to litigation only against the company. Often the board and/or senior officers can be sued in such cases. The law protects directors and officers through exculpation, indemnity, and advancement (legal fee payment) provisions in the company's charter and/or bylaws.

Most corporate statutes allow the company's governing documents to provide for exculpation of directors in certain circumstances. Delaware, for example, provides that directors may be exculpated against payment of judgments arising from a breach of the director's duty of care.

Likewise, corporate bylaws and/or the company's charter may include provisions relating to advancement of legal fees and indemnity against settlements or judgments. Directors should know whether such provisions exist and make sure that they are regularly reviewed so that they are current and properly protect the board to the full extent of the law.

The law also allows the company to purchase insurance for its directors and officers to insure against this type of litigation. In most cases, that insurance should be purchased, and the company should hire the services of competent coverage counsel to help review and negotiate the company's policies.

Key Questions

- ❑ What is the nature of each case reported in the company's financial statements or public reports?
- ❑ What is the potential for each such case to affect the long-term viability of the company, assuming that worst-case scenario?
- ❑ What is the strategy for the in-house and/or outside legal team dealing with each such case? How often does the board get reports on these cases and by whom?
- ❑ Has ADR been attempted in these cases? If so, what type and what was the result?

- ❑ Does the company's certificate of incorporation provide exculpation for the board? Does the company have indemnity and advancement bylaws? When was the last time that these provisions were reviewed and/or updated?
- ❑ Does the company purchase D&O (directors' and officers') insurance? What is the amount of the policy, with whom is the coverage placed, and what is the nature of the coverage? How often is it reviewed by competent outside experts to make sure that it is both adequate protection and as state of the art as possible?

Additional Reading

1. Varallo, Gregory V., Blake Rohrbacher, and John D. Hendershot. *The Practitioner's Guide to the Delaware Rapid Arbitration Act* (2015).
2. Varallo, Gregory V. and Sarah T. Toner. "The Delaware Rapid Arbitration Act: 5 Considerations for a Practitioner." *The Temple 10-Q* (August 7, 2015).
3. Zeberkiewicz, John Mark and Blake Rohrbacher. "The Right Protection: More on Advancement and Indemnification." *The Review of Securities & Commodities Regulation* (December 2008).
4. Veasey, E. Norman and Grover C. Brown. "An Overview of the General Counsel's Decision Making on Dispute-Resolution Strategies in Complex Business Transactions." 70 *The Business Lawyer* 407 (Spring 2015).

Notes

____

____

____

____

____

9.9 DEALING WITH A WHISTLEBLOWER

CONTRIBUTED BY
Michael D. Blanchard
Morgan, Lewis & Bockius LLP[1]

The last decade has witnessed a substantial expansion of whistleblower legislation, designed to incent every company's employees to serve as insider watchdogs for the government. As new whistleblower laws are passed—and as monetary rewards for successful whistleblowers are boosted and publicly touted—the incentives are higher than ever for employees with knowledge or suspicions of corporate impropriety to speak up. To protect against the reputational and financial harm occasioned when a whistleblower reports directly to the government, instead of to the company's management where the problems may be addressed in a cost efficient manner, boards of directors need to ensure that their company is proactively encouraging a culture of internal reporting without fear of retaliation.

There are numerous federal and state statutes that include whistleblower provisions. One primary example—and the source of a recent explosion in whistleblower activity in the private business sector—is the Dodd-Frank Act. In general, Dodd-Frank provides that an employee who provides original information to the SEC that leads to a successful judicial or administrative action shall be awarded between 10 and 30 percent of the collected

1. Michael Blanchard is a partner with Morgan, Lewis & Bockius LLP, where he specializes in securities and shareholder litigation. He wishes to thank Christopher Wasil for his assistance in preparing these materials.

monetary sanctions. Dodd-Frank also contains strong protections against retaliation for whistleblowers. Firing, demoting, threatening, or in any way discriminating against a whistleblower on the basis of her whistleblowing activities is expressly forbidden and can lead to significant money damages, fines, and penalties.

Given the increased likelihood that a company will at some point be faced with a potential whistleblower claim, there are at least two reasons why directors, specifically, should be involved in the company's approach to such situations. First, as a general matter, directors have a fiduciary duty to monitor the company's actions to ensure that it complies with applicable laws. Alleged breaches of this duty regularly give rise to class actions and derivative complaints, which often name the directors as individual defendants. Further, there is a developing body of case law suggesting that directors can be held personally liable under Sarbanes-Oxley and Dodd-Frank if the company improperly punishes purported whistleblowers. In other words, the unsuspecting director who allows the termination of a whistleblower employee could face civil liability.

While each company must assess its own needs, to minimize the risks just outlined, directors may want to consider the following points in fulfilling their duties with respect to whistleblower claims:

- If the company does not have a formal, written policy encouraging employees to report wrongdoing and setting forth a process for responding to whistleblowers, the board should require the company to adopt one.
- The policy should encourage employees to report internally any known or suspected impropriety. While whistleblower laws such as Dodd-Frank do not condition their statutory benefits upon the employee first raising complaints internally before providing a tip to the SEC (thus limiting the employee's incentive to report internally), providing a safe and convenient method to do so can often allow the company to take appropriate remedial measures itself or, if necessary, self-report to the SEC.
- To assuage employees' fears of retaliation, individuals outside the chain of command should be appointed to receive and process internal whistleblower complaints.
- The company should strive to maintain the confidentiality of whistleblowers where possible. This not only promotes internal reporting, but it also lowers the risk that the whistleblower's superiors will unlawfully retaliate.
- Careful consideration must be given to who is to conduct investigations sparked by whistleblower tips. While low-risk complaints may be handled by human resources, investigations of more serious whistleblower claims, such as those that would implicate Dodd-Frank, may best be led by in-house or even outside counsel. The depth and independence of the investigation may become a central issue in future litigation.

Finally, it is particularly incumbent upon directors to ensure that mechanisms are in place to prevent retaliation against an employee who has blown the whistle, either internally or to the SEC. In one cautionary tale, a California federal court in 2015 held that directors could be held personally liable for retaliation under Dodd-Frank where the board voted to terminate the company's general counsel after he reported potential violations of the Foreign Corrupt Practices Act. A working knowledge of whistleblower anti-retaliation laws can help prevent these missteps.

The SEC's statistics regarding the number of whistleblower tips it receives are staggering. Boards of directors, therefore, should treat the possibility of their company facing a whistleblower claim as a "when"—not an "if"—scenario. Boards must be proactive in developing the company's procedures for encouraging internal reporting, protecting the confidentiality of such reports, responding to and appropriately investigating whistleblower tips and then protecting the whistleblowers from retaliation.

Key Questions

To help a company manage the risks associated with potential whistleblowers, directors may ask themselves the following questions:

- ❑ Is the board satisfying its fiduciary duty to monitor the company for potential legal compliance deficiencies?
- ❑ Does the company provide a formal system for employees to report internally suspected or known improprieties?
- ❑ Who has the company appointed to receive and investigate internal complaints?
- ❑ What efforts does the company take to protect the whistleblower's confidentiality?
- ❑ What procedures are in place to ensure that whistleblower tips are investigated properly?
- ❑ Does the company take necessary precautions to ensure that whistleblowers are not subjected to retaliation?

Additional Reading

1. Whistleblowers: What the Board Needs to Know (2015)
https://global.theiia.org/knowledge/Public%20Documents/TaT-Sept-Oct-2015.pdf
2. How Companies Should Respond to Whistleblower Complaints (2014)
http://www.rmmagazine.com/2014/12/02/when-the-whistle-blows-how-companies-should-respond-to-whistleblower-complaints/
3. Dealing with Whistleblowers and Avoiding Retaliation Claims (2013)
http://www.nhbr.com/December-27-2013/Dealing-with-whistleblowers-and-avoiding-retaliation-claims/
4. Practical Solutions for Dealing with Whistleblowers (not dated)
http://corporate.findlaw.com/human-resources/practical-solutions-for-dealing-with-whistleblowers.html

5. Strategies for Keeping a Whistleblower In-House (2012)
   http://www.alixpartners.com/en/Publications/AllArticles/tabid/635/articleType/ArticleView/articleId/528/Strategies-for-Keeping-a-Whistleblower-In-House.aspx#sthash.2d3AYnCY.dpbs
6. How Nonprofit Directors Should Handle Whistleblower Complaints—Carefully! (2016)
   http://www.wagenmakerlaw.com/blog/how-nonprofit-directors-should-handle-whistleblower-complaints-%E2%80%93-carefully

Notes

PRACTICAL ISSUES CONCERNING THE ATTORNEY–CLIENT PRIVILEGE

CONTRIBUTED BY
Michael D. Blanchard
Morgan, Lewis & Bockius LP[1]

The attorney–client privilege is a legal doctrine that protects from disclosure communications between an attorney and his or her client, made in connection with rendering legal advice. It applies to protect from disclosure to third parties all communications between attorneys and corporate clients, including communications between in-house counsel and the company's agents. It also protects communications between in-house counsel or independent, outside counsel representing the board of directors or board committees. The attorney–client privilege, however, is construed narrowly by the courts, may be negated inadvertently by actions inconsistent with the privilege, and may be waived voluntarily by the client. Directors should be vigilant in establishing and maintaining the confidentiality of privileged communications between counsel and the company, while at the same time recognizing that those privileged communications may someday be disclosed.

Only communications made in connection with rendering legal advice are protected by the privilege. In the operating company context, where counsel (especially in-house counsel) are frequently involved in business discussions, the lines between protected

1. Michael Blanchard is a partner with Morgan, Lewis & Bockius LLP, where he specializes in securities and shareholder litigation.

attorney–client communications, and unprotected business discussions, are often blurred. Directors will serve their company well by taking care to differentiate between those communications with counsel that purely concern business and those that involve legal advice. Once a communication is identified as an attorney–client privileged communication, care must be taken to ensure that the communication is not disclosed to anyone outside the privilege (i.e., third parties), because disclosing a privileged communication to anyone outside the attorney–client relationship negates the privilege.

Even conduct that is merely inconsistent with maintaining the confidentiality of a privileged communication may effect a waiver of the privilege. Email communications between counsel and independent directors provide an excellent example of how the privilege might be inadvertently waived in this manner. Often, independent directors are employees of other companies—third parties insofar as the privilege between counsel and the independent director is concerned. Most companies' e-mail policies provide that employees have no expectation of privacy when using their company's e-mail systems. In many jurisdictions, if the independent director uses his employer's e-mail account to transmit attorney–client communications and that employer does not recognize the privacy of employee e-mails hosted on its server, the privilege may be deemed waived as the communications were exposed to third parties outside the privilege.

Directors should always remain cognizant of the fact that the privilege belongs to the company—not the individuals acting on the company's behalf (including directors). Accordingly, whoever is legally empowered to act on behalf of the company is entitled to waive the privilege, even with respect to earlier communications, preceding the person's authority to direct the affairs of the company. New management, a bankruptcy trustee, or an acquirer (post acquisition) all may have the authority to waive the privilege attached to earlier communications. In limited circumstances, the privilege might even be circumvented by a shareholder bringing a derivative action on behalf of the company.

In the post-Enron era, directors should also be aware that the government has become increasingly hostile to assertions of privilege in the context of investigations. For instance, the SEC has embedded in its official policies that a company's decision to voluntarily waive the privilege in responding to SEC inquiries will be perceived as "cooperation," potentially mitigating fines and penalties. While there may be benefits flowing from the waiver of the privilege vis a vis the SEC, directors should fully appreciate the collateral consequences of making such a waiver. If the privilege is waived vis a vis the SEC, it is waived as to all parties, including, for instance, class action and derivative plaintiffs suing the company and its officers and directors.

The attorney–client privilege is a powerful protection that extends to companies obtaining legal advice. Directors should always be mindful of protecting the privilege in furtherance of the company's objectives, while at the same time recognizing that the cloak of privacy for attorney–client communications may be lifted down the road.

Key Questions

When considering the operation of the attorney–client privilege while serving as a director, key questions that a board member might ask include the following:

- ❑ Is the attorney's involvement in any given discussion in connection with rendering legal advice? Or is it instead business focused?
- ❑ Are third parties privy, or even potentially privy, to the conversation, negating the privilege? Should those parties be excluded from participation in those conversations?
- ❑ Who is the client? Does the answer to that question impact who may be privy to attorney–client communications, consistent with protecting the privilege? For example, should the privileged communications between a special litigation committee and its counsel be disclosed to the full board?
- ❑ Is there a significant chance that the privilege may be waived at a later date? Are the communications at issue likely to be relevant to a government investigation?
- ❑ Has the board developed procedures for memorializing in meeting minutes the facts establishing the privilege for those portions of the board's discussions and deliberations that are in fact privileged?
- ❑ Has the board established rules for e-mail communications to ensure that privileged communications are not exposed to environments where there is no expectation of privacy?

Additional Reading

1. Directors' Exercise of the Corporate Privilege (2013)
   http://www.stblaw.com/docs/default-source/cold-fusion-existing-content/publications/pub1601.pdf?sfvrsn=2
2. Protecting Attorney–Client Privilege When Emailing with Outside Directors (2009)
   http://www.robinsonbradshaw.com/newsroom-publications-Protecting-Attorney-Client-Priviledge-09-30-2009.html
3. Attorney–Client Privilege in the Corporate Context: Can Corporate Officers Waive the Corporation's Privilege? (2012)
   http://www.frostbrowntodd.com/resources-attorney-client-privilege-in-the-corporate-context.html
4. Directors and Waiver of the Attorney–Client Privilege (2006)
   http://www.maglaw.com/publications/articles/00097/_res/id=Attachments/index=0/07002060007Morvillo.pdf

5. Attorney–Client Privilege between a Board Committee and Outside Counsel: An Outline of Authorities

   http://www.americanbar.org/content/dam/aba/administrative/professional_responsibility/39th_conference_session_11_confidentiality_and_atorney_client_privilege.authcheckdam.pdf

6. The Attorney–Client Privilege and SEC Examinations: To Waive or Not to Waive?

   http://apps.americanbar.org/buslaw/newsletter/0075/materials/pp3.pdf

Notes

SECTION TEN

TAKEOVER PREPAREDNESS

10.1 GENERAL TAKEOVER PLANNING

CONTRIBUTED BY
Trevor S. Norwitz
Wachtell, Lipton, Rosen & Katz[1]

One of the most challenging situations a board of directors can face is an unsolicited takeover bid. Historically about one-third of the time the "hostile" bidder has successfully acquired its target, one-third of the time the target was sold to another company (called a "white knight" if it is a preferred or higher bidder), and only about one-third of target companies have managed to fight off the hostile bidder and remain independent. Following years of shareholder activism to disarm corporate takeover defenses, it is likely that in the future, even fewer targets of hostile bids will be able to remain independent.

There are a multitude of factors that influence the likelihood of successfully defending against a hostile takeover bid, but takeover preparedness is one of the most important and can be decisive. Not all unsolicited takeover bids are undesirable, but it should surprise no one that they are often timed opportunistically to favor the bidder. It is important for directors and management of all companies, large and small, to lay the groundwork and to be prepared to respond to a takeover bid well in advance of an approach. Failure to prepare in advance for possible takeover bids (or demands by activists to sell the

1. Trevor S. Norwitz is a partner in the corporate department of Wachtell, Lipton, Rosen & Katz, located in New York City.

company) can reduce a company's ability to control its own destiny and the board's ability to achieve the best result for the company and its shareholders.

The likelihood of facing an unsolicited takeover bid has grown substantially in recent years. Deal activity generally has reached historically high levels recently, with global M&A volume hitting an all-time high of over $5 trillion dollars in 2015 (surpassing the previous record of $4.6 trillion in 2007). Growth in unsolicited or hostile M&A activity has surpassed even the rate of growth in the general M&A market, having increased from approximately 5 percent of total M&A volume in 2013 to approximately 20 percent of total M&A volume in 2015.

A takeover bid can unfold in a variety of ways. For example, an unsolicited bidder may accumulate a company's shares in the public market; make a "casual pass" indicating interest in a transaction to a director or executive; write a so-called bear hug letter offering to buy the company, which can be public or private and have a more or less friendly tone; make a tender offer for the company's shares; or launch a proxy contest or consent solicitation to remove directors or take other actions. Litigation often ensues. No two takeover bids are exactly alike.

Responding to takeover bids is more of an art than a science. The range of possible responsive actions available to a target board will depend in large part on the amount of advance preparation. Some of the structural elements impacting a company's ability to resist a takeover bid are required by applicable state law to be included in the company's certificate of incorporation if they are to have any effect. Once the company has become public, these typically cannot be implemented by the board alone but also require shareholder approval (which is unlikely to be achievable in the face of a takeover bid). In Delaware, for example, these provisions include a classified board structure, a requirement that shareholders act at a meeting and not by written consent, and the authority of the board to issue blank-check preferred stock. Other responsive actions can be effected by the board without shareholder action, like the establishment of advance notice provisions for shareholder nominations and proposals at meetings, authority for the board to expand its size and fill vacancies, and director qualification requirements. Similarly, the board's ability to consider a financial restructuring (such as incurring debt to finance a special dividend) or transactional alternatives (such as spinning off an undervalued division) will often depend on whether the groundwork for those responses has been laid in advance. Precipitous action is highly likely to face withering scrutiny in the market as well as judicial challenge. Ideally, directors should have a sense of the potential risks of a hostile takeover bid (including who might seek to buy the company and how they would approach it) and the range of possible responses should it come to pass.

In today's environment, shareholder engagement should also be considered an important element of takeover preparedness. To be sure, as soon as a hostile bid is announced, a significant amount of the target's stock trades into the hands of arbitrageurs, who are highly incented to press for and vote for a transaction in the near term. However, a large number of shares will necessarily remain in the hands of the company's traditional shareholders, primarily institutions, and their support will be critical. Having invested the time to build strong relationships with the company's key shareholders, ensuring that they understand and support the company's long-term strategy will be extremely valuable when approaching them to support the board in the face of a hostile takeover bid.

This chapter necessarily overlaps and is best read in context with some other topics focused on elsewhere in this Handbook: M&A as part of general corporate planning (i.e., in the context of a voluntary sale or takeover) (see Section Six); M&A that occurs in a distressed context (see Section Twelve); and board structure and governance as part of general corporate structure (see Section One), parts of which will come into play in various takeover contexts.

Key Questions

In order to best prepare a company for facing a potential takeover situation, directors may find it helpful to ask some of the following questions:

- ❑ Do we have a team on standby and easily reachable to deal with a takeover bid (typically a small group of key officers plus legal counsel, an investment banker, a proxy soliciting firm and a public relations firm)? Can we convene a special meeting of the board within 24 to 48 hours to address takeover situations?
- ❑ Do we have a policy of not commenting on takeover discussions and rumors?
- ❑ Are the board and management aware of who will be the sole spokesperson for the company on independence, merger, and takeover issues (typically it would be the CEO)?
- ❑ Do all directors understand their duties in a takeover context, including the enhanced fiduciary duties that may apply under state law to board decisions or actions?
- ❑ Are we prepared to deal with all of our corporate constituencies in the event of a takeover situation? These constituencies may include, in addition to shareholders, employees and unions, customers, suppliers, banks, regulators, media (including message boards, blogs, and other real time sources), stock exchanges, other directors, institutional investors and analysts, and government officials.
- ❑ Do we know who might be likely bidders for the company and which of them might "go hostile"?
- ❑ Do we know the range of companies that might be interested in a friendly merger or acquisition transaction with us (and so could be a potential "white knight") or in making a "white squire" investment in our company in the case of an inadequate hostile bid?
- ❑ How does the company's business portfolio and strategy, including its dividend policy, leverage, share repurchase history, divestitures, and spinoffs, affect its attractiveness as a takeover target?
- ❑ What structural "defenses" does the company have in place and what are its structural weaknesses? Are there additional structural elements impacting the company's ability to defend itself that the board should consider? (Which of these could be implemented by the board alone and which would require shareholder action?)
- ❑ Has our legal counsel reviewed the company's corporate profile, including the charter and bylaws, to ensure that our structural position is state-of-the-art?

- ❑ What are the applicable takeover laws of our state of incorporation? Have we opted into or out of any provisions that allow us the option?
- ❑ Do we have a shareholder rights plan (also known as a "poison pill") in place or "on the shelf" (which really just means having a law firm standing by to put one in on short notice)? Has the board been educated on what a rights plan is?
- ❑ What are the likely regulatory implications of a takeover bid? These may be industry- or party-specific, especially where there may be antitrust concerns. A foreign bidder may face Committee on Foreign Investment in the United States (CFIUS) review issues.
- ❑ Do our loan agreements and indentures have any provisions that would be triggered in the event of a change of control?
- ❑ How would the company's equity incentive plans, employment agreements, executive incentive plans, and severance arrangements be affected in the event of a takeover? Are they state-of-the-art or do we need to consider implementing change of control termination protections or retention incentives for any of our executives or employees who might be at risk of leaving once the takeover bid is made public? Has the board been fully briefed on the potential costs of the impact of a takeover on the forgoing?
- ❑ How will investors and investor advisory services (e.g., ISS, Glass Lewis) be likely to react to the announcement of a takeover bid, or to the implementation of certain takeover defenses and, if applicable, any change of control termination protections for the company's employees?
- ❑ Do we have earnings projections and liquidation values that may be helpful for evaluating a takeover bid and proposing alternative transactions?
- ❑ Do we monitor changes in the company's institutional holdings on a regular basis?
- ❑ Do we regularly review our dividend policy, analyst presentations, and other financial public relations?
- ❑ Are we regularly informed about activist hedge funds, activist institutional investors in our industry or among our shareholder base, and about emerging corporate governance and shareholder activism issues?
- ❑ Are there structural or strategic alternatives, such as acquisitions, dispositions, recapitalizations, separation transactions (like spin-offs and split-offs), and tracking stock alternatives that the company could utilize to "unlock" short-term shareholder value if the company was to receive an opportunistic takeover bid?
- ❑ What financial flexibility does the company have (for example to take on more debt to fund a special dividend or stock buy-back) if that is necessary to respond to an inadequate takeover bid?

Additional Reading

1. Gill, Stephen M., Kai Haakon E. Liekefett, and Leonard Wood. "Structural Defenses to Shareholder Activism." *The Review of Securities & Commodities Regulation* 47, no. 12 (June 18, 2014)
   http://www.law.harvard.edu/programs/corp_gov/shareholder-engagement-roundtable-2015-materials/vinson-elkins_structural-defenses-to-shareholder-activism.pdf
2. "Takeover Response Checklist and Dealing with Activist Hedge Funds," *Wachtell, Lipton, Rosen & Katz*
   http://www.wlrk.com/files/2016/TakeoverResponseChecklistandDealingwithActivistHedgeFunds.pdf
3. Zeberkiewicz, John Mark and Stephanie M. Norman. "A Brief Overview of Corporate Defensive Measures." *Business Law Today*
   http://www.americanbar.org/publications/blt/2015/08/03_norman.html
4. "Takeover Law and Practice (2016)," *Wachtell, Lipton, Rosen & Katz*, Chapter VI: "Advance Takeover Preparedness and Hostile M&A"
   http://www.wlrk.com/files/2016/TakeoverLawandPracticeGuide.pdf

Notes

10.2 SHAREHOLDER RIGHTS PLANS

CONTRIBUTED BY
Trevor S. Norwitz
Wachtell, Lipton, Rosen & Katz[1]

The shareholder rights plan, often called the "poison pill," is an important tool for a corporation to be able to control its own destiny. Originally developed to protect against abusive and coercive takeover tactics, the rights plan—which importantly can be implemented by a board of directors without shareholder involvement—empowers the board to buy the time necessary to respond appropriately to a takeover bid or threat of creeping control. Rights plans do not prevent or block unsolicited takeovers, nor do they interfere with the company's ordinary operations or negotiated transactions. Rights plans do have the desired effect of encouraging would-be acquirers to deal with a company's board, and empower the board to negotiate and to secure the best transaction or other outcome available for the company and its shareholders.

The use of rights plans has changed significantly since their development in response to the junk-bond driven bust-up takeovers of the 1980s. In those days, companies would adopt standing rights plans for 10 years at a time to discourage unsolicited transactions. Over 3,000 companies at one point had adopted rights plans, including over 60 percent

1. Trevor S. Norwitz is a partner in the corporate department of Wachtell, Lipton, Rosen & Katz located in New York City.

of S&P 500 companies. However, those rights plans were opposed by shareholder activist groups and institutions because they gave the board power to resist unsolicited transactions rather than leaving the decision entirely to shareholders. Accordingly, over years of shareholder activism, most companies have given up their standing shareholder rights plans. Today, less than 5 percent of S&P 500 companies have standing rights plans in effect and many of those plans are adopted for shorter terms and include other so-called shareholder-friendly provisions. However, there is broad support for boards' having the ability to adopt rights plans on short notice in response to specific threats, as long as they are not kept in place for too long before the shareholders have an opportunity to approve or reject them. Many companies have a rights plan "on the shelf," which essentially means that they are in a position to adopt one on short notice if needed.

Shareholder rights plans are typically implemented by way of a dividend to all of the existing shareholders of a company of a right to buy a fraction of a share of preferred stock (which is designed to be the economic equivalent of a share of common stock) at a price far out of the money (that is, well above the stock's trading value). The key feature of a rights plan is the "flip-in" of the rights, which is triggered when a shareholder crosses a certain specified threshold of ownership (generally an acquisition of between 10 and 20 percent of the company's stock). Once triggered, the rights grant all holders—except the holder that crossed the ownership threshold—the right to purchase these common stock equivalents at a discount, thereby diluting the shareholder who "triggered" the pill. Existing holders above the triggering threshold at the time the plan is adopted are typically grandfathered in and protected from dilution as long as they do not increase their ownership percentage.

The risk of dilution, combined with the authority of a company's board to redeem the rights prior to a triggering event, gives a potential acquirer a powerful incentive to negotiate with the company's board rather than proceeding unilaterally.

Unlike in some other jurisdictions where a target's board of directors is prohibited from taking action to frustrate a takeover bid once it is announced, American state courts and some legislatures have long recognized that an undervalued or opportunistically timed takeover bid can be a threat to a corporation, to which the board may legitimately respond. The adoption of a shareholder rights plan is a prime example of the sort of defensive response that is generally upheld by the courts, as long as it is a reasonable response to the threat posed.

Rights plans are specifically authorized by the corporate law statutes of several states and have been upheld by the courts of Delaware (which does not have statutory authorization) and other states. Rights plans are highly effective at preventing a third party—or a group of people acting in concert—from buying, in a tender offer or on the open market, shares above the triggering threshold. In the only known case in which someone triggered a flip-in rights plan (an unusual situation where the amount at stake was so small as to warrant risking the dilution to "test" the poison pill), the Delaware court upheld the rights plan. In this *Selectica* case (see the note in the Additional Readings section), the court upheld the exchange-and-reload feature of the rights plan, so that every shareholder other than the triggering shareholder was issued one new share for each right they owned, thus diluting the triggering shareholder, with each new share so issued bearing its own right so that any future triggering acquisitions would lead to further dilution.

In practice, because the rights can be redeemed by the board of directors, the rights plan is effective only as long as the board remains in place. Hostile takeover battles therefore often include proxy (or consent) battles by which the bidder seeks to replace a majority of the board with new directors who will redeem the rights and sell the company. A proxy fight generally plays out over several months (the exact timeline depending on many factors). The rights plan effectively buys that much time for the incumbent board to either convince shareholders not to sell, or to sell the company in the best available transaction.

A company that has a classified or "staggered" board (in which only one third of the board is up for election each year) is well positioned to defend against a hostile bid, because the combination of the rights plan with the staggered board means that a hostile bidder will have to persist through two election cycles in order to take control of the company. It was this combination that allowed Airgas to fend off an opportunistic bid by Air Products and sell itself for a much higher price a few years later. Years of shareholder activism have also resulted in most large companies giving up their staggered boards as well, with the result that the shareholder rights plan is a much less formidable defense than it once was.

A few states have allowed more aggressive forms of rights plans, which only allow the original directors who implemented the rights plan or their approved successors to redeem the rights (these are called "dead-hand" poison pills), or which limit the ability of new directors to redeem the rights for a period (called "slow-hand" pills), but these have been held invalid in Delaware and most other states.

While the traditional purpose of shareholder rights plans has been to defend against hostile takeover bids, in recent years, rights plans have been adapted and used to respond to other threats to the company. The Delaware courts have upheld a two-tiered rights plan designed to counter the threat by shareholder activists to effect a change in control without paying a control premium. They have also upheld a rights plan specifically designed to protect a company's net operating losses or NOLs (which plans uniquely set the trigger at a 5 percent level, because IRS rules only count shareholders of 5 percent or more in calculating whether there has been a chance of control that can limit the use of NOLs).

It may not be appropriate to adopt one in response to every takeover threat, but the shareholder rights plan (poison pill) is a vital tool that directors need to know about, as it may be the only thing that enables them to prevent a third party from taking control of the company without paying a proper control premium to all shareholders.

In recent years, takeover activity has increasingly involved the formation of so-called wolf packs of shareholders seeking to cause a company to be sold. These shareholders are careful not to engage in activity that would constitute them as a "group" under the securities laws, thereby aggregating their holdings (and thus triggering a rights plan).

Companies and their counsel have sought to deal with this specific threat by sometimes including "wolf pack" or "concerted actions" provisions in their rights plans. Although theoretically effective, these provisions have yet to be judicially tested and have risks that should be discussed and considered with legal counsel.

Key Questions

When assessing an existing shareholder rights plan or considering whether to adopt a rights plan, a board of directors may ask some of the following key questions:

- ❑ Does the company currently have a rights plan in place, and if so, what are the triggering conditions?
- ❑ If the company does not currently have a rights plan in place, are there circumstances existing that may warrant the adoption of a rights plan?
- ❑ How much time would a rights plan buy the board in the face of a takeover bid? (This will usually depend on whether the company has a staggered board and what rights the shareholders have to act, by meeting or by written consent, in between annual meetings.)
- ❑ Does the company have a rights plan "on the shelf" that may be adopted on short notice?
- ❑ Has the board been educated as to what a rights plan is and how it works so that they can approve its adoption on short notice if necessary?
- ❑ In the company's jurisdiction of incorporation, what are the laws regarding rights plans? What types of plans may be adopted?
- ❑ Is the adoption of a rights plan consistent with the board's fiduciary duties? (In Delaware, for example, a board action taken in response to a perceived threat to the company must be a "reasonable" and "proportionate" response.)
- ❑ Is the board authorized to unilaterally issue "blank check preferred stock"? If not, are other types of rights plans (such as a common stock rights plan) possible?
- ❑ What effect would the adoption of a rights plan have on investors and investor advisory services' recommendations? Does a proposed rights plan fit within the guidelines for "compliant" rights plans for investor advisory services?
- ❑ Are there tax assets that the company should seek to protect using a "Section 382" (NOL) rights plan?

Whether adopted or kept on the shelf, directors may consider different possible features of a shareholder rights plan and may ask some of the following questions:

- ❑ What should be the appropriate term for the plan?
- ❑ What should be the exercise price of the plan (the dollar amount of a company's shares that a shareholder may purchase upon a triggering event)? What should be the discount for such purchases?
- ❑ What should be the flip-in trigger threshold?
- ❑ What should be included in the definition of ownership for the purposes of the triggering event? Should derivative positions and group activity be included?
- ❑ Should there be exemptions for certain "qualifying offers" to purchase the whole company?
- ❑ Should the plan have a two-tier structure with a higher triggering threshold for passive institutional investors and a lower trigger for activists? (Note that this variation was accepted by the Delaware courts in the Sotheby's situation but may not be appropriate in all cases.)

- ❑ Should our rights plan include a "wolf pack" or concerted action provision?
- ❑ When and under what conditions may the board redeem the rights plan?
- ❑ Should our plan include any provisions to make it more palatable for institutional shareholders?
- ❑ Should our shareholders be asked to ratify the plan at our next annual meeting?

Additional Reading

1. "Takeover Law and Practice" (2016), *Wachtell, Lipton, Rosen & Katz*, Chapter VI, Section A: "Rights Plans or 'Poison Pills'"
   http://www.wlrk.com/files/2016/TakeoverLawandPracticeGuide.pdf
2. Alpert, Marc A., Kessar Nashat, and Garrett Lynam. "Rights Plans in a New Era: Recent Drafting Trends." *Bloomberg Law Reports* (March 12, 2012)
   http://www.chadbourne.com/sites/default/files/publications/03.12.12%20-%20rights%20plans%20in%20a%20new%20era.pdf
3. ISS 2016 U.S. Summary Proxy Voting Guidelines (December 18, 2015), Section 3. Shareholder Rights and Defenses—Shareholder Rights Plans (Poison Pills)
   https://www.issgovernance.com/file/policy/2016-us-summary-voting-guidelines-dec-2015.pdf
4. Laide, John. "2014 Poison Pill Impetus: Why Are U.S. Companies Adopting Poison Pills?" *FactSet Insight*
   http://www.factset.com/insight/2015/01/2014-poison-pill-impetus-why-are-u.s.-companies-adopting-poison-pills
5. Lipton, Martin et al. "'Just Say No'—The Long-Term Value of the Poison Pill." *Wachtell, Lipton, Rosen & Katz* (December 17, 2015)
   http://www.wlrk.com/webdocs/wlrknew/WLRKMemos/WLRK/WLRK.25026.15.pdf
6. "Poison Pills: Defending Against Takeovers/Stockholder Activism and Protecting NOLs," *Practical Law*
   http://us.practicallaw.com/3-386-0340
7. Mirvis, Theodore N. et al. "Delaware Supreme Court Affirms Approval of 4.99% Rights Plan to Protect NOLs." *Wachtell, Lipton, Rosen & Katz* (October 5, 2010)
   http://www.wlrk.com/webdocs/wlrknew/WLRKMemos/WLRK/WLRK.17941.10.pdf
8. Brownstein, Andrew R. et al. "Delaware Court of Chancery Upholds Rights Plans as a Defense to Activism." *Wachtell, Lipton, Rosen & Katz* (May 9, 2014)
   http://www.wlrk.com/webdocs/wlrknew/WLRKMemos/WLRK/WLRK.23328.14.pdf

Notes

10.3 CHANGE OF CONTROL SEVERANCE ARRANGEMENTS

CONTRIBUTED BY
Trevor S. Norwitz and Andrea K. Wahlquist
Wachtell, Lipton, Rosen & Katz[1]

In order to attract and retain executives, most major companies have adopted executive compensation programs containing change of control protections for senior management (which are often referred to as "golden parachutes"). Change of control severance or retention agreements and plans are not defensive devices intended to deter sales or mergers; rather they are intended to ensure that management teams are not deterred from engaging in corporate transactions that are in the best interests of shareholders on account of the potential adverse effects those transactions may have on their post-transaction employment. A well-designed change of control severance protection program—whether contained within change of control agreements, separate provisions in an executive's employment agreement, or standalone severance and equity incentive plans—should neither incentivize nor disincentivize management from engaging in a transaction on the basis of personal circumstances.

Some companies also have (or adopt in the face of an imminent threat) broader change of control protections for key employees and other lower level employees (sometimes

1. Trevor S. Norwitz is a partner in the corporate department, and Andrea K. Wahlquist is a partner in the executive compensation and employee benefits practice of Wachtell, Lipton, Rosen & Katz, located in New York City.

called "silver" or "tin" parachutes) to ensure that a destabilizing event like a takeover bid does not result in a loss of too many critical employees.

Although there continues to be a great deal of public and legal scrutiny of executive compensation arrangements, appropriately structured change of control arrangements are both legal and proper. Courts that have addressed the legality of change of control severance agreements and other benefit protections have almost universally found such arrangements to be enforceable and consistent with directors' fiduciary duties, so long as directors do not have a conflict of interest. A board's decision to adopt change of control protections for employees is usually analyzed under the business judgment rule. The scrutiny applied to such arrangements may be heightened if they are adopted during a pending or threatened takeover contest, thereby making careful advance planning all the more important. Public companies that do not already maintain reasonable change of control protections for senior management should consider implementing them, and companies that already maintain such arrangements should monitor and periodically review them.

Over the years, a generally consistent standard of change of control protections has emerged. Although some companies may still maintain certain "single-trigger" arrangements (e.g., which result in accelerated vesting of unvested equity-based awards or cash payments (such as severance or deferred compensation) upon a change of control event, even if there is no termination of the executive's employment), in recent years, such protections have become very unpopular with shareholder advisory services and many institutional shareholders. It is far more typical for change of control protections to now be triggered only once both a change of control event *and* a qualifying termination of an executive's employment in anticipation of, or within a specified period of time after, the change of control event has occurred. In general, such a period of time would not exceed one or two years following a change of control, due in no small part to the promulgation of certain standards by shareholder and proxy advisory firms, such as ISS and Glass Lewis, but also due to certain federal income tax rules (i.e., Section 409A of the Internal Revenue Code) relating to the timing of certain payments upon certain terminations of employment occurring within two years after certain change of control events, such as a takeover. Under these common types of change of control severance protections, if the executive's employment is terminated during the protected period by the employer without "cause" or by the executive for "good reason" (i.e., following a specific adverse change in the terms of the executive's employment), the executive is entitled to severance benefits. A typical "good reason" (sometimes called a "constructive termination") definition could include (i) a material diminution in the executive's compensation (e.g., annual rate of base salary and/or annual target bonus opportunity); (ii) a material change in the executive's primary work location; or (iii) importantly, a material diminution in the executive's authority, duty, or responsibility; such a triggering event often means that the most senior executives of acquired companies likely will be entitled to resign for good reason, even if they are retained by the acquiring company in some capacity (at the acquired company or otherwise below the parent-level acquiring company) after the change of control event. Note also that "silver" or "tin" parachutes for employees below senior management often only trigger on a termination of the employee's employment without "cause." This is because boards of directors often conclude that it is unlikely for an acquirer to take the kind of actions with respect to lower-tier employees that would constitute "good reason" for a senior executive, although certain change of control events, including a relocation of the employee's work location and/or a material reduction in annual base salary, could be considered "good reason" triggers for lower-tier employees as well.

The severance benefits due to an executive upon such a qualifying termination of employment also should be sufficient to ensure the executive's neutrality and retention through the closing of the proposed transaction, but not so great as to be excessive or to encourage the executive to encourage a change of control when it is not in the best interests of the company and its shareholders. For the most senior executives at public companies, a multiple of an executive's annual compensation (e.g., two to three times) is the standard severance formula in most industries, with silver and tin parachutes being at lower multiples (e.g., 12 to 18 months for silver parachutes and less than 12 months for tin parachutes). "Compensation" for this purpose generally includes base salary and annual bonus (with such based on a fixed formula, usually related to the executive's prior year's bonus, average annual bonus over some period, or target annual bonus). Note that the target board of directors or compensation committee may need to consider how shareholder advisory firms view severance packages, as firm guidelines continue to evolve. In addition, severance benefits often include payments in respect of welfare benefits continuation premiums in respect of the same multiple of years as the cash severance being paid. In the change of control context, severance is customarily paid in a lump sum within a specified period of time following a qualifying termination (generally, subject to the executive's execution of a release of employment-related claims against the company), as opposed to installment payments, but it is sometimes necessary in certain circumstances to structure severance in installments in order to comply with the compensation tax rules previously referenced.

Also, to the extent a company's equity incentive plans do not provide for so-called double-trigger vesting of equity awards (i.e., upon a severance-qualifying termination of employment in connection with a change of control event), the company may wish to consider including such provisions in the change of control severance protection arrangements. Note that the target board of directors or compensation committee may also need to consider how performance-based awards should vest; based on most recent shareholder advisory firm guidelines, the new standards require vesting either a prorated target number of awards (based on the date the change of control event occurs relative to the award's performance period) and/or based on achievement of targets as of the change of control event.

Finally, change of control arrangements typically provide that any payments and benefits in the nature of compensation (whether severance payments, vesting of equity awards, or otherwise) that become due to executives in connection with a change of control event (which may also include a termination of employment that occurs on or after the change of control) that would be subject to a "golden parachute" excise tax (i.e., taxes imposed under Section 4999 of the Internal Revenue Code) will be reduced to just below the individual's statutorily determined threshold above which the excise tax applies (the analysis of which is beyond the scope of this chapter, but which threshold, in general, is equal to 2.99 times the executive's prior five-year average reported taxable compensation), unless the executive would retain a higher net after-tax amount if the executive were to pay the excise tax in full (often called a "better of net after-tax" provision). Another approach would be to simply reduce the payments to just below the executive's applicable threshold. It is worth noting that although excise tax "gross-up" provisions have fallen out of favor due to shareholder and proxy advisor firms' dislike of such provisions, a target company's board of directors may still wish to consider approving such provisions for certain executives, if the impact of the transaction could have a disproportionately adverse impact on certain executives (e.g., a newly hired chief executive officer brought in specifically to aid in the turnaround of the target company may not have a high applicable threshold, as compared to longer-tenured executives who may have recognized greater amounts of income over time due to bonus payments and vesting of equity awards).

Target company boards of directors also often consider approving a cash or equity-based (or both) pool to be set aside and used to grant retention bonuses or other awards to key employees who may be identified as flight risks once a deal is announced. Typically, these pools are negotiated with the acquirer and are allocated in the discretion of the compensation committee and/or chief executive officer, payable subject to continued employment through the closing of the transaction (and otherwise payable if the company terminates the employee's employment without cause prior to the closing). Often, these retention bonus amounts are based on percentages of annual salary, with such percentages larger or smaller depending upon the length of time between the signing of the definitive transaction agreement and the closing of the transaction and/or the equity award values of the at-risk key employees.

In recent years, the SEC has adopted rules under the Dodd-Frank Wall Street Reform and Consumer Protection Act requiring companies engaging in M&A transactions to give shareholders the opportunity, when voting on the transaction, to cast an advisory vote on any "golden parachute" benefits triggered by the transaction. Although this vote is non-binding and separate from the vote to approve the transaction, it can be (and on rare occasions is) an embarrassing rebuke for a target company's board of directors.

Key Questions

Some key questions regarding change of control protections are the following:

- ❑ Does the company currently have change of control arrangements in place with senior management? Do the arrangements incentivize or disincentivize management to pursue change of control transactions?
- ❑ Has the company benchmarked the current (or proposed) change of control protection arrangements and clearly advised the board of directors of the potential costs of any such arrangements?
- ❑ Has the company considered the impact of the golden parachute excise taxes on senior management? Do the arrangements incorporate provisions to address the impact of the golden parachute excise tax on payments using "better of net after-tax" provision or some other approach?
- ❑ What disclosure requirements apply to change of control arrangements when the company's shareholders are asked to approve a merger or sale of the company?

- ❑ Does the company currently have silver or tin parachute change of control arrangements in place with lower level employees? What effect would the cost of these plans have in a potential transaction scenario?
- ❑ What is the potential impact of a change of control on the company's equity-based compensation plans?
- ❑ Do the company's equity-based compensation plans have single-trigger vesting (acceleration of equity compensation awards upon a change of control) or double-trigger vesting (acceleration of equity compensation awards upon a severance-qualifying termination event in connection with a change of control)?
- ❑ Do the change of control arrangements—both the severance protection and equity award vesting provisions—comply with Section 409A of the Internal Revenue Code governing certain compensation arrangements?
- ❑ Has the company considered whether a retention bonus plan should be adopted, in order to ensure the retention of employees through the closing of the transaction?

Additional Reading

1. "Change of Control Clauses," *Practical Law*
http://us.practicallaw.com/8-203-1642
2. "Compensation Committee Guide" (2017), *Wachtell, Lipton, Rosen & Katz*
http://www.wlrk.com/docs/CompensationCommitteeGuide2017.pdf
3. O'Brien, Jeannemarie. "The Continuing Relevance of Change-of-Control Arrangements," in *Hot Issues in Executive Compensation 2016*, Practicing Law Institute Course Handbook (September 2016)
4. Frederic W. Cook and Co., Inc., "Executive Severance and Change in Control Practices" (March 2016)
http://www.fwcook.com/content/Documents/Publications/Executive_Severance_and_Change-in-Control_Practices.pdf
5. Segal, Michael J. et al., "Compensation Season 2017," *Wachtell, Lipton, Rosen & Katz*
http://www.wlrk.com/webdocs/wlrknew/AttorneyPubs/WLRK.25479.17.pdf
6. "Takeover Law and Practice" (2016), *Wachtell, Lipton, Rosen & Katz*, Chapter VI, Section D: "Change-of-Control Employment Arrangements"
http://www.wlrk.com/files/2016/TakeoverLawandPracticeGuide.pdf

Notes

10.4 DEALING WITH AN UNSOLICITED ACQUISITION PROPOSAL

CONTRIBUTED BY
Trevor S. Norwitz
Wachtell, Lipton, Rosen & Katz[1]

In the event that you are a director of a company that receives an unsolicited acquisition proposal, you should keep in mind a few general principles regarding both your company's general policies and advance preparation regarding takeovers (see Chapter 10.1, General Takeover Planning), as well as your duties as a director, in order to preserve the board's capacity to act in the best interests of the company. When facing an unsolicited bid, psychological and perception factors can be as important as, or even more decisive than, legal and financial considerations. Once a company is publicly put "in play," its range of options narrows substantially.

Unsolicited bidders (and shareholder activists) sometimes directly contact outside directors as an initial matter to gauge the intended target company's receptiveness to a proposal or to create division in its boardroom. In such situations, directors should refuse to engage in the discussion and should refer all approaches to the company's CEO. Directors should treat all conversations with interested parties as being "on the record"; any comments may be later used by the potential acquirer.

1. Trevor S. Norwitz is a partner in the corporate department of Wachtell, Lipton, Rosen & Katz, located in New York City.

A board's appropriate response to an unsolicited proposal depends on the situation. For casual approaches and nonpublic "bear hug" letters, the board has no duty to discuss or negotiate these approaches. There is no requirement to give a "fair hearing" to a potential bidder that expresses an interest but does not make a specific proposal. Furthermore, a company has no duty to disclose these approaches publicly (although this may change if the information leaks and the leak is attributable to the company). For public offers (in the form of public "bear-hug" letters, tender offers, or otherwise), a company response will be necessary in practice if not in law. If a tender offer is launched, the board must consider and formally respond to it on an SEC form called a Schedule 14D-9 within 10 business days. Until the board does express its view in this formal SEC filing, the company must remain silent and may only put out a short "stop, look, and listen" press release encouraging shareholders to wait for the board's response before acting. The company's response should be determined by the board after considering the advice of the company's financial and legal advisors and presentations by the company's management. Once the company has filed its Schedule 14D-9, it will have to disclose promptly material developments, such as if it is negotiating with a third party. These public disclosure considerations can have great strategic importance.

In considering unsolicited proposals, directors should be aware of their fiduciary duties to the company under applicable state law. In some states, like Delaware, there may be an elevated level of fiduciary duty and judicial scrutiny that applies in certain types of takeover situations (such as when a company has already agreed to sell itself or when the board adopts takeover defenses), whereas in other states no special duties apply in these situations. If the board opposes the unsolicited proposal, it will of course have to take into account in determining its response the company's defensive profile and the assessment of its expert advisors as to how long it will be able to resist until the decision is out of its hands and in the control of the company's shareholders. This will depend in large part on whether the company has a staggered board and whether the shareholders are able to act in between annual meetings. (See Chapter 10.1, General Takeover Planning.)

In general, a board is legally permitted to "just say no" to a proposal if the board has a good faith belief, arrived at after reasonable investigation, that it would be in the company's best interests to remain independent and pursue its own strategic plan or that the price offered is inadequate. A premium over market is not necessarily a fair price; and a price may be fair, but the board may reject it because it is inadequate or an inopportune time to sell the company. In practice, however, it may be difficult for the board to "just say no" as the shareholders ultimately have the power to remove and replace the board.

In evaluating an unsolicited acquisition proposal, a board should consider, among other things, the following:

- The nature and timing of the offer, specifically whether this is a good time to consider a sale of the company
- Whether the offer is fair and adequate
- Whether the bidder has existing resources to consummate the offer or will require external financing that makes the transaction less certain
- The risk of non-consummation of a proposed transaction
- The quality and type of consideration offered (if the bid is not all cash) and the adequacy of the bidder's financing

- The company's strategic plans
- The company's business prospects and intrinsic value
- Whether a full review of strategic alternatives is appropriate under the circumstances
- Potential regulatory issues (such as antitrust hurdles) presented by the offer
- How the company's shareholder base is likely to change following announcement of the takeover proposal
- The company's "defensive" profile and how long the board will be able to resist before the shareholders will have the opportunity to vote the board out if they want to accept an offer

Key Questions

Once a company has received an unsolicited acquisition proposal, a board should consider some of the following key questions:

- ❑ Who is the key spokesperson for the company in the takeover context to whom directors and management should refer unsolicited proposals? (This should be the CEO in most cases.)
- ❑ What is the identity of the unsolicited bidder? Is it a strategic or financial party? What is the bidder's history?
- ❑ What is the seriousness and specificity of the proposal?
- ❑ What kind of approach is the bidder making?
- ❑ Is the offer fully financed or subject to a financing contingency? How likely is the bidder to obtain the requisite financing?
- ❑ What are the bidder's goals? Has the bidder made additional requests or stated other objectives? Has the bidder worked with an activist that has lobbied for other objectives?
- ❑ Does the board have any legal obligation to respond to the offer?
- ❑ What are the board's fiduciary duties under applicable state law? Do any heightened fiduciary duties apply in the specific takeover context?
- ❑ If the takeover approach is private, how can the company and the board best maintain confidentiality? (If the board does not consider it a good time to sell the company, it is far preferable if the situation is never made public; once a company is "in play" it is much more difficult to control the destiny of the company.)
- ❑ Is it appropriate to convene a board meeting to consider the offer? What is the input of management and outside advisors?
- ❑ Does the board have any conflicts related to the unsolicited bid?
- ❑ If there are board conflicts, is it appropriate to form a special committee to consider the offer? (Generally speaking, except in conflict situations, special committees are not necessary and may add complication and expense.)
- ❑ In the event an unsolicited proposal turns hostile, what takeover defenses does the company have in place? What are the company's prospects for remaining independent? Does the company have a staggered board? What is the range of potential "white knights"? Is it appropriate or advisable to implement additional defenses?
- ❑ If the bid has been made public, what are the responses to it among shareholders, investors, analysts, media, regulators, employees, customers, and other constituencies?

Additional Reading

1. "Defending Against Hostile Takeovers," *Practical Law*
   http://us.practicallaw.com/9-386-7206
2. Kotran, Stephen M., Trevor S. Norwitz, and Paul J. Shim, "It's a Hostile World: Responding to Unsolicited Take-Over Proposals"
   http://pli.edu/Content/Seminar/Doing_Deals_2016_The_Art_of_MA_Transactional/_/N-4kZ1z11iak?ID=259602
3. Sparks, A. Gilchrist, "Responding to Unsolicited Takeover Offers." *Harvard Law School Forum on Corporate Governance and Financial Regulation* (July 16, 2009)
   https://corpgov.law.harvard.edu/2009/07/16/responding-to-unsolicited-takeover-offers
4. "Takeover Response Checklist and Dealing with Activist Hedge Funds," *Wachtell, Lipton, Rosen & Katz*
   http://www.wlrk.com/files/2016/TakeoverResponseChecklistandDealingwithActivistHedgeFunds.pdf
5. Emmerich, Adam O. and Trevor S. Norwitz, "The Nancy Reagan Defence in 2015: Can a Board Still Just Say No?" *The International Comparative Legal Guide to: Mergers and Acquisitions* 2016, 10th ed., published by Global Legal Group Ltd., London
   http://www.wlrk.com/webdocs/wlrknew/AttorneyPubs/WLRK.25171.16.pdf
6. "Takeover Law and Practice" (2016), *Wachtell, Lipton, Rosen & Katz*, Chapter VI: "Advance Takeover Preparedness and Hostile M&A"
   http://www.wlrk.com/files/2016/TakeoverLawandPracticeGuide.pdf

Notes

10.5 ENGAGING AN INVESTMENT BANKER IN A BUSINESS COMBINATION

CONTRIBUTED BY
Trevor S. Norwitz
Wachtell, Lipton, Rosen & Katz[1]

Companies engage investment bankers as financial advisors in M&A transactions for many reasons. Good bankers have industry expertise and know the key players (including competitors of the company), so they can help structure the transaction and negotiate its terms. They can also provide insight (and a degree of legal protection—see Chapter 10.7, Fairness Opinions) as to the fairness of the financial terms of the transaction. A company's management team may be able to play many of these roles and often does so without outside financial advisors in smaller transactions. However, in situations where the management team may have its own interest in a transaction, the company's financial advisor also plays the important role of providing the board with an independent view on the transaction. Investment bankers have their own interests as well, and there has been increasing scrutiny by investors, boards, and courts regarding perceived conflicts of interest (see Chapter 10.6, Dealing with Investment Banker Conflicts of Interest). As a result, boards should be more active and careful in their engagement with their financial advisors in connection with a material transaction, both on the buy side and on the sell side.

1. Trevor S. Norwitz is a partner in the corporate department of Wachtell, Lipton, Rosen & Katz, located in New York City.

There are several stages over the course of an M&A process at which the board's interaction with its financial advisors should be considered:

- Identifying potential financial advisors
- Interviewing and selecting the financial advisor(s)
- Terms of engagement
- Monitoring the deal process
- Reviewing, analyzing, and interpreting financial analysis

In engaging a financial advisor for a material transaction, directors should, of course, consider their qualifications, expertise, and helpful relationships, but should also attempt to assess whether a potential advisor has or is likely to develop a conflict of interest in the proposed transaction. Boards should be generally be aware of the terms of engagement with the advisor or advisors that are ultimately selected (including any provisions to guard against investment banker conflicts) and remain proactive in monitoring the deal process throughout.

In many situations companies have close, long-standing relations with their advisors, and it may be perfectly acceptable to engage those advisors to advise the company and the board. The board of course, and not the management team, are the representatives of the company and its shareholders. In some situations, it may be more appropriate for the board, or a special committee of the board, to have advisors (legal as well as financial) who are independent of management. In those situations, the board may choose to interview a number of potential advisors. In some cases, such as where the board is dealing with a transaction in which management or some directors are conflicted, it may be advisable for the unconflicted directors to engage legal counsel first. The directors and their legal counsel should discuss any potentially meaningful actual or potential conflict of interests of which they are aware and how best to deal with them. The interview process can be important in soliciting sufficient information to determine if a conflict exists or is likely to arise during the transaction.

After the financial advisors have been selected, the board should continue to monitor and engage with them throughout the deal process. It should be understood that if any significant conflict develops that could impact the advisor's ability to give the board unbiased advice (or which would create the impression that their advice is tainted), the advisor should inform the board so that they can consider whether or how to mitigate the problem. Given the complexities and sensitivities around confidentiality and information gathering concerns, this is not an area that is well served by hard and fast rules but by common sense, good judgment, and a determination to do what is right.

When bankers present their financial analysis to the board, directors should not be passive but should be engaged and ask questions to develop a reasonable understanding of the analysis, including key valuation assumptions, judgments made, and limitations (see Chapter 10.7, Fairness Opinions).

Key Questions

When selecting an investment banker to act as a financial advisor, boards may wish to consider the following questions (with the degree of focus depending on whether the board is overseeing or actually managing the engagement):

- ❑ What comparable transactions has the advisor completed in recent years?
- ❑ Does the advisor have experience with your company's industry and competitive landscape?
- ❑ What size companies and transactions does the advisor typically work with?
- ❑ What relationships and other connections does the advisor have that could help or, conversely, create a conflict of interest? (See the Key Questions in Chapter 10.6, Dealing with Investment Banker Conflicts of Interest.)

When considering and negotiating the terms of engagement of a financial advisor, directors should ask the following (if the board is managing the engagement process):

- ❑ What advisory services will be provided? Is the scope sufficient to allow the board to exercise its fiduciary duties?
- ❑ How is the advisor being compensated for its services? Structure may be more important for board consideration than absolute amount.
- ❑ What provisions should be included to address and communicate the incurrence of new conflicts that arise during the course of the proposed transaction?
- ❑ Is the engagement exclusive? May the company hire more than one advisor if the board deems that necessary or appropriate?

If the company is considering hiring a second advisor, directors should ask the following:

- ❑ Why is the second advisor being retained? Is the purpose additional expertise or to mitigate a potential conflict on the part of the first advisor? And if the purpose is to address a potential conflict, will the arrangement be effective to address the concern?
- ❑ How will the roles and responsibilities of the two advisors overlap or be distinct?
- ❑ How should the compensation of the two advisors be structured?
- ❑ When should the second advisor begin involvement in the process to avoid disruption and delay?

As the deal process progresses, the board should monitor the proceedings and, if it is appropriate for the board to be actively engaged in the process, directors should ask the following:

- ❑ If on the sell side, how are potential bidders identified? Is the bidding pool limited, and if so, why? Any bidder/type of bidder favored?
- ❑ How is information being shared with potential bidders? Are communications centralized? Do all bidders have appropriate access to information?

- ❑ How are communications with management, among bidders, and the potential formation of bidder consortiums being controlled?
- ❑ Is the board restricting premature conversations regarding retention of senior management post-transaction?
- ❑ How are decisions being made regarding advancing bidders, standstill provisions, and exclusivity?

Additional Reading

1. "Takeover Law and Practice" (2016), *Wachtell, Lipton, Rosen & Katz*, Chapter III, Section C: "Investment Bankers and Fairness Opinions"
   http://www.wlrk.com/files/2016/TakeoverLawandPracticeGuide.pdf
2. Strine, Leo E., Jr. "Documenting the Deal: How Quality Control and Candor Can Improve Boardroom Decision-Making and Reduce the Litigation Target Zone." *The Business Lawyer* 70 (Summer 2015)
   http://files.mwe.com/files/uploads/Documents/Pubs/TBL-Vol.70-2015.pdf
3. Sikora, Martin. "The Role and Fee Structure of an M&A Advisor." *Business Insider* (January 13, 2011)
   http://www.businessinsider.com/the-role-and-fee-structure-of-an-ma-advisor-2011-2

Notes

106 DEALING WITH INVESTMENT BANKER CONFLICTS OF INTEREST

CONTRIBUTED BY
Trevor S. Norwitz
Wachtell, Lipton, Rosen & Katz[1]

Directors rely on their financial advisors for unbiased advice. Especially in situations where management is conflicted, directors need to be able to trust that their advisors are acting loyally in the interests of the company and not in their own interests. Investment bankers' own interests can conflict with those of their clients' in many ways. The most common perceived conflict is that their fees are often largely contingent on the transaction being completed, which incentivizes them to opine that the consideration offered is fair. However, this is largely unavoidable, as companies are generally unwilling to pay transaction fees when there is no transaction. More serious conflicts can arise when an investment banker has a substantial investment in, or a long and valuable relationship with, a party on the other side of the table, or tries to use its role in one transaction to get financing or other business from a party on the other side or in a totally different transaction.

In recent years, following some cases in which investment banks were found by courts to have acted egregiously, courts and regulators have focused intensely and critically on perceived conflicts of interests of investment banks and are ensuring that there is adequate

1. Trevor S. Norwitz is a partner in the corporate department of Wachtell, Lipton, Rosen & Katz, located in New York City.

disclosure of these to investors. Since 2007, FINRA's rules require specific disclosures and procedures addressing conflicts of interest when member firms provide fairness opinions in change of control transactions. The SEC also requires, in transactions subject to the proxy rules, detailed disclosure of the procedures followed by an investment banker in preparing their fairness opinion, including a summary of the underlying financial analyses, and about previous relationships between the investment banker and the parties to the transaction.

In an important decision concerning the role played by outside financial advisors in the board's decision-making process, the Delaware Court of Chancery held in *In re Del Monte Foods Co. Shareholders Litigation* (2011) that a financial advisor was so conflicted that the board's failure to actively oversee the financial advisor's conflict gave rise to a likelihood of a breach of fiduciary duty by the board. The court stated that, when overseeing a financial advisor's role in a transaction, "the buck stops with the board," because "Delaware law requires that a board take an active and direct role in the sale process." In 2015, the Delaware courts further clarified the board's role in overseeing a conflicted financial advisor in *In re Rural Metro Corporation Stockholders Litigation* and again put the onus on directors to be "especially diligent in overseeing the conflicted advisor's role in the sale process."

Del Monte and *Rural Metro* are rare cases where the courts have found serious improper behavior by investment bank advisors, but because the courts were only able to reach the bankers by finding that the directors had breached their fiduciary duties and the bankers had aided and abetted (or caused) those breaches, these cases highlight the importance of directors taking a proactive role in overseeing and managing conflicts. Directors cannot know and do not have a responsibility to identify every conflict their financial advisors may have, but they should seek to ensure that these conflicts are brought to light if they arise during the transaction process and seek to appropriately manage any such conflicts.

Key Questions

When selecting and interviewing potential financial advisors, directors should ask some of the following key questions (again the degree of focus expected of directors will depend on whether the board is overseeing or actually managing the engagement):

- ❑ Does the bank have a prior relationship with the company's management or controlling shareholder?
- ❑ Does the bank have a prior relationship with the proposed or likely acquirer(s) or target(s), as applicable?
- ❑ Does the bank have a financial interest in the company or the proposed or likely acquirer(s) or target(s)?
- ❑ Does the bank have contingent fee arrangements with any of the relevant parties in the proposed transaction (and if so are these appropriately structured)?
- ❑ Does the bank have any other financial interest in the deal outcome (for example, through its interest in providing financing to a party)?
- ❑ What protective provisions regarding investment banker conflicts should be included in our engagement letter?

If a potential conflict is identified, a board should understand as much as possible regarding the nature of the conflict, keeping in mind that the nature and timeliness of responses from the bank may be impacted by confidentiality requirements, information walls between divisions of the bank, and bank policies and recordkeeping:

- ❑ Which individuals at the bank (or which divisions of the bank) are potentially conflicted?
- ❑ Over what period of time?
- ❑ Are there relevant dollar thresholds?

In response to a potential conflict, the board may seek ways to mitigate or avoid the conflict:

- ❑ Would disclosure to shareholders be curative of the conflict?
- ❑ Would "ethical walls" alleviate the conflict?
- ❑ What are the costs and benefits of retaining the conflicted banker?
- ❑ Are there other curative approaches possible (e.g., retaining a second bank, etc.)?

Additional Reading

1. "Takeover Law and Practice" (2016), *Wachtell, Lipton, Rosen & Katz*, Chapter III, Section C: "Investment Bankers and Fairness Opinions"
   http://www.wlrk.com/files/2016/TakeoverLawandPracticeGuide.pdf
2. Hoffman, Liz. "In Deal Boom, More Firms Ask: Is My Banker Conflicted?" *Wall Street Journal* (March 2, 2016)
   http://www.wsj.com/articles/in-deal-boom-more-firms-ask-is-my-banker-conflicted-1456957142
3. Indap, Sujeet and James Fontanella-Khan. "Court Case Forces M&A Bankers to Take Conflicts Seriously." *Financial Times* (December 1, 2015)
   http://www.ft.com/cms/s/0/9ec910d0-981e-11e5-9228-87e603d47bdc.html
4. Katz, David A. and Laura A. McIntosh. "Corporate Governance Update: *Del Monte* and Responsibility of Board in a Sales Process" (March 24, 2011)
   http://www.wlrk.com/webdocs/wlrknew/WLRKMemos/WLRK/WLRK.18503.11.pdf
5. Reder, Robert S. and Stephanie Stroup Estey. "Sell-Side Financial Advisors in the M&A Crosshairs." 68 *Vand. L. Rev. En Banc* 279 (2014)
   https://www.vanderbiltlawreview.org/wp-content/uploads/sites/89/2015/12/Sell-Side-Financial-Advisors-in-the-MA-Crosshairs.pdf
6. "The Delaware Supreme Court Speaks to Boards and the Investment Banks," *Wachtell, Lipton, Rosen & Katz* (December 3, 2015)
   https://higherlogicdownload.s3.amazonaws.com/GOVERNANCEPROFESSIONALS/a8892c7c-6297-4149-b9fc-378577d0b150/UploadedImages/Landing%20Page%20Documents/The%20Delaware%20Supreme%20Court%20Speaks%20to%20Boards%20and%20the%20Investment%20Banks.pdf

7. Tuch, Andrew F. "Banker Loyalty in Mergers and Acquisitions." *Harvard Law School Forum on Corporate Governance and Financial Regulation* (September 29, 2015)
https://corpgov.law.harvard.edu/2015/09/29/banker-loyalty-in-mergers-and-acquisitions-2

Notes

10.7 FAIRNESS OPINIONS

CONTRIBUTED BY
Trevor S. Norwitz
Wachtell, Lipton, Rosen & Katz[1]

Since Delaware's 1985 *Smith v. Van Gorkom* decision, it has been typical in a merger transaction involving a public company for a "fairness opinion" to be rendered by an investment bank to the board of the selling company. Sometimes, but far less often, boards of acquiring companies also seek fairness opinions in large transactions to have the benefit of the expert opinion that the price they are paying is fair to their own shareholders.

Fairness opinions are not rooted in a requirement of "black letter" law but in directors' fiduciary duties. Directors, in exercising their business judgment and satisfying their duty of care, may rely on experts, including investment bankers, selected with reasonable care and whom they reasonably believe to be acting within the scope of their expertise. In merger and acquisition transactions, an investment banker's unbiased view of the fairness of the consideration to be paid and the analyses underlying that view provide a board with significant information with which to evaluate the transaction. The analyses and opinions presented to a board, combined with presentations by management and

1. Trevor S. Norwitz is a partner in the corporate department of Wachtell, Lipton, Rosen & Katz, located in New York City.

the board's own long-term strategic reviews, provide the key foundation for the exercise of the directors' business judgment. Courts reviewing the actions of boards have commented favorably on the use by boards of investment bankers in evaluating mergers and other transactions.

The fairness opinion itself is very short and narrowly worded, expressing the banker's opinion that the consideration to be paid is fair "from a financial point of view." The opinion does not speak to the business decision to enter into the transaction itself, even if the investment bank may have helped the company source, negotiate, and implement the transaction. The fact that the consideration offered in a transaction is "fair" does not necessarily mean that it is adequate, but fairness is a minimal requirement for a board to approve a transaction.

Particularly in situations where directors are choosing among competing common stock (or other noncash) business combinations, a board's decision-making may be susceptible to claims of bias, faulty judgment, and inadequate investigation of the relative values of competing offers. Because the stock valuation process inherently involves greater exercise of judgment by a board than that required in an all-cash deal, consideration of the informed analyses of financial advisors is helpful in establishing the fulfillment of the applicable legal duties. In a stock-for-stock fixed exchange ratio merger, the fairness of the consideration often turns on the relative contributions of each party to the combined company in terms of revenues, earnings, and assets, not the absolute dollar value of the stock being received by one party's shareholders based on its trading price at a particular point in time.

A fairness opinion is typically delivered at the meeting at which the board makes the decision to engage in the transaction and speaks as of that time. Parties to a merger (especially a stock-for-stock merger) do not usually seek a "bring-down" of the fairness opinion as a condition to the closing, which would introduce a significant risk that a party might have a right to walk away if the fairness opinion would otherwise have changed between signing and closing. Often the board will also receive financial presentations from their investment bankers at earlier meetings as well.

Directors should ensure that they take the time (and ask all the questions necessary) to understand the analyses used and assumptions made by their investment bankers to support their opinion, such as the discounted cash flow (DCF), comparable company, and comparable transaction analyses. Typically these are reflected in summary form on a page of the investment banker's presentation called the "football field" (because that is what it resembles) which shows how the proposed consideration in the particular transaction compares to the mean and median values in their analyses. Needless to say, these analyses are very sensitive to the inputs used and assumptions made. Directors should satisfy themselves that these analyses were prepared on a fair and reasonable basis, that the valuation methodologies were appropriate, and that any customary methodologies that were not employed were discarded for good reason (and not simply because they contradicted a finding of fairness).

Fairness opinions take on a special significance in the context of "going private" transactions where a controlling party "squeezes out" the minority shareholders. The Schedule 13E-3 filing required by the federal securities laws in those situations calls for disclosure regarding both the selling directors' and the bidder's consideration regarding the fairness of the transaction to the minority shareholders.

A close cousin of the fairness opinion, a board of directors of a company that has received an unsolicited takeover proposal will sometimes ask their investment bankers to render an "inadequacy opinion" reflecting their view that the consideration offered is not fair. This too is not a legal requirement but can provide support for a board to reject an offer. Whether (and when) to request an inadequacy opinion is a tactical decision the board should make in consultation with its advisors.

Key Questions

When an investment banker presents its fairness opinion, generally accompanied by a presentation to the board, directors may consider the following key questions:

- ❑ What are the key valuation assumptions in the fairness analysis? Are these assumptions reasonable and appropriate? Have there been changes in these assumptions since the last time the board saw a version of the analysis?
- ❑ How were comparable companies and precedent transactions selected? Were there clear selection criteria and explanations for exceptions?
- ❑ How were the projections for the business prepared? How does it compare to the process for projections normally used to manage the business or used by management in seeking financing for a "going private" transaction? Are these projections reasonable?
- ❑ If the banker relied on management projections, did the banker modify any of these projections? For example, were they "normalized" or extended beyond management's original forecast?
- ❑ Do the projections reflect undue influence of a controlling shareholder or entrenched management?
- ❑ What discount rate and terminal multiple were used in the DCF analysis and why were they chosen? Were they reasonable assumptions and how sensitive is the fairness analysis to changes in these inputs?
- ❑ Did the banker rely on valuation tools and models that are accepted and generally used in applicable industry? If not, why not?

Additional Reading

1. Brown, Chip and Steve Whittington. "The Role of the Independent Financial Adviser in M&A Fairness Opinions." *Financial Adviser Insights* (Winter 2009), p. 64 http://www.willamette.com/insights/articles_practice/brown_role_of_indep endent_winter2009.pdf
2. Gottlieb, Mark S. "A Guide to Fairness Opinions." *MSG* (October 2014) http://www.msgcpa.com/forensicperspectives/a-guide-to-fairness-opinions

3. "SEC Approves New NASD Rule 2290 Regarding Fairness Opinions," *FINRA* (December 8, 2007)
https://www.finra.org/sites/default/files/NoticeDocument/p037445.pdf
4. "Takeover Law and Practice" (2016), *Wachtell, Lipton, Rosen & Katz*, Chapter III, Section C: "Investment Bankers and Fairness Opinions"
http://www.wlrk.com/files/2016/TakeoverLawandPracticeGuide.pdf

Notes

SECTION ELEVEN

TRANSACTIONS IN COMPANY SECURITIES

11.1 STOCK BUY-BACK PROGRAMS

CONTRIBUTED BY
Katherine J. Blair
Manatt, Phelps & Phillips, LLP[1]

A public company may repurchase its publicly traded stock in the open market. A company may have several reasons to buy back its stock, such as the stock is perceived to be undervalued in the market, the company wants to return excess capital to its shareholders, the company may wish to show confidence in its business and prospects, or the company may be facing pressure from activist shareholders to do so.

A stock buy-back program should be approved by the company's board of directors, with the approval determining a maximum amount of shares (either by number or dollar amount) that may be repurchased, the price at which shares may be repurchased (a market price or set price), and whether the program has a specific duration. Repurchased shares may be held as treasury stock or canceled by action of the company's board, with the former being the norm.

Stock buy-back programs present the risk of being used to manipulate the market in the company's stock. Rule 10b-18 of the Securities Exchange Act of 1934 (Exchange Act) provides companies with a nonexclusive safe-harbor to effect repurchases. If a

1. Katherine J. Blair is a partner in the Capital Markets group at Manatt, Phelps & Phillips, LLP, where she practices in the firm's Los Angeles office.

company satisfies the requirements of Rule 10b-18, then it will be "safe" from potential liability for market manipulation under Section 9(a)(2) and Rule 10b-5 under the Exchange Act.

For a stock repurchase to qualify for the protection of the Rule 10b-18 safe harbor, a company must generally satisfy four conditions:

1. *Manner of Purchase*. Purchases must be effected using a single broker or, if a broker is not used, with only one dealer, on any single day.
2. *Timing of Purchase.* The company's stock repurchase cannot be the opening purchase on a trading day, and purchases must be effected during either 10 or 30 minutes before the scheduled close of the trading session, with the specific deadline depending on the company's average daily trading volume (also known as ADTV) or public float.
3. *Price*. Purchases are only permitted at a price that does not exceed (i) the highest independent bid or (ii) the last independent transaction, whichever is higher, quoted, or reported in the consolidated system at the time the Rule 10b-18 purchase is effected.
4. *Volume.* Purchases on any single day must not exceed 25 percent of the ADTV for that security. As an alternative, a company may effect a "block" purchase if it occurs only once per week, no other Rule 10b-18 purchases are effected that day, and the block purchase is not included in future calculations of a security's ADTV.

Rule 10b-18 applies to issuers as well as "affiliated purchasers" who act, directly or indirectly, in concert with the issuer for the purpose of acquiring the issuer's securities.

Once a company implements a stock buy-back program, it is required to report in its Forms 10-Q and 10-K purchases made during the applicable quarter, disclosing for each month the number of shares purchased, the average price paid per share, and the maximum number of shares that may be purchased under the program.

In implementing a stock buy-back program, a company should also consider state corporation laws with respect to stock redemptions and director fiduciary duties, any contractual limitations (such as those found in credit agreements or indentures), and stock exchange continued listing requirements.

A company should be cautioned that Rule 10b-18 does not shield a company from insider trading liability under Rule 10b-5 or violation of Regulation M with respect to distribution of securities. To mitigate any Rule 10b-5 liability concerns, a company may use the affirmative defense of Rule 10b5-1 by conducting the program through a prearranged written formula plan. A company must also ensure that a stock buy-back program does not constitute an issuer tender offer, or a going private transaction, subject to Rule 13e-3 under the Exchange Act. These topics are discussed elsewhere in this Handbook.

Companies will generally announce the board's decision to approve a repurchase program by a press release at the time of their decision.

Key Questions

In considering a potential stock buy back, questions a board may wish to address include the following:

- ❑ What are the company's reasons for implementing a stock buy-back program? What are the other uses for the cash that management has considered? What are the pros and cons compared to a dividend?
- ❑ Is there a particular broker that may be contacted to assist the company in repurchasing shares of its stock?
- ❑ What procedures does the broker have in place to implement the company's buy-back program?
- ❑ What internal control procedures will the company implement to ensure compliance with Rule 10b-18?
- ❑ Is the company also in the process of distributing its securities or may do so in the near future?
- ❑ Will the company also use Rule 10b5-1 to mitigate insider trading liability, and, if so, how will this be accomplished?
- ❑ Is there any existing material; nonpublic information, such as merger negotiations; any activity or action that would be a material deviation from the results of operations, financial condition, or prospects of the company as currently presented; or any other material facts regarding the company that have not been disclosed to the public?
- ❑ Will the company continue to satisfy the continued listing requirements of its principal stock exchange?
- ❑ Does the company satisfy the redemption requirements of the corporation laws of its state of incorporation?
- ❑ Will the company issue a press release and file a Form 8-K in connection with the adoption of a stock buy-back program?
- ❑ If shareholder activism has played a role in bringing about the repurchase, what special communication efforts, if any, are appropriate?
- ❑ Does the company plan to make any block repurchased or participate in an accelerated repurchase program instead?
- ❑ How will the repurchase of the company's stock effect the percentage ownership of the company's existing shareholders?

Additional Reading

1. Rule 10b-18 of the Securities Exchange Act of 1934
   http://www.ecfr.gov/cgi-bin/text-idx?SID=8e0ed509ccc65e983f9eca72ceb26753&node=17:4.0.1.1.1&rgn=div5#se17.4.240_110b_618

2. SEC Division of Market Regulation: Answers to Frequently Asked Questions Concerning Rule 10b-18 ("Safe Harbor" for Issuer Repurchases)
https://www.sec.gov/divisions/marketreg/r10b18faq0504.htm
3. SEC Final Rule, Purchases of Certain Equity Securities by the Issuer and Others, Release No. 33-8335
https://www.sec.gov/rules/final/33-8335.htm
4. "Buybacks vs. Backlash: The Board's Role in Weighing the Pros and Cons of Stock Repurchases," EY Center for Board Matters, June 2016
http://ey.com/gl/en/issues/governance-and-reporting/ey-center-for-board-matters-buybacks-vs-backlash
5. "Buybacks and the Board: Director Perspectives on the Share Repurchase Revolution," The Investor Responsibility Research Center Institute, August 2016
http://irrcinstitute.org/wp-content/uploads/2016/08/FINAL-Buybacks-Report-Aug-22-2016.pdf

Notes

11.2 SELLING COMPANY SECURITIES TO THE PUBLIC

CONTRIBUTED BY
Anne C. Meyer
Georgeson LLC[1]

In connection with the public offering of securities, a company's board of directors must exercise adequate oversight and ensure, among other things, that the offering and related matters are properly authorized and that there are no material misstatements or omissions in the offering disclosure. The extent to which a company's board is directly involved in the offering process may vary depending upon several factors, including whether the company is a seasoned issuer and whether the offering and use of proceeds are part of a broader transaction, such as a material acquisition.

The board is typically responsible for approving a range of matters related to a public offering, including the following:

- The hiring of one or more investment banks to act as underwriters for the offering
- The offering, issuance, and sale of the securities to the public
- The use of proceeds

1. Anne C. Meyer is senior managing director, Corporate Governance, at Georgeson LLC and is based in the company's New York office.

- The form and content of the registration statement and prospectus as well as any registration of the securities under the '34 Act
- The terms of the securities, including (i) for common stock, the number of shares to be sold and the price to the public; and (ii) for debt, terms such as the aggregate principal amount, the coupon or interest rate, restrictive covenants, and redemption features
- Listing of the securities on a stock exchange, if applicable
- The entry into and terms of the underwriting agreement (including the price at which the securities will be sold to the underwriters) and other material agreements in connection with the public offering (including, for debt offerings, one or more indentures)

The board may determine to delegate some of its responsibilities to a "pricing committee" or other committee of the board (which may, in some cases, include executive officers) that has the ability to meet and take action more quickly than the entire board. In addition, the board's resolutions will frequently authorize identified "authorized officers" to take broad actions with respect to the offering, outside of the material action items reserved to the board.

When a company sells securities to the public, directors have certain responsibilities and potential liabilities pursuant to the Securities Act and the Exchange Act. Under Sections 11 and 12 of the Securities Act and Rule 10b-5 under the Exchange Act, a person who has acquired securities pursuant to a registration statement that contained a material misstatement or omission may sue (among others), the issuer, directors of the issuer (whether or not such directors sign the registration statement), and officers of the issuer who sign the registration statement. Under Sections 11 and 12 of the Securities Act, the issuer itself is strictly liable for any material misstatement in or omission from a registration statement. In contrast, other parties, including directors and officers, can generally assert a "due diligence" defense if he or she can establish that, after reasonable investigation, he or she reasonably believed that the statement was true or that there was no omission. A director or officer may also avoid liability if he or she can prove he or she had no reasonable ground to believe, and did not believe, that there was a material misstatement or omission contained in a part of the registration statement that has been certified by an expert or made on the authority of an expert, such as the audited financial statements. In view of the potential liability that the company and directors face in connection with a public offering of securities, a director should be prepared to establish that he or she has made a reasonable effort to determine the accuracy and completeness of the registration statement.

In addition to compliance with federal securities laws, the laws of the company's state of incorporation as well as the company's charter and bylaws and other corporate governance policies and procedures may contain terms that are relevant to the offering process.

Key Questions

When a company is undertaking a public offering of securities, key questions that a board member might ask include the following:

- ❑ Given the company's capital structure and strategic goals, what type of securities should be offered—debt or equity? Is the targeted amount of proceeds appropriate?
- ❑ Does the underwriting team have the industry knowledge and market insight necessary to run a successful offering process?
- ❑ Did the board make all necessary approvals in connection with the offering and sale of securities?
- ❑ Is there any material nonpublic information, such as a proposed significant transaction, that the company would be compelled to disclose in connection with the offering before it would otherwise be required to do so?
- ❑ Does the board believe there was a robust due diligence process in connection with the offering and preparation of the registration statement?
- ❑ Did the board have adequate time to review the registration statement and prospectus and ask any questions of management and outside advisors?
- ❑ Is the director comfortable that (i) the registration statement is accurate in all material respects, (ii) information in the registration statement is not presented in such a way that would be likely to mislead a potential purchaser of the company's securities, and (iii) that there are no material omissions from the registration statement.
- ❑ Were the appropriate members of senior management and other employees involved in the process of preparing and vetting the company's disclosure?
- ❑ Is the new offering impacted by any terms of the company's constituent documents? For example, is there a class of securities that has preemptive rights or approval rights? Are there enough authorized shares to complete the offering and have sufficient capital flexibility on a pro forma basis?
- ❑ Is the new offering impacted by any terms of the company's outstanding securities? For example, are there covenants associated with outstanding debt that limit the amount or type of securities that may be offered or limit the use of proceeds of any offering?
- ❑ Were there any issues raised by the accountants in connection with reviewing the financial information contained or incorporated by reference in the registration statement? If so, were they properly addressed by the audit committee?

Additional Reading

1. ABA Business Law Section, Committee on Corporate Laws, *Corporate Director's Guidebook*, 5th ed.
2. Johnson, McLaughlin & Haueter, *Corporate Finance and The Securities Laws*, Copyright (2015)

Notes

13 BOARD AND MANAGEMENT STOCK OWNERSHIP GUIDELINES

CONTRIBUTED BY
Katherine J. Blair and Darren Kerstien
Manatt, Phelps & Phillips, LLP[1]

The implementation of stock ownership guidelines has risen significantly in recent years. The guidelines typically set forth stock ownership requirements for executive officers and directors, provide a timeframe for compliance, and provide possible penalties for noncompliance. Stock ownership guidelines are being adopted, at least partially, in response to the focus by institutional investors and proxy advisors on more closely aligning the interests of executives and directors with those of shareholders. Supporters of stock ownership guidelines also argue that the guidelines

- encourage company management to act like owners in its decision-making;
- produce a long-term perspective among management regarding value creation; and
- minimize unwise decisions and inappropriate risks driven by a short-term focus on quarterly results and stock price.

1. Katherine J. Blair is a partner in the Capital Markets group at Manatt, Phelps & Phillips, LLP, where she practices in the firm's Los Angeles office. Darren Kerstien is an associate in the Corporate and Finance group, where he practices in the firm's Orange County office.

Not Required . . . But Encouraged

Stock ownership guidelines are not specifically required by any federal or state law, or any stock exchange rule. However, executive officer and director stock ownership is highly encouraged by certain constituencies of the company. In its Rules of Corporate Responsibility, the New York Stock Exchange (NYSE) notes that many shareholders feel that directors and officers should have a meaningful investment in the companies they manage.

Institutional investors and shareholder proxy advisory firms, such as Institutional Shareholder Services (ISS), may also take into account in their voting policies the presence or absence of "robust" stock ownership guidelines and their terms with respect to voting on compensation matters and shareholder proposals. In reviewing compensation-related proposals, shareholder proxy advisory firms may take into account stock ownership factors, including the following:

- The time period required to retain shares
- Post-termination holding requirement policies
- The percentage of shares required to be retained
- The robustness of the company's equity retention, holding period, and/or stock ownership requirements
- Executives' actual stock ownership and the degree to which it meets or exceeds a stockholder proponent's suggested holding period/retention ratio or the company's existing requirements

In its Policies on Corporate Governance, the Council of Institutional Investors (CII) states that executives and directors should own, after a reasonable period of time, a meaningful position in the company's common stock. Executives should be required to own stock—excluding unexercised options and unvested stock awards—equal to a multiple of salary.

Participants

In most cases, stock ownership guidelines apply to executive officers and nonemployee directors of the company. Virtually all companies apply the stock ownership guidelines to the chief executive officer, the chief financial officer, and the next three most highly paid executive officers (named executive officers or NEOs). Some companies also include other senior executives (such as Section 16 reporting officers).

Stock Ownership Requirements

Stock ownership guidelines vary widely among companies. They may suggest or require that officers and directors own a certain amount or percentage of the company's stock, which may differ based on their respective positions and compensation. Companies typically allow directors and newly hired or promoted executives a period of time to comply with the ownership requirements, which may range from months to five years or more.

Officers. For executive officers, the amount is usually based on a multiple of salary, with different multiples for different executives. Almost universally, the multiple for the chief executive officer is higher than other officers. Multiples may range from 1x to 10x or higher for large companies. Other metrics used include a fixed number of shares, a specific dollar value of shares, or the lesser of a dollar value and specific number.

Directors. For nonemployee directors, companies stock ownership requirements are usually based on a multiple of their annual cash retainer. For example, ISS currently favors a minimum of three times the annual cash retainer for nonemployee directors.

Shares Counted

Although not always included, guidelines may specify the types of equity interests that qualify toward the ownership requirements. Unrestricted stock owned outright by the executive or director (e.g., purchased in the open market) always counts toward the required stock ownership level. Shares owned indirectly, such as through family members, trusts, entities, and company retirement benefit plans (e.g., 401(k) plans), may also count toward meeting the stock ownership requirement. Restricted stock awards and restricted stock units may only count with respect to the after-tax value of shares since shares can be sold to pay income taxes on the vesting date. Although some companies do not count shares underlying the company's stock options, if option shares are counted then the company may further specify whether it will only count vested options, vested and in-the-money options, or all options. Like most governance polices, the type of ownership that satisfies the company's ownership requirement can depend on the company, its industry, and its size.

Retention Requirements

Some companies also implement retention requirements in connection with equity awards. A retention requirement means that the officer or director must retain a certain percentage of shares in connection with the exercise or vesting of an equity award. It may also require that the shares be held for a certain period, such as 12 months, after such exercise or vesting. In most cases, a company will have retention requirements until such time as the officer or director has satisfied the required stock ownership level.

Enforcement

Enforcement of the guidelines is an ongoing issue because companies generally do not impose penalties on executives or directors for noncompliance. When utilized, possible penalties may include prohibiting sales of stock, requiring future compensation typically paid in cash to be paid in stock, reducing or eliminating future awards, reducing aggregate compensation, and adverse employment action. More commonly, if required levels have not been met within the given timeframe, companies may impose stock holding or retention requirements.

Disclosure

When a company adopts stock ownership guidelines, it needs to also consider disclosure of the guidelines. Although not required, many companies post their guidelines on the investor relations and/or corporate governance sections of their websites. Form 8-K does not require disclosure at the time of adoption of stock ownership guidelines but it may be reported under Item 8.01—Other Events. It can also be noted in connection with reporting an insider entering into a 10b5-1 plan for the purchase of stock. (See Chapter 11.7, Basics about 10b5-1 Plans.)

The company's proxy statement is usually the most common place for a discussion of the company's stock ownership guidelines. The Compensation Discussion and Analysis in the proxy statement can discuss the ownership requirements and any retention periods in connection with the company compensation policies. Stock ownership guidelines may also be discussed under Director Compensation in the proxy statement.

Key Questions

In considering whether to adopt and how to configure stock ownership guidelines, issues to consider include the following:

- ❑ Are there compelling reasons to adopt stock ownership guidelines?
- ❑ Which executives should be covered?
- ❑ What ownership levels are appropriate? Should there be different levels for different types of executives?
- ❑ What types of equity interests should count toward meeting ownership requirements? Should there be a distinction between restricted stock and stock options?
- ❑ Should stock ownership by affiliates or holdings by family members count toward meeting ownership requirements? Should ownership through company 401(k) or employee stock purchase plans count?
- ❑ What should be the time period for compliance after adoption of guidelines and after a new hire or promotion?
- ❑ How and when are these guidelines communicated to new hires or board members?
- ❑ Who will be charged with implementation and oversight of the guidelines? Does the company have a compensation committee?
- ❑ What are the implications of noncompliance with the guidelines?
- ❑ Will exceptions to compliance be made? Under what circumstances and by whom?
- ❑ How often are the guidelines reviewed? When were they last reviewed and what were the results?
- ❑ When and how often will the stock ownership of the covered individuals be reviewed?
- ❑ Is disclosure of the guidelines required? Should the company highlight the guidelines in investor relations materials?

Additional Reading

1. Center on Executive Compensation, Stock Ownership Guidelines
http://www.execcomp.org/Issues/Issue/corporate-governance/stock-ownership-guidelines

2. Equilar, Executive Stock Ownership Guidelines (March 9, 2016)
http://www.equilar.com/reports/34-executive-stock-ownership-guidelines.html
3. Stock Ownership Guidelines, Compensation Committee Handbook, Meridian Compensation Partners, LLC
http://www.meridiancp.com/images/uploads/31_Stock_Ownership_Guidelines.pdf
4. National Association of Stock Plan Professional, A New Reach for Stock Ownership Guidelines? (February 20, 2014)
http://www.naspp.com/blog/2014/02/over-the-past-5-years.html
5. Bowie, Michael. Executive Compensation Bulletin: A New analysis reveals moderate increases in *Fortune* 500 outside director pay, *Willis Towers Watson* (July 19, 2016)
https://www.towerswatson.com/en/Insights/Newsletters/Global/executive-pay-matters/2016/Executive-Compensation-Bulletin-New-analysis-moderate-increases-Fortune500-director-pay
6. 2016 Americas Policy Updates at Hold Equity Past Retirement or for a Significant Period of Time, https://www.issgovernance.com/policy-gateway/2016-policy-information/, and voting polices at www.issgovernance.com
7. CII Policies on Corporate Governance, Section 5.15 Stock Ownership
http://www.cii.org/corp_gov_policies#exec_comp
8. ISS 2016 U.S. Summary Proxy Voting Guidelines, Director Compensation—Equity Plans for Non-Employee Directors
https://www.issgovernance.com/file/policy/2016-us-summary-voting-guidelines-23-feb-2016.pdf.

Notes

14 THE SEC'S BENEFICIAL OWNERSHIP REPORTING REGIME

CONTRIBUTED BY
Katherine J. Blair
Manatt, Phelps & Phillips, LLP[1]

Officers, directors, and certain stockholders of public companies with securities registered under Section 12 of the Securities Exchange Act of 1934, as amended (Exchange Act), are subject to a number of reporting requirements designed to, among other things, give the investing public information regarding their holdings and trading activity. These reporting requirements are based on the SEC's definition of "beneficial ownership" and primarily include the following:

- *Table of Security Ownership:* This table is included in registration statements, proxy statements, and Form 10-K annual reports.
- *Section 16: Forms 3, 4 and 5:* These forms report ownership of and changes in beneficial ownership of officers, directors, and principal stockholders (persons who own more than 10 percent of a class of security).
- *Schedules 13D and 13G:* These filings are made by stockholders who beneficially own more than 5 percent of a company's securities.

1. Katherine J. Blair is a partner in the Capital Markets Group at Manatt, Phelps & Phillips, LLP, where she practices in the firm's Los Angeles office.

Beneficial Ownership

The determination of beneficial ownership is based on Rule 13d-3 of the Exchange Act. A person is considered the beneficial owner of any securities over which the person, directly or indirectly, through any contract, arrangement, understanding, relationship or otherwise, has or shares (i) *voting power*, which includes the power to vote or direct the voting of a security, or (ii) *investment power*, which includes the power to dispose of, or direct the disposition of, a security. It is not required that a person have *both* voting and investment power; either attribute alone is sufficient for beneficial ownership.

Indirect beneficial ownership may be based on relationships, such as shares held through family members, corporations, partnerships, limited liability companies, trusts, and other entities. A person also may be deemed to be a beneficial owner of securities if that person has the right to *acquire beneficial ownership of shares within 60 days*. This includes options, warrants, convertible notes, a power to revoke a trust, discretionary account, or similar arrangement. For example, a person is deemed to own beneficially a company's common stock if the person owns a presently exercisable option to purchase common stock or owns an option to purchase common stock that will become exercisable within 60 days.

Beneficial ownership may be acquired either individually or as a group. If two or more persons agree to act together to acquire, dispose of, or vote shares, a group is considered to have acquired the shares of each member thereof as of the date of that agreement. The share ownership of group members is aggregated in applying the test of beneficial ownership.

The SEC rules discourage arrangements to avoid beneficial ownership and specifically provide that a person who, directly or indirectly, creates or uses a trust, proxy, power of attorney, pooling arrangement, or any other contract, arrangement, or device with the purpose or effect of divesting such person of beneficial ownership as part of a plan or scheme to evade the reporting requirements, will be deemed to be the beneficial owner of such security.

Determination of beneficial ownership often requires an in-depth analysis and should be made on a case-by-case basis with the assistance of securities counsel.

Table of Security Ownership

The Table of Security Ownership of Certain Beneficial Owners and Management provides a snap shot of the beneficial ownership of a company's securities of its named executive officers (those officers who are listed in the executive compensation tables), directors, current officers and directors as a group, and stockholders owning more than 5 percent of the outstanding securities.

Pursuant to the disclosure requirements set forth in Item 403 of Regulation S-K, the table must include the number and percentage of securities beneficially owned as of the most recent practicable date. Based on the determination of "beneficial ownership," as discussed above, if a security holder also has the right to acquire beneficial ownership of shares within 60 days, such as an option, warrant, or convertible note, then the shares underlying the convertible security are also included in such person's beneficial ownership. For example, shares underlying currently exercisable stock options will be included in a stockholder's beneficial ownership as well as shares underlying options that may vest within 60 days. Plus, the percentage ownership must also be calculated to include those underlying shares. In calculating the percentage ownership for each person, the denominator will consist of all shares outstanding, plus shares underlying currently exercisable options and those options exercisable within 60 days, but only with respect to options held by that person as opposed to all outstanding options.

The table needs to disclose whether the holder possesses shared or sole voting power or investment power over the securities and the name and address of each holder (officers and directors typically use the company's address). The rules encourage the use of footnotes disclosing the securities for which the holder has the right to acquire. Information about 5 percent holders can be obtained from Schedule 13D and 13G filings (discussed below) and the company may disclose the source and date of such information. Companies are deemed to have knowledge of any Schedule 13Ds and 13Gs filed with the SEC.

Section 16(a): Forms 3, 4, and 5—Pecuniary Interest

Under Section 16(a) and Rules 16a-1 through 16a-13 of the Exchange Act, persons who are insiders of a company are required to report transactions in the company's securities on Forms 3, 4, and 5. Insiders are officers, directors, and beneficial owners of more than 10 percent of the securities of the company. Companies are also required to post the Section 16 reports on their websites by the end of the business day following the filing. An officer is an issuer's president, principal financial officer or principal accounting officer (or controller when there is no principal accounting officer), any vice president of the issuer in charge of a principal business unit, division or function (such as sales, administration or finance), any other officer who performs a policy-making function, or any other person who performs similar policy-making functions for the issuer. In addition, officers of an issuer's parent or subsidiaries will be deemed officers of the issuer if they perform policy-making functions for the issuer. See Rule 3b-7 of the Exchange Act.

Once beneficial ownership is determined, officers, directors, and beneficial owners of more than 10 percent of the company's shares need only report holdings and transactions in shares in which they have a "pecuniary interest." *Pecuniary interest* means the opportunity, directly or indirectly, to profit or share in any profit derived from a transaction in the subject securities. In general, an indirect pecuniary interest would include (i) an interest in securities held by members of a person's immediate family sharing the same household, (ii) a general partner's proportionate interest in the portfolio securities held by a general or limited partnership, (iii) a person's right to dividends that is separated or separable from the underlying securities, (iv) a person's interest in securities held by a trust, and (v) a person's right to acquire common stock upon the exercise or conversion of a derivative security, whether or not presently exercisable.

A Form 3 is an initial report filed upon becoming an insider and is due within 10 days. A Form 4 or Form 5 reports changes in beneficial ownership. A Form 4 reports transactions such as sales, purchases, equity grants, and exercises and is due within two business days following a transaction. A Form 5 is filed 45 days after the end of the company's fiscal year and may report certain transactions exempt from Section 16(b) (e.g., gifts—if they were not voluntarily reported on a Form 4) and transactions that were not previously reported on Form 4 but should have been. All insiders are personally responsible for ensuring that they comply with the reporting requirements of Section 16.

Proper Section 16 reporting is important because SEC rules require companies to disclose in proxy statements, information statements, and Form 10-K annual reports information regarding delinquent Section 16 filings, including the name of each insider involved and the number of delinquent filings for each insider.

Schedules 13D and 13G—5 Percent Stockholders

Security holders that beneficially own more than 5 percent of any registered class of a company's equity securities, either individually or as a group, are subject to special reporting and disclosure requirements under Section 13 and Regulation 13G-D (specifically, Rule 13d-1 through 13d-7) of the Exchange Act, which is commonly referred to as the Williams Act. Such owners are required to make certain disclosures by filing with the SEC either a Schedule 13D or Schedule 13G. Beneficial ownership for purposes of Schedule 13D and 13G filings is determined based on Rule 13d-3, as previously discussed. Plus, if a group of persons is deemed to beneficially own securities, then each member of the group must file either a Schedule 13D or Schedule 13G. A person may disclaim beneficial ownership in a Schedule 13D or 13G filing if there is a bona fide basis that a doubt exists as a matter of law with respect to beneficial ownership, but the sole purpose to disclaim beneficial ownership cannot be to avoid disclosure.

A long-form Schedule 13D is the default form that is required to be filed unless the security holder is qualified to file on a short-form Schedule 13G as a passive investor (an investor who has no intent to acquire or influence control of the company) or a qualified institutional investor based on an enumerated list (set forth in Rule 13d-1). Both Schedule 13D and Schedule 13G require disclosure of the identity and background of the reporting person or group, the class of equity securities, and beneficial ownership; however, the disclosures required under the short-form Schedule 13G are less extensive than those required under Schedule 13D. Schedule 13D requires certain additional information concerning the source and amount of funds used to acquire the securities, the purpose for which the securities were acquired, and any agreements between the person making the filing and the company or otherwise relating to the shares owned. Depending on circumstances, Schedule 13G eligibility may be lost by an investor, in which case a Schedule 13D would be required. For example, a passive investor whose beneficial ownership exceeds 20 percent of the company's securities would be required to file on a Schedule 13D.

Schedule 13D must be filed within 10 days of a triggering acquisition. Amendments must be promptly filed to reflect changes in beneficial ownership of one percent or more or other material changes in previously reported facts. Schedule 13G must be filed either within 45 days after the end of the calendar year in which registration under the Exchange Act becomes effective (e.g., an IPO) or within 10 days following a triggering acquisition. Amendments to Schedule 13G must be filed within 45 days after the end of each succeeding year to reflect any changes as of the most recent year end.

Key Questions

When reviewing the beneficial ownership reporting, questions to address include the following:

- ❑ Do questionnaires distributed to officers and directors seek information about beneficial ownership of the company's securities?
- ❑ Has each officer and director of the company provided the number of shares over which they possess voting or investment power?
- ❑ Is voting or investment power shared with anyone else, and if so, who?
- ❑ Has the company reviewed and checked its security ownership records against Form 4 and 5 filings?
- ❑ Does the company need to contact any departed named executive officer to obtain beneficial ownership information for the Form 10-K or proxy statement?
- ❑ Do the company's officers and directors hold any securities convertible into or exercisable for the company's equity securities, such as options, warrants, or notes? If so, what are the vesting periods for any convertible securities?
- ❑ Do officers and directors indirectly hold securities, such as through a family member, an entity, or trust, and, if so, does the company have information about how the securities are held?
- ❑ Is the company aware of any contracts, understandings, or arrangements with respect to the voting or investment of the company's equity securities?
- ❑ Has the company implemented procedures to ensure that its officers and directors file their required Form 3, 4, and 5 filings?
- ❑ Are any security holdings reported differently on Form 3, 4, or 5 filings by any officers or directors based on pecuniary interest?
- ❑ Has the company reviewed all Schedule 13D and 13G filings made with the SEC?
- ❑ Does the company know or have reason to believe any information provided on Schedule 13D or 13G is not complete or accurate or that a statement or amendment should have been filed and was not?

Additional Reading

1. Regulation 13D-G of the Exchange Act of 1934, as amended
   http://www.ecfr.gov/cgi-bin/text-idx?node=pt17.4.240&rgn=div5#sg17.4.240_113b2_62.sg29

2. Regulation S-K, Item 403, Security Ownership of Certain Beneficial Owners and Management
   http://www.ecfr.gov/cgi-bin/text-idx?SID=8e0ed509ccc65e983f9eca72ceb26753&node=17:3.0.1.1.11&rgn=div5#se17.3.229_1403

3. Schedule 13D
   http://www.ecfr.gov/cgi-bin/text-idx?node=pt17.4.240&rgn=div5#se17.4.240_113d_6101
4. SEC Fast Answers: Schedule 13D
   https://www.sec.gov/answers/sched13.htm
5. Schedule 13G
   http://www.ecfr.gov/cgi-bin/text-idx?node=pt17.4.240&rgn=div5#se17.4.240_113d_6102
6. SEC Compliance and Disclosure Interpretations: Exchange Act Sections 13(d) and 13(g) and Regulation 13D-G Beneficial Ownership Reporting
   https://www.sec.gov/divisions/corpfin/guidance/reg13d-interp.htm
7. SEC Fast Answers, Forms 3, 4, 5
   https://www.sec.gov/answers/form345.htm

Notes

11.5 INSIDER TRADING POLICIES AND PROTECTIONS

CONTRIBUTED BY
Anne C. Meyer
Georgeson LLC[1]

Insider trading law has been developed by the courts on a case-by-case basis under the antifraud provisions of Section 10(b) of the Exchange Act and Rule 10b-5 thereunder. As a result, the standards are not always entirely clear, and application of those standards to a particular factual situation can be complex. Illegal insider trading generally refers to the purchase or sale of a security, on the basis of material nonpublic information, in breach of a duty of trust or confidence owed, directly or indirectly, to the issuer, its shareholders, or any other person (e.g., the trader's employer) who is the source of the material nonpublic information.

There are two established theories of insider trading: (i) the "classic" theory, in which a corporate insider, such as an officer or director, trades in an issuer's securities on the basis of material, nonpublic information; and (ii) the "misappropriation" theory, in which a corporate "outsider" trades on the basis of confidential information in breach of a fiduciary duty owed to the source of the information. Insider trading violations may include

1. Anne C. Meyer is senior managing director, Corporate Governance, at Georgeson LLC and is based in the company's New York office.

sharing information, or "tipping," trading by the person "tipped," and trading by others who misappropriate such information.

Illegal insider trading is a focus of enforcement activity by the SEC and the U.S. Department of Justice. Potential penalties for an insider trading violation under federal securities laws include imprisonment, criminal fines, and civil penalties. If a company fails to take appropriate steps to prevent illegal insider trading, the company may have "control person" liability for trading violations, and civil penalties can extend personal liability to a company's directors, officers, and other supervisory personnel if they fail to take appropriate steps to prevent insider trading.

Corporate insiders may, of course, also engage in *legal* insider trading. For example, a director may purchase shares on the open market to satisfy a mandated director stock ownership requirement or an executive may sell shares received pursuant to an incentive or compensation plan in order to diversify his or her personal assets. The SEC requires disclosure of legal insider trading in company securities by directors, officers, and other Section 16 insiders on Forms 3, 4, or 5. Doing so at a time when the director has no knowledge of material nonpublic information presents no legal issues.

Members of a company's board of directors are insiders who have access to material nonpublic information with respect to the company and, potentially, other organizations with which the company does business. Directors should ensure that all of their personal transactions in securities conform to federal securities laws and avoid even the appearance of impropriety. In addition, in exercising their fiduciary duties, directors should ensure that the company has appropriate policies and procedures in place to minimize the risks of insider trading by company directors, officers, employees, and other relevant parties. Allegations of insider trading can quickly and irreparably harm an individual's or a company's reputation for integrity and high ethical standards. At times, a determination of whether a director can permissibly trade will not be straightforward. In such cases, legal advice should be sought (often from the company's general counsel). Given the legal and reputational stakes, "close cases" should normally be resolved in favor of the more conservative course of action.

Company insider trading policies are not currently required under federal securities laws or U.S. stock exchange listing standards. However, companies frequently adopt written insider trading policies and procedures to help prevent and detect unlawful trading. Insider trading policies should be tailored to a company's specific circumstances, including the nature of its business, number of employees, management structure and culture, trading market for securities, and safeguards for material nonpublic information. In addition, many companies implement related controls, such as quarterly blackout periods or trading windows related to the company's financial reporting cycle and special blackout periods which limit trading in company securities at times when insiders and designated outsiders are likely to be in possession of material nonpublic information. The existence of an effective insider-trading program can provide the company with a good faith defense against control person liability for the actions of employees.

Key Questions

When considering the form and scope of a company's insider trading policies and protections, key questions that a board member might ask include the following:

- ❑ Does the company have a written insider trading policy? If not, should the company adopt one?
- ❑ Who should be covered by the company's insider trading policy? In addition to directors, officers, and employees, are there consultants, advisors, or other "temporary insiders" who should be subject to the policy?
- ❑ Should the company's insider trading policies and procedures cover potentially problematic transactions, such as short positions, hedging transactions, collars, and margin accounts? If so, should these transactions be prohibited or subject to pre-clearance?
- ❑ Does the company have effective mandatory pre-clearance procedures for trading in the company's securities? If not the general counsel, who should be responsible for pre-clearing trades? Are the correct people subject to pre-clearance procedures?
- ❑ Does the company have an effective quarterly trading window or blackout period? Does the company put appropriate blackout periods in place when material circumstances exist, such as potential M&A activity or a significant enforcement situation, that heighten the risk associated with inside information? How are these trading periods communicated to applicable parties?
- ❑ Do the company's policies and procedures adequately cover the use of social media?
- ❑ Does the company effectively monitor and support Section 16 reporting by the company's directors and officers? Has the director, in his or her capacity as a director, reported all relevant transactions in accordance with the company's policies and procedures and made all required filings with the SEC?
- ❑ Does the company encourage or require the use of 10b5-1 plans by officers and directors? If not, should it do so? If so, how does the company monitor entry into, amendment, or termination of 10b5-1 plans?
- ❑ Are directors, officers, and employees adequately educated and trained with respect to insider trading? Are the complicated legal concepts explained in a clear manner?
- ❑ Is quarterly or annual certification of compliance with the company's insider trading policies and procedures required? If not, should it be?
- ❑ How will my proposed trade look "in 20-20 hindsight"?

Additional Reading

1. SEC's Guide to Insider Trading, Online Publication of the SEC https://www.sec.gov/answers/insider.htm
2. ABA Business Law Section, Committee on Corporate Laws. *Corporate Director's Guidebook*, 5th ed.

3. Insider Trading Policies Handbook, Publication of TheCorporateCounsel.net, Copyright (2016)
4. Best Practices for Drafting Insider Trading Policies, Publication of Law360, Copyright (2015)
http://www.law360.com/articles/674725/best-practices-for-drafting-insider-trading-policies

Notes

11.6 "SHORT-SWING" TRADING

CONTRIBUTED BY
Katherine J. Blair
Manatt, Phelps & Phillips, LLP[1]

Officers, directors, and beneficial owners of more than 10 percent (also known as "reporting persons") of a company's equity securities registered under the Exchange Act of 1934, as amended (Exchange Act), are subject to special rules concerning "short-swing" trading. In general, Section 16(b) of the Exchange Act provides that if any reporting person realizes a profit on a purchase and subsequent sale, or a sale and subsequent purchase (also referred to as "opposite-way transactions"), of any class of equity securities of the company (other than an exempted security or transaction) or a security-based swap agreement involving any such equity security *within a six-month period*, they must return (i.e., disgorge) to the company the statutory profit (also known as "short-swing profits").

Under Section 16(b), any profit realized by a reporting person from nonexempt opposite-way transactions within a period of less than six months is recoverable by the company or by a stockholder in an action on behalf of the company. Many law firms actively monitor public filings on behalf of stockholders and will contact companies when they identify a potential short-swing trading profit.

1. Katherine J. Blair is a partner in the Capital Markets group at Manatt, Phelps & Phillips, LLP, where she practices in the firm's Los Angeles office.

Strict Liability

Section 16(b) imposes strict liability to reporting persons. No misuse or even possession of insider information need be shown. The lack of possession of undisclosed information is not a defense to the recovery of these statutory profits. A reporting person's good faith, inadvertence, or misunderstanding of the law is not relevant. Plus, the company cannot look the other way when faced with a violation, even if the violation was unintended and did not harm the company or its stockholders. Any acquisition or disposition is required to be "matched" against any opposite way disposition or acquisition within the preceding or following six months.

General Rule

The general rule governing opposite-way transactions, unless otherwise exempt (see further on for a discussion of exemptions) for Section 16(b) short swing-profits is

- a voluntary (i.e., discretionary transactions)
- change in beneficial ownership (i.e., a purchase or sale)
- by the beneficial owner
- for value
- within a six-month period.

Reporting persons should be mindful that for Section 16(b) purposes, the extent to which a transaction is voluntary need not be great and depends on the facts and circumstances of each case. Any transaction where the security holder was not the beneficial owner of the securities both at the time of the purchase and sale, or the sale and purchase, is not subject to Section 16(b) short-swing profit liability.

Recovery by Company or on Behalf of Company

The party entitled to recover short-swing profits under Section 16(b) is the company—not an enforcing stockholder. However, if the company fails to bring a suit against a reporting person within 60 days after demand by a security holder of the company to do so or fails to prosecute the suit diligently, suit may be brought on behalf of the company by the security holder.

Some lawyers actively review computerized databases of all Form 3, 4, and 5 filings in search of finding matching transactions that result in Section 16 liability. If a potential short-swing profit is discovered, a lawyer will write the company on behalf of its security holders to bring suit seeking to recover the profits for the company. Plus, the lawyers may be able to collect attorneys' fees from the company if they are successful in recovering the profits from the insider.

Measuring the Six-Month Period

The accepted method to calculate the six-month period for determining short-swing profits is measured from the date of the first transaction to the *second day* before the date in the sixth month period that corresponds numerically with the date of the month in which the first transaction occurred. The second preceding day is the last day during the six-month period for which profits are recoverable. For example,

February 1	Date on which first transaction occurs
August 1	Six months later
July 30	The second day preceding the last day in the six-month period

Based on this example, any profits realized starting on and after July 31 are outside of the scope of the Section 16(b) six-month period and are not recoverable.

The date of a sale or purchase through a broker is the date on which the broker executes the transaction.

Measuring Short Swing Profit: Lowest In, Highest Out

For a single opposite-way transaction, the profit recoverable equals the aggregate sale price minus the aggregate purchase price.

To compute statutory short-swing profits for multiple transactions, the highest sale price and lowest purchase price during the six-month period are matched, regardless of whether the sale and purchase involved the same shares and regardless of the order in which they occurred. All securities are fungible for purposes of measuring profit under Section 16(b) but only each transaction may be matched once. Any sales and any purchases within a given six-month period will be matched, and the highest price received in any sale will be matched with the lowest price paid in any purchase. The aggregate differences are then totaled to determine "profit realized" in the series of transactions.

Recovery of short-swing trading profits under Section 16(b) can actually exceed an insider's actual profit, and it is possible to recover profits even if a reporting person loses money on the transactions.

Sales and purchases of different types of equity securities of the company, for example, shares and options exercisable for shares, can be matched for determining short-swing profits. For example, purchases or sales of the corporation's Series A preferred stock would not be matched with sales or purchases of the corporation's common stock or Series B preferred stock, but purchases or sales of the corporation's Series B preferred stock (which is convertible into common stock) would be matched with sales or purchases of the corporation's common stock.

Plus, matching occurs between any securities beneficially owned, even if not owned in the same capacity. For example, a sale as a trustee for a director's minor children or by a child sharing the director's home may be matched against a purchase by the director as an individual or by the director's spouse.

Exempt Transactions

Certain transactions are exempt from short-swing liability and so are not deemed purchases or sales under Section 16(b). Rules 16b-1 through 16b-8 under the Exchange Act provide a list of exempt transactions, some of which are discussed next.

Derivative Securities (Rule 16b-6). Generally, establishment of a derivative, such as a put or call equivalent or an option, is deemed a purchase or sale of the underlying security. Most exercises or conversions of derivative securities are exempt transactions not subject to matching under Section 16(b). In addition, an exercise of in-the-money (as opposed to out-of-the-money or priced above the market price options) long call option (referred to as a "call equivalent position" and is a right to acquire equity securities) is exempt from Section 16 and will not constitute a purchase of the underlying security. Rule 16b-6 provides other circumstances under which a transaction in a derivative security may be exempt.

Transactions with the Issuer; Equity Awards (Rule 16b-3(d)). This exemption is relied upon the most by companies and officers and directors. A transaction between a company and an officer or director of the company is exempt if certain conditions under the rule are satisfied. For example, acquisitions of stock from the company, including equity and option awards, are exempt from Section 16(b) if

- the transaction is approved in advance by the board of directors or a committee of the board composed solely of two or more non-employee directors;
- the transaction is approved or ratified by a majority of the issuer's shareholders at a meeting or by written consent; or
- the securities (or underlying securities in the case of a derivative security, such as an option) are held for six months since acquisition.

Qualified Plans (Rule 16b-3(c)). Transactions pursuant to a qualified plan (such as a 401(k) plan or a Section 423 qualified employee stock purchase plan) are generally exempt from Section 16(b), unless they are discretionary transactions (at the volition of the participant) in which case, they are not exempt.

Dispositions to the Issuer (Rule 16b-3(e)). Transactions (other than discretionary transactions) involving the disposition to the issuer of its equity securities are exempt if the transaction is approved in advance by the board of directors or a committee of the board composed solely of two or more nonemployee directors, or the transaction is approved in advance by a majority of the issuer's shareholders at a meeting or by written consent.

Bona Fide Gifts and Inheritance (Rule 16b-5). Bona fide gifts and transfer of securities by will or the laws of descent and distribution are exempt from Section 16(b) short-swing profit liability.

Mergers, Reclassifications, and Consolidations (Rule 16b-7). An acquisition of securities in a merger, reclassification, or consolidation is exempt from Section 16(b) if the entities involved have at least 85 percent cross ownership.

Section 16(a) Reporting Exemptions (Rule 16a-10). Any transaction that is exempt from reporting under Section 16(a) is also exempt from Section 16(b) short-swing trading liability. For example, shares acquired as a result of dividends are exempt unless the Section 16 insider influenced the dividend declaration. See Rule 16a-9. The acquisition of securities based on the reinvestment of dividends of the same issuer are exempt as long as the acquisition is made under a plan with broad-based participation that does not discriminate in favor of the company's employees providing for the regular reinvestment of dividends (usually called a dividend reinvestment plan). See Rule 16a-11.

Statute of Limitations

Section 16(b) has a two-year statute of limitations from the date profits are realized. However, the Supreme Court has held that the period is tolled and a claim can be made after the statutory period has expired if inequitable circumstances have prevented the plaintiff from bringing the action within the applicable statute of limitations. The tolling ends when fraudulently concealed facts are, or should have been, discovered by the plaintiff. Previously, courts generally ruled that the period is tolled until the reporting person files the Section 16(a) beneficial ownership report (i.e., Form 4).

Transactions before Reporting Person Status

Generally, a reporting person becomes subject to Section 16(b) short-swing trading upon becoming an officer or director or once they hold more than 10 percent of the company's securities. Any transactions prior to that time are not subject to Section 16(b) liability. This means that the transaction that causes a person to become a 10 percent stockholder is exempt from, and will not be matched for purposes of, Section 16(b). However, when a company registers a class of equity securities for the first time, existing officers and directors may be liable for transactions during the six months prior to registration.

Transactions after Insider Status

Section 16 may apply to transactions entered into after an individual's insider status ends. Any purchase or sale within six months after ceasing to be a director or officer subject to Section 16 can be matched against any sale or purchase effected less than six months earlier at the time the individual was still an insider, and any profit from the transaction is subject to short-swing profit recovery.

What to Do

The liability that results from the short-swing profit rules is not based on inside information or bad intent. The rule is mechanically applied to sales and purchases of stock. As a result, insiders must monitor every purchase or sale of stock to avoid liability. The responsibility for compliance belongs to the insider. Although companies generally assist insiders in monitoring compliance with the rules, they may not forgive the liability, despite the good faith of the insider or the failure of the corporation to remind the insider of that person's responsibilities. A company should ensure that it establishes an insider trading policy and educates its insiders of short-swing profit liability and its consequences.

Key Questions

When faced with insider trading policy issues, some questions a board should consider include the following:

- ❑ Does the company have an insider trading policy or educational materials describing Section 16(b) liability?

- ❑ Does the company assist or have procedures to ensure that all insiders make timely Section 16 filings?
- ❑ Does the company monitor all Form 4 and 5 filings to determine if there are any short-swing trades?
- ❑ Are grants made under the company's equity plans approved in advance by the board of directors or a committee of the board composed solely of two or more nonemployee directors?
- ❑ Does the company's benefit plans qualify under the rules of Section 16(b) so that stock transactions are exempt?
- ❑ Does the company have procedures to assist former officers and directors to watch for possible opposite-way transactions after their departure?

Additional Reading

1. Section 16(b) of the Exchange Act of 1934, as amended, Profits from Purchase and Sale of Security within Six Months

   https://www.law.cornell.edu/uscode/text/15/78p

2. Rules 16b-1 to 16b-8 of the Exchange Act: Exemption of Certain Transactions from Section 16(b)

   https://lawblogs.uc.edu/sld/the-deskbook-table-of-contents/the-securities-acts-statutory-law/the-securities-exchange-act-of-1934-15-usc-%c2%a7-78a-et-seq/general-rules-and-regulations-promulgated-under-the-securities-exchange-act-of-1934-17-cfr-part-240/exemption-of-certain-transactions-from-section-16b-rules-16b-1-to-16b-8

3. SEC Compliance and Disclosure Interpretations: Exchange Act Section 16 and Related Rules and Forms

   https://www.sec.gov/divisions/corpfin/guidance/sec16interp.htm

4. Ownership Reports and Trading By Officers, Directors and Principal Security Holders, SEC Release No. 33-8600 (April 3, 2005) re: Rules 16b-3 and 16b-7

   https://www.sec.gov/rules/final/33-8600.pdf

5. *Credit Suisse Securities (USA) LLC v. Simmonds,* 132 S. Ct. 1414 (2012)—Tolling for Short-Swing Trading Claims

   https://www.supremecourt.gov/opinions/11pdf/10-1261.pdf

6. Speech by SEC Staff: Insider Trading—A U.S. Perspective, Remarks by Thomas C. Newkirk, Associate Director, Division of Enforcement (September 19, 1998)

   https://www.sec.gov/news/speech/speecharchive/1998/spch221.htm

7. The Genius of Section 16: Regulating the Management of Publicly Held Companies, Steve Thel, 42 *Hastings L. J.* 391 (1990–91)

   http://ir.lawnet.fordham.edu/faculty_scholarship/679

Notes

11.7 BASICS ABOUT 10B5-1 PLANS

CONTRIBUTED BY
Katherine J. Blair
Manatt, Phelps & Phillips, LLP[1]

Rule 10b-5 is the general anti-fraud rule of the Exchange Act. It prohibits any person from engaging in a purchase or sale of a company's securities if the person trades on the basis of material nonpublic information. Rule 10b5-1 goes further and provides that a person trades "on the basis of" material nonpublic information if such person is aware of the material nonpublic information when the person makes a purchase or sale.

Rule 10b5-1 provides an affirmative defense from insider trading liability and permits a person to trade in certain specified circumstances where it is clear that the information they are aware of is not a factor in the decision to trade. An affirmative defense must be proven in the event there is an insider-trading lawsuit; however, an affirmative defense does not prevent someone from bringing a lawsuit.

Officers and directors of public companies are subject to insider trading liability as they are usually aware of material nonpublic information about the company as a result of their positions. In order to benefit from the affirmative defense provided under Rule 10b5-1 and not be considered to trade on the basis of material nonpublic information,

1. Katherine Blair is a partner in the Capital Markets group at Manatt, Phelps & Phillips, LLP, where she practices in the firm's Los Angeles office.

an executive officer or director of the company may demonstrate that *before* becoming aware of any material nonpublic information, he or she had, in good faith, entered into a plan, contract, or instruction about trading securities, commonly known as a "10b5-1 Plan." In other words, a 10b5-1 Plan permits pre-arranged transactions in the company's securities.

10b5-1 Plans have become fairly common since 2000 when Rule 10b5-1 was adopted. Although it is typical for officers and directors to enter into 10b5-1 Plans, anyone, including company employees, may establish 10b5-1 Plans. As a matter of fact, some companies may require certain employees, beyond executive officers, who may have access to material nonpublic information to enter into 10b5-1 Plans. Companies may also establish polices related to 10b5-1 Plans, such as when persons are allowed to establish plans, the minimum duration of the plan, the "cooling off" period, and plan amendments.

10b5-1 Plan Requirements

Under Rule 10b5-1, a person may establish an affirmative defense and demonstrate that a purchase or sale of securities is not "on the basis of" material nonpublic information by implementing a plan of securities trading that satisfies ALL of the following three requirements:

1. BEFORE becoming aware of the information, the person had
   - entered into a binding contract to purchase or sell the security; or
   - instructed another person to purchase or sell the security for the instructing person's account; or
   - adopted a written plan for trading securities; and
2. The contract, instruction, or plan must
   - specify the amount of securities to be purchased or sold (number of shares or dollar value), the price (market price on a particular date, limit price, or particular dollar price), and date on which securities are to be purchased or sold, or include a written formula or algorithm, or computer program, for determining the amount of securities to be transacted and the price and the date; and
   - not permit the person to exercise any subsequent influence over how, when, or whether to effect purchases or sales, and any other person who, pursuant to the plan, exercises influence must also not be aware of material nonpublic information (e.g., a blind trust type of arrangement); and
3. The purchase or sale was actually pursuant to the contract, instruction, or plan.

CAUTION!

A securities trade will NOT be deemed pursuant to a plan and qualify for a Rule 10b5-1 affirmative defense if the person **deviates** from the 10b5-1 Plan (whether by changing the amount, price, or timing of the purchase or sale) or enters into a hedging position or corresponding position with respect to the securities purchased according to the 10b5-1 Plan.

In Good Faith/Cooling-Off Period

Rule 10b5-1 requires that the insider enter into the plan in good faith and not as part of a plan or scheme to evade the prohibitions of Rule 10b5-1. A 10b5-1 Plan may not be entered into while the insider is aware of material nonpublic information nor during a blackout period. Furthermore, an insider cannot rely on the 10b5-1 affirmative defense even if he/she enters into a 10b5-1 Plan while aware of material nonpublic information but trades are not implemented until after such information is made public. The best time to adopt a 10b5-1 Plan is during the company's open trading window.

As described in Rule 10b5-1, elements that establish good faith include (1) a specified amount of securities (number of shares or dollar amount) covered by the 10b5-1 Plan; (2) the price and dates of transactions, or, alternatively, a formula that determines the amount, price and dates of transactions; and (3) giving discretion to a third party.

Although there is no per se requirement for a waiting period between the time of adoption of the 10b5-1 Plan and commencement of securities trades, the imposition of a cooling-off period helps negate an evasion claim and shows good faith. Generally, the gap between establishing a 10b5-1 Plan and the first transaction typically ranges from 14 to 90 days, with 30 days being the most common.

CAUTION!

A Rule 10b5-1 affirmative defense is available only if the person enters into the contract, instruction, or plan **in good faith** and not as part of a scheme to avoid complying with insider trading laws.

Duration

There is no required duration for a 10b5-1 Plan. However, a 10b5-1 Plan that is very short or a series of shorter duration plans could raise good faith issues. It is easier to argue that the good faith requirement has been met for longer plans. A 10b5-1 Plan usually lasts between six months and two years. Some companies require a minimum duration period of one year.

Insider Trading Policies/Pre-Clearance

A 10b5-1 Plan may contemplate trades in a company's securities regardless of restrictions of windows or blackout periods. If the company has an insider trading policy, and the insider trading policy does not contemplate trades effected through a 10b5-1 Plan, then the insider trading policy may need to be amended to provide an exemption for trades made pursuant to a 10b5-1 Plan. (See Chapter 11.5, Insider Trading Policies and Protections, in this Handbook.)

The insider should disclose to the company's board of directors the adoption of a 10b5-1 Plan; however, while not required, the board of directors may also pre-approve the adoption of the 10b5-1 Plan by the insider. Alternatively, the company's compliance officer, or an independent officer with equivalent responsibilities, may pre-clear a 10b5-1 Plan and any related arrangements or trading instructions involving option exercises.

Public Disclosure of 10b5-1 Plan

Rule 10b5-1 does not require public disclosure of the adoption of a 10b5-1 Plan. However, disclosure can strengthen the good faith defense and may minimize the risk of adverse publicity regarding future sales by an insider, especially during blackout periods. The adoption of a 10b5-1 Plan may be made in a press release, on the company's website (if it is compliant with Regulation FD), or in a Form 8-K (under Item 8.01 "Other Events"). Some companies may also disclose 10b5-1 Plans of executive officers during their earning calls, which permit the executive officer to provide context for the adoption of the 10b5-1 Plan. The disclosure about a 10b5-1 Plan usually includes the number or dollar amount of shares involved, but not the trading details and investment strategies of the plan.

Issuer Certificate

An insider's broker plays an important role in creating and executing a 10b5-1 Plan, but in most cases, the broker is just implementing the investment strategies of its client (i.e., the insider). The broker for a 10b5-1 Plan may require the company to provide certain representations, such as notifying the broker when the company becomes aware of an inconsistency between the 10b5-1 Plan and the company's insider trading policy or the company becomes aware of restrictions applicable to the insider that would prohibit any sale pursuant to the 10b5-1 Plan.

Amendments and Termination

Amending a 10b5-1 Plan is permitted but risky, especially if multiple amendments are made. Amending the plan may mean that the insider possessed influence over how, when, or whether to effect trades, thereby weakening the affirmative defenses under Rule 10b5-1. If the insider amends, modifies, or suspends a 10b5-1 Plan, it should always be done when he/she is not aware of material nonpublic information.

The act of terminating a 10b5-1 Plan even while aware of material nonpublic information, and thereby not engaging in the planned securities transactions, does not result in liability under Rule 10b-5. Rule 10b-5 applies to any fraudulent conduct "in connection with the purchase or sale of any security." The "in connection with" requirement is satisfied when a fraud "coincides" with a securities transaction. The 10b5-1 Plan should permit termination by the insider with written notice. However, termination of a 10b5-1 Plan, or the cancellation of one or more plan transactions, could affect the availability of the Rule 10b5-1 affirmative defense for prior plan transactions if it calls into question whether the plan was "entered into in good faith and not as part of a plan or scheme to evade" the insider trading rules within the meaning of Rule 10b5-1. (See SEC Compliance and Disclosure Interpretations Exchange Act Rules, Section 120. Manipulative and Deceptive Devices and Contrivances: Rule 10b5-1, Questions (CDI 10b5-1) 120.17 through 120.19.)

Multiple 10b5-1 Plans

An insider is not prohibited from implementing multiple, overlapping 10b5-1 Plans. However, usually brokers and companies highly discourage this practice as it may jeopardize the good faith requirement and trades under the plans or create confusion.

Reporting Requirements and Other Matters

Section 16; Form 4 Filings. Rule 10b5-1 does not exempt transactions from any of the provisions of Section 16. Whenever a trade occurs pursuant to a 10b5-1 Plan, the officer or director will be required to file a Form 4 within two business days. As such, the insider should ensure that the broker actively coordinates with him/her so that a Form 4 can be filed in a timely manner and to avoid disclosure of late Form 4 filings in the company's proxy statement. Each Form 4 reporting trades made pursuant to a 10b5-1 Plan should include a footnote with a statement indicating that the sales were made pursuant to a pre-existing 10b5-1 Plan so that the public is aware of the arrangement, especially for sales that occur during blackout periods.

Open market purchases and sales under a 10b5-1 Plan are subject to Section 16(b) and must be monitored to ensure that they will not result in matches under Section 16(b) with opposite-way nonexempt transactions within or without the plan. (See Short-Swing Trading, Chapter 11.6 in this Handbook.) Some 10b5-1 Plans provided by brokers prohibit any securities trades by the insider outside of the plan.

Form 144 Filings. Officers and directors, who are usually deemed "affiliates" of the company for purposes of Rule 144 of the Securities Act, will most likely need to report sales on Form 144. (See Chapter 11.2, Selling Company Securities to the Public, in this Handbook.) The broker usually takes the lead in preparing and filing the Form 144, but it is ultimately the insider's responsibility. The Form 144 must be transmitted for filing concurrently with either the placement of a sell order for a brokerage transaction, or the execution of such sale directly with a market maker, as provided in Rule 144(h). (See CDI 10b5-1, Question 120.01.) Each Form 144 should note that the reported sales are being made pursuant to a pre-existing 10b5-1 Plan so that the public is aware of the arrangement, especially for sales that occur during blackout periods.

Schedule 13D. An insider who beneficially owns, or acquires beneficial ownership of, more than 5 percent of the company's voting equity securities may need to also disclose transactions on a Schedule 13D. Officers and directors usually report on Schedule 13D as opposed to Schedule 13G (the short form) since the SEC has provided guidance that officers and directors are most likely not eligible to be passive investors qualified to file on Schedule 13G. (See SEC Compliance and Disclosure Interpretations, Exchange Act Sections 13(d) and 13(g) and Regulation 13D-G Beneficial Ownership Reporting, Section 103. Rule 13d-1—Filing of Schedules 13D and 13G, Question 103.04.) A Schedule 13D must be filed within 10 days of acquisition, and amendments must be filed to reflect changes in beneficial ownership of one percent or more or other material changes in previously reported facts.

Key Questions

In considering a 10b5-1 Plan, questions to address include the following:

- ❑ Does the company's insider trading policy address adoption of and trade made under 10b5-1 Plans?
- ❑ Pursuant to any company policy, is the 10b5-1 Plan required to be disclosed and approved by the board of directors or compliance officer?

- ❑ Is the company currently in a blackout period or is the insider aware of material nonpublic information?
- ❑ Who will be responsible for the preparing and filing of each Form 144 and Form 4?
- ❑ Will the insider also be required to file or amend a Schedule 13D?
- ❑ Does the 10b5-1 Plan prohibit the insider from conducting any trades in the company's securities outside of the plan?
- ❑ Is the company required to make any representations or provide any notices or covenants in connection with the 10b5-1 Plan?
- ❑ Will there be a waiting period between execution of the 10b5-1 Plan and implementation of trades? If so, how long?
- ❑ Does the company contemplate a share repurchase program in the near future? (See Stock Buy-Back Programs, Chapter 11.1, in this Handbook.)
- ❑ Will the company announce the adoption of a 10b5-1 Plan, and if so, how?

Additional Reading

1. Rule 10b5-1—Trading "on the Basis of" Material Nonpublic Information in Insider Trading Cases

   https://www.law.cornell.edu/cfr/text/17/240.10b5-1

2. SEC Compliance and Disclosure Interpretations, Exchange Act Rules, Section 120. Manipulative and Deceptive Devices and Contrivances: Rule 10b5-1

   https://www.sec.gov/divisions/corpfin/guidance/exchangeactrules-interps.htm

3. Final Rule: Selective Disclosure and Insider Trading, Release No. 33-7881, August 15, 2000

   http://www.thecorporatecounsel.net/member/SEC/33-7881.htm

4. Opening Remarks Before the 15th Annual NASPP Conference, Linda Chatman Thomsen, Director, Division of Enforcement U.S. Securities and Exchange Commission, October 10, 2007

   https://www.sec.gov/news/speech/2007/spch101007lct.htm

5. LaCroix, Kevin. The D&O Diary: Rule 10b5-1 Trading Plans Under Scrutiny Once Again. (November 29, 2012)

   http://www.dandodiary.com/2012/11/articles/securities-litigation/rule-10b5-1-trading-plans-under-scrutiny-once-again/

6. Society of Corporate Secretaries and Governance Professionals Survey on Rule 10b5-1 Finds That Two-Thirds of Corporate Boards Review Their Company's Insider Trading Policy (June 23, 2016)

   http://www.marketwired.com/press-release/society-corporate-secretaries-governance-professionals-survey-on-rule-10b5-1-finds-2137143.htm

Notes

SECTION TWELVE

THE TROUBLED COMPANY

THE BOARD'S FIDUCIARY DUTIES IN AN INSOLVENT (OR NEARLY INSOLVENT) CORPORATION

12.1

CONTRIBUTED BY
Rolin P. Bissell
Young Conaway Stargatt & Taylor LLP[1]

As a corporation becomes financially distressed, insolvent, or files for bankruptcy, directors' and officers' fiduciary duties remain the same—duty of care and duty of loyalty. Regardless of whether a corporation is solvent, in the zone of insolvency, or insolvent, the primary job of directors remains the same—to continue to maximize the value of the corporation by exercising judgment in an informed, good faith effort to maximize the corporation's long-term wealth-creating capacity. Moreover, distress or insolvency does not change the standard of review that Delaware courts apply to directors' decisions as to how to fulfill their fiduciary duties. Their decision-making, when not conflicted, retains the traditional deference of the business judgment rule. Entire fairness review will apply to conflicted decision making.

But insolvency does change who may seek to enforce the director's duties. As poor economic performance drives a troubled corporation toward little or negative equity (i.e., insolvency), the corporation's stockholders may find themselves "out of the money." With a diminished economic stake in the corporation's performance, the stockholders may be

1. Rolin P. Bissell is a partner in the Corporate Counseling and Litigation section of Young Conaway Stargatt & Taylor LLP and practices in Wilmington, Delaware.

without means or incentive to use the stockholder franchise to elect the board, approve fundamental transactions, or bring derivative claims against derelict directors.

Under ordinary circumstances, the board does not owe creditors duties, fiduciary or otherwise, beyond the contractual rights the creditor has bargained for. With the insolvent corporation, the creditors' contractual rights under lending agreements, particularly when secured by liens, may make the creditors the de facto economic owners of the distressed corporation and the parties with the greatest interest in the corporation's restructuring, reorganization, or liquidation. Thus, once insolvent, the corporation's creditors become the beneficiaries of any residual increase in the corporation's value and thus gain the incentive to monitor the directors for breaches of fiduciary duty. Reflecting the shifting interests and incentives insolvency brings, the creditors of an insolvent corporation gain standing to bring claims derivatively to enforce a director's fiduciary duties.

With a troubled or insolvent corporation, the business risk tolerances of the stockholders and the company's creditors may diverge. Out-of-the-money stockholders may favor a riskier path that plays out over a longer time horizon than that favored by the corporation's creditors, who are looking for repayment of what is owed to them quickly, before things might turn even worse. Common stockholders may lose control in favor of preferred stockholders as a corporation acknowledges its financial distress. Junior creditors may favor riskier strategies than senior creditors who feel as though repayment of their credit is secure. In addition, due to the active market for trading in the debt of distressed companies, there may be conflicts between creditors at the same level of priority who have different cost bases in the debt and, often, different investment horizons. Creditors who buy into their position at a steep discount with a short investment horizon may favor near-term liquidation of the debtor—even at a "fire sale" price—if it would yield them their targeted internal rate of return within the targeted time frame. The directors of an insolvent corporation may need to consider these competing interests in making decisions about how to manage, financially restructure, or liquidate the corporation.

Under Delaware law, creditor standing to bring derivative litigation does not arise until the corporation is insolvent. Creditors of a corporation that is "in the zone of insolvency," but not yet insolvent, do not have standing to bring derivative litigation. The Delaware courts have yet to give a test that would allow a board to tell with any precision when a corporation enters the "zone of insolvency" or the where the "zone of insolvency" becomes actual insolvency. Creditors need only plead—and later prove—that the corporation was insolvent at the time the suit was filed to have standing. Creditors are not required to show that corporate debtor was irretrievably insolvent to have standing. The balance sheet test is used for determining whether a company is insolvent for the purpose of determining creditor standing.

Unlike stockholders, creditors do not have standing to bring "direct" claims against directors and officers for breach of fiduciary duty. When a corporation is distressed, it may be the one in most need of effective and proactive leadership—as well as the ability to negotiate in good faith with its creditors—goals which would likely be significantly undermined by the prospect of individual liability arising from the pursuit of direct claims by creditors. It is also clear that Delaware law does not allow claims for "deepening insolvency"—claims that directors improperly continued to operate an insolvent corporation or lenders lent to an insolvent corporation, damaging the corporation's stockholders or creditors. The board of an insolvent Delaware corporation remains entitled to exercise its good faith business judgment when determining whether the corporation should continue operating; the decision for the corporation to continue operating when insolvent is not subject to a heightened standard of review by reason of the corporation's insolvency.

The laws of other states should be consulted if the corporation in question is incorporated in a state other than Delaware. Although most states' law is consistent with Delaware corporation law on the issues of creditor standing to bring derivative claims on behalf of an insolvent corporation and the nonexistence of creditor direct claims for breach of fiduciary duty and claims of deepening insolvency, a few are not. A prudent board of a distressed corporation will want to receive an update concerning developments of this still emerging area of law that is specific to their corporation's state of incorporation.

Key Questions

When considering how to meet the duties of care and loyalty duties, key questions that a board member of a distressed corporation might ask include the following:

- ❑ How close to insolvency is the corporation?
- ❑ What has management done to monitor the liquidity and financial position of the corporation?
- ❑ What is the corporation's debt structure and who are the corporation's largest creditors? How reliable are the sources of that information? Do any of the individuals providing it (e.g., management) have a personal interest that I should be aware of?
- ❑ Is the corporation receiving advice on addressing its financial distress (out-of-court restructuring, prepack, reorganization, asset sale in bankruptcy)?
- ❑ Are there potential conflicts of interest between stockholder and creditors? Is controlling stockholder also a creditor?
- ❑ Do the managers have sense of what "runway" exists before insolvency becomes inevitable?
- ❑ Do I or any of my fellow board members have experience with distressed situations? Should we bring in some additional directors with that experience?
- ❑ Have we considered hiring a restructuring firm or chief restructuring officer?
- ❑ What effect would filing for reorganization have on our business operations?

Additional Reading

1. Moringiello, Juliet M., Andrew B. Dawson. *Bankruptcy Overview: Issues Law and Policy,* 7th ed., American Bankruptcy Institute (2016).

2. Hansen, Craig D, et al. *Pre-bankruptcy Planning for Commercial Reorganization*, 2nd ed., American Bankruptcy Institute.

3. Baker, D.J., J. Butler, and M. McDermott, "Corporate Governance of Troubled Companies and the Role of Restructuring Counsel," 63 *Bus. Law* 855–80 (May 2008).

4. Shein, James B., *Reversing the Slide, a Strategic Guide to Turnaround and Corporate Renewal*, Jossey-Bass (2011).

Notes

____

____

____

____

____

12 OVERSIGHT OF A DISTRESSED OR INSOLVENT CORPORATION

CONTRIBUTED BY
Rolin P. Bissell
Young Conaway Stargatt & Taylor LLP[1]

As discussed in the previous chapter, distress or insolvency do not change the nature of a director's fiduciary duties, but they do increase the number of constituencies that directors must consider in their decision-making. Although a director's role in governance may be terminated due to the decision to liquidate or because of misconduct, corporate distress or insolvency alone does not change a director's duties to oversee the affairs of the corporation. Even after filing for reorganization, directors retain the authority to manage the affairs of the corporation and their obligation to manage it consistent with their fiduciary duties. There is no obligation on the part of the director to cease the corporation's operations and liquidate. Absent a conflict of interest, director decision making will be reviewed under the business judgment rule, meaning that decisions short of "waste" will not be the source of liability.

1. Rolin P. Bissell is a partner in the Corporate Counseling and Litigation section of Young Conaway Stargatt & Taylor LLP and practices in Wilmington, Delaware.

Directors May Remain in Control, or Not

A reorganization under Chapter 11 of the Bankruptcy Code presumes that the debtor's business will continue to operate and that the debtor (and its directors) will remain in possession and control of its assets as a "debtor in possession." Nonetheless, the continuing directors of a reorganizing debtor will likely find that the board's role is circumscribed by the realities of a reorganization proceeding. First, because the debtor's board must submit all nonordinary course business decisions to the bankruptcy court for review and approval, the bankruptcy court supervision is constant. Second, during a reorganization the board typically retains and places heavy reliance upon outside "restructuring professionals," such as chief restructuring officers, bankruptcy lawyers, investment bankers, and others. Third, the debtor's creditors are involved in governance. Debtors will typically agree to conditions in debtor-in-possession (DIP) financing that tightly cabin the discretion of the debtor's management. Creditors also have standing to challenge the debtor's decisions in bankruptcy court.

Insolvency can lead to situations in which the directors are removed from any significant corporate governance role. When a company liquidates under Chapter 7 of the Bankruptcy Code, a trustee is appointed to sell the debtor's assets and use the proceeds to pay the debtor's creditors; there is no job for the directors to perform. Similarly, the appointment of a receiver under state corporation law will typically end the board of director's role in corporate governance. In a Chapter 11 reorganization, the debtor's creditors may seek the appointment of a Chapter 11 trustee to manage the debtor's affairs if there is evidence that the debtor's management has engaged in fraud or other misconduct. The appointment of the Chapter 11 trustee will end the board's role in governance.

Recurring Conflict of Interest Scenarios

When directors remain in control, distress and insolvency can give rise to conflicts of interest that can infect director decision-making and subject a board's decision to attack. Some recurring conflict of interest flashpoints are described in the next sections.

Continued Employment by the Corporation

Continued employment by the corporation can create a conflict of interest. Delaware law presumes that a director does not have a material interest in remaining a director, with limited exceptions. And the receipt of ordinary directors' fees will generally not create a conflict of interest for a director. However, where a director is an employee of the company as well as a director, the director likely has a material interest in the director's continued employment, unless neither the job nor the compensation received is material to the director. Where a director has a material interest in ongoing employment, the director suffers a conflict of interest wherever the director is asked to make a decision potentially affecting the director's employment. The director also suffers a conflict of interest with respect to any transaction in which someone with control over the director's employment, such as a controlling stockholder, has an interest. Such conflicts may easily arise where the corporation is in financial distress, if, for example, the board considers whether to liquidate the corporation or to engage in a merger or other transaction that would foreseeably affect the employment of the director.

Conflicts between Companies within a Corporate Family

When one member of a corporate family is in financial distress the interests of that corporation may differ materially from the interests of other members of the corporate family, which may be stockholders, creditors, or potential acquirers of assets from the financially troubled corporation. A director or officer may face a conflict of interest where the individual serves as a director or officer of multiple entities within the corporate family.

When a wholly-owned subsidiary is solvent, it may be managed exclusively for the benefit of its parent entity. Directors do not breach fiduciary duties when they cause a wholly-owned, solvent, subsidiary to engage in transactions with the subsidiary's parent that are disadvantageous to the subsidiary. Such transactions may include transferring assets to a different subsidiary of the same parent, allowing the parent to use the subsidiary's assets to secure a loan to the parent, or entering into service agreements with the parent or other subsidiaries of the parent that are not set at a market rate.

But, when a wholly-owned corporation becomes insolvent, its dealings with its parent entity may be subject to greater scrutiny. This shift is the result of creditors becoming residual interest holders. At that point, the creditors, not the controlling stockholder, pay the price of any lopsided transactions between the subsidiary and its parent.

Thus, insolvency curtails the freedom that a parent has to engage in transactions with its subsidiaries. As a result, directors of an insolvent subsidiary must scrutinize transaction between the parent and affiliates for fairness to the subsidiary itself. In these situations, it may be prudent to appoint directors to the subsidiaries board that are independent of the parent and for the board of the subsidiary to obtain its own advisors.

Personal Financial Interest in Distressed Company

Directors' ownership of stock of the corporation on whose board they serve is ubiquitous. Outside of bankruptcy, a director's ownership of stock generally does not give rise to a conflict of interest, because generally the stockholders' interests are aligned with the corporation's interests and the beneficiary of the directors' fiduciary duties.

When an insolvent corporation's interests diverge from those of its stockholders, stock ownership may present a conflict of interest for directors. Similarly where a transaction is beneficial or detrimental to various classes of a corporation's equity, a director's financial interest can present a conflict. These types of conflicts may well emerge in times of financial distress despite not existing previously.

Ties to a Controlling Shareholder or Creditor

Perhaps the most common conflict of interest that a director may suffer arises where the director has ties to a creditor of the corporation or to the controlling stockholder of the corporation. In either case, the director's lack of independence from the creditor or controlling stockholder creates a conflict of interest for the director wherever the interests of the creditor or the controlling stockholder differ from those of the corporation.

Other Business Dealings with the Distressed Company

Directors and officers will also suffer a conflict of interest with respect to their management of a financially troubled corporation in any other situation in which their interests differ from those of the corporation or its stockholders generally. Thus, for example, where a financially troubled corporation sells assets in an effort to repair its balance sheet, its directors will have a conflict of interest if they are affiliated with the buyer of the corporation's assets.

In a refinancing or recapitalization, it is not unusual for the new capital to come from someone who already has a position in the troubled company's capital structure. This can create conflicts of interest to the extent the new financing impairs the position of the other members of the capital structure.

Key Questions

When considering how to meet the duties of care and loyalty, key questions that a board member of a distressed corporation might ask include the following:

- ❑ How close to insolvency is the corporation?
- ❑ Do the managers have a sense of what "runway" exists before insolvency becomes inevitable?
- ❑ What has management done to monitor the liquidity and financial position of the corporation?
- ❑ What is the corporation's debt structure and who are the corporation's largest creditors? How reliable are the sources of that information? Do any of the individuals providing it (e.g., management) have a personal interest that I should be aware of?
- ❑ Is the corporation receiving advice on addressing its financial distress (out-of-court restructuring, prepack, reorganization, asset sale in bankruptcy)?
- ❑ Are there potential conflicts of interest between stockholder and creditors? Is the controlling stockholder also a creditor?
- ❑ Do I or any of my fellow board members have experience with distressed situations? Should we bring in some additional directors with that experience?
- ❑ Have we considered hiring a restructuring firm or chief restructuring officer?
- ❑ What effect would filing for reorganization have on our business operations?

Additional Reading

1. Hansen, Craig D, et al. *Pre-bankruptcy Planning for Commercial Reorganization*, 2nd ed., American Bankruptcy Institute.

2. Shein, James B. *Reversing the Slide, a Strategic Guide to Turnaround and Corporate Renewal*, Jossey-Bass (2011).

Notes

12.3 THE BOARD'S ROLE IN CRISIS MANAGEMENT

CONTRIBUTED BY
Ryan M. Philp and Fritz Lark
Bracewell LLP[1]

Corporate crises come in many different shapes and sizes, including hostile takeovers, allegations of executive malfeasance, CEO departures, cybersecurity breaches, government investigations, accounting restatements, operating failures, and financial scandals, to name but a few examples. Prior to a crisis unfolding, the board's role is to ensure that sufficient analysis and advance planning has occurred, with the goal of implementing a detailed crisis response plan.

A thoughtful crisis response plan sets out a proper governance framework for crisis response initiatives and provides management with a roadmap for decisive action that minimizes business disruption and preserves shareholder value. Crisis response plans should be revisited periodically to ensure that they reflect current economic and cultural realities as well as legal requirements. However, no board has a crystal ball. Some corporate crises simply cannot be predicted even by a diligent and dedicated board and

1. Ryan M. Philp, a partner in the litigation group at the New York City office of Bracewell LLP, concentrates his practice on litigation and counseling in the areas of corporate governance, securities litigation, and other business disputes. Fritz Lark, a partner in the corporate group at the New York City office of Bracewell LLP, represents clients on a broad range of transactions and corporate governance matters and frequently advises clients on mergers and acquisitions in the energy and utility industries.

management team. Even those that are foreseen and planned for often present unanticipated twists and turns. Therefore, when a crisis hits, the board should be prepared to roll up its sleeves to ensure that the company has considered, analyzed, and addressed all potential risks and liabilities to the greatest extent possible.

The key to effectively managing a crisis is a good process. At the outset, the board should determine whether the circumstances require it to take a lead role in the company's crisis response, which often turns on the board's assessment whether company management is implicated in the crisis or otherwise compromised. This decision should be made promptly with the aid of *independent* outside advisors. To this end, the board should consider looking outside the company's usual stable of advisors to ensure it is receiving advice untainted by any institutional loyalties, allegiances, or other influences. Where key members of senior management are compromised, embroiled in controversy, or otherwise deemed not up to the task, the board should ramp up its involvement and should be prepared to quickly transition crisis management roles to those better equipped to deliver timely and effective results untainted by any allegation of conflict or ulterior motives. In this regard, it may be prudent for the board to consider the formation of a crisis committee comprised of independent outside directors to avoid any appearance that the board's decision-making is subject to improper influences.

With the aid of its advisors, the board should work quickly to implement a carefully orchestrated crisis management plan that maps out a clear division of duties; ensures the proper flow of information between key players, advisors, and the board; and documents the board's deliberative process. This plan should include a centralized communications plan that designates responsible personnel and shapes the company's message. Implementing such a plan will ensure the company delivers a clear and consistent message and, in turn, will communicate to shareholders and other constituencies that the crisis is under control. In addition, a process should be put in place to monitor additional developments, litigation, and media coverage, including social media. At all times, the board's goal should be to ensure the company responds in a timely and decisive manner to mitigate company risks and liabilities while projecting an image of honesty and integrity.

The board's crisis response tasks can be divided into five principal categories:

1. *Advance Preparations*. It is important that the company not be caught "flat footed" in the face of a crisis. As part of its oversight function, the board should ensure that the company has in place a reasonably detailed crisis management plan that includes the identification and retention of appropriate outside experts, including an investor relations firm, a crisis communications firm, legal counsel, and any other advisor appropriate to the company's particular circumstances. Communication protocols should be established. The list of advisors should be updated periodically to ensure that organizational departures are taken into consideration and contacts are replaced and refreshed as appropriate. Many companies engage in rehearsals to ensure that members of the team can be assembled promptly in the face of a crisis.

Advanced measures also include identifying and training those individuals who can serve as a corporate spokesman under appropriate circumstances. The CEO is often the most appropriate spokesman, but not always, and alternatives should be available and trained.

Appropriate checklists should be prepared for major categories of corporate crises, and these checklists should also be reviewed and updated periodically. It is not the duty of directors to perform all of these functions. Rather, directors should exercise sufficient oversight to ensure that these functions have been performed.

2. *Investigation and Fact Gathering*. When a crisis does arise, the board must act immediately to determine whether the company has marshaled all necessary facts to formulate a comprehensive action plan. With the aid of independent advisors, this requires an initial determination whether additional investigation or analysis is necessary to evaluate the full scope of the crisis, its business impact, and potential ripple effects, including potential liabilities, litigation, and other exposure. The board also must make a prompt determination whether the company adequately has marshaled all personnel and resources necessary to tackle the problem(s). The time for shifting responsibilities, forming dedicated committees, and engaging additional resources, including legal and professional advisors, is at the outset.

3. *Planning and Implementation*. While the board should endeavor to implement a plan as quickly as possible, the need for expedition should be balanced against the need to develop as robust a factual backdrop as possible. At the earliest reasonable opportunity in light of these factors, the board should engage with management and other advisors to construct and implement a crisis response plan that sets out a detailed division of responsibilities, deliverables, and deadlines. Given management's greater familiarity with the day-to-day activities of the company, the board should task management with developing the plan, subject to the board's input and ultimate approval. When considering the division of duties, the board should be mindful of management's day-to-day responsibilities to ensure that crisis management tasks do not result in neglect of the company's ongoing business operations. However, where management is implicated in this crisis or otherwise not well-positioned to take the lead, the board should transition responsibilities and, if necessary, take a leading role in the company's response.

4. *Active and Continuous Oversight*. Once a crisis response plan is put into action, the board should schedule regular—and in severe situations, daily—updates with management. The board should encourage an open and honest dialogue with management and implement a plan to this end. Likewise, the board should receive routine updates from outside advisors regarding the company's progress. The board should react diligently to the information it is provided and should suggest modifications to the crisis response plan as necessary and appropriate, including shifting responsibilities and priorities.

5. *Remedial Actions*. Many corporate crises lead to the need for remedial actions, which can include the following:

- Reporting to government, regulatory authorities or the applicable stock exchange
- Improving processes, procedures, and business methodologies
- Accounting restatements
- Improving accounting or internal controls
- Changes in business practices
- Remediating corporate infrastructure, particularly IT infrastructure

- Disciplinary action with respect to one or more employees
- Replacement of senior management personnel
- Branding restoration or communication efforts

Once these actions have been taken, the board may also wish to determine whether an "after action" or "post-mortem" session is appropriate to identify the need for any modifications to the company's operations or its future crisis management planning.

Key Questions

Some important questions board members should ask before and during a crisis include the following:

- ❑ Do we have a crisis management plan in place that addresses the circumstances at hand?
- ❑ If so, when was the last time the crisis management plan was updated and does it reflect the company's current economic and cultural realities?
- ❑ Should we consider any modifications to the applicable crisis management plan?
- ❑ Do we have all relevant information regarding the crisis, or do we believe further investigation and fact-finding is necessary to determine the full scope of all actual and potential impacts and liabilities to the company?
- ❑ Have any members of management engaged in improper behavior or otherwise contributed to the crisis such that they should not be involved in the company's crisis response and/or should be subject to company discipline, such as being divested of responsibilities, placed on leave, or terminated?
- ❑ Do any of the members of the board have any actual or potential conflicts that may be perceived to dilute the credibility of the board's process, such as personal interests or loyalties to affected members of management or other impacted constituencies, such that the board should consider delegating its authority to a committee of the board?
- ❑ Does the board believe that the management personnel tasked with crisis response initiatives are capable of performing their assigned duties in a capable and timely manner?
- ❑ Has the company retained all necessary advisors, including legal advisors and strategic communications advisors, to assist with the company's crisis response?
- ❑ To the extent the company routinely works with outside advisors, does the board believe that those advisors are qualified and well-positioned to assist the company and are they free from conflicts or other influences that may impact their ability to provide timely and independent advice?
- ❑ Does the crisis create any reporting obligations that the company must satisfy to regulators, government authorities, or other governing bodies?
- ❑ Do any members of the board or management have experience or expertise dealing with the subject matter of the crisis at issue?

- ❑ What are the company's actual and potential liabilities arising from the crisis and what steps need to be taken to mitigate all such actual and potential liabilities?
- ❑ Does the company have any applicable insurance and have the relevant carriers been put on notice of the crisis?
- ❑ Has the company prepared a written holding statement, with credible double-checked facts, that can be presented to the media, shareholders, and other interested constituencies?
- ❑ What systems have been put in place to monitor litigation and media coverage, including social media, arising out of or related to the crisis?
- ❑ Have procedures been put in place to ensure that the board is regularly updated and kept abreast of all developments?

Additional Reading

1. The Board's Role in Crisis Management
   https://www.osler.com/osler/media/Osler/reports/risk-management/Board-of-directors-role-in-crisis-management.pdf
2. Crisis Management and the Board of Directors
   http://www.national.ca/Bold-Thinking/Crisis-Management-and-the-Board-of-Directors.aspx
3. In the Eye of the Storm—Governing in a Crisis
   https://www.cpacanada.ca/~/media/site/business-and-accounting-resources/docs/challenges%20and%20changes-%20in%20the%20eye%20of%20the%20storm%20-%20governing%20in%20a%20crisis.pdf

Notes

12.4 DEVELOPING A CRISIS MANAGEMENT PLAN

CONTRIBUTED BY
Julia M. Tosi
Squire Patton Boggs (US) LLP[1]

"Crises result from a single devastating event or a combination of escalating events and present a severe threat to an organization's strategic objectives, reputation and viability. Crises are episodic and of more significant magnitude."

—*A Crisis of Confidence*, joint study by Deloitte Touche Tohmatsu Limited and Forbes Insights (2016) (See Additional Reading, 2.)

No company is immune from being confronted with a "crisis." Crises come in all forms, shapes, and sizes and generally are complex and multifaceted situations. They can quickly develop out of seemingly "non-crisis" situations and can escalate in severity as the facts and responses unfold. By way of example, crisis situations and triggers can include environmental or natural disasters, data or cyber attacks, product liability issues, financial restatements, financial reporting or accounting issues, liquidity issues, fraud or allegations of fraud, labor or management issues, regulatory scrutiny or investigations, damaging social media, rumors or reputational issues, activist investor or hostile takeover situations, and terrorism situations.

1. Julia M. Tosi is a partner at Squire Patton Boggs (US) LLP, where she is a member of the firm's Corporate group, practicing in its Cleveland, Ohio office.

Crisis management plans and preparations are top of mind for management and boards alike. How a crisis situation is handled can dramatically impact its duration, outcome, and short- and long-term effects. Advance planning and preparation for crisis situations in general and for the most foreseeable or likely crises for your company are key.

Crisis management planning and preparations go hand in hand with organizational risk management and oversight and should be a regular part of the board's agenda. A company's crisis management plan generally should be developed and updated by management and reviewed and approved by the board. Board members can provide valuable input on the plan, both from their own experiences with other organizations and from the perspective of their general company and risk management oversight. Equally important to having a plan is ensuring that those on the crisis response team understand it and stand ready to implement it.

What an appropriate and ideal crisis management plan is for one organization versus another varies significantly based on the company's particular circumstances. A plan generally will not attempt to foresee or address every possible crisis or facet of a crisis, but should provide a framework for responding to any situation that arises and, as appropriate, should address specific situations where a company has heightened risk. Key parts of a crisis management plan include identification of a core crisis management/response team, identification of others who may need to be included in a response team (including in specific risk situations), protocols for a crisis assessment and initial action steps, a communications plan (internal and external) and clear articulation of roles and responsibilities.

Key Questions

With respect to developing a crisis management plan, key questions that a board member might ask include the following:

General

- ❑ Does the company have a crisis management plan? When was it established, last reviewed, updated, and tested? Who in management "owns" the plan, reviews it with the board, and is responsible for updating and implementing it?
- ❑ Is the crisis management plan specific enough to be useful but flexible enough to adapt to the nature of the crisis?
- ❑ Is the crisis management plan tailored to our company's unique situation, vulnerabilities, and stakeholders? For example:
  - Has there been a risk assessment, and what do I think the greatest areas of risk are for the company?
  - Are there certain company risks/potential crisis situations that I think should be addressed specifically in the plan?

Crisis Response Team

- ❑ Do we have the right core crisis response/management team in place? Are there protocols to quickly identify and mobilize others who should be on the response team once a specific crisis arises?

- ❑ Who is the team leader and who are the other essential members of the core response/management team?
- ❑ Does that team have the confidence of the board and senior management? Do they have the knowledge, authority, and ability to engage appropriate internal and external resources and demonstrated judgment?
- ❑ Is the core group the right size for our company? Who (or what group) has decision-making authority and what decisions must be made at the board level?
- ❑ Are there other individuals (internal or external) who would be on the response team in addition to the core group (i) for any crisis situation, or (ii) for any specific crisis situations? Are they identified in the plan?
- ❑ Are there outside experts who should be identified, approved for retention, and/or retained in advance?
- ❑ In what circumstances might board members need to lead or be the core team? Which board member(s) would be on the core team in those situations?
- ❑ Is there an up-to-date, emergency contact list for all of these team members? Who has and maintains it?

Communications Plan

- ❑ Does the communications plan address whether and when to notify and communicate with the board?
- ❑ Is the communications plan designed to ensure that the company is speaking with one voice and is accurate, consistent, and timely in communications? Is there a designated spokesperson?
- ❑ What are the protocols for determining whether and when to notify and communicate with other stakeholders and constituents?
- ❑ Does the plan include an assessment of who the potential stakeholders and audiences are and their interests and motivations?
- ❑ Does the plan appropriately account for public disclosure obligations and potential legal implications and other consequences?

Other

- ❑ Has the crisis management team discussed steps to take as part of
  - causation determination, correction and mitigation;
  - restoration of physical assets, business operations, or reputation;
  - information gathering and preservation;
  - managing potential dispute resolution;
  - managing insurance issues?
- ❑ Should the crisis management plan include any protocols or frameworks for these items?
- ❑ Has the plan been updated to incorporate any lessons learned from prior company crisis situations?

Additional Reading

1. DeHaas, Deborah and Ashish Patwardhan. Crisis Management—Assessing the Board's Role Before the Next Crisis. Director Advisory, NACDonline.org (March/April 2016)

   https://www2.deloitte.com/content/dam/Deloitte/us/Documents/center-for-corporate-governance/us-ccg-crisis-management.pdf

2. A Crisis of Confidence, joint study by Deloitte Touche Tohmatsu Limited and Forbes Insights (2016)

   http://www2.deloitte.com/content/dam/Deloitte/global/Documents/Risk/gx-cm-acoc-surveyreport.pdf

3. PwC's 2015 Annual Corporate Directors Survey—Governing for the Long Term: Looking down the Road with an Eye on the Rear-View Mirror, p. 31, PricewaterhouseCoopers LLP (2015)

   http://www.pwc.com/us/en/governance-insights-center/annual-corporate-directors-survey/assets/pwc-2015-annual-corporate-directors-survey.pdf

4. Crisis Management—Does Your Board Have a Plan?, Board Questions to Ask Today, The Governance Solutions Group (March 3, 2014)

   http://www.gsgboards.com/wpcnt/uploads/2014/03/GSG-BQs-3.2014-Crisis-Management-Plan.pdf

5. All About Crisis Management

   http://managementhelp.org/crisismanagement/ (featuring articles and links to various resources)

6. Crisis Management and Communications, posted on October 30, 2007 by W. Timothy Coombs, Institute for Public Relations

   http://www.instituteforpr.org/crisis-management-and-communications/ (featuring a bibliography of additional articles and titles)

Notes

25 DEREGISTRATION AND STOCK EXCHANGE DELISTING, OR "GOING DARK"

CONTRIBUTED BY
Toby D. Merchant
Squire Patton Boggs (US) LLP[1]

A public company engaged in the process of voluntarily terminating its securities listings with one or more national stock exchanges (e.g., the NYSE or NASDAQ) and/or quotation system (if applicable) and exiting the periodic reporting regime of the Securities Exchange Act of 1934 (the Exchange Act) is commonly referred to as "going dark." The primary effect of going dark is that a company's shares will no longer be traded on the applicable stock exchange (although its shares may still be traded on an OTC Market as noted later), and the company's obligation to file periodic reports under the Exchange Act will be terminated and/or suspended.

The process of going dark is complex and the specific regulatory filings that must be made will vary depending upon a variety of factors. These factors include the sections of the Securities and Exchange Commission (SEC) regulations that give rise to the company's reporting obligations, the stock exchange from which the shares will be delisted, and the company's contractual obligations (e.g., credit facilities and insurance policies). Conceptually, it is generally easier to understand the "going dark" process by first understanding

1. Toby D. Merchant is a partner at Squire Patton Boggs (US) LLP, where he is a member of the corporate and financial institutions practice groups.

why companies are required to file periodic reports under the Exchange Act. Companies are required to file periodic reports under the Exchange Act due to three sections of the Exchange Act, which are as follows:

- Section 12(b) if any of a company's shares are listed on a national securities exchange (e.g., the NYSE and NASDAQ)
- Section 12(g) if the company has over 2,000 holders of record or 500 holders of record who are not "accredited investors" (as defined in the Securities Act of 1933 (the Securities Act)) of a class of securities and totals assets exceeding $10 million
- Section 15(d) if the company has an effective registration statement under the Securities Act

The first step in the process of going dark is to delist the company's shares from the applicable stock exchange. Once the company's shares have been delisted, the company can terminate its reporting obligations under the Exchange Act; this process will vary depending on which of the foregoing sections gives rise to a company's reporting obligations (more than one section may apply). For example, deregistration under Section 12(b) of the Exchange Act requires the filing of a Form 25 with the SEC (which also requires that the company give notice of an intention to file such form and give a press release publicly announcing such intention at least 10 days prior to the filing of the form), while deregistration under Section 12(g) and suspension of the obligations pursuant to Section 15(d) of the Exchange Act, if applicable, require the filing of a Form 15 (which will have the effect of immediately suspending any reporting obligations and become effective 90 days after filing). From a timing perspective, the delisting and deregistration process can take in excess of 100 days to complete.

Although a board is not generally expected to completely understand the technical legal requirements, process, and other minutiae applicable to a company that is going dark, it is important for the board to have at least a basic understanding of the process due to some important consequences that could occur depending on the company's circumstances. For example, a company may be able to delist its shares from the applicable national securities exchange but not be able to completely terminate and/or suspend its obligations to file reports under the Exchange Act. Many companies might consider this circumstance to be the worst of both worlds—its shares will no longer be listed on a national securities exchange and it would still be subject to the reporting requirements of the Exchange Act. This circumstance occurs when a company has a shareholder base that consists of more than 300 holders of record and/or has an effective registration statement on file under the Securities Act. In short, a company that delists its shares from a national securities exchange will no longer be registered pursuant to Section 12(b) of the Exchange Act but such registration will automatically continue under Section 12(g) in the event that the company continues to have 300 or more holders of record and/or Section 15(d) if the company has an effective registration statement under the Securities Act. Consequently, before beginning the process of going dark, it is imperative that a board involve counsel and management in order to fully understand the applicable requirements and how they will apply to the company's particular circumstances.

Notably, even after a company completes the process of going dark, its shareholder base will remain unchanged due to the fact that no shares are cashed out in the process (as opposed to a going private transaction whereby a significant number of shares are cashed out) and its shares will likely continue to be traded on the OTC Market, which consists of the OTCQX, OTCQB, and OTCPink markets, although typically with a significant drop in share price and volume and reduced analyst coverage. This fact is important to keep in mind due to the possibility that a company's requirement to file reports under the Exchange Act could be revived in the event the company's shareholder base exceeds the applicable number of holders of record after the company deregisters under the Exchange Act by filing a Form 15.

A company may wish to go dark for a variety of reasons. Many companies that go dark do so in order to reduce their reporting and corporate governance requirements and avoid the rising costs of compliance (particularly in the case of smaller public companies, whose costs typically comprise a significantly higher percentage of revenues than larger public companies). Minimizing management's attention to compliance matters and allowing management to direct its full attention to the company's business is another commonly cited reason for going dark. Other reasons for going dark include voluntary or involuntary delisting from a stock exchange (whether due to potential issues with a company's listing status, lack of an active trading market in a company's shares, or otherwise), an acquisition, or its dissolution.

Regardless of a company's rationale or motivation for going dark, there are a number of items that the board should carefully consider before making a decision on whether going dark is in the best interest of the company and its shareholders. The board should, for example, understand and evaluate the relative merits of remaining a public company as well as the expected cost savings and/or other economic benefits that may be realized as a result of going dark. The board should also consider how going dark is likely to be perceived by, among others, its shareholders, employees, customers, and the public in general. The possible impacts on the market price of the company's shares, incentive compensation plans (particularly if shares are issued to employees as incentive compensation), ability to use its shares as a currency for acquisitions, existing contractual arrangements, D&O insurance policies, and business should also not be ignored.

The board should also be mindful of its fiduciary duties and the potential for litigation when making a decision regarding going dark. In particular, boards should ensure that there are no conflicts of interest, whether actual or potential, that could unduly influence a member of the board in determining whether to approve the delisting of a company's shares and deregistration under the Exchange Act. As for litigation, a variety of claims could be brought against a board for matters such as breach of fiduciary duty (particularly a breach of the duty of loyalty) and insider trading (in the event of repurchases of shares by the company or transactions in company shares by the board or company executive officers due to the fact that information will not be provided about a company following deregistration).

Key Questions

When pondering the potential to deregister, issues to consider include the following:

- ❑ What are the specific reasons for desiring to go dark and what evidence or information does the board have to support such reasons? If not, what information does it need? Are there reasons to not go dark?

- ❑ How will going dark be perceived by the company's employees, shareholders, customers, suppliers, etc.?
- ❑ How many holders of record does the company have, and will the company be able to delist its shares from the applicable stock exchange *and* terminate and/or suspend its reporting obligations under the Exchange Act?
- ❑ Has the company considered the implications of having its shares listed on the OTC Market? Are any of the three OTC Markets more desirable than others for the company? Has the company considered whether such markets will require that information about the company be periodically disclosed?
- ❑ Do any members of the board have an actual or potential conflict of interest in determining whether going dark is in the best interests of the company and its shareholders? Does the board expect litigation to be initiated if it determines to go dark?
- ❑ Does the company have any contractual obligations, such as a credit facility or D&O insurance policy(ies), that would be impacted by going dark? If so, do any modifications to such contracts and/or insurance policies need to be made prior to beginning the process of going dark?
- ❑ How will the timing constraints on the process impact the company and its business, if at all?

Additional Reading

1. United States Securities and Exchange Commission, Fast Answers: Going Private (September 2, 2011)

   https://www.sec.gov/answers/gopriv.htm

2. Leuz, Christian et al. "Why Do Firms Go Dark? Causes and Economic Consequences of Voluntary SEC Deregistrations." *J. Acctg. & Econ*, 45 (2008) 181–208

   http://www.sciencedirect.com/science/article/pii/S0165410108000025

Notes

______

______

______

______

______

12.6 FILING FOR BANKRUPTCY

CONTRIBUTED BY
Rolin P. Bissell
Young Conaway Stargatt & Taylor LLP[1]

The Decision to File

The decision whether to file for bankruptcy belongs to the directors of the corporation and that decision (absent a conflict of interest, a breach of the duty of care, or the failure to act in good faith) is protected by the business judgment rule under state corporation law. The directors have broad discretion in making this decision. A corporation has no obligation to file for bankruptcy or liquidate when it becomes insolvent, and a board may opt to pursue strategies outside of bankruptcy in an attempt to maximize the value of the corporation. When a corporation files for bankruptcy, the corporation is placed immediately under the supervision of the bankruptcy court and automatic stay of the bankruptcy court goes into effect immediately to prevent creditor actions against the corporation.

Although the directors of a corporation are in firm control of the decision to file, that decision can be challenged by the corporation's creditors. A board's decision to file for reorganization under Chapter 11 can be challenged under bankruptcy law on the basis

1. Rolin P. Bissell is a partner in the Corporate Counseling and Litigation section of Young Conaway Stargatt & Taylor LLP and practices in Wilmington, Delaware.

the bankruptcy petition was not filed in good faith. In assessing a debtor's good faith, courts may consider the totality of facts and circumstances to determine where the bankruptcy petition is abusive and not in good faith. Factors considered include the following:

- *The debtor must be suffering "financial distress."* Insolvency is *not* required. But at a minimum, the debtor must "face such financial difficulty that, if it did not file at that time, it could anticipate the need to file in the future."
- *The Chapter 11 filing must serve a "valid bankruptcy purpose."* The two valid purposes of Chapter 11 that have been recognized by the case law are (i) preserving going concerns, and (ii) maximizing property available to satisfy creditors.
- *The filing cannot have been "merely to obtain a tactical litigation advantage."* Thus, a case that is filed solely for the purpose of obtaining the protection of the automatic stay, with no prospect of rehabilitation of the debtor, may be deemed to have been filed in bad faith.

Although dismissal of a Chapter 11 petition for bad faith is a rare occurrence, a board considering commencing a Chapter 11 proceeding should evaluate critically its goals in seeking Chapter 11 relief and assess the risk that the decision is vulnerable to attack as not in good faith.

Similarly, if a corporation is unwilling to file for bankruptcy, its creditors (provided they meet certain minimums in number and amount claimed) may file an involuntary petition in the bankruptcy court. An involuntary petition functions as a complaint seeking a declaration that the corporation should be put into bankruptcy. The corporation can respond by opposing the involuntary petition, in which litigation ensues over whether the corporation should be placed into bankruptcy. Because of the potential cost of litigation and damages for lender liability, the creditors seldom use the involuntary petition.

A debtor cannot contractually waive its right to file for bankruptcy. An advance agreement to waive the benefits conferred by the bankruptcy laws is wholly void as against public policy and unenforceable. Nonetheless, a corporation's formation or governing documents may contain provisions that place limitations or preconditions on the corporation's ability to file for bankruptcy case. Examples of enforceable governance provisions include requirements that a super-majority of directors or stockholders vote to authorize the bankruptcy filing or that a particular class of equity securities consent to the filing. A governance provision requiring unanimous director approval when a lender has the right to appoint a director, or requiring consent of a series of preferred stock that is owned by the lender, or has the practical effect of giving a lender veto power over the decision to file for bankruptcy, may be vulnerable to attack as disguised advanced waiver.

Choosing between Liquidation and Reorganization

A board that decides a corporation should file for bankruptcy must choose whether to seek liquidation or reorganization. If the corporation's distress reflects a failure in its business operations and there is no viable business to reorganize, liquidation pursuant to Chapter 7 will likely be the best way to maximize the recovery of the corporation's creditors. For the board of an insolvent corporation, the decision to pursue Chapter 7 liquidation is the end of the governance road. It requires the appointment of a Chapter 7 trustee who takes exclusive control of the corporation's assets and the management of its business. Directors and officers of a Chapter 7 debtor typically resign upon the filing of the bankruptcy petition.

But if the corporation's operations are healthy and the source of its distress is a burdensome capital structure, reorganization may be preferable because it may preserve the otherwise viable business's going concern value that would be lost in liquidation. In a Chapter 11 reorganization, the debtor retains control of its assets and business (as a "debtor in possession") and the insolvent corporation's existing directors and management often continue managing the reorganizing corporation's affairs. Because the reorganization process involves numerous and frequent strategic decision, it will require substantial attention from a corporation's directors. For example, a "reorganization" may take the form of a going-concern sale of all or a substantial portion of the corporation's assets, a merger or strategic acquisition, a recapitalization of the business, or a refinancing or restructuring of existing debt. The directors' control of the reorganizing debtor is constrained by the supervision of the bankruptcy court (e.g., the requirement of bankruptcy court approval for transactions outside the ordinary course of business) and potential challenges by an official committee of creditors, which has the right to participate and be heard on most issues in the reorganization.

Given the specialized nature of bankruptcy proceedings and the complexity of a reorganization, it will typically be prudent for a board to engage insolvency professionals (e.g., bankruptcy counsel, financial advisors, turnaround managers, independent board members) to assist in the decision whether to file for bankruptcy and guide the board through the Chapter 11 process. These advisors can also provide significant protection against personal liability for board members who rely in good faith on their advice. The board's resolution authorizing the bankruptcy filing will typically ratify the corporation's prior retention of insolvency professionals and authorize the continued retention of such professionals in the Chapter 11 case. In addition, given the dynamic nature of Chapter 11 proceedings and the need for flexibility on the part of the debtor's management, the resolutions will typically delegate authority to make decisions and act on behalf of the corporation to specific individuals. Even though a board may delegate to advisors, the board may not abdicate its authority, must continue to provide oversight, and will remain ultimately responsible for the management of the corporation during the Chapter 11 case.

Key Questions

When considering whether to file for bankruptcy, key questions that a board member of a distressed corporation might ask include the following:

- ❑ Can the corporation be reorganized outside of bankruptcy?
- ❑ Are there any governance provisions that require the consent of more than a majority of the directors or the consent of certain securities holders before filing for bankruptcy? Are they enforceable?
- ❑ Has the board received sufficient advice from insolvency specialists that it can make an advised and informed decision about whether to file for bankruptcy?
- ❑ Can the corporation successfully reorganize? Are its problems with the viability of its underlying business (for example, technological advances have made the

corporation's product obsolescent) or is it a good business but with the wrong financial structure?

- ❑ Does the board have a clear picture of how the corporation's creditors and other stakeholders will fare?
- ❑ Is there a creditor who might challenge the filing for bankruptcy as not in good faith?
- ❑ Are there a sufficient number of creditors who might file an involuntary petition?
- ❑ Are there any directors with potential conflicts of interest or independence issues participating in the decision to file for bankruptcy?
- ❑ Are the current directors and officers staying with the corporation while it reorganizes?

Additional Reading

1. Hansen, Craig D, et al. *Pre-Bankruptcy Planning for Commercial Reorganization,* 2nd ed., American Bankruptcy Institute.
2. Shein, James B. *Reversing the Slide, a Strategic Guide to Turnaround and Corporate Renewal*, Jossey-Bass (2011).

Notes

___

___

___

___

___

INDEX

A